THE INTERNET
FINANCING ILLUSION

THE INTERNET FINANCING ILLUSION

A Diary of Global Scams

Vincent Panettiere

iUniverse, Inc.
New York Lincoln Shanghai

THE INTERNET FINANCING ILLUSION
A Diary of Global Scams

iUniverse books may be ordered through booksellers or by contacting:

iUniverse
2021 Pine Lake Road, Suite 100
Lincoln, NE 68512
www.iuniverse.com
1-800-Authors (1-800-288-4677)

ISBN: 978-0-595-38567-6 (pbk)
ISBN: 978-0-595-82945-3 (ebk)

Printed in the United States of America

CONTENTS

ACKNOWLEDGMENTS

This book could not have been written without the assistance and support of many people—both actual and virtual.

While those in cyberspace will never realize the depth of their anonymous contributions, I am grateful just the same.

I would like to thank:

The steadfast group of Anamika supporters who provided mutual encouragement while forming a bond with me during eight months in 2003. They are: Alan of England, Allen of Phoenix, Brian, Jack, Jody and Kevin.

And: Debbie McCurdy, who listened to my experiences and said "so, write a book"; Sumit Das Gupta, Metro Editor of the *Kolkata Telegraph* and *Telegraph* reporter Nisha Lahiri; Kristin Oomen, who knew how to soothe the savage beast; Karl Biniarz, who knew better, but never said "I told you so"; Annie McGuire of www.fraudaid.com who graciously gave me permission to use the material in the Appendix.

Most especially I am grateful to my wife Penny for her love and support through the ages.

PREFACE

At its core, *The Internet Financing Illusion* is a non-fiction detective story. One could even call it a virtual mystery since much of it occurs in cyberspace. Where it differs from a traditional who-dunnit—real or fictitious—is the absence of violence and a material corpse.

There are plenty of clues and more twists than a hair pin. However, all that is deceased in this story are hopes, dreams, aspirations, beliefs, trusts, and good intentions, i.e. much of what makes up the fabric of a civilized society.

Those bottom line losses, therefore, are more devastating than any financial ones.

Early in 2003, I never considered writing any book. Most importantly, I didn't have a subject even if there was the slightest inclination to face several hundred blank pages and attempt to impart on them some cohesiveness of thought. But, a book about the Internet and financing schemes was beyond fantasy.

As the year began, my foremost concern was financing a slate of films I wanted to produce. I intended to identify and locate a non-traditional source or sources, which I fervently expected would provide the necessary funds and enable me to produce the films independently.

By non-traditional I mean a financing source apart from a film studio or distributor and thereby avoid the elaborate film development (more on this inside) dance.

As a literary agent for more than a decade and before that a writer with four sold, but not produced, projects, I'd read thousands of scripts and seen hundreds of films. My sense of story, structure, plot arc, characterization and history of film were as well honed, I believed, and commercial as any production executive in the business. All I needed was the chance to prove my bone fides. Money would give me that chance.

I'd been searching for financing, on my own and with the help of various "finders" for nearly two years. It was a slow process continually entailing two steps forward and one and a half steps back. I believed the funds I sought were out in the universe somewhere and kept myself steeled with such banalities as "nothing hard is ever easy", "if it were easy, everybody would be doing it," "all you need is one person to say yes", etc.

On reflection these mantras were self induced and necessary for my equilibrium—meaning sanity. They were needed to prevent the cold sweat of fear from spreading throughout my body at three in the morning.

"Once more into the breach" was the trumpet blare inside my head as I faced each day with an optimism that ever so slightly obscured reality.

Eleven months into 2004, a book idea started pecking at my consciousness. Gradually, I felt the necessity to spread my thoughts on paper, if for no other reason than to "debrief" myself concerning my experiences. What was reality? What fantasy, delusion, denial, disillusion, and dishonesty had I created?

While others were involved in the same venture, this book represents only my perspective based not only on my phone notes, email and memory but also on my perception of the email of some of those also in this group, who may recall events differently.

Primarily and selfishly, this book was written to help me. If, by extension of my humanity, others can benefit it will be a bonus of extraordinary proportions. This book was written based on my reaction and exposure to the enormity and complexity of potential and actual Internet scams.

I'm not a crusader, but I've had my fill of hubris, chutzpah, guile, gall, etc., whatever it's called. This is not a cautionary tale for those with an uncontrollable need to squander money; who are determined to go through hell and back, or fill an insatiable addiction to get "something for nothing". Unfortunately, those who offered SFN wanted thousands of dollars for which they were prepared and determined to provide nothing.

The first two chapters covering Nigerian up front fee scams, which I'd also experienced first hand, can be seen as prelude to my primary focus for eight months—a woman named Anamika Biswas who led me and more than 20 other individuals and companies on a merry chase with the precision of a military commander leading the enemy into a blind canyon.

As the end of the chase, and its realization that she could not and would not provide any funding, neared I remembered one of those witticisms newspaper columnists and other cognoscenti toss around to provide encouragement and relief. "When the world gives you lemons, make lemonade."

I had hundreds of pages of email and Instant Messages on my hard drive as well as hand written notes based on numerous phone conversations. I also had the evaporated dreams, fantasies and aching disappointments which each page validated.

My world had given me a wealth of source material. What else was there to do but write a book to purge the hurt through commerce and income?

Or is this another fantasy?

Author's Note: All of the email received by the Author has been reproduced as it was written. None has been corrected for spelling or grammar.

1. THE TRIPLE PLAY

SIERRA-LEONE TO BENIN TO LONDON

When T.S. Eliot wrote "April is the cruelest month," he had not met a group of 24 individuals searching for the financing that would launch their dreams and propel them into a level of security none had previously ever known.

Had Eliot consulted these entrepreneurs—at once idealistic, obsessive, naive, greedy, loyal, supportive, empathic—he'd have written April, May, June, July, August, September, October and November 2003 were the cruelest months. That is how long the journey from hope to despair through realization to resignation took for eight Americans and one Canadian, more than one third of the group, who kept the faith with the investor, seeking a better, nontraditional way for their businesses to grow and prosper.

While the other two thirds of the group went elsewhere for capital infusion, the nine clung to whatever sliver of hope they could glean.

I am one of the nine. This is mostly my story. I should have known better, but instead I spent my time, some money most of the hope, enthusiasm and positive thinking of a life time during eight months of 2003 searching for a way to finance my company Thistle Productions, Inc.

My enterprise re-defined the term "starting from scratch". I'd let a moderately successful literary agency slowly sink under the horizon and decided in a fit of altruistic fervor to "package" film writer and film director clients.

Packaging entails joining the script written by a client to a director the agency also represented. The theory being that a single script floating around in the universe could not be considered seriously by those who might be interested in investing at least several millions in the venture. But a director with a "track record" who is not only "interested" in the "material", but has also committed a year of his life bringing the script to life—that surely could, would, should make the investor more willing to part with his cash.

More than that I was burnt out by the Hollywood system which all but guarantees that only the top tier fill their bellies while everyone else pecks in the yard for a scrap of cracked corn.

This applies across the board and is patently obvious. Whether actor, director, writer, cinematographer, production designer, editor—no matter the craft or skill—talent does not naturally and automatically rise to the top. It is managed, manipulated, massaged and hyped by those whose only job is to find the needle in the haystack, pea in the mattress, diamond in the coal mine—insert here countless other clichés, and conventional pieces of wisdom—and turn them into a money machine.

They are human sluice boxes who sift people instead of silt to find bright nuggets. But, what they discover is no less a product, an object with but one value—to bring them—profit. Like gold miners from the beginning of time, whether the ore they find is turned into Piaget or dental filling is no concern once they get their price. So too, with the human managers, agents, lawyers, casting directors, so-called development personnel, etc. the ca-ching factor is the be all and end all.

George C. Scott, standing before a huge American flag as General George S. Patton told his troops they had the option of fighting and dying for their country or "shoveling shit in Louisiana." Whether moving insurance forms from one pile to the next, separating Grade A apples from the puny ones, packaging chocolates like Lucy Ricardo or discovering the next (fill in the celebrity of your choice), we are all on a cosmic conveyor belt bombarded by decisions and choices, spending our lives battling through the obstacles to reach pay dirt. In short most of us are shoveling shit in Louisiana.

In the approximately ten years I ran my literary agency, representing writers, directors and directors of photography for movies and TV, I'd made several thousand submissions. Ultimately, each submission was the end product of multiple phone calls. Film scripts were sold, some were even produced. A book was published, a play produced, some writers got jobs re-writing scripts others sold episodes to TV series and others directed for TV. The only deals I didn't make were for directors of comedy episodes and movies of the week. But the totality of effort expended never produced a comparable reward.

Rather than spending another decade trying to improve on my somewhat modest results, I decided to take my destiny in my own hands and raise financing so that the most worthy and commercial of my clients could get a place in the sun, with me along as producer.

In my most altruistic moments, I was taking this leap, more off the cliff than of faith, to demonstrate my support and belief in their scripts and by projection their ideas and selves as humans, even if hundreds of so-called development people in Hollywood had passed on their material or talent.

By aiding their careers and lives, I'd be moving myself up the ladder to achieve the one commodity money, fame, rich parents, or a government grant couldn't buy—control over my life. Hah!

In November of 1999, I started modestly. I intended to raise only $500,000 as the initial funds to produce my first film. While some films have been made for that amount, most end up being vanity fare and if extremely lucky get seen on the film festival circuit. By that I don't even mean "Sundance", the grand daddy of film festivals which started out with lofty ideals and eventually slid, propelled by its own self importance back down to earth i.e. commercialism. By vanity film festival fare, I mean the backwater film festivals from Ottumwa to Oswego and all stops in between.

I intended to make commercial, main stream films with not a jots worth of pretense toward art. In my mind film was and still is a commodity like shoes or soup. It costs X and can be sold for X plus Y, not X minus Y. I wanted to create a profitable venture not something just to make my family and a coterie of dentists proud.

The budget of my film would be at max about $6 million. I intended to use the "seed" money i.e. $500,000 to legitimately and correctly option the script and attach a director and one lead actor. Here we need to digress.

The elements of a film traditionally are assembled in a fashion similar to real estate development. First a script is acquired. *This is akin to acquiring a parcel of land.* The option on a script reserves it for the production company over a period of time. Usually, there are provisions to extend the option beyond the initial period. Money usually is paid to the writer for each option and extension which, if the gods are favorable, leads to the purchase of the script at the end of the final option and production of the film.

An option gives the production entity control of the script during the option period and time to develop the script further. Development comes in at least two forms—work is done to improve the script with the original writer or a new writer or writers. *This is like buying a house and adding an extension or tearing it down and building a new one.* Another part of the development process is attracting some casting element.

Attaching actors and possibly a director increases the risk, since the money needed to keep them "attached" to a project is greater than that needed for the script (there is a certain inequity here the explanation of which will be reserved for another time). Plainly, actors and directors make a greater impression on distribution companies, crucial for the success of any film, than writers.

The risk to the neophyte producer occurs while juggling all the ingredients for a movie long enough for all the financing to be put in place. Once the various options expire, if the production funds are not firmly set, the producer stands to lose all the money he or she has put up front to hold the actors. This is musical chairs with greater stakes.

That was my plan. Raise $500,000. Option the script and attach an actor who would be attractive to a distribution company. My clients had written the script and I knew they'd be amenable to making some money. The director was another client who'd read and liked the script.

Very simple and straightforward. All I needed was the half a million.

No one was interested in investing $500,000!

Too little!

After a dozen or so conversations via phone and email with possible investors and brokers, it was clearly apparent that size counted.

Five hundred thousand dollars was a puny amount. It was then I got a shot of "eureka." Too small didn't mean too small for me, or too small to recoup the investment. Too small meant the commission for the brokers and assorted middle men would be too small for <u>them.</u>

Like adding more water to the soup when unexpected company arrives at dinner time, I added more zeros to the proposal. Voila! I now had a four film, $25 million business plan!

This reminded me of how I'd learned to submit expense accounts the summer I interned at one of the Big Three auto companies in Detroit. A deflated expense account was as liable to be scrutinized as an inflated one. "How could Harry be on the road for seven days and only spend $105 while Tom is on the road for seven days and spent $405?"

The key to both film funding and expense accounting was expectation.

Expectation should not be confused with reality.

With a business plan for $25,000,000 I started contacting prospective investors and those who could lead me to investors. In my case, having zip-a-dee-do-da, I started with an Internet Search Engine.

Typing in "non traditional investors" brought a list of sites to my screen and great enthusiasm to my heart. It was a new day and the Internet would set me free. To hell with tradition. I'd raise the money, then contact the distributors and dictate terms to <u>them</u>. Now, striking a substantial blow for the little guy was as much a goal as actually producing the film.

More than 200 submissions and 20 months later, I not only had experienced a great deal but was ripe to be sucked into the adventure that would be the all consuming part of my life for the next seven months.

That is how I ended up on the virtual doorstep of Anamika Biswas, whose doorstep, by the way, is located in Kolkata, India.

I'd never heard of the city and could not find it in my atlas, but soon learned it was the new name given to Calcutta. Could this be the first step in the beautification of India's image? Better trying and failing to find Kolkata on a map than preceding Calcutta with the words black hole, which to those of a certain age was a combo, the late lamented and soon-to-be-sainted Mother Teresa aside, as easy to mind and tongue as ham and eggs.

Soon, to me black hole of Calcutta was the term that most accurately described where I resided during the next seven months rather than the Kiplingesque house of pestilence.

Yet, like every journey of thousands of miles, my single step would be taken from California to British Columbia and then to Tasmania. Yep. That Tasmania. Ass end of the world Tasmania. And, why not?

Why not, indeed? Why not me? Why shouldn't it be true?

This is the story of expectation gone awry.

In the beginning there was Larry and Chris. And they begat twenty four companies, none of which full disclosure forces me to add, were on the Fortune 500 list. Mine included.

It all began with an email.

But, here I digress again.

Expectation does not develop in a Petri dish, or in a vacuum. It is the fusion of one's life experiences with one's heart's desire. Given the right ingredients all possibilities have potential, just like all sows ears can become silk purses, with the proper perception. Naturally.

Part of my life experience came directly from the distribution of my executive summary and/or business plan to 200 plus brokers and potential investors. I'd turned over any number of rocks and found a corresponding amount of creepy crawlies.

I remember it began one summer morning in 2000, about eight months after my quest to raise $500,000 mutated into $25,000,000. A new broker I'd engaged set a meeting with an attorney in a law firm located high atop Madison Avenue in Manhattan. Reaching the address I soon realized the building was one in which I'd had an office more than 20 years earlier. Was this a positive sign? There was no time to speculate since I'd parked in the Helmsley Palace garage and I knew a lengthy meeting would require a hefty ransom to get my car back.

A hush of respectability screamed at the visitor immediately after exiting the elevator. The suite of offices were paneled and decorated to imitate chambers of English barristers and affect suitable substance and probity. Soon, a bright, young, wire-rimmed bespectacled attorney entered the conference room in summer dress, which meant without a tie but with suspenders over his open-necked white, of course, shirt.

His voice barely rose above the general hush, which forced me to lean closer to the attorney, thereby being drawn ever deeper into his force field. Any attempt or instinct I might have to negotiate was sublimated to the physical act of trying to hear what he said.

This distraction, which I saw as a ploy, later became a snare of the most heinous and destructive sort. However, it served as my first important lesson in the journey to Kolkata. Just because someone is cloaked in the aura of respectability and virtue does not mean they are respectable and virtuous. Beggars can have more nobility than kings.

Ultimately I learned the attorney was a manipulative, lying, deceitful child of God who used my business plan to move himself forward, but that is another more complicated story. As a lesson, it prepared me for a more ingenious ruse.

The lady from Sierra Leone contacted me in 2001, which was the tenth year in the civil war being fought in Sierra Leone between the government and the Revolutionary United Front. With an area approximately the size of South Carolina, Sierra Leone located in West Africa is one of the most impoverished countries in the world. It's GDP per capita was estimated at $580 in 2002. It has a population of more than five million people whose median age is 17.5 and life expectancy 42.8 years. Less than twenty percent of the female population was literate compared to forty five percent of males. This is also the country where a visitor, not properly immunized, could contract cholera, hepatitis A, malaria, schistosomiasis, tuberculosis, typhoid fever and yellow fever.

It wasn't until I wrote this book that I looked any deeper into life in Sierra Leone. However, when contacted I was determined to give equal opportunity to all investors. This particular potential investor said she was from Sierra Leone. Her name was.... Actually I don't really know what her name was, but she identified herself through email as Diana Theodoritou, a widow residing in what I knew to be a war-torn African country.

Our story officially begins on

April 25, 2001—09:42:22 MDT

An email was sent to me with the subject "jonit venture investment." It was a year and five months since I started looking for financing and I was not about to quibble about a misspelled word. Diana Theodoritou sent the email from her address at theodotmines@usa.net. The following is what she sent, including all spelling and punctuation/grammar errors.

> *Dear sir,*
> *I found your proposal at … listings through search engine on Internet, and I am interested to invest into the project. I am 62yrs old widow, a Greek by birth but currently living in Africa. I am into Gold and Diamond Mining in Sierra-leone. Please contact me as soon as you can for further details about the Investment.*
> *Thank you and best regards,*
> *Madam Diana Theodoritou*

Who knew? The Internet spans the globe, right? The listings site was a legitimate one and is not identified here since the person who runs it has my utmost respect and confidence. As with all predatory creatures, once prey is spotted they swoop. Why not? Why not me?

At 09:19:58—0700 I responded to Madam Diana.

> Thank you for your e-mail. As I was not sure what you meant about contacting you "for further details about the investment—from you or me—I've attached the business plan for my project.
> With that additional information, I would hope that you'd provide me with your investment intentions/interests or "next steps" as you perceive them.
> I appreciate your interest and look forward to discussing this at length in the future.
> Best regards,
> Vincent Panettiere

I attached my executive summary for the $25,000,000 business plan.

April 26—16:20:49 +0100 (BST)

I received a response from the Madam.

> *Dear sir,*
> *I am currently having problem with my usa.net address.*
> *Please send your response to this address.*
> *Thank you and best regards.*
> *Diana Theodoritou*

The email address she used was theodotmines@yahoo.co.uk. Clearly we were now on friendlier terms since she dropped the Madam in her closing.

April 30—19:51:36 +0100 9BST

She sent a more substantial response to me.

> *Thank you. I have gone through the executive summary of the project and it's alright.*

I will most probably can work with you as you are already in the business. I could put anything between USD2 million to USD5 million but it MUST be a joint venture.

If I invest this amount in your project, could you guarantee me 17% annual income???

As previously mentioned in my msg, I am 59yrs old widow, a Greek but have lived in Guinea, Angola and now Sierra-Leone for the past 30 years.

I am into Gold and Diamond mining. I am half deaf can't hear very well due to bomb blast by the Rebels when they invaded my mines field during the recent civil war in Sierra Leone.

Diana Theodoritou

She found my business plan to be "alright"? This is the plan I wrote and refined for months and her left-handed acceptance bruised my ego which quickly recovered when she indicated a willingness to invest $2-5 million in my company.

As I write this, I notice for the first time that after five days of correspondence, Madam Theodoritou's age had decreased by three years. Had I been aware of that discrepancy two years ago some kind of flag, not exactly red, might have been raised. Odd for a woman to reveal her age at all, particularly one in her sixth decade, and most especially upon introduction. To provide a different age some days later is even more unusual. Either she found my e-mails so charming that she was being flirtatious or the blast by the Rebels damaged more than her hearing or she was a complete fiction. Now this is intriguing hindsight. Then, I was oblivious.

I proposed, for her security that she become involved in a co-financing opportunity I'd discovered which required her to provide a letter of credit. I thought living in a far away country which, even as I write this, is barely civilized; she'd be better protected than simply wiring funds.

May 3—13:10:17 +0100 (BST) she replied:

Thank you for the msg. Though raising the said fund through LC is indeed a relatively risk free way for investment, but unfortunately we do not have a Commercial bank in Sierra-leone that can raise LC on huge amount.

Diana

A check of the Internet would have revealed Sierra-Leone had the Standard Chartered, Union Trust and Sierra Leone Commercial Bank with connections to HSBC and SCB in the U.S. and U.K. I didn't check the Internet and simply advised her that she could determine the next steps in this courtship. She punctually replied the same day at 18:36:29 +0100 (BST).

> How about if fund is moved to Europe through high profile Diplomatic Mission Agency???Wii you be comfortable with this arrangement? pls advice—Diana

What the hell is a high profile Diplomatic Mission Agency anyway? As the co-financing partner needed the funds verified in a U.S. bank, I asked if her" funds would be moved to a bank account in Europe?"

May 4—12:08:28 +0100 (BST) she responded.

> No, it will be moved to a security bank in Europe and after collection we can then arrange for onward transfer into any desired bank account.
> Diana

I agreed in essence as long as "the funds—in an escrow account or LC—end up in a U.S. bank and the terms of escrow or LC are for 12 months, there is no problem." She did not respond for five days.

May 9—15:01:25 +0100 (BST):

> ... I've been attacked with Malaria fever since couple of days ago, so I was at my private clinic receiving treatment. Thank God am okay now. Could you pls send the executive summary of the project once again to my lawyer at this address. fransawyer@usa.net—Diana

I wished her a speedy recovery and told her the executive summary would be sent to her lawyer. Her lawyer! Now we're moving ahead. Surely this is a sign of sincerity, good faith and honest intentions. Otherwise, why employ a lawyer? Even if the hourly fees in Sierra Leone were infinitesimal by comparison to Beverly Hills, they'd have to be exorbitant by local standards as that's the nature of lawyers—which of course is the punch line to the joke about the scorpion who asks the frog to take him across the river. The frog refuses fearing the scorpion, known by its reputation, will sting and kill him. The scorpion begs and pleads. The frog relents. All is fine until half way across and the frog is suddenly stung. "Why"? The frog asks with his dying breath. "It's my nature," the scorpion replies.

So it must be for lawyers everywhere, the need to batter, bludgeon, wheedle, cajole and gouge is part of the genetic fabric of all lawyers no matter country, culture or continent.

However, while engaging in this flight of fancy the lawyer's email was returned since it "had permanent fatal errors." The executive summary was resent, but Mr. Sawyer had difficulty opening it and provided an alternate email address fsawyyer@yahoo.fr.

On May 11, the ES was resent. I also proposed sending a hard copy by Federal Express. There was no response for five days. Just before leaving on a week-long business trip I advised Ms. Theodoritou I'd be out of email contact and asked that I receive some response from her attorney before I left. I also expressed my pleasure that the UN had stepped into the conflict in Sierra-Leone and hoped she was safe and in improved health. Couldn't hurt to be considerate and kind, even if perfunctory.

May 18—10:26:05 +0100 (CEST)

Just prior to my leaving for the East Coast, Mr. Sawyyer responded.

> *I just received information from Madam Theodoritou's secretary that she's at the moment undergoing a Ear surgery at the Medical Institution in Guinea and won't be available untill May 27,2001. I will inform you as soon as she back from Guinea*
> *Thank you and best regards.*
> *Francis Sawyyer*

First Sierra Leone and now Guinea. I was being taken on a tour of all the countries I knew nothing about and cared to know less. I sent word wishing her a speedy recovery and left for my trip.

Two days after returning, and with no word, I informed Mr. Sawyyer and Madam Theodoritou that I was back in Los Angeles and requested a status check regarding their interest.

May 29—11:30:14 +0200 (CEST) Sawyyer replied.

> *I have been directed by Madam Diana Theodoritou to inform you that she is willing to proceed into the investment. But, however, she expects 17% annual return on the amount invested or 40% equity offer of the company she's investing into.*
> *Please let me know if this is workable for you or not. Are you directly involved with the daily management of this project??? Your personal bio-data and cv is welcome.*
> *Sincerely yours*
> *Francis Sawyyer.*

As Sawyyer was nine hours ahead of me in California, I was able to respond the same day. I expressed my pleasure that Madam Theodoritou was willing to invest in my company, then advised Sawyyer that I was directly and totally involved in the management of the company and the production of the films. The tricky part was her expectation of a 17% return on her investment. No film production company, particularly a small, independent one, can guarantee what the annual return on its films will be. We are all trying to catch lightning in a bottle and most often, the lightning blazes over head and disappears without even illuminating the empty bottle.

I came up with two scenarios for the Madam. She could invest $5 million in one film and receive her initial investment plus 50% of the profits after distribution expenses had been deducted. Or, she could provide an LC for $2.5 million which would be returned after 12 months and receive 10% more than her bank interest as well as 10% of the profits of all four films I had been preparing to produce. In this way, I felt she would have the least amount of risk.

Two days later his response arrived via email. For some reason communication fell into a rhythm of two day delays. Realistically, they might have other investments to consider. Perhaps it took two days for Sawyyer and the Madam to make contact by phone. Why use the phone when each had email capability? I never discovered the reason for the delay and after a bit it didn't matter.

May 31—14:01:33 +0200 (CEST) Sawyyer replied:

> *Yes, I do received the executive summary and having reviewed it, I immediately recommended she proceeds with the investment.*
> *Concerning the two options mentioned in your mail, she will most certainly opt for the USD5 million investment because raising LC is almost difficult and time wasting. Actually, raising an LC normally*

takes 3 months if one has inside connection in a bank, but without connection we are talking about almost 3 to 6 months. And considering time factor which in this business is of essence, the first proposal is much more preferable.

So long as you can guarantee her investment return and 50% equal share with your company, I think she mostly likely will go for it.

Is there any time factor as to when this fund will be needed? Anyhow, I will contact her and if she confirms her willingness I will send you a draft agreement.

Looking forward to hearing from you.

Sincerely yours

Francis Sawyyer.

Taking stock of the situation, I had an investor willing to provide my company with five million of Uncle Sam's dollars for my first film. The fact that the Madam did not live in Monte Carlo, Beverly Hills or Shaker Heights was of no significance. She could just as easily have been a resident of Tierra del Fuego or Ayres Rock. Money is money. Someone had reviewed my business plan, thought it worthy of their time and money and was prepared to step up to the plate.

Her lawyer was going to write the contract. We were getting serious. And, it felt good to be treated seriously.

However, I had an ethical and rational responsibility to Madam. Most likely she was not very sophisticated in the labyrinthine ways of the film business. Who is? Therefore, I owed her an opportunity to pull out of the deal.

In my response to her on May 31, once again I expressed pleasure in her intent to invest. However, I added "You both (Sawyyer was copied) should be acutely aware that investment in motion picture production entails a high degree of risk and is suitable for those who can afford a total loss of their investment. Further, risk factors as contained in my previously sent Executive Summary should be carefully evaluated by you both.

"It is important that we all understand the risk. I cannot guarantee Ms. Theodoritou's investment. I can guarantee her 50% of all profits from the film in perpetuity."

As I typed that last sentence of email, the fingers of both hands were crossed behind my back.

Little did I know at the time that I was the one most at risk.

June 1—11:05:54 +0200 (CEST) Sawyyer replied:

> *Thank you for your sincereity. I will need time to discuss this issue with Madam Theodoritou I'll get back to you as soon as possible.*

Though my sincerity was applauded several days went by without any email from Madam or Sawyyer. Had I shot myself in the foot with my own honesty and need to be above board? Did this intrusion of reality deflate Madam's hopes and dreams, depriving her of a chance to rise out of the swamp of death and destruction to bask in the warm glow of Hollywood and fat profits? Did she find the prose in my email too purple? I had no way of knowing.

Absent their response, I took the initiative by trying to place film risk in a broader perspective.

June 5—01:06:26—0700 I wrote:

> You'll recall in my last e-mail I stated that I could not guarantee any investment from anyone in my films. That is the nature of the business. Investment in the stock market has its risks as well, regardless of the quality of the company.
>
> Naturally, no one enters any business expecting or anticipating failure. This is true of the film business as well. I can assure you I believe the films I have developed for production will make a profit. How big would be speculation. They have been designed to make a profit based on size of budget, genre and a knowledge of what the market place will return.
>
> In my last email you'll note that our income projections for "The Agenda" are positive and optimistic.
>
> What I didn't explain is the way revenue is returned.
>
> For example:
>
> Let's say $10 is paid for a ticket to a film. Half ($5) goes to the theater owner; 30% of the remaining $5 ($1.50) goes for distribution expenses which include the cost of making and distributing prints of the film as well as advertising.
>
> The remaining $3.50 is returned to the production company—for example my production company Thistle Productions. It is from these proceeds that the producer (Thistle) pays back its investor in full—and in the process pays for the cost of producing the film.
>
> Once the investment/cost of production has been recouped, the investor and production company (Thistle) share the resulting

profits according to a negotiated percentage. I am offering Madam Theodoritou 50% of the profits.

I hope the above will be helpful in determining your ultimate decision and look forward to the prospect of working with you both.

Nineteen minutes—01:27:04–0700—later I sent a follow up. This was approximately one thirty in the morning. I continued my mini course in the film business as I knew it with a discussion of the function of "pre-sales" an exposition on "paying down" the cost of production followed by the intent of "minimums" and the creation of "break even" positions.

Had I been living in a war torn, backward country for decades and suddenly was exposed to such language it would all read like Greek to me, even if I was a Greek.

Satisfied I'd tortured Madam and Sawyyer enough for one night; I went to bed and woke to find an email from "herself". She was able to translate my Greek at 1:59:55 +0100 (BST):

> *Please confirm if you have received a drafted agreement from my lawyer. Pls respond ASAP.*

I guessed my mini course in the film biz had impressed them enough to send an agreement and dashed off a quick email letting Madam know I had not received the agreement, but would let her know as soon as it arrived.

June 6

On this morning, memorialized for all above a certain age as D-Day, the beginning of the end of Nazi domination in Europe, I awoke with thoughts that this day would be the beginning of my burgeoning career.

Sawyyer sent me an email at 11:39:07 +0200 (CEST):

> *As per Madam Theodoritou's request, attached a drafted agreement for your perusal. Pls review, fill in the dotted lines, correct if necessary and return it back via e-mail ASAP. Please do not sign.*
> *Sincerely Yours,*
> *F. Sawyyer.*

I opened the Word attachment and indeed up popped his Draft Agreement. It was two pages in length. A quick look and all seemed to be consistent with the rudimentary language of a draft agreement as I had experienced deal memos while an agent. Maybe not as fulsome, but the requisite clauses were in place.

The following is the agreement, warts and all:

DRAFT AGREEMENT.

This agreement made and concluded this ... day of June 2001 by and between Madam diana Theodoritou of 25, Association avenue Freetown, Sierra-leone. Herein after referred to as the INVESTOR being party of the first part,
          AND
Mr Vincent Panettiere of ... in USA. Herein after referred to as the COMPANY being party of the second part.

WHEREAS, the INVESTOR being desirous in placing an investment in a profitable venture in Brisko International Inc. in USA in Consideration for a secured and guaranteed annual income. And the COMPANY, being interested in attracting fresh capital funding for it's ever expanding activities.

WHEREFORE it is hereby agreed that the INVESTOR Madam Diana Theodoritou agrees to invest the sum of USD ... (.... million US dollars) in the commercial activities of the COMPANY after the execution of this contract. That in consideration for this investment, the COMPANY agrees to offer 17 % of the COMPANY'S equity in the form of common stock to the INVESTOR Madam Diana Theodoritou.

That the INVESTOR agrees to respect and protect any CONFIDENTIAL and PROPRIETY information and rights of the COMPANY.

That both parties agree that any dispute to any part or section of this agreement shall be settled by arbitration under the prevailing Laws of the state of.... in USA.

That this agreement is signed, sealed and executed this.... day of.... 2001 Before me

_____ JP and the presence of the following witnesses

_____ for INVESTOR
_____ for COMPANY.

That the INVESTOR (*Madam Diana Theodotritou*) has her own independent due diligence of the COMPANY (...) and is entering this
Agreement based upon that due diligence.

That the COMPANY agrees that the INVESTOR or her ASSIGNEE will hold seats on the Board of the COMPANY equivalent to the percentage of equity held.

That while the INVESTOR agrees to accept future profit and loss account of the COMPANY, the INVESTOR will not be liable or share liability in any and ALL previous loss incurred or contracted by the COMPANY prior to the signing of this agreement.

That the COMPANY agrees, upon reasonable notice, to open the Financial Records of the COMPANY to the INVESTOR or her ASSIGNEE for scrutiny and due diligence.

The following signatories voluntary accept the terms of this Agreement and its legal implications under the laws of USA.

INVESTOR: *Madam Diana Theodotritou.*

COMPANY:(represented by Mr Vincent Panettierre).

N.B: This faxed copy shall enjoy the same validity as the original hard copy.

I immediately sent Madam an email giving her and Sawyyer conditional acceptance of the draft which would have to be reviewed by my attorney and chief financial officer. I expressed the hope that I would give them complete approval by the weekend, this being Wednesday.

Two days later I informed Madam and Sawyyer that my CFO thought the draft was a "simple and straight forward agreement" but asked that a funding schedule be included. My attorney was out of town until the next week.

By June 12 my attorney had read my revised version of the draft, which I sent on. We were ready to proceed with whatever next steps were in store.

We continued to have difficulty communicating, which required another series of email with attachments to Sawyyer on June 13. There was a four day lapse in communication which caused me to contact Sawyyer on June 17. Tentatively I tried not to be demanding or apply pressure.

June 17

> I realize you may have not formalized the next version of my agreement with Madam Theodoritou in such short a time. However, due to the distance of time and space between us, please at least advise me if you have received my several e-mails to you of last week.

The reply from Madam came two days later.

June 19—08:43:44 +0100 (BST).

> *Funds will leave Sierra-leone for London, UK as scheduled. You are required to be in London for further transfer arrangement of funds to it's final destination. However, before you leave, you are to contact handler's offshore office in London for informations. After agreement has been formalised, handler's offshore phone details shall be given to you including password.*
>
> *Meanwhile, my lawyer said he couldn't find the amended agreement you sent in his file. In other to formalise agreement, pls re-send the amended agreement using Doc via email to him including your fax number ASAP.*
>
> *For your information, I will be visiting your company in August 2001. As previously mentioned in my message, all voice messages should be directed to my lawyer Mr. Francis Sawyyer, should you have any questions or need more informations regarding this arrangement do not hesistate to contact him.*
>
> *Tel: (229) country code, no city code, number 985980.*
> *Diana Theodoritou*

Whoa! Quite a chunk to digest. I started reading from the top.

Funds will leave Sierra-leone for London, UK as scheduled. Great. But, who knew? What schedule? What day?

You are required to be in London for further transfer arrangement of funds to it's final destination. I have to go to <u>London</u>? What, nobody heard of wire transfer? SWIFT code?

However, before you leave, you are to contact handler's offshore office in London for informations. After agreement has been formalised, handler's offshore phone details shall be given to you including password. I had to contact a <u>handler</u>? Not an auspicious word. There are baggage handlers and elephant handlers, public relations handlers and assistants-fawning-over-the-rich-and-famous handlers. Now a financial handler? Both the word and context were strange. This handler had an offshore office in London? What does this mean? He's living on a house boat or 50-foot yacht?

But, I couldn't contact the handler until after my agreement with Madam had been formalized. Then and only then would I get the handler's phone details and PASSWORD. Now I felt I was entering the world of secret handshakes, spies in Lisbon, etc.

For your information, I will be visiting your company in August 2001. This was quite a surprise. If I had been questioning the legitimacy of handlers and passwords, etc. her plans to visit me in Los Angeles in only a few weeks was disarming and blew all doubts away. Madam was serious. So was I.

By now, where I might have become suspicious, this odyssey was making me curiouser and curiouser. Off went another email with my revised draft of the contract.

DRAFT AGREEMENT

This agreement made and concluded this 6th day of June 2001 by and between Madam Diana Theodoritou of 25 Association Avenue Freetown, Sierra Leone, Herein after referred to as the INVESTOR being party of the first part, AND Mr. Vincent Panettiere of Thistle Productions, Inc. Los Angeles, CA 90046 USA, Herein after referred to as the COMPANY being party of the second part.

WHEREAS, the INVESTOR being desirous in placing an investment in a profitable venture in Thistle Productions, Inc. in USA in consideration for a secured and guaranteed annual income. And the COMPANY, being interested in attracting fresh capital funding for its every expanding activities.
WHEREFORE, it is hereby agreed that the INVESTOR madam Diana Theodoritou agrees to invest the sum of USD$5 million in the commercial activities of the COMPANY after the execution of the contract. That in consideration for this investment, the COMPANY agrees to offer 17% of the COMPANY's equity in the form of common stock to the INVESTOR Madam Diana Theodoritou.

That the INVESTOR agrees to respect and protect any CONFIDENTIAL and PROPRIETY information and rights of the COMPANY.

That both parties agree that any dispute to any part or section of this agreement shall be settled by arbitration under the prevailing Laws of the State of California in USA.

That this agreement is signed, sealed and executed this _____ day of _____ 2001

Before me

_____ JP and the presence of the following witnesses

_____ INVESTOR

Before me

_____ JP and the presence of the following witnesses

_____ for COMPANY

That the INVESTOR (*Madam Diana Theodoritou*) has her own independent due diligence of the COMPANY (Thistle Productions, Inc.) and is entering this Agreement based upon that due diligence.

That the COMPANY agrees that the INVESTOR or her ASSIGNEE will hold one (1) seat on the Board of the COMPANY equivalent to the percentage of equity held.

That while the INVESTOR agrees to accept future profit and loss accounts of the COMPANY, the INVESTOR will not be liable or share liability in any and ALL previous loss incurred or contracted by the COMPANY prior to the signing of this agreement.

That the COMPANY agrees, upon reasonable notice, but no more than semi-annually, to open the Financial Records of the COMPANY to the INVESTOR or her ASSIGNEE for scrutiny and due diligence.

The following signatories voluntary accept the terms of this Agreement and its legal implications under the laws of the USA

INVESTOR: *Madam Diana Theodoritou*
COMPANY:
Vincent Panettiere
President
Thistle Productions, Inc.
N.B. This faxed copy shall enjoy the same validity as the original hard copy.

While my changes were being reviewed by Sawyyer and Madam, I checked Sawyyer's area code. He lived where? In Benin? A country so small one needs a magnifying glass <u>and</u> bifocals to find it in an atlas.

Now for the geography lesson on Benin. The country, about two thirds the size of Portugal, is located on the Gulf of Guinea on the west coast of Africa, but south east of Sierra Leone. As a former French colony, the official language is—surprise—French. There is also a risk of contracting cholera, dengue fever, hepatitis A, malaria, meningitis, schistomiasis, tuberculosis, typhoid fever and yellow fever. At the time I thought "her lawyer is in Benin? So?"

June 19—06:59:24—0700

I responded to Madam on the very same day.

> Is it your intent … that I go to London to arrange for the funds to be transferred to my US bank after we finalize the Agreement between you and Thistle Productions?
> As I am scheduling meetings sometime in August outside of California, please advise asap when you plan to arrive in Los Angeles and I will change my schedule. I am looking forward to meeting and working together with you.

I was curious and naive, but that didn't mean I had to be a blooming idiot. I had no plans to travel and was determined not to go to London. But I also wanted to smoke Madam out. If she were coming to Los Angeles at a time when she thought I'd be away at my "meetings" perhaps she could confirm her schedule sooner than she wished. Magnanimously I offered to change my "schedule" to suit hers.

June 20—09:40:35 +0100 (BST) she replied

> *Yes, according to the arrangement agreed upon with handlers you will need to be in London as indicated in my previous msg.*
> *Concerning my trip; to L.A., I'll send my flight itinerary in due course.*

I called Sawyyer in Benin. His accent might have been British or the faux British accent affected by those who want to seem cultured. As Benin was a former French colony, Sawyyer did not have to be of Gallic descent to live there. The spelling of his last name was peculiar, but not suspicious. We exchanged brief information among chamber-of-commerce pleasantries. For me it was a feeling-out call. I wondered how he regarded it, but determined by his tone of voice that he didn't seem unnerved or surprised.

I followed up with an email in which I asked him to advise me as soon as possible when the funds would be in London so that I could make appropriate arrangements to commit to some Italian and German co-producing partners. I did not mention going to London.

Additionally, I contacted Madam and requested further information.

> As we are moving toward a more formal relationship, please send me your biography so that I can share it with my Board of Directors and better prepare for your trip in August.

There was no board of directors, in the true corporate sense. However I was relying on colleagues and advisors who, if Madam arrived in Los Angeles and a meeting arranged, could be called upon to vet my investor.

June 22—09:18:33 +0100 (BST)

Back came Madam.

> *Dear Mr. Panettiere,*
> *As per your request, below my personal bio-data.*
>
> *MY ABREVIATED C.V.*
>
> *NAME: DIANA AGNES THEODORITOU (NEE AGRIPOLLOUS)*
> *D.O.B.: January 05 1942, Athens Greece.*
> *NATIONALITY: Greek*
> *QUALIFICATION: Bsc. Geo, Bsc. Mech Eng.*
> *LANGUAGE: Greek, English, SwahiliSwahili, and many African lan-*
> *guages.*
> *OWNER: Penta Gold&Diamond Mining holdings l.t.d*
> *I have spent virtually a lifetime in the Mining industry and has been actively involved in the exploration and development of both underground ALLUVIAL Diamond Mining projects through the influence of my late husband Mr. Staveras Theodoritou also an Engineer who had worked for several years in the Diamond mines fields in South Africa, Zaire, Angola before he died of Malaria fever in Angola in 1985. After my husband's death, a Mining company Zouthpa*

Diamonds (pty) l.t.d. with International operations in South Africa, Nambia, Zambia, Zaire, Guinea, Sierra-Leone offered me a position as strategic business Manager a position I accepted with the challenge of broadening my horizons internationally.

I was mandated to negotiate mineral and Mining rights and to establish corporate and company structures in various jurisdictions as either holding entities for rights, or operational entities for exploration activities. I gained invaluable experience in various African countries and built up a network of profession relationships and contacts during the fulfillment of my contract period. After my resignation, I established my own mining company in Sierra-leone through the help of my Sierra-leoneans partners. I have a daughter, she is married to a German and they are currently living in Australia with their two children. I gave my grandchildren African names Zatola (boy) and Jemila (girl) they so much cherish this names.

Regards

Diana

Whew! This woman had lived, with experience in places I never thought of and certainly never planned to visit. Soon after reviewing her CV, I thanked Madam for sending it and shared it with my colleagues who were pleased and intrigued by her unusual—from the first world/corporate world viewpoint—experiences.

Two days later I contacted Sawyyer to advise him that I had not received the new agreement.

June 25—08:06:05 +0100 (BST)

The next day Diana replied instead of Sawyyer.

This is to let you know that funds have arrived UK as scheduled. You are required to contact Mr. Chris Brown of Global Security and Fund Managers L.T.D. in London for details Tel:+44 7930639969 your password when contacting him is MTD SIERRA-LEONE.

Agreement has been formalised it will be faxed to you shortly. Should you have any questions do not hesistate to contact my lawyer Mr. Francis Sawyyer on Tel: (229) country code, no city code, number 985980.

Diana

Later that day at 19:58:20 +0200 (CEST) Sawyyer sent me an email.

> *Agreement will be completed tomorrow Tuesday 26th June 2001. It will be faxed immediately to the fax number given in your previous msg.*
> *Please you are to sign and return it by fax to the fax following fax number; (229) 315910.*
> *Best regards,*
> *F. Sawyyer*

I received the agreement by fax, as Sawyyer said I would. Before signing it and sending it back I checked with Karl and John my financial and business advisors. In an email Karl responded:

> Stranger things have happened. If there is a 0.001% chance, take it. You have. Now, let's see what the "terms" are.
> I'm pretty sure the "Sting" will be in there. I.e., a flat, one time advance $12,500 or something of that order which will trigger the release of the funds automatically to you. Sincerely Diana. Etc. But we are hip to that, eh Watson?

This was a pail of cold water in my face and across my ego. Karl's banking experience was deep and broad. His resume included senior positions with Citibank, Bank of America, Dai Ichi Kangyo and other major banks, working in the U.S., Europe, Russia, Egypt, Oman and Kuwait. We'd talked on numerous occasions about his experience uncovering members of a Nigerian scam operation in San Diego County. I respected his knowledge and experience, yet.

The "yet" was my reluctance to let go of an opportunity that, until further proof to the contrary existed, was a possibility with the potential to launch my first film as well as my company, my career and the careers of my writer and director clients. That was too much to discard without actually placing my fingers in an "open wound" like St. Thomas. I conceded the possibility he was right but reserved making a final conclusion until more information was forthcoming.

On cue, John, a man I respected as an honorable businessman and advisor sent me his reaction to the agreement by email, June 26, 2001 15:06:41–0400:

Thanks for the fax of the agreement. Her agreement is pretty much identical to others from her I have seen. Nothing has closed. It will all come down to up front money to "couriers".

Strangely or prophetically my mother's words from years gone by rang in my head. "You don't have to put your hand on the flame to know the stove is hot." Then I heard my voice answering her "I know, I know … mom." At the time I was not aware that D. H. Lawrence had written "… failures are usually the most conceited of men …"

I signed the agreement and sent it to Sawyyer by fax. I also informed Madam that I'd be travelling in August and asked her to advise the days she would be in Los Angeles.

June 29—08:24:22 =0100 (BST)

> *I will be in US from August 22nd to 28th 1\2001. I will let you know in good time in case there is change of schedule.*
> *Diana*

She had plans to visit Los Angeles which were freely communicated. This was a sign of positive intent. All we had to do was keep in touch, establish rapport and all would be well. I wrote back to Madam looking forward to our meeting.

Later that day Sawyyer sent an email—9:41:39 +0200 (CST):

> *Please call Global Security and Fund Managers immediately for transfer procedures.*
> *I will be out of town on week end trip to Accra, Ghana.*
> *Should you need information pls contact me if you can as from Monday July 2nd 2001.*
> *Francis Sawyyer*
> *(Tel) 985980*

So, that's where folks in Benin go for the weekend, Accra, Ghana. A life-long puzzle had been solved. With more than ninety thousand square miles, Ghana was almost twice the size of Benin. I imagined the opportunities to shop at better malls and meet more attractive women must propel many citizens of Benin across the border—actually two borders by land since Togo separates them—come Friday night.

Two months had passed since Madam's initial email to me on April 25. At this point I felt a true entrepreneur, which loosely translated can mean "between the pullers". On the one side were the experienced, knowledgeable and well intentioned advisors. Intellectually I gave considerable weight to their assessment.

But on the other side was the potential for growth and expansion, which might require a leap of faith, several grains of salt and the benefit of more than one doubt. Should all this be over come, we'd be on our way and rolling. This, of course, was the emotional, subjective side. As I'd been involved in mostly creative endeavours during my business career, I gave this side more weight.

At the same time I realized the one side of the "pullers" had divided. I was in the middle between Madam and Sawyyer. She was nurturing me with visions of a serendipitous meeting in Los Angles where, as partners, we would plan our future success. At the same time, Sawyyer was pulling me to call London where there was a 50/50 chance reality would bite my buns.

I thought it might be wise to keep them both in play. I was juggling all the balls in the air while moving forward. I wrote to Madam and told her how much I anticipated our meeting. Then I told Sawyyer, June 29 being Friday, I'd call Global on Monday.

July 2

That Monday I called the London number Madam provided several times and always got a busy signal. I asked her to check if the number was correct and added that I felt the London city code of either 71 or 81 was required.

The next day—12:13:43 +0100 she told me:

Please dial the given number directly like this 44 7930639967.

I did as instructed and sent Madam a follow up email regarding the conversation I'd had with Chris Brown.

July 3—08:54:42—0700:

Diana:
I spoke with Chris Brown in London today.
The following are notes from our conversation:
Brown asked "how much do you think we have here for you".
I said "I don't know". He said $5,000,000. I said that's what we'd agreed on.

He told me the procedure—that "Global Securities acts on behalf of its clients when a consignment comes in to us, providing all verifications."

They have to verify me "so we're not paying the wrong person. It's a security check so we don't get into trouble."

I asked if the money was in a bank and he said it was.

He asked for my cel phone and fax number. I gave him my fax number, but my cel is not usually on.

Then he asked me how old I was, what part of America do I live in, what business I was in and what films I produced.

He asked when I could come to London.

I told him I'm travelling through mid-July and then the second week in August.

As a result of my schedule he said it was not possible to make an appointment until August.

I told him my attorney in London could handle the details as I am travelling due to being in pre-production on my slate of four feature films—having just returned from a trip at the end of last week.

He said "normally we want to see the person for our selves".

He said he'd touch base with you.

I told him I'd send you an e-mail as well.

He said he didn't know how long he could hold the money. I told him that if you wanted to invest in my company she could do so at any time.

That my attorney with power of attorney could handle the details and have the funds wired to my account.

Diana, I hope you realize this is an excellent investment opportunity for you, not just in profits but as an annuity over the long term.

I am very much looking forward having you as my partner, introducing you to my board of directors and spending time with you in August.

I hope these technical details can be worked out for our mutual satisfaction so that we can. make progress together.

Best regards,
Vincent

As Brown didn't know I had an inkling he might ask for up front fees, I tried dodging and weaving until his intentions became clearer.

But, he started out taking the wrong approach with me. As I listened, his accent with its lilting cadences sounded Jamaican. Accent is one thing, but his question—*How much do you think we have for you?* This said in a sing song, ostensibly playful tone seemed more mocking than friendly. And, why that question? I made the deal and I knew how much to expect.

I listened as he went on about verifying identification so they didn't pay the *wrong person.* With some idea that Brown was setting me up for an up-front fee scam, his rationalization and explanation of probity was both transparent and galling.

More than anything I was determined not to go to London. If this was a scam, going to London with my foreknowledge would be akin to tripping the trap door at my own hanging. I did the best tap dancing I could around the subject of the trip by introducing a very full travel schedule and a fictitious attorney in London. How long would this play out? How much would he swallow?

Brown was sophisticated, or wily, enough in the ways of negotiation to "defer to a higher power". He'd check with Madam, but added some uncertainty—*he didn't know how long he could hold the money.* If the money was in a bank, what's the problem? The bank is not charging them rent, unless the money was stashed in a safe deposit box instead of a pass book or checking account. If the money was not in a bank, why wasn't it? I imagined canvas bags or steamer trunks filled with Uncle Sam's tender. How much does five million in bills weigh? What were its measurements when boxed and packaged? Whatever.

I tried to provide my own incentive to Madam in the email account of my conversation with Brown. I offered a way out of the misery of war and a glimmer of a stable, fruitful future with me and my company. I had the capacity to tug on heart strings to keep my balance between the pullers.

July 4—Madam sent an email—08:24:22+0100 (BST)

> *I have been informed already by my lawyer that due to your engagements throught this month you won't be able to be in London to complete the transfer transaction and that your lawyer will be there on your behalf. In any case, it is okay by me if there is no other options but however, an official letter will have to be written by my lawyer first authorising Global Security and Fund Manager's to allow your lawyer represent you for the transaction and copy of your power of*

attorney must be sent to me and my lawyer as well. I will give direc-tives to my lawyer Mr. francis Sawyyer to have this letter done ASAP. Diana

July 5—16:50:01—0700 I responded to Madam:

I appreciate your willingness to allow my attorney with my power of attorney handle the transaction with Chris Brown.

Chris Brown called me this morning to tell me he'd spoken with your attorney—Francis Sawyyer I guess—and they agreed I can send my attorney with power of attorney. He told me he doesn't usually agree to this procedure.

He told me once I put together the power of attorney I am to get back to him (Chris) and book an appointment with him—usually it takes a one week notice to get an appointment with Chris, he said.

I asked him about procedure and he told me once I book an appointment he'll tell me "what we're going to do". I'll get back to him as soon as we put together the power of attorney.

Sincerely
Vincent Panettiere

On balance, I'd come out of this first skirmish fairly intact. There was some give and take without any heavy handed demands. If the money was in London and this was a straight deal I now had a means of "taking their temperature."

Later that day I learned that power of attorney in the UK was different than power of attorney in the U.S. Madam T was promptly apprised of that along with some stretched truth i.e. I was working on the language with my attorney in London and had wired him funds to cover the power of attorney.

As an after thought, I asked her "might there be any ancillary fees connected with the Chris Brown transaction, other than my attorney fees which I will bear myself?"

For me, this was my attempt at getting every one "a little bit pregnant"—so involved that they couldn't or wouldn't back out for fear of losing a good deal i.e. money. I saw my deception as first and foremost a means of protection.

Additionally, the ruse was not that complex that it couldn't be undone immediately, if all was kosher.

July 6—11:44:25 +0100 (BST) Madam surprised me with an email.

> *As a matter of fact, I am thinking of having my lawyer arrange with Mr. Brown to have the funds wired directly to your nominated account in the US.*
> *I think this arrangement will be much more better as it will minimixed your expenses.*
> *I will advice you stop the power of attorney for the meantime until I hear from my lawyer latest Monday 9th July 2001*
> *Diana*

Oh joy! Oh Rapture! O, what a clever boy am I!

Suppressing a self satisfied grin, for fear it might be read in cyberspace, I sent her an email that said "I will wait until I hear from you." Simple yet deferential and hopefully disarming.

While waiting for Sawyyer to return from swinging Ghana or wherever, I contacted an editor at www.goldsheetlinks.com to get additional information on Penta Gold and Diamond Mining Ltd, Madam's company. The editor could not find any information on the company, neither a website nor an exchange where they might be listed.

However, he advised "the situation in Sierra Leone regarding conflict diamonds is very serious, and I would probably avoid the country based on its political risk." Fair enough, I knew about the violence and the child soldiers but had no intention of travelling there or investing. All I cared about was the opportunity to receive an investment from Madam.

July 10—10:01:36 +0100 (BST)

Madam promptly returned to my mail box with another pleasant surprise.

> *Arrangement to wire funds directly to your designated account as been concluded.*
> *Please contact Mr. Chris Brown immediately for procedures*
> *Diana*

My conversation with Chris Brown was a variation on the same theme as the first. I reported back to Madam the following:

I was pleased to receive your e-mail that arrangements have been made to wire your investment funds to me directly.

As you requested, I contacted Chris Brown this morning in London.

Chris confirmed my agreement with you to wire the funds and asked me to fax him a copy of the information portion of my passport so he could "open the file and start the documentation".

He then asked that I send him USD$8,000 to pay the "diplomatic courier who brought" your funds to London. He said he'd send hard copies of a contract to me and 72 hours after I sign and return the contract, the funds will be delivered to me.

1. I am confused by the $8,000 payment as you indicated in your e-mail of July 6 you were wiring the funds to minimize my expenses.

2. I believe the $8,000 is your cost of doing business.

You have agreed to invest in my company.

We have agreed on the size of your investment, percentage of ownership and return on investment.

How your investment gets to me, I believe, is your responsibility.

3. HOWEVER

As I am very interested in having you as a partner and believe we can make great progress for our mutual benefit, let me suggest the following:

a. I will pay the $8,000 by wire to your account immediately after your investment—$5,000,000 is received by my account. Or b. You can deduct the $8,000 from the total amount—as closing costs for bank loans and real estate mortgages are deducted—and then wire me the balance which is $4,992,000.

Naturally I will credit your investment at $5,000,000.

4. I don't see any reason why it should take 72 hours to wire funds to my account. You and I have already agreed on your investment. The next step should be that I supply you with my routing number and the funds are sent.

Once I receive your funds I will send you the appropriate shares of stock.

I do believe we can work out these technical details and look forward to your response as well as seeing you in Los Angeles in August.

When we meet I expect to demonstrate to you how your investment is being turned into revenue.

First, Karl's prediction of up front fees was $4,500 high and John had correctly advised there would be "courier fees" involved. I was 0 for 2 and batting .000.

Clearly, the reasoning behind my approach was to determine how "real" Madam, Sawyyer and Brown were. If they were only after up front fees, then no amount of alternatives would be satisfactory for them. Assuming they did five to ten deals a month at eight thousand a pop, in no time it could add up to real money. Conversely, I had no way of knowing if this "courier fee" was an established way to do business in certain parts of the world and others I asked were unclear as well. Knowledge rules more than gold. And those who have it—doctors, lawyers and Indian chiefs establishing casinos in California—can speak ex cathedra from the chair of St. Peter, infallible to all the civilians.

When I was five, a doctor told my mother I had leukemia. He was a pediatrician, a fairly new speciality in those days, and therefore the capo de tutti capo when it came to information about children. Right? My mother, bless her soul, had her doubts or maybe had a stubborn determination that her first born would not die. Obviously my mother was right and Mr-big-shot-pediatrician was wrong. Dead wrong—which means by now I'd be dead for many decades if my mother had listened to him.

How could I know if the courier fee was legitimate or not? I couldn't, but felt the need to err on the side of my mother. Damn the experts, full speed ahead. Two days later Madam contacted me. Now it was apparent that Madam, Sawyyer and Brown—either all three or in combination—had direct contact with each other.

July 12—14:25:03 +0100 (BST) she wrote:

> *Thank you for the mail sent. The $8,000 requested by Mr. Brown as I was told was a miscellaneous charges and is expected to be paid before the funds could be released to its designated account.*
> *Actually, I have spent over $165,000 for this arrangement excluding kick backs from Customs and airport officials both in Sierra-leone and abroad.*
> *Of course I agree that it is my responsibility to foot the bills but as a partner I will implore you assist to have the fees paid so that there won't be any hold up on the transfer.*
> *You said you are confused, well, I thought arranging for a direct wiring of funds to your account will minimised your expenses since you won't need to pay your lawyer any service fees. And the truth of the matter is I never knew there will be additional fees required apart from the one paid earlier on.*
> *Please contact Mr. Brown and endeavor to have this problem solved soon as possible.—Diana*

A gullible person might conclude that eight thousand dollars was not much to pay when his benefactor had already shelled out one hundred and sixty five thousand dollars for assorted venal customs inspectors and border guards. The per capita income of Sierra-leone and neighbouring countries being less than a thousand dollars per year her bribes could satisfy the yearly wages of 160 individuals with countless family members.

Then, her feminine, at least I hoped they were feminine, wiles began to show. She only had my best interest at heart by agreeing to wire the funds to my account from London. *I thought arranging for a direct wiring of funds to your account will minimised your expenses since you won't need to pay your lawyer any service fees.*

And, then she implored me to assist her. Finally came the protestation of ignorance—*I never knew there will be additional fees required apart from the one paid earlier on.*

In my response to her at 07:27:17–0700—I stood firm.

The Partnership Agreement you sent me and we signed is predicated on your investment of $5,000,000 in my company, Thistle Productions, Inc.

Until those funds are deposited in my account, all we have is an intention which is activated and turns into a partnership immediately upon investment.

I regret your considerable expenditure on the process to cause our intention to be realized. But we are not yet partners. Therefore, I can be of no immediate assistance and must stand fast on my determination that the $8,000 is and continues to be your cost of doing business—until we are partners.

HOWEVER—once your investment is made i.e. your funds wired to my account—I will be in fact your partner and can act in that manner.
As your partner, I will authorize the Company to reimburse you $50,000 toward your expenses. This sum will be immediately wired to an account of your choice from the $5,000,000.

My Chief Financial Officer, a banker in the U.S., Europe, the Mideast, etc. for more than 25 years, assures me the transfer can be made—both from you and to you—in rapid fashion and certainly not 72 hours as Mr. Brown suggests.

Time is of the essence as I'm sure you do not want your funds sitting idle in London.

Therefore, should my offer to reimburse you for your expenses meet with your approval, let me know and I will send you my bank routing/account numbers, etc.

Tuesday July 17 I leave for the first of two business trips that will prevent me from having e-mail contact with you for some days.

If we cannot accomplish this transfer by close of business on Monday, we'll have to wait until the last week of July.

I look forward to your favorable response to the above as well as to a very successful partnership and business relationship.

I felt I'd been too abrupt with Madam and sent her a follow up email at 12:33:38–0700:

I have sent a notarized copy of my passport to Chris Brown as he requested so that he can start the process.

I've been trying to reach you by phone, but the Sierra Leone consulate in Washington cannot find the number for me.

I think, if we can talk by phone we can speed up the process.

Can you provide me with your phone number?

Additionally, please provide me with the sorting code for your bank so that I can prepare to reimburse you for your expenses once your funds are received in my account?

I look forward to making progress—and movies—with you.

Part of me hoped that if we could talk by phone we could work out a solution, IF she was on the level.

July 13—12:59:14 +0100 (BST) my answer arrived:

As previous mentioned in my message for any voice message ple call my lawyer.
Diana

Clearly, I could reach out and touch anyone except Madam.

Even though his instincts were correct, I sensed that Karl understood the conflict between my intellect and my emotions. He suggested I propose to Madam that shares in my company

"… could be held in escrow so that the transfer of same are assured … That way she will be assured ownership while funds flow. Although its 99% certain there are no funds. But let's see what their reply will be."

To this day I appreciate his understanding and the fact that he never once said "I told you so," as many experts would do. But, Karl, in addition to being a banking expert, was also a good friend.

July 17—6:19:34—0700 I sent Madam the following:

> I leave today on the first of two business trips that will keep me travelling through mid-August.
> I hope we can work out these technical difficulties and look forward to meeting with you when you come here next month.

July 27—13:41:37 +0100 (BST) Madam sent me the following:

> *This is to let you know that my trip to USA has been postponed to September 2001 due to my health problem. I will abreast you on the new date later.*
> *Meanwhile arrangement is on to have the funds transferred to your account in US.*
> *Please re-send your Bank details to my lawyer including phone number and your office and mobile phones incase they want to contact you.*
> *Diana*

The delay of her trip by one month seemed like a stratagem to force my hand and keep me at a distance. If Diana were a facade, an imaginary investor who was invented to give the scheme a sense of reality and believability, then it made sense to <u>never</u> have me speak with her on the phone or meet in person.

Yet, Madam indicated she was making arrangements to have the funds transferred. This was part of a constant "give and take" in a sense. With every questionable or doubtful action or statement there was a counterbalancing believable action. A whipsaw of sorts made it difficult to keep one's head stable enough to accurately focus.

I was determined to play my part as well. At 14:00:22–0700—I sent an email to Madam.

> I regret that you are not feeling better and wish you a speedy recovery so that we can meet in September.

I am pleased that your recent e-mail indicated that "arrangement is on to have the funds transferred" to my account.

The information you requested will be sent to your attorney in a separate e-mail.

Meanwhile please instruct your attorney to inform me what value date you will assign to the transfer of funds.

Also, deduct the $8,000 in expenses from the transfer, if possible. If not I will wire transfer same amount upon receipt of funds in my account.

Please let me know if you have any questions or need additional information.

Later that day I sent the following email to Sawyyer:

Per the instructions of Diana Theodoritou in her e-mail of 7/27, the following is information she requested I send to you

Bank of America account for Thistle Productions, Inc.
XXXXX XXXXX

Routing # 12100358

Phone# (323) XXX-XXXX
Fax #   (323) XXX-XXXX

cel (323) XXX-XXXX—not always on, but you can leave a message

Please inform me ASAP what value date you will assign to transfer of funds.

I have advised Madam Theodoritou that $8,000 can be deducted from the total of $5 million, if possible. If not possible I will wire transfer back to her the same amount after receipt of funds in my account.

You or she will have to supply me with her bank account # and routing number.

Please let me know if you have any questions or need additional information.

I delayed sending the banking information to Sawyyer until after talking with Karl who advised me that as long as Madam/Sawyyer/Brown et al did not have borrowing authority over my account or the ability to make a transfer I did not have high exposure. He also assured me that any transfer out of my account without signature authorization would be denied due to insufficient funds. My plan was to keep only one hundred dollars in the account.

In a follow up email to me Karl concluded "If it's real, you will see ca$$$sh soon."

July 30—10:58:25 +0200 (CEST)

Sawyyer responded:

I got the info. I will abreast you about the transfer as soon as is concluded.

It was now more than three months since Madam's initial email to me.

Dutifully, and in keeping with my role as the unsuspecting innocent, I replied at 05:20:48–0700:

Kindly let me know when transfer begins so I can take necessary steps to prepare.

Also advise me how I can transfer appropriate shares of stock to Diana Theodoritou.

Within hours—22:41:41 +0200 (CEST)—he sent another email.

I will let you know as soon as I get the actual date. Concerning shares of stock I will advice you later on how it will be transferred to Madam Diana.

Sawyyer was close to burning the midnight oil in Benin sending me an email at what I presumed was nearly eleven at night. Later that day I replied at 17:32:34–0700:

> Thank you for your response. As I indicated several weeks ago, I am scheduled to leave for the second of two business trips on Aug. 5 and will not return until Aug. 11. During that time I will be out of touch with email but will be able to get voice mail messages either at 323-XXX-XXXX or 323-XXX-XXXX. Should you need to call either of those numbers be sure and leave me a number where I can reach you.
>
> I appreciate your assistance and look forward to a successful conclusion of our efforts.

July 31—15:25:06 +0200 (CEST)

Sawyyer was brief

> *Thank you, I'll contact you if there is any news.*
> *Sawyyer.*

I did not want to wait for Sawyyer to deliver news and decided to "prime the pump" via an email that asked if he knew what time frame was involved. How long before the transfer began and how long would completion of the transfer take? These questions were as much a sign of my anxiety as they were an attempt to demonstrate that I was an organized businessman who let nothing slide between the cracks. Sawyyer et al keyed in on the first part—anxiety.

August 1—17:35:59 +0200 (CEST)—came his reply.

> *According to my findings, Global Security will not release the funds until $8,000 is paid for their services.*
> *However, I have requested to have this amount paid with Bank guarramtee letter. If my request is granted I will contact you so that an arrangement will be made to have the letter issued as quickly as possible.*
> *Sincerely,*
> *Sawyyer*

The payment of $8,000 was a dead issue. It would not happen. Sawyyer's introduction of a Bank Guarantee could be a solution. But, it depended on who was putting up the BG, what it would cost me, if in fact I'd be asked to pay the cost, and when that cost was due. I was prepared to make a reasonable deal on the BG, which could possibly include reimbursement of the guarantor's expenses plus a bonus and even back end points in the film. Anyone who would help me out on the if-come deserved to be rewarded, but upon funding and not any sooner.

Unfortunately my response to Sawyyer was not conciliatory. Somehow I skipped a level and was somewhat strident. Quite possibly it was the frustration and the delay with obstacles of time space and procedure. On reflection I should have given Sawyyer a chance to present me with the Guarantor. With all I've learned since, the eternal optimist in me still wonders if the deal was real. No matter. My email at 09:03:30–0700.

> Diana sent me an e-mail on July 27 informing me that the "agreement is on to have the funds transferred".
>
> That day I responded that she could have the $8,000 deducted from the total amount, which means that $4,992,000 would be wired into my account. I added to her that if that amount could not be deducted I would immediately wire her the $8,000 once her investment funds ($5,000,000) had been received in my account.
>
> As far as I am concerned, any payment due Global Security has been satisfied by the above procedure—i.e. deduct and send or send and get reimbursed.
>
> If you need to get a bank guarantee to facilitate the transfer, please do so.
>
> However—I WILL NOT PAY THAT COST!
>
> The only fee I am willing to pay, or ever will be willing to pay is $8,000 in the manner indicated above—deduct and send or send and get reimbursed.
>
> I await your response and hope we can conclude these arrangements before Diana arrives in September as I have much important

and exciting news to discuss about pending, profit making business.

The next day I informed Madam that I'd be away on business for about six days and hoped the wire transfer was progressing. I also sent wishes for her to feel better so that our meeting in September would go as scheduled.

Ten days later I returned from my trip and sent Sawyyer and Madam an email asking for a status report on the transfer of the investment funds.

August 13—14:52:32 +0200 (CEST)

Sawyyer's email was brief and clear:

> *I am afraid without payment of the cost required we cannot proceed*
> *I'll suggest you contact madam Diana.*

Shortly after getting Sawyyer's email I contacted Madam at 07:19:41–0700.

> I have returned from my business trip. Please advise me as to the status of your investment transfer as well as the details of your trip to the U.S.
> I look forward to meeting you and working with you.

August 14—11:06:18 +0100 (BST) Madam sent me an email.

> *Dear Vincent*
> *The status of my investment still stands as agreed however, being my partner I expect you also contribute both morally and financially in order to achieve our aim.*
> *My lawyer said some certain amount must be paid before the funds is transfered to your account and you said you would not pay it why?the amount required is too small comparing to what you'll receive thereafter. Actually, I'll suggest you do as my lawyer says so that we can conclude the transfer process.*
> *I look forward to seeing you soon in US.*
> *Diana*

Even though it was apparent as the scar from a knife fight, I believed my strength of logic and problem solving expertise would be not only impeccable but irresistible. Later that day, 18:46:19–0700 I replied.

Dear Diana

Re your e-mail of August 14, I am pleased that your "investment still stands as agreed".

However, we are not partners until our deal is concluded.

That means when I receive the full amount of your investment — approximately USD$5,000,000 and you receive appropriate shares in Thistle Productions, Inc.—we are partners. Your appeal for me to contribute "both morally and financially" is misplaced. I am not your partner until the above is consummated. However I have demonstrated both a moral and financial commitment to you nevertheless.

On August 1, I sent an e-mail to Francis Sawyyer with a copy to you, the essence of which is as follows: "… I responded that she could have the $8,000 deducted from the total amount, which means that $4,992,000 would be wired into my account. I added to her that if that amount could not be deducted I would immediately wire her the $8,000 once her investment funds ($5,000,000) had been received in my account …"

The above is my position. I HAVE AGREED TO PAY THE $8,000, BUT ON MY TERMS!

In case you think I am being too stubborn, I will also help defray some of the cost of $165,000 you indicated to me in your e-mail of July 12. I will give you 33 1/3% or USD$55,000 upon delivery of your investment to my account.

In sum I will reimburse you a total of $63,000 from the proceeds of your investment.

I give you permission to deduct this amount from the $5,000,000 before it is wired or—on my honor—I will immediately wire to you that sum when your investment is in my account.

Please consider the above a sincere expression of my moral and financial commitment to you—once we become partners. I too look forward to our meeting in the US.

One week elapsed and did not hear from Madam or Sawyyer.

August 21—08:01:54 0700

I sent her an email. In it I expressed concern for her health and hoped she was preparing for her trip to the U.S. so that we could solve whatever "technical difficulties" existed. I asked her to advise me of her schedule "asap."

September 2—14:25:56—0700, once again without any contact from Sawyyer or Madam, I sent my last email to her.

> Please advise your schedule during your trip to U.S. this month.
> Hope you are well.
> Thank you
> Vincent Panettiere

I never heard from Madam or Sawyyer again.

Anyone who tries to contact either of them by email will have it returned with the message from Yahoo "This account has been disabled or discontinued."

2. THE EFFEXBANK

THE CONGO-IVORY COAST-ANGOLA-LONDON CONNECTION

One year passed since deafening silence descended over Madam, Francis and Mr. Brown Despite numerous meetings with prospective investors I still had not raised financing for my slate of films or even one film. However, toward the end of September 2002 possibility once again steamed in off the horizon.

Clifford Newton contacted me regarding my business plan, which had been posted on various Internet sites. To some this might seem an efficient way to raise financing. To date, I wouldn't know. But in the underworld of the Internet it could be easily read as the cyberspace version of a "kick me" sign or in this context "scam me." But, after my experience with Madam et al—my motto was—<u>try</u> to scam me.

I sent him the Executive Summary for my package and within a few days.

October 1, 2002—8:49 EST—he replied.

> *I have tried calling you unsuccessfully. Please try to reach me on 243 88 43294.*
> *I am ready to infuse US$7.5 Millions in your film production if I am guaranteed that fantastic return envisage in your business plan.*
> *Please respond soonest.*
> *Clifford.*

I thought "infuse" was a strange and significant word. The first dictionary meaning for infuse is "to put in or introduce into by or as if by pouring." It is the fourth definition that made the most sense to me "to steep or soak without boiling, in order to extract soluble elements or active principles." My antenna told me the soluble elements good ol' Clifford's infusion would extract—or try to—from me would be money. Nevertheless my expectation level, on a scale of 1 to 100, lingered around five.

A sane person would ask why even that high? Once again where the majority of folks would ask "why" I continued to ask "why not." This time with low, for me, expectations, I'd go along for the ride, see where it took me and in the event that every planet and every star was aligned to my advantage, Clifford actually would invest, not infuse, US$7.5 million in my film production company.

Almost immediately, I had to give pause. There I was, feet on the starting blocks, every muscle of my being poised to blast down the straight away. The gun goes off. I push off the line, take one step and pause?

Clifford's email address was clifford@newton.ca, which I took to be located in Canada. His area code—243—was in Zaire! That Zaire. The one famous or infamous, depending on who you bet on, for "Rumble in the Jungle" where

Muhammad Ali knocked out George Foreman in the eighth round on October 29, 1974.

A check of the CIA's The World Factbook reveals that my AT&T International Dialing Guide was outdated. Zaire is no longer. Since 1997 it has been called the Democratic Republic of the Congo. Prior to receiving its independence from Belgium in 1960, it had been known as, naturally, the Belgian Congo.

The Factbook also revealed that DRC was located in Central Africa, northeast of Angola. Slightly less than one-fourth the size of the US, the DRC's median age was 15.8 years. Life expectancy was 48.9 years, with females living on average three years more.

On the last page of the report under "Transnational Issues," the boys and girls from Langley listed "Illicit drugs", with this explanation: "illicit producer of cannabis, mostly for domestic consumption; while rampant corruption and inadequate supervision leaves the banking system vulnerable to money laundering, the lack of a well-developed financial system limits the country's utility as a money-laundering center." Similarly, by their logic, if I was six feet 11 inches tall, I could play basketball for the New York Knicks.

This time I knew the arena and the opposition. All of the golly, gee-whizzes I had dealing with Madam Theodoritou were gone, replaced by an optimistic wariness.

October 2—8:55 EST, I sent Clifford an email.

We would start off this relationship with me calling the tune, taking the lead, in the driver's seat and all the other clichés meant to instill courage and boil the blood.

> Clifford
> I tried calling at 6:30am this morning, but got the same recording in French, once again.
> For the contract please provide me with the following information:
> 1. Name of investor—names of individuals, if more than one, and name of corporation.
> 2. Address of investor both company and individuals if more than one.
> 3. Phone/fax and email addresses of company and investors. FYI—investors will have to affirm in contract that funds provided are clean, value dated and wire transferred Fed funds.

Thistle reserves the right to reject any source of funds not in compliance with the above, which will be so stated in the contract.
I appreciate your interest in an investment in Thistle Productions and look forward to working with you toward that end.
Vincent

Several weeks went by as I tried to make contact. Towards the end of October I sent Clifford another email complaining about my phone difficulties and asking "… what's going on with investors?"

October 22—3:16 EST came his response.

Please try again. You may also fax papers to 31 20 600 9936
Funding available.
Clifford

I'd prepared a draft agreement and to save time I wanted to include the names of all the investors from the very beginning. However, before sending another fax I checked the area code for Clifford's new number. It was in the Netherlands! In the past 20 days Clifford had not furnished me with any of the information I'd requested on October 2. Had he been traveling, or … there was no telling what he was doing or where he physically existed

About 9:30 Los Angeles time I sent him another email advising him that before I can send him any documents I needed the names of investors, company name, phone/fax, passport number, etc. Three hours later I faxed him a draft of the investment agreement, concluding it was better to have it there to be reviewed than sitting in my computer gathering dust.

DRAFT AGREEMENT
This agreement made and concluded this 21st day of October 2002 by and between _____, Herein after referred to as the INVESTOR(S) being party of the first part, AND Mr. Vincent Panettiere of Thistle Productions, Inc. Los Angeles, CA 90046 USA, Herein after referred to as the COMPANY being party of the second part.

WHEREAS, the INVESTOR(S) being desirous of placing an investment in Thistle Productions, Inc. in USA in consideration for a secured and guaranteed annual income. And the COMPANY, being interested in attracting fresh capital funding for its ever expanding activities.

WHEREFORE, it is hereby agreed that the INVESTOR(S) agrees to invest the sum of USD $7.5 million in the commercial activities of the COMPANY after the execution of the contract.

That in consideration for this investment, the COMPANY agrees to offer 10% of the COMPANY's equity in the form of common stock to the INVESTOR(S).

That INVESTOR(S) agrees to provide COMPANY with clean, value dated and wire transferred Fed funds. COMPANY reserves the right to reject any source of funds not in compliance with the above.

That INVESTOR(S) agrees to respect and protect any CONFI-DENTIAL and PROPRIETY information and rights of the COM-PANY.

That INVESTOR(S) agrees it/they have its/their own independent due diligence of the COMPANY and is entering this Agreement based upon that due diligence.

That COMPANY agrees that the INVESTOR(S) or its/their ASSIGNEE will hold one (1) seat on the Board of the COMPANY equivalent to the percentage of equity held.

That while the INVESTOR(S) agrees to accept future profit and loss accounts of the COMPANY, the INVESTOR(S) will not be liable or share liability in any and ALL previous loss incurred or contracted by the COMPANY prior to the signing of this agreement.

That the COMPANY agrees, upon reasonable notice, but no more than semi-annually, to open the Financial Records of the COM-PANY to the INVESTOR(S) or its/their ASSIGNEE for scrutiny and due diligence.

The following signatories voluntary accept the terms of this Agreement and its legal implications under the laws of the USA

That both parties agree that any dispute to any part or section of this agreement shall be settled by arbitration under the prevailing Laws of the State of California in USA.

That this agreement is signed, sealed and executed this _____ day of _____ 2002

Subscribed and sworn before me this _____ day of _____, 2002
_____   _____ County/City/Country _____
Notary Public

My Commission expires _____

INVESTOR(S): *{LIST ALL WITH NAMES, ADDRESSES, PASSPORT NUM-BERS, ETC}*

1.
2.
3.
4
5.

That this agreement is signed, sealed and executed this _____ day of _____ 2002

Subscribed and sworn before me this _____ day of _____, 2002

_____   _____ County/City/Country _____
Notary Public
                                   _____

My Commission expires _____

COMPANY:

Vincent Panettiere

President
Thistle Productions, Inc.

N.B. This faxed copy shall enjoy the same validity as the original hard copy.

October 23—7:55 EST

I got an email from one Joseph McGrath whose email address was jmcgrath1950@yahoo.co.uk. He said:

> *I CONFIRM* THE RECEIPT OF YOUR FAX OF *YESTERDAY. UNFORTUNATELY, MR. CLIFF HAS TRAVELLED BUT I WILL SEND THE DOCUMENTS TO HIM THIS AFTERNOON THROUGH DHL COURIER SERVICE*
> *BEST REGARDS*
> *JOSEPH MCGRATH*

I waited a few days and sent another email to Clifford.

October 26—6:52 EST he replied;

> *Thanks. I think everything okay. Completed papers along with phop-tocopies of identity papers should reach you earliest Tuesday of next week.*
> *Clifford*

I wrote back to Clifford that I was pleased I'd be receiving the requested information by next week and continued:

> Are you one of the investors?
> When you say "everything okay" do you mean you have read the draft agreement and it is acceptable to you?
> Or, are you dealing with the investors and have discussed it with them and they approve the draft?
> Will there be any further discussion of the substance of the agreement I sent you?
> Once I have the name(s) of investors, I will include in agreement and send to you for signature.
> Please answer the questions above with as much detail as you can.

November 1—22:41 EST—three days after the "Tuesday of next week".

I contacted Clifford to ask about the status of the draft agreement. More than a month later I got a response, but not from Clifford.

December 11—10:15 EST, the email was from sierrawellfare@yahoo.co.uk and signed by Sam Smith. Too bad it wasn't signed Sam Spade, then I could have ended each email to him with "… this is the stuff that dreams are made of." As if, he'd understand the reference. But maybe I'm being too cynical toward my fellow man.

> *ATTENTION MR. VINCENT*
> *DEAR SIR*
> *I WAS MADE TO CONTACT YOU BY MR CLIFFORD NEWTON,*
> *IN KINSHASHA.*
> *FOR A SECURITY AND PRIVATE REASONS, MR NEWTON HAS*
> *APPOINTED ME TO CONCLUDE THE TRANSACTION WITH*
> *YOU ON HIS BEHALF. CURRENTLY MR NEWTON IS AN*
> *EMPLOYEE OF A BIG FIRM IN CONGO AND WOULD NOT*
> *WANT TO REVEAL HIS IDENTITY FOR NOW.*
> *WAITING TO HEAR FROM YOU URGENTELY, SO THAT I WILL*
> *GIVE YOU MORE DETAILS REGARD TO ME*
> *MY REGARDS*
> *SAM*

I immediately sent an email to Sam.

> I received your email this morning informing me that Clifford Newton appointed you for security and private reasons to conclude the transaction Clifford and I negotiated.
>
> Please advise me of the following:
>
> 1. Are you aware of the nature of the deal?
> 2. Have you seen the draft agreement I sent him on October 22 and to which I have not received any reply?
> 3. Are you prepared to supply me with the names addresses, phone/fax numbers, passport, country and numbers of all individual investors?

4. If a company, I will need the above information on all who own the company or who are permitted to enter into this agreement on its behalf.

I look forward to receiving answers to the above as well as your providing me with whatever additional details you indicated in your email.

Smith replied

AM SORRY FOR THE DELAY, ALL IS BEEN SET REGARDS TO THE TRANSACTION.
I WILL FORWARD TO YOU ALL YOUR REQUID INFORMA-
TION BY TOMORROW
THANKS
SAM SMITH

In dealing with Madam, I learned it was necessary for expediting the process, as well as one's sanity, to be as specific as possible. I asked Sam to let me know if the information was being sent by email or DHL courier. His answer was brief and surprising.

I JUST SEND IT TO YOU, IN A COPLE MINUTS AGO, GO
THROUGH IT AND GET BACK TO ME AS TIME IS NO LONGER
ON OUR SIDE.

Oh, yeah? *Time is no longer on our side?* More than two months without a response from Newton or his associates and now some guy in the middle of the jungle is hustling me. I wonder what the Kingwana (one of the languages spoken in the DROC which is a dialect of Kiswahili or Swahili) word for chutzpah is?

I decided on a civilized response.

In your last email you indicate "time is no longer on our side", yet I have not received any reaction to the agreement or a signed agreement, nor have I received a copy of the investor's passport—either by email or fax.

I am ready to move forward and hope you are too. For future reference—once I receive the signed agreement from the investor, his investment can be wired to my account—info to be provided at the appropriate time.

January 9, 2003—9:47 EST came "Sam Smith's" email.

> *ATTN/VINCENT*
> *DEAR SIR,*
> *REGARDS TO THE PROMISE I MADE TO YOU YESTERDAY THAT I WILL BE SENDING ALL THE REQUID INFORMATION.*
> *1] AM AWARE OF THE NATURE OF THE DEAL*
>
> *2]I HAVE SEE THE DRAFT AGREMENT, AND YOUR EXECU-TIVE SUMMARY WHICH YOU SEND, I HAVE GONE THROUGH AND CERTIFIED.*
> *3] THIS ARE THE NAMES OF THE INVESTORS.*
>
> *MR BAVION PIRES PAIRA [FRANCISCO]*
> *PORTUGAL NATIONAL INDENTITY 12221390*
> *ADDRESS/137 BLVD DU 30 JUIN GOMBE, KINSHASA*
> *CONGO DEM, REP*
> *TEL/FAX 243 88 423274*
>
> *I TRIED TO FAX YOU THE COPY OF HIS INTERNATIONAL PASSPORT, BUT YOU LINE IS NOT GOING THROUGH, OR SHOULD I SCAN IT TO YOU?*
> *I HOPE ALL YOUR QUESTION HAVE BEEN ASNWERD IF ANY OTHER DON'T HASITATE TO DO SO AM WAITING TO HEAR YOUR NEXT LINE OF ACTION SO THAT WE COULD FNALISE THIS DEAL AS WE SCHEDULLED.*
> *MY REGARDS*
> *SAM SMITH.*

Four hours after Sam's transmission, 13:55 EST, I replied thanking him for providing the name of the investor and asking him to resubmit the passport information. I also reminded him that I needed the investor to sign the agreement I'd sent weeks before to Clifford Newton, if there were no changes.

We exchanged a series of emails over the next four days.

> *mr barion is out of town to back by Monday, the agrement will on you desk latest Tuesday morning*

thank you for understanding.
sam smith

My response was to thank "Mr. Smith" for his prompt response.

January 13—14:00 EST I received another email from Sam

> MR. BAVION JUST ARRIVE FROM HIS TRAVEL THIS
> EVENING, PLEASE IS LIKE HE MISPLACE THE AGREMENT
> SOME WHERE, SO PLEASE RESEND IT TO ME, BECASE HE
> WILL BE IN MY OFFICE TOMORROW MORNING, WHEN WE
> RECEIVE IT HE WILL SIGN THE SAME TIME AND SEND BACK
> TO YOU
> WAITING TO HEAR FROM YOU URGENTELY
> MY REGARDS
> SAM SMITH

I decided to treat Mr. Bavion Pires Paira (Francisco) as a real person, who in fact would be in the office of "Mr. Sam Smith" and sent a letter and contract to him by fax—as follows:

{THISTLE PRODUCTIONS, INC. Letterhead}

January 13, 2002
Mr. Bavion Pires Paira
137 Blvd. du 30 Juin Gombe
Kinshasa, Congo Dem. Rep.

Dear Sir:

DRAFT AGREEMENT

Sam Adams advised me to resend to you the draft agreement for your investment in Thistle Productions.

Enclosed by fax is the draft agreement. Please make whatever changes you feel necessary and return it to me. Should I agree, I will make the necessary changes, sign it and return it to you for your signature.

If you have no changes to the draft, let me know and I will send you a final version for your signature.

I continue to need the names, addresses, phone/fax numbers, passport country and numbers of any and all additional investors, who might be your associates.

If a company is the investor involved, I will need the above information for those who own the company or are permitted to enter into this agreement on its behalf.

I look forward to your response and to the prospect of working together in the future.

Sincerely,
SIGNED BY
Vincent Panettiere
President
Thistle Productions, Inc.
VP/srs
enc.

This was followed by a copy of the agreement.

{THISTLE PRODUCTIONS, INC. Letterhead}

DRAFT AGREEMENT

This agreement made and concluded this 13th day of January 2003 by and between Bavion Pires Paira of 137 Blvd. Du 30 Juin Gombe, Kinshasa, Congo Dem. Rep., Herein after referred to as the INVESTOR(S) being party of the first part, AND Mr. Vincent Panettiere of Thistle Productions, Inc. Los Angeles, CA, USA, Herein after referred to as the COMPANY being party of the second part.

WHEREAS, the INVESTOR(S) being desirous of placing an investment in Thistle Productions, Inc. in USA in consideration for a secured and guaranteed annual income. And the COMPANY, being interested in attracting fresh capital funding for its ever expanding activities.

WHEREFORE, it is hereby agreed that the INVESTOR(S) agrees to invest the sum of USD $7.5 million in the commercial activities of the COMPANY after the execution of the contract.

That in consideration for this investment, the COMPANY agrees to offer 10% of the COMPANY's equity in the form of common stock to the INVESTOR(S).

That INVESTOR(S) agrees to provide COMPANY with clean, value dated and wire transferred Fed funds. COMPANY reserves the right to reject any source of funds not in compliance with the above.

That INVESTOR(S) agrees to respect and protect any CONFIDENTIAL and PROPRIETY information and rights of the COMPANY.

That INVESTOR(S) agrees it/they have its/their own independent due diligence of the COMPANY and is entering this Agreement based upon that due diligence.

That COMPANY agrees that the INVESTOR(S) or its/their ASSIGNEE will hold one (1) seat on the Board of the COMPANY equivalent to the percentage of equity held.

That while the INVESTOR(S) agrees to accept future profit and loss accounts of the COMPANY, the INVESTOR(S) will not be liable or share liability in any and ALL previous loss incurred or contracted by the COMPANY prior to the signing of this agreement.

That the COMPANY agrees, upon reasonable notice, but no more than semi-annually, to open the Financial Records of the COMPANY to the INVESTOR(S) or its/their ASSIGNEE for scrutiny and due diligence.

The following signatories voluntary accept the terms of this Agreement and its legal implications under the laws of the USA

That both parties agree that any dispute to any part or section of this agreement shall be settled by arbitration under the prevailing Laws of the State of California in USA.

That this agreement is signed, sealed and executed this _____ day of _____ 2002

Subscribed and sworn before me this _____ day of _____, 2002

_____   _____ County/City/Country _____
Notary Public

My Commission expires _____

INVESTOR(S): *{LIST ALL WITH NAMES, ADDRESSES, PASSPORT NUM-BERS, ETC}*

1.
2.
3.
4
5.

That this agreement is signed, sealed and executed this _____ day of _____ 2002

Subscribed and sworn before me this _____ day of _____, 2002

_____   _____ County/City/Country _____
Notary Public

My Commission expires _____

COMPANY:

Vincent Panettiere
President
Thistle Productions, Inc.

N.B. This faxed copy shall enjoy the same validity as the original hard copy.

January 14

I experienced my first LO AND BEHOLD! moment. The email from Sam Smith had two attachments identified as Pict0036.JPG and Pict0037.JPG

> *DEAR SIR*
> *THESE ATTACHED AGREEMENT. PLEASE SEND YOUR BANK-*
> *ING INFORMATION AS SOON AS YOU RECEIVE AGREEMENT.*
> *SAM SMITH*

I opened the JPGs and found a signed and sealed copy of my "Draft Agreement". It was dated 14th—1–2003. The signature did not resemble anything that could remotely be identified as Bavion Pires Paira or even Sam Smith. However, I sent the banking information with a silent wish and hope that dealing with a Portuguese national would be more successful than my experience with Madam Theodoritou. Why did I feel that? For the very unscientific and rational reason that hope springs eternal. I also requested once again Mr. Bavion Pires Paira's passport number.

January 15—5:39 EST Sam Smith sent the following:

> *Dear sir,*
> *many thanks to your mail, your bank information will forwarded to our banker this morning for onward transfer of the fund.*
>
> *Mr Bavion PASSPORT NUMBER IS/130892*
>
> *WAITING TO TALK TO YOU LATTER*
> *SAM SMITH*

January 17

I had enough of dealing with intermediaries and sent an email to Sam Smith, a copy of which is missing, attempting to move him out of the communication link so that I could deal directly with my investor "Francisco", AKA, Bavion Pires Paira.

Shortly thereafter, Smith sent me a EUREKA, EUREKA email. It was twice Eureka because at first it was a surprise and secondly it was a revelation. After receiving the information on Francisco and the signed contract I felt a certain comfort that we would move forward successfully. The surprise was that

Smith's letter came when it did, but its contents immediately reminded me of Madam Theodoritou and Sierra Leone.

Two clichés circled in my head: "if at first you don't succeed, try, try again," which most likely was translated into Kingwana. The other was "whoever doesn't learn from history is bound to repeat it", which needed no translation.

Smith wrote:

> *Dear sir,*
> *These are the situation report, we have tried all we could to make sure that the fund is been transferd, but no way because the bank said since September 11th 2001 problem, all the banks in this part of the world has been giving instructions not to transfer more than $10,000, for this reason we are making an alternative arrengement to see if it could go through a diplomatic means as a cargo to europe or asia, which means that you are to be there to claim it. are you ready to travel out to europe or asia? because we are on talk with the diplomat more details will be relaying to you immediately we finalise all the arrengement.*
> *Please indicate your opinion on this.*
> *waiting to hear from you urgentely.*
> *my regards*

I curtly replied that I would "investigate alternative solutions at this end and get back to you." Sam knew he had a live one at the end of his line and wasted no time firing back an email he thought would motivate me.

> *am waiting to hear from you urgentely, as time is no longer on our side, because am planing to move down to my nebouring country where i will stay to finalise the move.*
> *my regards.*

Sam Smith's lack of rock and roll history was beginning to tick me off. Didn't he know, in the immortal words of the Rolling Stones, that "time, time, time, is on our side?" Yes it is. At the time I didn't remember that the refrain "you'll come running back to me, yes you will" was also part of that song. I'd be reminded soon enough.

The task at hand demanded a response to Sam.

Mr. Smith

I suggest you should have known of the restrictions before you contacted me.

Send me $9,500 as a good faith gesture and I'll consider going to Europe to meet with your courier.

At the same time I will investigate limits on wire transfers with my banker.

I'm offering a solid and real investment opportunity for the investor. His money will be safe and receive an ample return.

However, I won't be rushed with "time is no longer on our side."

You and Clifford Brown wasted a lot of time.

Let's see your good faith transfer.

February 3—14:33 EST Sam deflected my thrust and parried.

Dear sir,
am still waiting to hear from you, because mr francisco told me he will
be talking to you.
regards
sam smith

Enough of this crap. The odds that Sam, Francisco or Newton were real and that I had an investor was 1000, if not more, to 1. I decided to pepper them with as many on the nose jabs as I could get in. At 17:10 EST, I wrote:

Dear Mr. Smith:

On January 17th I sent you an email in which I requested that the principals communicate directly. The following is a direct quote from that email:

"Francisco needs to contact Vincent so that we can establish this partnership properly. When he contacts me, we can discuss future strategy."

Your email today says: "am still waiting to hear from you, because mr francisco told me he will be talking to you."

Mr. Francisco has not contacted me. There is no reason for me to contact you in the future since I will be dealing directly with Mr. Francisco, the investor. Please refer to my email to you of Jan. 17.

Mr. Francisco either will wire his investment to the account number provided and become my partner or he will not and our deal will be ended.

You might suggest that Mr. Francisco wire his investment from Portugal, since he is a citizen of that country.

The total responsibility is on your end. Either you invest or you don't.

Please let me know when and how (email, phone, etc.) Mr. Francisco will be contacting me and if you have any questions regarding the above.

February 4—4:21 EST an email came from clifford@newton.ca. It read:

Dear Mr. Vincent
I am Clifford's wife and as I am told, you are aware that he had a heart attack a few months and although recovering, he has been restricted from conducting any business. I understand that he was in the process of concluding a business arrangement with you and that he subsequently authorised a business partner, Mr. Bavion Paira to close the business in his behalf. He apparently gave an amount of US$4Million to Mr. Paira and Mr. Paira was to have added an amount of US$3.5 Million to this and send the total of US$7.5 Million to you. We are in Angola and Mr. Paira is in Congo Democratic Republic. We last communicated with Mr. Paira about 18 days ago at which time he assured that the money was in the process of being sent to you or collected by your agent. However, there has been some difficulties in communication lines between here and Kinshasa and I am now writing to you in effort to establish the current status of arrangements.
Agnes

This email was a filled with surprises. First, no one told me Clifford had a heart attack (imaginary or real). I was never informed that Newton and Francisco were partners, or that Newton lived in Angola and had a wife named Agnes, who obviously had a very good command of the English language—spelling, punctuation, syntax, etc. Much better than Newton and Sam combined.

But, the biggest surprise of all was that Agnes contacted me by using the email string I'd established with Newton going back to October. Specifically, what Agnes had done was to send me an email by hitting the reply button on the last email I'd sent to Clifford, rather than to type in my email address to start fresh correspondence. I don't fault her since hitting reply is a quick and easy way to respond. However, the significance to me was that someone somewhere had kept a file of my correspondence with Clifford. In itself, this was not surprising yet I was disoriented.

Was this deal real? The business about going to Europe or Asia seemed to be another version of Madam's trip to London. And yet, if Agnes was as real as her command of the English language maybe this deal could be done. And yet? The "and yet(s)" still would not disappear.

At 10:10 EST I wrote back to Agnes.

> Dear Mrs. Newton:
> I am sorry to learn for the first time through your email that Clifford suffered a heart attack. I hope he is now much improved and wish him a complete and speedy recovery.
>
> After a period of time, when I didn't hear from Clifford, I was contacted by Sam Adams(sic). He said he'd been appointed by Clifford for security and personal reasons to conclude the agreement. He never mentioned the heart attack, however we continued to discuss investment and reached an agreement for $7.5 million, to come from Bavion Pires Paira, who he also referred to as Francisco. He never mentioned that part of the funds would come from Clifford.
>
> I have provided Mr. Adams(sic) with my banking information and the funds have not been sent as of this date. Yesterday I informed him it was time for the two principals—Francisco and myself—to communicate directly so that the matter could be efficiently concluded. I have not as yet heard back.
>
> I look forward to your response and to any suggestions that may successfully conclude this matter for all concerned.

February 6—4:08 EST, Agnes wrote back:

> *Mr. Vincent,*
> *Thank you for kind and warm letter—Clifford sends his regards.*

*Francisco called us late last night and he is going to be calling you
later today.* •
*This matter is now clearer and there should be a conclusion in the
next few days.*
Agnes

February 20

Two weeks passed. At 4:41 EST I received an email with the address of barry-goldman2003@yahoo.co.uk. The yahoo address in the United Kingdom was appearing often enough as to not be a coincidence. Madam Theodoritou had her address at yahoo.uk as did Sam Smith. Now, along comes Barry Goldman. This should be interesting.

DEAR VINCENT PANETTIERE
*MY NAME IS BARRY GOLDMAN, PRESIDENT OF GLOBAL
FINANCE COMPANY AND A LAWYER, WITH OFFICE IN ABID-
JAN—IVORY COAST.*

*MY FIRM HAS BEEN CONTRACTED TO HANDLING THE
TRANSFER OF THE FUND TO YOUR ACCOUNT, IT'S MY
PLEASURE TO INFORM YOU THAT ARRANGEMENT HAS
BEEN CONCLUDED TO TRANSFER THE MONEY,*

*HOWEVER, YOU'RE REQUIRED TO OPEN AN ACCOUNT
WITH THE BANK WE INTENT TO USE IN LONDON, DETAILS
SHALL BE GIVEN TO YOU ONCE I RECEIVE YOUR REPLY.*

*I CAN BE REACHED ON TELEPHONE NO/+22505419755 OR
SAT/+8821652300908*

HOPE TO HEAR FROM YOU SOON

WE CONTINUE TO WORK TO THE GLORY OF GOD

IN HIS NAME

BARRY GOLDMAN

Chutzpah had indeed been translated into the Swahili dialect. Barry Goldman, a lawyer, was working for the glory of God! I'd believe that as soon as God came down from wherever and verified it in person. Some bushman (I know it's not PC and I don't care) in (I presumed) western dress who most likely is participating in an Internet scam is evoking the name of God for what end? To make me believe he is more sincere? So that I believe in him more than anyone else?

With no more than a moment's consideration I decided—why not? Why shouldn't the name of God be exploited by some bozo in the Ivory Coast. After all, the name of God has been abused down the centuries to rationalize all kinds of evil and violence. Why shouldn't it be used to relieve unsuspecting Internet users of their money in the same manner as His name has been used to bilk the parishioners of Televangelists?

February 21—3:46 EST Sam Smith reappeared in my email box:

> *The finance company that we set to handle this transaction will be calling you, pls. don't hasitate to give any information he may need from you.*
>
> *Due to the regulation on bank's here we have to apply to the finance company to help in trasfering the fund.*
>
> *his name Mr Barry Goldman, he also a lawyer.*
>
> *waiting to hear from you urgentely*
> *regards*
> *sam smith*

Sam Smith was now back on my email screen, but he was a day late, though I'd bet the way he and the others were working this deal they'd never be a dollar short. I told Sam that I'd in fact spoken to Goldman.

Quickly he requested:

> *please don't hasitate to give me whatever is the out come of your discussion with mr goldman.*
> *waiting to hear from you urgentely*
> *sam smith*

Goldman gave me the name of the bank they wanted to use in London. It was called the Effexbank. It existed only in cyberspace at www.effexbank.com. I knew FX or effex were terms used in the banking industry to designate foreign exchange. Naively, I thought the similarly named bank was established to act as a liaison between clients from various countries needing a central location to handle transactions of varied currency.

February 22

The email I received from accounts@efrexbank.com informed me that my account was open.

> *DEAR VINCENT PANETTIERE*
> *THANK YOU FOR OPENING ACCOUNT WITH EFFEXBANK.*
> *YOUR USER NAME IS kwaaak*
> *YOUR PASSWORD IS stromb*
>
> *YOUR ACCOUNT IS NOW ACTIVE*
> *BELOW IS THE INFORMATIONS OF YOUR ACCOUNT*
>
> *EFFEXBANK LONDON UK*
> *SORT CODE: 23.41.12*
> *ACCOUNT NUMBER; 0005411-235*
> *ACCOUNT NAME; VINCENT PANETTIERE*
>
> *YOU CAN LOG IN AT ANY TIME TO CHECK THE ACTIVITIES*
> *OF YOUR ACCOUNT BY USING YOUR USER NAME AND PASS*
> *WORD*
>
> *THANK YOU FOR USING EFFEXBANK*
> *SINCERELY*
> *RONALD WILLIAMS*

At this point it was getting more comical and fantastic by the minute. I had opened an account in a bank that existed only in cyberspace which was operated by someone in London waiting to receive $7,500,000 from two investors who may not be real living in Angola and the Democratic Republic of the Congo. Not to mention a lawyer in the Ivory Coast. There was Agnes and Clifford Newton, Sam Smith, Barry Goldman and now Ronald Williams.

Assuming they all used fictitious names at least I had spoken to Barry Goldman and Ronald Williams using the numbers they provided in the Ivory Coast and London, respectively. Agnes, Clifford and Sam could be at least two people, one who could write in the English language and the other who had not one clue.

I needed to see where all this would lead and dutifully informed Barry Goldman that I had been contacted by Ronald Williams of Effexbank and he had opened an account for me.

February 23—9:44 EST I contacted Sam:

> Where is Clifford Newton's wife? I thought I was dealing with her, now?
> I discussed opening an account with Effexbank with Mr. Goldman and have done so.

I also called Ronald Williams and asked about the procedure for making a deposit in my account. He told me I had to deposit at least one hundred dollars to keep the account open. I reminded him that I expected a deposit of more than seven million dollars, which was coming into his bank on the advice of Barry Goldman and that should be sufficient.

Williams later informed me by email:

> *WE HAVE GIVEN YOU A CREDIT OF $100.00. YOU CAN DEPOSIT AND WITHDRAW ANY AMOUNT YOU LIKE. THE $100.00 CREDIT MUST ALWAYS REMAIN IN YOUR ACCOUNT WE CANNOT GIVE YOU AUTHORIZATION TO WITHDRAW THE $100.00 UNLESS YOU DEPOSIT ANY AMOUNT THAT EXCEEDS $5000.00 YOU CAN ALSO DEPOSIT LESS THAN $5000.00 AND WITHDRAW IT AT ANY TIME.*
> *SINCERELY—RONALD WILLIAMS*

Clearly, this told me they were afraid that I'd steal one hundred dollars from them!

February 24—6:56 EST Goldman asked me to confirm that the account had been credited.

As if on cue I got the following email from Ronald Williams at 8:42 EST:

WE RECEIVED TODAY FROM FEDERAL REPUBLIC OF THE CONGO THE SUM OF $7,500,000.00. WE ARE GOING TO CREDIT YOUR ACCOUNT LATER ON TODAY. YOU CAN LOG IN WITH YOUR USER NAME AND PASSWORD TO CHECK YOUR BALANCE AND TRANSFER FUNDS IN BETWEEN BANKS.
SINCERELY
RONALD WILLIAMS

I checked my online account and sure enough my opening balance was $7,500,100. However Available Input/Deposit was $0.00, while Today's Available Output was $7,500,100. Today's Total available balance stood at $7,500,100 and no interest earned to date. In short, I had a balance of more than seven million dollars but none of it was available to me.

About three hours later I thanked Williams for the information and advised him that the name on the account had to be changed from me individually to the corporation Thistle Entertainment Corp.

While I didn't particularly like not being able to spend money I really didn't have, I thought just to be prudent I needed to contact an expert on the matter—Bankers' Almanac. I wanted to know how legitimate and viable Effexbank was for anyone who would make a deposit and also wanted to learn the British government entity which might regulate the performance of such a bank.

At 15:40:13 Rosemary Palmer, a Financial Editorial Assistant at Bankers' Almanac responded:

> *The Bankers' Almanac, at present, does no hold information on Internet Banks, so I am unable to answer your queries.*
> *The Financial Services Authority (FSA) holds information on banks operating in the UK, so they are the best people to contact about this bank.*

She then provided contact details for the FSA.

Later that day, at 22:48 EST, I received email with the subject "Fraud Warning—African Money Transaction." from <u>security_team@ananzi.co.za.</u>. The following is that letter:

Fraud Warning—African Money Transaction

We are following up on fraudulent transactions identified by our mail router and we feel it necessary to advise you that you are almost certainly the intended victim of a Nigerian 419 Advance Fee Scam.

Plese look at the Anti-419 Coalition homepage at:
http://homerica.net/alphae/419coal/

or the U.S. secret service page at:
http://www.secretservice.gov/alert419.shtml
for detailed information about this fraudulent activity.

You can also read a specific account of the scam here:
http://www.freep.com/money/tech/mwendi19_20020419.htm

Unless you want to lose a lot of money—do not advance ANY money for a "business" transaction involving millions of dollars. If you have already paid any money it is almost certainly lost for good.

Additionally, your participation in such activities could amount to consorting with criminals and you could be subject to prosecution by relevent law enforcement agencies.

For your own safety and protection, it is in your best interests to investigate this matter thoroughly and to cease all contact with the scammers immediately.

Regards

Joseph (for Anzani.co.za Mail Services)

If it sounds too good to be true—It probably is.

This pissed me off no end. Somebody was reading my mail or if not actually reading it, they were following mail coming into my mailbox, which to me was as good as opening it. Imagine if someone kept track of the return address on every hard copy letter sent to you? It may not be a stretch to consider such a practice actually happening, but at least the U.S. Government has the good taste to keep it a secret.

The second affront was the indirect accusation that by participating I could be accused of "consorting with criminals" and threatened with prosecution. If this wasn't an example of Big Brother! Anyone who thinks my assessment to be hyperbolic or paranoid, need only substitute the words Boy Scouts or Baptist Church instead of Nigerian 419 Advance Fee Scam and see how that sounds.

While the email was a generalized form type document, I decided Joseph needed to hear from me directly. I replied the same day at 18:58:24–0500, as follows:

> To: Joseph
> Thank you for your recent email regarding Fraudulent Nigerian money transactions.
>
> I appreciate your concern.
>
> I have been aware of that activity for many years and laugh at each new solicitation.
>
> I HAVE NOT PARTICIPATED. DO NOT INTEND TO PARTICIPATE AND HAVE NOT GIVEN ANY MONEY NOR WILL I GIVE ANY MONEY.
>
> While I appreciate your concern, I also regard your email as an unnecessary and unwarranted intrusion into my life and business.
>
> Be so kind in the future, to mind your own business.
> Thank you,
> Vincent Panettiere

February 25

Ronald Williams informed me that the name on my account at Effexbank had been changed as I requested to Thistle Entertainment Corp. I decided to check and found that my account's opening balance was still $7,500,100.00 which was the same amount available. However the "available output" was $15,000,200 as was "today's available" balance. Somehow my balance was double what anyone had imagined—with stress placed on the word "imagined".

I contacted Ronald Williams to let him know that:

I tried learning your transfer process and after pushing the transfer button received an "access denied" message and advice to contact the foreign exchange department. When I clicked that, nothing happened.
Please advise.

Early that morning, I called the Financial Services Authority at Canary Wharf in London using the information provided by Bankers' Almanac. I spoke with Simon Kattle who told me that the Effex Bank was "not on the register", "not regulated by anyone" and something that "we need to look into." I never heard from or spoke with Simon Kattle again.

Later on at 10:08 EST Williams sent another email.

Please contact Douglas Townsend on douglastownsend@juno.com or you can call him direct on 008821652305653. He will issue the access code for transfer or wire transfer.

Towards the end of the day at 13:14 EST I advised Williams about the discrepancy in my balance as well as my inability to transfer any funds. Furthermore, I added:

I am advising the attorney for my investor of this matter and hope you will provide an explanation as soon as possible.

Once again, at 15:08 EST, I received an email the subject of which was African Money Transaction—Fraud Warning.

Dear Sir/Madam,
You are receiving this email because our span detection software has identified you as the potential victim of a Nigerian 419 Advance Fee Fraud. This fraud typically originates with the scam operator (Effex Bank) soliciting your assistance to move millions of dollars from Africa to a different continent. You will eventually be asked to pay fees ranging from a few thousand dollars to hundreds of dollars for storage fees, transportation costs, clearance documents, and in the final stage you will be asked for hundreds of thousands of dollars to pay for chemicals to "clean" the money.

Be advised that this is an ongoing scam that has been happening for over twenty years and to date has successfully bilked unwary victims of billions of dollars. There are currently thousands of persons of West African origin perpetuating this scam.

There is no money. The only persons who stand to gain in this business are the criminals operating this scam. If it sounds too good to be true then it is. If you have already paid any money to these criminals it is almost certainly lost for good. If you are still in contact with the criminals it is in your best interests to cease all communications and forward all correspondence to the authorities in your country.

For detailed information on this scam please refer to the following websites:
The 419 Coalitions homepage: http://home.rica.net/alphae/419coal/
The 419 Fraud homepage: http://www.419fraud.com/

You can read a specific account of this fraud here:
http://www.freep.com/money/tech/mwendi19_20020419.htm

If you reside in the United States and have lost money to the criminals please contact the United

States Secret Service financial crimes division by referring to their page at:
http://www.secretservice.gov/alert419.shtml
Sincerely
Fastmail.fm 419 Alerts
Postmaster
alert419@fastmail.fm

While another form letter, this one was at least more respectful, provided more information and was not threatening. Additionally, the fact that it identified Effex Bank by name did not dissuade me from continuing my counter scam.

February 26

I checked my Effexbank account at 6:24am Los Angeles time to find that the Today's Total available balance was $15,000,200. But by 8:30am my available balance reflected the correction and was restored to the "accurate" amount of $7,500,100.00.

Later that morning, at 9:47 EST I wrote to Barry Goldman:

> I spoke with Ronald Williams of Effexbank this morning and asked
> him the same questions in my email. When do I get my access code
> and why the discrepancy in the balance.
>
> He gave me no specific answers, but said he would "send email
> tomorrow and it will work out fine." Whatever that means.
>
> Who did you make the deposit with? Maybe you can contact him
> to help sort this out.
>
> I have made a deal with a film distributor and must start accessing
> the funds to pay actors so that we can begin production.

Once again I tried to use the old film distributor deal to provoke a bite out
of the carrot at the end of <u>my</u> stick and waited to see how effective that ruse
would be this time.

Barry Goldman contacted me by email at 10:03 EST:

> *I HAVE MADE CONTACT REGARDING THE DISCREPENCY*
> *AND ITS BEING SORTED OUT NOW*
> *ONCE I HAVE ANY WORD I KEEP YOU POSTED*
> *KEEP HOPE AND GOD HELP US?*
> *TRULY?*
> *BARRY GOLDMAN*

Did Barry really want to use a question mark at the end of God Help Us and
Truly. I hoped it wasn't some kind of private joke at my expense, but soon dismissed it as using the wrong key on his computer.

At 10:14am EST on February I replied to Barry.

> I appreciate your response. However, it is very general. Please
> inform me who did you speak with at the bank, why is there a dis-
> crepancy and when will I have access to the funds.
>
> I am concerned about Francisco's investment, as I'm sure you are as
> his attorney. I'd feel more comfortable with the funds in an estab-
> lished land-based bank like Bank of America, but since you insisted
> on Effex … let us hope for the best.

I await your response.

At 10:38am my Opening Balance read $7,500,100.00 but Available Input/Deposit "blinked" back at me $0.00 ON HOLD.

Before I could write a complaining email, Douglas Townsend contacted me at 11:23 EST.

DEAR MR. VINCENT

Ronald Williams of Effexbank contacted me demanding the transfer code to enable him wire the $7,500,100.00 to your account in another bank. But before we can proceed to issue the transfer code you need to pay a 0.1% vat tax for the $7,500,100.00

However we have placed your account with the effexbank on hold until you pay the 0.1% vat tax totaling $7,500.00. You have five working days to pay this money otherwise the funds will be marked as a terrorist money and will be handed over to the American government.

There will be no negotiation of any kind in this matter. I can be reached through this email address or my direct phone (0118821652305653. Below is where to wire the Funds:

CHANGHWA COMM. BANK LTD
CHENG BRANCH 123 NANKING W ROAD
TAIPEI TAIWAN

SWIFT: CCBCTWTP505
A/C NAME: CHEN MENGHSUN
A/C NUMBER; 50502252300700

IN FAVOR OF: International fund transfer department

Email me as soon as the funds are wire (sic)
Best regards
Douglas Townsend
International fund transfer department

I had negotiated on behalf of writers, directors, directors of photography and professional baseball players for about ten years. Being told by some fraudster in London that the demands of his extortion scheme were not negotiable did not make my knees buckle or fear spread through my heart. It made me boiling angry.

A reader of the above rightfully could ask "what did you expect?" After all, I am a willing, even active participant in this elaborate mutual charade. By what new definition of chutzpah did "Douglas Townsend" believe that he could intimidate anyone with a non-negotiable demand. Then Townsend doubles his chutzpah with the threat that <u>he</u> will send the money to the U.S. Government and *the funds will be marked as terrorist money*!

I was convinced that anyone intimidated by such a threat had to be dumb as a stone or he or she was so convinced the money was real that they suspended any perception, ability to discriminate and common sense.

My next email went to Barry Goldman at 12:03. My position was that Barry's client was being defrauded and waited to see what that would provoke.

> Barry
> Am forwarding recent email from Douglas Townsend. I don't know who he is or what is his connection to Effex Bank, but the letter is self explanatory. I will pay no vat tax until I have access to the funds.
>
> Don't you think it is strange that the vat tax has to be paid to a bank in Taiwan instead of a bank in England. Don't you agree. If the funds are paid to the U.S. government Francisco loses his money. Since I've not received the funds I am not liable. However, you are the one who picked the Effex Bank.
>
> I suggest you contact whoever you know there and strongly advise them to release the funds to me. Then IF there is a vat tax, I will pay it to the appropriate British authority— like the Financial Services Authority, etc.
>
> Mr. Townsend can send the money to the U.S. government if he wants and I'm sure it will be grateful to use it to pay a lot of bills.
>
> It is now up to you. Either you save Francisco's investment or it goes to Uncle Sam.
>
> I await your response.

Before Barry could respond, my caring friend Joseph reappeared at 12:17 EST responding to my email of two days previous.

> *Dear Sir*
> *Thank you for your reply.*
> *It is pleasing to know that you are fully aware of the fraudulent activity and that any involvement you have with the scammers is simply to tease/waste their time; we applaud this.*
>
> *We feel that warnings such as the one you received are by no means unnecessary. You would probably be suprised to hear that many people do become victims of the scammers and end up losing money.*
>
> *If you use alternative identities/email addresses to contact scammers then we cannot guarantee that you will not receive standard fraud warnings again.*
>
> *However, I will keep your email in a folder called "Pricks" (quite apt considering your thistleprods@aol address) to remind us in the future.*
>
> *If we took your ill-informed 'advice' and 'minded our own business' then many people would fall victim not realising what they are getting into.*
>
> *Thanks*
> *Joseph*

I'd never been called a prick, at least not in print, before. I searched for a feeling. Was I insulted, offended, outraged, ashamed, embarrassed or contrite? No. Not at all. I was exhilarated. If I had pricked Joseph's hide, perhaps Clifford, Agnes, Sam, Barry, Ronald and Douglas felt the same.

February 27—4:04 EST:

Email from Agnes Newton appeared in my email box for the first time since February sixth.

Dear Mr Vincent
I am sorry that I have been out of touch for a few days. Clifford's condition worsened and I had a full hand. He is again stable. Have you had the funds sent into your account? This seems to be a source of worry for Clifford.
Please advise.
Agnes

I decided to lay it all out for Agnes. It would be one blast to end the merry-go-round ride and get on with life.

Dear Agnes
I regret that Clifford had a set back and am pleased that he recovered.
Funds were deposited in the Effex Bank account that Barry Goldman insisted I open—much against my wishes. I was never given an access code, so have not gained access to any of the funds. Yesterday I was informed that I would not be given the code until I wired $7,500 into an account at a bank in Taiwan. Should I fail to do that within five days starting yesterday, I was told the funds would be regarded as "terrorist" funds and given to the U.S. government.

In that case, poor Mr. Francisco would lose all of his money and Mr. Goldman would be totally responsible, along with the bank for the theft of those funds.

No one ever told me there would be a "vat tax" to receive the funds. Most banks charge a fee for wire funds, but they are paid directly to the bank and not to an account in an obscure bank in Taiwan.

I am not pleased at what has transpired and will take suitable measures if and when I do not receive satisfaction—which means getting access to all of my funds.

Please do not trouble Clifford with this news as I am concerned about his health.

Vincent

Meanwhile I spoke with Barry Goldman at his Ivory Coast number that day. He told me he "contacted the bank and you have to pay a fee." I told Barry there was not a chance in the world I would pay the fee. Either it's deducted from the total amount or I'd wire it upon receiving the funding.

Agnes also sent another email.

> *Dear Mr. Vincent*
>
> *I am rather troubled by the news that I have just received from you about this matter. I am not conversant with International Business matters but considering that the bulk of this money belongs to Clifford and by extension to myself in the event of his demise, I shall implore you to PLEASE see if you can possibly accomodate this process. If I could have afforded it, I would't have minded sending the money to you but at the moment I am having to cover ALL of expenses until Clifford is fully recovered.*
>
> *Mr. Vincent, please see if you can at least do it for*
> *my sake.*
> *Agnes*

There is nothing like blatant manipulation to make any semblance of Christian charity in my bones dissolve into dust. I figured Agnes deserved another salvo.

February 28—9:17 EST I sent her another email.

> Dear Agnes
> The Effex Bank, which Francisco's attorney selected, has been iden-tified to me by several authorities as a major participant in the Nigerian 419 scam.
>
> If Clifford and Francisco have their money in that bank, I suggest they remove it immediately, if they can, and put it in a more reli-able bank. From that point, they can wire me their investment and we can restore some sanity to the proceedings.
>
> I have no problem with the bank reducing the total by $7,500 AFTER I get access to the funds—if that is the wire fee.

However, no one will get a crumb of bread from me—let alone some vat tax—until I get the investment as promised in writing and by signature in my contract with Francisco.

This has nothing to do with the understanding international business, it is all about common sense—not to mention, honesty, morality, etc.

This is my suggestion to you, Clifford and Francisco AND IT IS MY FIRM AND IRREVOCABLE POSITION.
Vincent

Goldman called me later that morning to tell me he was "working hard to sort out the complications and working hard to raise the money." He assured me he "will try to sort it out"; an assurance that I knew could not be taken to any bank in the world. I asked for a number where he could be reached and he gave me (225) 05 41 9755.

March 1—3:36 EST I received my last email from Agnes.

Mr. Vincent
I am a bit troubled by the content of your last mail. I shall have to discuss this with Clifford. The money was originally with the Congolese Bank for Trade and Industry before that Bank collapsed during the war and Clifford only managed to get the funds out in the nick of time. I am not sure which Bank the money went into eventually. I will get back to you later.
Agnes

I gave no more thought to Agnes, Clifford, Barry et al and was soon involved with the matters that will occupy the rest of this book, namely spending from April to November living on India time.

April 21

Seven weeks after I'd severed contact with the boys and girls from West Africa Ronald Williams popped up again. There was that refrain from the Rolling Stones "you'll come running back ... to me." Indeed he had.

Williams advised me that I could "wire funds from you account site to any other bank in the world. Your Approved balance is now $7,500,000.00. Effex

Bank Ltd. would like to introduce itself as a leader in Offshore Banking and Corporate Services in the International market today."

In similar fashion, I would like to introduce my self as Brad Pitt.

At least I still had more than seven million dollars at my disposal. I'd always been good at Monopoly and figured this was just another game. Then I recalled, playing against my sisters, I usually cheated at Monopoly. Taking the role of the banker a few hundred dollars were always kept neatly tucked under my leg. Now I knew what it felt like when the tables were reversed.

Nevertheless, I took Williams at his word, naif that I am, and the next day decided to wire funds from my account at Effex Bank to my account at Bank of America in Los Angeles.

Faster than you can say Effex Bank, I received an email from Martha Stevens with the email address of interwiretransfernetwork@juno.com. Martha Stevens is an excellent name to use when trying to levy reprimand. It conjures up another Martha with similar initials, whose reputation for exactitude is legendary. No one would accuse Ronald and the boys and girls in West Africa of not being au courant.

April 23—17:26:36 GMT my Martha wrote:

> *Dear Vincent Panettiere*
> *I am sorry to inform you that your wire transfer failed. The wire transfer network did not accept your authorization code. Your account has been frozen and the funds has been credited back into your frozen account number (45330-671009) by the wire transfer network. You cannot withdraw or deposit any funds into your account until you get a new authorization code. To get a new authorization code you have to pay a total of $21,500.00 for vat on the new authorization code.*
>
> *However we are not authorize to make any deduction from your account. Because your account is already frozen by the wire transfer network. Your account can only be reactivated by the new authorization code. We are very sorry for this inconvenience. Contact me when you are ready to make Payment. Contact effexbank for more details.*
> *Sincerely*
> *Martha Stevens*

Even in Monopoly I had my standards. Increasing the vat by almost three times was outrageous. I sent off an email to Williams in protest at 10:53:00–0700(PDT)

> Your email to me indicated I could wire funds from my account in the Effexbank to any bank in the world.
>
> There was no mention of a $21,000 payment. Why?
>
> Advise me how that amount can be deducted from my balance so that I can proceed.
>
> Funds are urgently needed here for film production.

A few minutes later, 11:05:35-0700 (PDT), I also directed my displeasure at Martha.

> Am quite surprised by your email since no one at Effexbank ever informed me regarding the need for an authorization code, let alone a payment for one.
>
> When the account was opened I was informed that I could wire funds to any bank in the world.
>
> Please provide me with phone number for the wire transfer network so that I may sort this out and arrange for payment.
>
> Am surprised the network has the authority to freeze my funds and want to know the reason why they have done so.
>
> No payment will be made until I receive satisfactory answers and explanations.
>
> Please advise ASAP.

That should put the fear of God into her. Not only did I express outrageous indignation, but I diminished her authority over me by insisting on speaking with the higher authority. Surely she would be well put her in her place.

Williams was the first to respond at 19:34:11 GMT.

I tried to deduct the money but your account is already frozen. To reactivate your account you need to settle the payment with international wire transfer network. Since September 11th issue happened any wire transfer have to be properly investigated before proceeding. The $21,500.00 is value added tax (VAT) that is due to your funds. When ever a huge amount is deposited in UK a VAT is needed. So I think they want to collect the VAT before issuing a new authorization code. This is how it works here. It is normal thing as soon as you settle the payment with them all will be fine.
Sincerely
Ronald Williams

Gee that Ronald fellow was earnest. You could just sense in his email that he gave a yeoman effort to have the VAT deducted from my account, but to no avail. All that was left was for me to simply pay twenty one thousand dollars "all will be fine"; something like God's in his heaven all's right with the world.

Didn't September 11th become a convenient excuse for all kinds of chicanery? I wouldn't be surprised if that date wasn't credited or blamed for the increase or decrease of births nine months later. Surely, it was being used as an emotional wedge to leverage funds out of unsuspecting victims. Whether or not there is a legitimate VAT imposed by the British government I didn't know at the time. If there is, under the guise of some anti money laundering scheme, then governments are equally guilty of exploiting 9/11 to line their own coffers.

Six minutes after the Williams email, our Miss Martha responded. Makes one pause, doesn't it. Do we conjure up two distinct individuals working feverishly into the night on their separate enterprises? Or, are they sitting next to each other hatching an orchestrated response to my indignant email?

"You write first, Ronnie. Be the good cop."

"Okay, Martha."

Or were Martha and Ronald one and the same, but in fact neither. Which means that since we've never been able to accurately identify Ronald Williams and Martha Stevens as real people, they most likely have another name like Chauncey Montague or some such name.

Miss Martha wrote at 19:40:01 GMT:

You should have known that you suppose to pay a vat of $21,500.00 before doing any wire transfer. Don't you want to pay your tax again?

or am I not suppose to do my job? This is nothing personal but a must thing to do. I will reactivate your account as soon as the payment is made.
Below is the wiring Informations for the $21,500.00

CHANGHWA COMM BANK
CHIEN CHENG BRANCH 123
NANKING RD TAIPEI TAIWAN
SWIFT: CCBCTWTP505
ACCOUNT NUMBER: 5050225300700
A/C NAME: CHEN MENG HSUN
BENEFICIARY: (IWTN) XX V. PENETTIERE

Inform me when you have wired the funds.
Sincerely
Martha Stevens

My Miss Martha was sounding too authoritarian for my taste. But, before dealing with her, I noticed something very familiar about the banking information she provided.

In his February 26 email to me, Douglas Townsend instructed me to send $7,500 to the following:

CHANGHWA COMM. BANK LTD
CHENG BRANCH 123 NANKING W ROAD
TAIPEI TAIWAN

SWIFT: CCBCTWTP505
A/C NAME: CHEN MENGHSUN
A/C NUMBER; 50502252300700

IN FAVOR OF: International fund transfer department

Martha wanted me to send $21,000 to the same bank, same branch with the same address. In addition the SWIFT code and account name and number had not changed. I was most curious about how Chen Meng Hsun got involved in this deal. Was he real? Was he Chinese or Taiwanese and if so how did a bunch of African con artists connect with their Asian counterpart? Finally, I realized this is what was meant by the term "global economy."

The difference now was that I was named as "beneficiary" while Townsend had the funds sent to the International fund transfer department. What was the benefit? I still had to fork over twenty one thousand dollars to receive more than an imaginary seven million dollars. The obvious answer was—not much.

Similarities aside, I sent Martha an angry email at 13:20:35–0700 (PDT).

> Don't you tell me what I'm supposed to know! The bank never mentioned that in its email. First I heard of it was from you.
>
> I'm supposed to pay a vat to a bank in Taiwan for an account in England????
>
> Get real.
>
> Who are you and your organization that you have the power to freeze my account. Show me the government statute and direct me to the government office.
>
> Unfreeze my account and I will wire the funds.

Two hours later I remembered that it takes at least two to play liars poker. At 15:48:40–0700 (PDT), I sent Martha another email.

> The vat was wired to Taiwan at 2:51pm Los Angeles time.
>
> Please advise me when received and immediately unfreeze my account.

April 24

The next morning I decided to stir the pot even more by contacting Agnes Newton, with copies to Barry Goldman and Sam Smith.

> Agnes
> Please be advised that Effexbank continues to refuse to release the funds your husband and his Portuguese partner invested in my company. They want a vat of $21,500, which I insist be deducted from the proceeds in my account for Thistle Entertainment Corp. at the bank.

I am told the funds are on hold until the vat is paid.

Since we are at a standstill, I suggest you withdraw or have your representatives withdraw the funds so that they are not stolen.

I have contacted by someone in Toronto who posed as a representative of the bank and tried to fraudulently collect those funds for himself.

I do not wish for anyone to lose money and would feel better if the funds were returned to you.

At some later date, should you want to invest in my films, you can send the funds to the Bank of America in Los Angeles and I will supply the necessary sorting codes, account numbers, etc.

I hope Clifford is well.

Good luck.
Vincent Panettiere

If nothing else I hoped the email would provide a spot of humor and bit of respite to those living in such sinkholes as the Congo, Angola and Ivory Coast. One could look on my spurious email as a true humanitarian act.

As I was engaging in self reverence, Ronald responded at 08:07:01 GMT.

Send us by email attarchment the receipt of payment or payment slip. We will reactivate as soon as we receive confirmation and the new code that will be when they receive your payment.
Ronald

Interestingly, Ronald responded using the email I'd sent to Martha. Once again in explanation, instead of typing in my email address and start fresh correspondence, he simply hit the reply button on Martha's email. Coincidence?

Four—count them one, two, three, four—minutes later, at 08:11:00 GMT, Martha sent me an email.

I will notify you as soon as we confirm payment. Make sure that you email a copy of your payment slip to us and the effexbank. Keep in touch.
Sincerely
Martha Stevens

I decided to throw a spanner (wrench to Americans) into the machinery of the London-based Effex Bank by sending them both an email at 09:46:24–0700 (PDT).

Dear Martha and Ronald
I've discussed the need for a VAT payment with my chief financial officer, a man with more than 30 years experience as a banker in the U.S., Europe, Russia and the Middle East. He informs me the best way for me to provide the VAT is as follows:

1. Transfer the funds in Effexbank account #45330-671009 to your correspondant bank offshore in Ireland, Jersey or the Isle of Man and open an account in my name and the corporate name Thistle Entertainment Corp in that bank.

2. I will complete the required forms to transfer the VAT to the Effexbank in the UK or elsewhere as the case may be.

3. British Inland authorities will accept the $21,500 Vat payment to them from an offshore account and will take no issue with us if the bank is offshore so that we both thereby comply fully with the British authorities request for VAT.

4. I will make instructions to debit my account irrevocable so that you may obtain the proceeds of $21,500.

Please advise soonest commencement of the above.

Ronald was the first to respond at 18:32:19 GMT.

That will be very good idea please contact martha Ronald

Twelve minutes later, 18:45:16 GMT, before I could even think about an email to write to Martha, she wrote to me. Another coincidence.

Thank you for your email. I have just given permission to effex bank to unfreeze your account. Your account will be active in 5 mins but you will not be able to wire funds without the authorization code. The funds will continue to bounce back unless a new authorization code is issued.

Let me know when payment is made.
Sincerely
Martha Stevens

If my email two hours before had convinced them to unfreeze my account, I thought one more ruse might work to get me an authorization code without paying the VAT. I wrote to Ronald at 11:49:49–0700 (PDT).

Ronald
I sent you the VAT but can't fax you the receipt because the number you gave me is not a working number according to the operator.

Let me know how you want to proceed.

I also received your email suggesting I contact Martha. I assume this was sent before we spoke.

As of our conversation, the following has and will happen:

1. You informed me on the phone this morning that my account is unfrozen. I have sent from those funds $21,500 to the bank in Taiwan. (Funds sent at 11:35 am Los Angeles time.)

2. I tried to fax you the computer screen page of that transaction (fax number doesn't work) and will fax it to any working number you select.

3. When you receive confirmation that the VAT has been received in Taiwan you will call me by Tuesday, at which time I will be able to wire my funds anywhere in the world.

This is our agreement today by phone.

Please advise immediately if this is not your understanding.

He responded at 19:05:04 GMT.

> *All will happen like we discussed. Our agreement holds Don't have*
> *any douting mind. I sent the email to contact martha before we spoke*
> *before we spoke on the phone. You can fax the slip of payment to this*
> *American fax number 1-775-320-2775. I will email you when i*
> *receive it.*
> *Sincerely*
> *Ronald Williams*

Twenty eight minutes later a resounding AH HAH! could be heard bellowing out of my office window. At 19:33:36 GMT Ronald wrote:

> *If you try to wire funds out of your account here the money will keep*
> *coming back. You need authorization code before you can wire funds*
> *out of your account although it is unfrezen. Please wire funds from*
> *your other account.*
> *Thank you.*
> *Ronald Williams*

AH HAH again. I have to send the VAT from my other account, which means the account where Ronald, Martha, et al believe I have real money deposited. They were smart enough to know not to receive imaginary money from an imaginary account. Bet they never took a wooden nickel in their lives, either.

Karl's reaction to Ronald's request for real money was very supportive.

> *Their reply is meaningless and has absolutely nothing to do with what*
> *you sent them. Therefore the only thing to do is to ask them to specifi-*
> *cally reply to your email's contents and to not b.s.*
> *What they sent you is "bait".*
> *Regards*
> *Karl*

April 26

Two days later at 19:54:25 GMT Ronald had a new idea.

> *We can put your funds in a CD account. our interest rate is 20%. You can be making money while looking for the money for vat.*
> *Ron*

He figured Americans are a friendly people why not get familiar and shorten his name to Ron, which rhymes with con and where time is always on his side.

What Ron also did was to reply to me from an email I'd sent to Martha on April 23. Don't tell me this is another coincidence?

More than anything, Ron's email gave me a sense of euphoria.

He promised to make me money on phantom money so that I'd pay him real money.

The mind whirls. Wheeeeeeeeeeeeeeeeeeeeeeeeee!

April 27—05:41:16—0700 (PDT) I told Mr. Williams that I appreciated his proposal and would discuss it carefully with my Chief Financial Officer. And, that we'd get back to him with our reaction and any questions in due course.

Monday morning I informed Ronald, this time, that my CFO thought putting a portion of the funds in a CD with Effexbank was a good idea.

"Can we put $2 million in a CD for 90 days as a test to see how it works out?" I asked.

Tuesday morning he replied that "we will do that as soon as possible."

The obvious seven million dollar question is if Ronald, Martha et al can move two million from the "frozen" funds to place in a CD, why can't they move $21,000 to pay the vat tax? In addition, was the CD suggestion part of a scripted ploy toward their end game?

May 1

On Thursday I queried Ronald on the status of the CD. It was now seven months since my initial contact with Clifford Newton. How time flies when you're having fun.

May 2—13:07:18 GMT, Ronald told me:

> *I have fixed your funds for three months. I will give you details on 1st of Augus 2003*

Any body with a calendar and an acquaintance with rudimentary math would know that August 1st was 90 days away from May 1st. But what I needed to know was the process by which this would be accomplished. At 08:18:57–0700 (PDT) I contacted Ronald to ask

> "Will you remove $2 million from my account? How does this work? Does interest begin accruing from May 1 to August 1?

I checked my balance on May 2nd and 3rd. On both days the total available balance was $7,500,000, meaning no money had been deducted for a CD.

May 11

Nine days later, and with no response, I contacted Mr. Williams at 10:45:15–0700 (PDT).

> Please advise status of establishment of $2,000,000 CD from Thistle Entertainment funds in Effexbank?

May 12—06:08:44 GMT—Williams told me by email:

> *You will be notified in due time.*

Vague enough to be true. At 06:12:54–0700 (PDT) I wrote him:

> Mr. Williams
> What does "in due time mean." I cannot find that date on any calendar, please be more precise.

The next sound I heard, at18:48:25 GMT, was BABOOOOOM!

> *Dear Vincent*
> *You have five days to comply with our demands. After five days and we don't hear from you I will contact the IRS of United States for help to secure our VAT. It has worked before and it will work again.*
> *Ronald*

Oh, Yeah?!

Those guys really know how to make a fella's knees knock and boots quake. Going to the IRS for money was like going to a bull for milk.

At 11:53:42–0700 (PDT) I wrote to Ronald.

> Your "demands" are extortion and thievery. If that money actually exists in your bank, and you can actually put it into a CD, then you have the ability to subtract the VAT and pay it as I have authorized.
>
> Otherwise you are a bunch of scammeisters who should be arrested for fraud, theft and extortion.
>
> Do as I have instructed and you will get your money for the VAT.
>
> Otherwise go try to steal from somebody else.

Not surprisingly, I never heard from Ronald again. Guess he must have taken my criticism much too personally.

September 2003

FAST FORWARD to the end of September 2003, approximately one year to the day that Clifford Newton had made his initial contact with me.

It's email from Sam Smith—"you'll be coming back, you'll be coming back to meeeee." Sam wanted me to confirm my phone and fax number because "the finance company have been trying to get hold of you for conversation but you number not going through."

Sam was contacting me through the email I'd sent to Agnes, with copy to him and Barry Goldman on April 24. Somebody must like the way I write and was keeping my email to remind him of how good the English language sounded when properly written.

September 30

I sent Sam my phone and fax numbers.

October 2

Paul Morris called me. He said he was with the International Fund Management Corp. and spoke with a street wise New York accent. Being a born and bred New Yorker, it takes one to know one. He sounded like the kind of guy you wouldn't/shouldn't buy an umbrella from on the corner of Broadway and 47th Street if it was in the middle of Hurricane Andrew. I listened.

October 4

As a result of my conversation with Paul Morris I sent an email to Sam.

> I was contacted by Paul Morris of International Fund Management Corp on October 2, 2003
>
> He told me a condition of my receiving the investment from Clifford Newton was that I open an account with his bank for a minimum of $5,000.
>
> I told him I had a bank account and he should wire the funds directly. He refused to do this and offered that in lieu of the bank account he would set up a "legal structure" to trace the funds and find if any taxes were owed.
>
> I told him that taxes were my concern not his. He told me the taxes in question were on the funder. I also told him it was not his concern.
>
> Ultimately, I advised him to return the funds.
>
> I've told you before and I'll tell you again. If Mr. Newton sincerely wants to invest in my company—as our signed agreement indicates—he is to wire the funds DIRECTLY into my account.
>
> Anything less is unacceptable.
>
> If there are fees involved THEY WILL BE PAID AFTER I RECEIVE THE INVESTMENT FUNDS!
>
> Nothing else is acceptable. I hope you are all clear on the matter and will act accordingly.

In checking my notes to write this chapter I discovered that I'd spoken to Paul Morris on more than one occasion and he'd given me several cel phone numbers, which seems to be a standard practice going back to my dealings with Madam Diana and her "agent" Chris Brown in London.

At one point Morris told me the funds were "at the Federal Reserve now"; that there was no tracking number for the funds because they had been sent by "telex" and later that he had the tracking number, but "I won't tell you."

I asked him to send me an annual report for the bank, which he refused to do because it was "a private bank." He gave me the bank's address as 1440 Broadway in Manhattan. To New Yorkers 1440 Broadway is one of those familiar addresses like 30 Rock or 666 Fifth Avenue. They are well rounded, even addresses that are easy to remember.

When I asked for the main office phone number he gave me (212) 202-4320, which the day before he'd given me as the fax number.

International Fund Management Corporation has a website—www.ifmcor poration.com that indicates it is located in George Town on Grand Cayman in the Cayman Islands.

October 5—1:11:20 PM EDT, Sam Smith answered my latest email to him.

> *Dear Vin*
> *Thanks for all your effort, i will advice you to find out acturelly if is the way in doing transaction in U.S. A before you conclude.*
>
> *If the condition is okay you go ahead and open the new account, even if the business didnt take place you can go back and collect you money, hence are to open it with your name and signature.*
>
> *For the fact the organasation exist in america, because asking mr newton to call his fund remeber they will still move some money out of the original fund that was deposited.*
>
> *The way i see it they never ask you for any upfront fee or taxies, is only to open an account with them so that it will directely their.*
>
> *The issue of wireing the fund directelly to your nominated account, we have tried all we could but no success, because since the problem of September 11, no bank wire's money directly to U.S A, EITHER THROUGH THEIR AFFILIATE.*
>
> *PLEASE CONSIDER IT FROM YOUR SIDE TO IF YOU ARE TO OPEN THE NEW ACCOUNT FOR EASY TRANSFER.*

WAITING TO HEAR FROM YOU, TO KNOW THE
NEXT STAGE
RGDS
SAM SMITH

October 6—11:21:03 AM EDT I let loose on Sam Smith.

Dear Mr. Smith
PAY CLOSE ATTENTION TO THE FOLLOWING

I WILL NOT, REPEAT NOT, REPEAT NOT, REPEAT NOT—
OPEN AN ACCOUNT WITH THAT BANK!!!!!!!!!!!!!!!!!!!!!!!!!!!!!!!!!!!!

I HAVE A BANK ACCOUNT. WIRE THE INVESTMENT FUNDS
TO MY ACCOUNT.

OTHERS HAVE WIRED WITH NO PROBLEM. 9/11 IS AN
EXCUSE THAT IS NOT ACCEPTABLE.

WIRE THE MONEY OR GET LOST!!!!!!!!!!

October 8

Sam Smith did not shrink from my yelling at him and replied—9:24:33 AM
EDT.

Dear sir
thanks for your email, do you want someone to bring the fund to your
door step in u.s.a?if yes you are going to paid for the expencied on his
arrival.

waiting to hear from you for more details regards to it.
Rgds
Sam Smith

About two hours later that morning 11:44:23 AM EDT I tersely wrote back
to Sam:

WIRE THE FUNDS OR GET LOST

That was the last I wrote to Sam Smith or any one else connected with the Effex Bank deal.

However, as I began writing this book, I tried to access the Bank's website only to find it was no longer available. At least that is what I intuited when I got a page marked HTTP 403 (Forbidden) and in large type "You are not authorized to view this page", but did provide www.effexbank.com home page.

I tried once again and received the same forbidden message. Next I did an Internet Search for Effexbank.

The most important reference came from the Office of the Comptroller of the Currency, Enforcement and Compliance Division in Washington, DC.

On December 5, 2003 OCC ALERT 2003-14 was sent to the Chief Executive Officers of all National Banks; all state banking authorities, the Chairman and Board of Governors of the Federal Reserve System, the Chairman of the Federal Deposit Insurance Corporation, Conference of State Bank Supervisors, etc. In short the alert went to the U.S. banking community.

The alert put all on notice that Effex Bank NA; Effex Bank Ltd; Effexbank Bank, Ltd; or Effexbank International Bank Limited, located electronically at www.effexbank.com and physically at 350 Fifth Avenue, New York, NY 10118 was "operating a banking business without authorization."

By December 7th a posting online in the The Diligizer Board indicated that the Effex Bank "web site is no longer accessible" which brought the comment "looks like the powers that be are successful for once."

I don't know if the OCC actually read through all of the information posted on Effex Bank's web site.

If it had, it might have noticed the last line: "The laws of the Federal Republic of Nigeria shall apply to this agreement." What laws?

3. APRIL 2003

THE JOURNEY BEGINS

In April 2003, keeping a diary to write a book about my experiences trying to raise money from a 24-year-old woman in Kolkata, India was as far removed from my consciousness as Alpha Centauri. Otherwise, I would be able to report precisely when I was first contacted about this particular funding possibility. Best as I can recall the most unusual, curious, absurd and nonsensical adventure of my life began on or about April 27, 2003.

An email from Larry Kronebusch, who operated the company J.J.'s Concept & Design, arrived. It proclaimed in full caps, indented in the center of the first page:

ABSOLUTELY NO FEE, 100% FINANCING.

At this same time Ronald Williams of Effexbank was proposing to put my phantom $7,500,000 in an equally non-existent CD to provide an additionally imaginary 20% interest.

Stumbling out of that desert Larry's email was very welcome. I'd had a passing acquaintance with Larry about a year earlier. He sent me an unsolicited email listing all of his possible funding sources, claiming to be a "broker" from British Columbia. Now, as I was recovering from my EffexBank experience this possibility became a ready substitute.

The email explained that Chris Catlin, (Catlin Enterprises) his partner in Tasmania, "was approached for some top quality projects from a referral through an associate in India and this family has some very large funds they wish to bring offshore and invest into projects requiring funding."

Larry explained that he and Chris were "still around a week aways from actually confirmed bank transferred confirmation of this investor's true capabilities. We are going through the motions and we want to know if anyone who is receiving this notation wants to participate."

As further inducement, Larry admitted they were still trying to "verify this lender, but we are in constant contact with her and her family; we have their names and business names and addresses and we have been working very hard this month directly with her so we believe that if anything else you and we have an excellent shot at some serious amounts of capital."

Furthermore, he continued "we already had the first wave approved and arranged, but … five projects failed to perform." The investor needed to take sixteen projects to her banker and now had only 11. I didn't know why the others "failed to perform" and cared less. I only wanted to be one of the five replacements; eagerly read through the remainder of the email to determine what information was required.

First, I needed to have my business plan converted to html, because the investor/lender was "wary of viruses." Then I needed to hook up to Yahoo Messenger so that I could communicate online with Larry and Chris in real time.

Larry and Chris required a two percent fee agreement with them as brokers.

A message from Chris was appended to Larry's email. He required all new applicants to prepare an official letter from the company (Thistle Productions, Inc.) informing the investor I was authorized by the company to raise money for the business; the amount of funding needed per stage and return on the investment over a specified period.

In this letter I also had to reveal any current loans or liens against the company and provide banking information for the transfer of funds. The letter had to be signed by the CEO and its corporate seal had to be affixed as well. I sent the following:

April 30, 2003
Ms. Anamika Biswas
A.B. Exports
#84 Jatindra Mohan Avenue
Kolkata, 700005 India

Dear Ms. Biswas:

INVESTOR'S CONTRACT FOR THISTLE PRODUCTIONS

This agreement made and concluded this 30th day of April 003 by and between Anamika Biswas of A.B. Imports, #84 Jatindra Mohan Avenue, Kolkata, India, Herein after referred to as the INVESTOR(S) being party of the first part, AND Mr. Vincent Panettiere of Thistle Productions, Inc. Los Angeles, CA USA, Herein after referred to as the COMPANY being party of the second part.

WHEREAS, the INVESTOR(S) being desirous of placing an investment in Thistle Productions, Inc. And the COMPANY, being interested in attracting fresh capital funding for its ever expanding film production activities;

WHEREFORE, it is hereby agreed that the INVESTOR(S) agrees to invest the sum of USD $28.5 million in the commercial activities of the COMPANY within fifteen (15) days after the execution of the contract;

That in consideration for this investment, the COMPANY agrees to share revenue from its feature films, produced with the above funds, in tandem with INVESTOR(S) on a pari passu basis until INVESTOR(S) have received 115% of its investment after which INVESTOR(S) will receive twenty five (25%) percent of additional revenue generated by said films COMPANY produces with these funds.

That INVESTOR(S) agrees to provide COMPANY with clean, value dated and wire transferred Fed funds. COMPANY reserves the right to reject any source of funds not in compliance with the above.

That INVESTOR(S) agrees to respect and protect any CONFIDENTIAL and PROPRIETARY information and rights of the COMPANY. Similarly, COMPANY agrees to respect and protect any CONFIDENTIAL and PROPRIETARY information and rights of INVESTOR(S).

That INVESTOR(S) agrees it/they have its/their own independent due diligence of the COMPANY and is entering this Agreement based upon that due diligence.

That while the INVESTOR(S) agrees to accept future profit and loss accounts of the COMPANY, the INVESTOR(S) will not be liable or share liability in any and ALL previous loss incurred or contracted by the COMPANY prior to the signing of this agreement.

That the COMPANY agrees, upon reasonable notice, but no more than semi-annually, to open the Financial Records of the COMPANY to the INVESTOR(S) or its/their ASSIGNEE for scrutiny and due diligence.

The following signatories voluntary accept the terms of this Agreement and its legal implications under the laws of the USA

That both parties agree that any dispute to any part or section of this agreement shall be settled by arbitration under the prevailing Laws of the State of California in USA.

Contract confirmed legal and binding by Anamika Biswas of the company known as A.B. Exports, Kolkata, India.

This agreement is signed and executed this _____ day of _____ 2003

_____

Anamika Biswas

Contract confirmed legal and binding by Vincent Panettiere of the company known as Thistle Productions, Inc. _____ USA.

This agreement is signed and executed this 30th day of April 2003

_____

Vincent Panettiere
N.B. This faxed copy shall enjoy the same validity as the original hard copy.

Chris explained that the information requested in the corporate letters was "a requirement of the bank that money is in and a requirement of the government, otherwise no money will be invested as the bank and the government demand they know how much is going out and how much of a return is supposed to be coming back in if all investments are successful."

Larry concluded the email by delineating the steps and stages which had been and would be taken for funding.

Once Chris received my fee agreement he would send me contact information for Anamika Biswas and then he and I would coordinate the time to reach her by cel phone before sending our information to her by fax. At that time, India was twelve and a half hours ahead of Los Angeles. This meant that noon in Los Angeles was 12:30 am in Kolkata, India—the new name for Calcutta.

It also meant that for the next seven months I would be living on India time—twelve and a half hours behind during Pacific Daylight Time and thirteen and a half during Pacific Standard Time.

Beyond the need to add and subtract, living on India time had a mental impact as well. Each communication was sent aware of the time difference and with the expectation of a response that would arrive from India during my interval of sleep. The ebb and flow of email produced a similar psychological rhythm so that failure to receive a reaction to the previous day's email could cause twenty four hours of frustration and disappointment until the next morning, when, if no email from India were forthcoming, the cycle would be repeated.

Larry's explanation of next steps indicated "investor received the contracts and letters and then signs them and sends them back to the clients as a completed package and when all are completed (16 projects minimum) she then within a few days arranges for the transferring of the funds."

He suggested "All clients as they receive their capital write a nice letter to Chris and the lender confirming safe transfer of funds." Then, "all clients transfer the commissions as directed by Chris and Larry within the time frame listed on the fee agreement...."

What could be simpler and more direct? This is what I heard and what motivated me:

- an investor needed additional projects
- I had an excellent project
- no up front fees/100% funding
- finders' fees 2%
- fees paid after funding received

After months of dealing with the folks in London, Sierra Leone, Benin, Congo, Ivory Coast and Angola, this proposal for financing from a woman in Kolkata, India seemed to be just perfect (note to remind my self—nothing is perfect in life or in nature).

April 30, 2003

Chris sent me an email providing Anamika's phone and fax numbers and asking that I call between 10am and 8pm India time or 9:30 PM to 6:30 AM Los Angeles time.

It would take another five days before I finally completed sending my documents to Anamika by fax on the seventh try. Each error message indicated NG—poor line condition.

Communication might not be as easy and convenient as in the U.S., but I felt assured funding would be easier.

What I didn't know at that time was that Larry was trying to verify Anamika's proof of funds. It was a noble and responsible effort, but it became the initial irritant for Anamika which ultimately would destroy whatever relationship he had with her. At least, that's what it seemed at the time. This was an omen of things to come which we either failed to recognize or saw, but chose to ignore.

Larry wrote:

Hello Anamika

Anamika it is Larry here and I have some things we need to discuss on this project funding affair and I know in my heart that you are really doing your very best and so far I have been very proud to have been a big part of this affair.

And I am not sure how you will accept me discussing with you some issues but there are some things that we need to talk about ok? So here goes and if you would be so kind as to send in your answers in bold letters below each point then it will make things clear for us all. In other words I will list the items of interest then you please make your answers directly below the topic.

If you need more space just type in what you wish to say and the document will expand as needed and then simply save your work every few minutes or so.

Clearly, as good as were his intentions, Larry did not display any talent at writing business letters. This is the first of what would be many discoursive, rambling emails and attached word documents which showed no indication they were ever re-read for spelling, grammatical or contextual errors.

After a number of these, I offered to help edit his email but Larry took offense. I reminded myself my goal was not to teach Larry how to write a business letter, but to find financing for my company. It was necessary, but not satisfying.

Larry enumerated what he wanted answered by Anamika.

1. International investing is never easy I do not think and has much investigations and introductions for everyone involved, for the investor(s) and for the clients chosen for funding.

reply …

2. we know that you are trying your very best and are really doing an outstanding job so far and that you simply wish to have top quality projects as an investment avenue in order so that you can make the best possible profits for you, your family and companies as we too wish this for you.

reply …

3. *We are very proud to have captured your and your family and friends interest with our projects and we too feel that we offer an incredible amount in value and in large profit potentials for you as our investors.*

reply …

4. *This funding affair is one of the THE VERY BEST EVER OFFERRED on the world STAGE and really is an incredible opportunity for you, your family and associates and for all of us, our families and associates and nobody know this better than us.*

This funding offered by your family and associates has been a very serious affair to us right from day one and especially with the fact that you have offered to give us full 100% financing as this is very important to us as we are all mostly start-up situations.

WE NEED THIS LOAN/INVESTMENT from you more than anything in the world as we have some SUPURB projects to accomplish and bring to life.

However we need this loan/investment in a combination of your working capital investment AND your friendship and partnership as well as that too is a big part of us working parnershiping together.

So, it is a TEAM EFFORT between us and you and your fine people that will bring us together as SERIOUS ENTITIES that will allow us to accomplish our tasks and bring forward these large profit dollars over a period of time.

We only hope that you feel as comfortable about investing/working with us as we do in working with you and returning profits to you.

reply …

5. *However anamika PLEASE UNDERSTAND THIS VERY IMPORTANT FACTOR that I am mentioning now as it is one of the most important ones. We are TRUE POFESSIONALS in ALL aspects of our business's and ALL of the clients HAVE TOP COLLEGE DEGREES and extremely talented teams to support them.*

WE ARE SOME OF THE VERY BEST START-UP SITUATIONS in ALL OF THE WORLD and when you ask something from us we deliver and we deliver FAST as we possibly can.

*WE DELIVER THE BEST WE CAN AND WE EXPECT THE BEST
FROM ALL OF OUR PARTNERS AS WE CAN GET.*

this is very simple and what it takes to succeed in business.

*We MUST be able to perform daily at the TOP of our industries and
because this funding is really a SUPER HUGE AFFAIR, $33 Billion in
total we really maybe are expecting too much from you too fast and if
we are, we seriously appologize.*

I know this letter is fascinating you, but we need to stop and note what
Larry has affirmed with Anamika. She is going to invest $33 billion in the proj-
ects Larry packaged and sent to her!

With my nose pressed to the window pane I didn't pay much attention to
the number 33 as my concern was raising the $28,500,000 required by my
business plan. To be sure that was a sizable amount of money. Had she or anyone, offered twenty percent of that figure, I'd be more than grateful and ready
to charge ahead. Only several months before I tried raising five hundred thousand dollars and was rebuffed. Having learned my lesson, my mind was fixated
on the propriety and legitimacy of $28.5M.

As I write this now with impeccable hindsight I am appalled at myself for
not immediately recognizing the folly of relying on a woman from half a world
away who only offered her intentions to fund.

What does $33 billion actually represent?

- The U.S. receives $2 billion in fresh financing from foreign
  investors every day.
- The News Corporation bought the DirecTV satellite system from
  General Motors for $6.6 billion
- The U.S. Export/Import Bank has the authority to issue at least $15
  billion in loans.
- Bank of America, fifth largest in the U.S. merged with
  NationsBank(#3) for $57.7 billion
- Bank of America bought Fleet Bank of New England for $47 billion
- Biogen, Inc. merged with IDEC Pharmaceutical Corp. for $6.8 bil-
  lion to create the third largest biotech firm.

Now this is a perspective I didn't have in April 2003. Larry continues:

We do not mean to be pushy or rush you.... it is just that we all have family's and associates who are really depending upon us to come through with the capital that it will take for our projects.

and time is moving along and many of us while we try to be very patient, are getting anxious as to the final stages being completed ON TIME as you indicate you can do.

We do NOT really care that it takes you some time to prepare documents and get your things accomplished as we know it will and does take time.

We simply wish for when you set a date to send something over for us to receive or review that those dates are met without delay....

That is all we are asking of you.

and we too ask that if you are not going to proceed with the funding of our company's to please tell us right up front and if you are going to be funding our companies then please tell us what final states do we need to go through to accomplish this fact??

Please advise whatever you can on these topic. (thank you for your understanding)

6. we also very very soon need what is called all around the world as PROF of FUNDS PROOF of CAPABILITY ok.

now we do NOT conduct buisenss like you do i nyour country so pelase forgive us if we are ignortant of your ways, but pelase think like a lein fo r a moment.

Say you had a project and you were patiently for REAL PROOF that your project is going to get funded from an interantional invetor, but say that they offer no confirmable proof of who they are or what they own or how they plan on funding your company. ok??

Wouldn't you, after a while say the very same as us??

WHERE IS THE PROOF PLEASE???

Very simple business Anamika as we all know you well enough and seriously respect your businesss intelligence enough to know that you are trying hard to do this well and properly but we feel that there has to be some docuemnts sent over to us very soon to PROVE to us all and our associates that inded this affair is moving forward in as fast a pace as possible with FULL DOCUMENTATION from the Biswas Family and Empire to clarify beyond ANY SHADOW OF DOUBT that funding will be soon forthcoming to us for your projects.

What be used in America IS a photo copy of the actual drafts, front and back or a verifiable letter from your bankers that we can call to verify (one call) that you have the funds for this amount of funding.

and please work with us on this fact as this is a very important stage for us to get over.

Once you have verified funds w can all relax and chill out and simply do what you direct as you get a chance toas again we understand you are governed by rules and regulation from the RBI so if we can help you out please just ask.

This is a VERY HUGE International Investment affair Anamika and if you need some help from us to get everything accomplished we are here are your new found partners to do whatever it takes to get this funding on its way.

Maybe what is best is one of our group coming to India to assist you in our western ways and manenrs of international investment say one or two clients and a lawyer to come over as reperesentatives of our entire group and if this is acceptable to you we will do our very best to arrange this in a very short period of time.

We all look forward to meeting you and your friends anyways so this would really speed things up possibly.

We truly believe t hat you are one of the very sharpest business ladies in the entire world and you insight and ability is going to be world known and very highly respected all over the world soon but we also believe that you may need a bit of assistance and/or guidance to pull this large of a funding affair off.

This is NOT just for one man or one woman to accomplish but a TEAM EFFORT with EVERYONE who can pitching in to help as directed by the director of the affair, which is you.

So your comments if any please are respected and welcomed.

reply ...

Reading this again, I now realize we were doomed from the start. If I were Anamika with the slightest notion to invest $33 BILLION! after receiving Larry's, at best, poorly written letter which patronized me as a woman and as a citizen of a third world country, and was alternatively sappy and whiny, I wouldn't invest a stamp to tell Larry to buzz off.

Reading it originally, I cringed, shoved back my shoulders, saluted smartly, probably in the same manner as Oliver North, and marched over the cliff with the others.

ABSOLUTELY NO FEE, 100% FINANCING

Had it been a neon sign blinking LIVE, NUDE GIRLS nothing would have been brighter, more disorienting and alluring. It was a reminder than I could find non-traditional funding, but I'd have to take sloppy email as part of the package.

At the same time $33 billion from one person or entity or consortium of companies in India was a figure I never questioned. Nor did I check with any source to determine who the wealthiest families in India were.

Anamika told Larry and Chris that she could invest $33 billion in approximately twenty four companies and we all said "why not"?

Larry provided all the clients with an update that listed each company submitted to Anamika and the total funding for each. I scanned the list in an amazement which, rather than repel, drew me closer into the process.

The first company was to receive $2 billion, another $5 billion and a third $7 billion. Larry and Chris, the brokers, were also clients who stood to realize $10 billion in funding!

My need of twenty eight million, five hundred thousand was puny in comparison.

Before moving on to the rest of the journey with Anamika in Wonderland, it is enlightening to examine other factors which may have caused "intellectual blindness" or rather "intellectually sight-impaired" as the PCers would prefer.

BLINDNESS FACTOR #1—We were dealing with a woman from a "third world" country who in her infinite generosity said she was willing to invest a fortune by any standard in twenty four companies that were in dire need of start up and/or expansion capital. As critical thinking in the United States has been acculturated out of our population through under education and threat of social, financial and legal censure by the politically correct—two words flashed at us.

WOMAN + THIRD WORLD = FUZZY WUZZY

Not only would we be financed beyond our wildest hopes and dreams, but we could achieve a warm feeling by taking the money from a "woman of color" thereby proving we had raised our consciousness and were progressive, inclusive, enlightened beings.

When it comes to warm, fuzzy feelings in situations where they are not required or warranted, I recall the expression of one of my clients when I was in the public relations business.

He would remind us, when judging the limited efficacy of a suggested tactic, that the result would be similar to "pissing in your pants while wearing a dark blue suit—no one would know, but we'd get a warm, fuzzy feeling." When he expressed that opinion, we knew our suggestion had to be changed.

While warm, fuzzy feelings may not be the root of all evil, they can deflect focus and cause one to veer off course in the wrong direction.

BLINDNESS FACTOR #2—Once our intellects were softened by the PC need to suspend critical thinking comforted by the warm fuzzies, the rest came easy. We were open to relying on the power of our hopes, dreams, expectations and desire to short circuit for at least eight months any objective view of the unfolding events in this journey, as will be explained in following chapters.

4. MAY, 2003

THE INVESTORS ARE COMING! THE INVESTORS ARE COMING!

May 1, 2003

Larry informed me and a client from Philadelphia by email that "things are going as far as i know right on schedule." Nevertheless, I spent each day waiting for "India time" (12+ hours later in the day) to send Anamika my documents by fax. Nothing went through.

Larry reported in his May Day missive that he and Chris had added another twelve submissions, bringing the total to nearly twenty four, after a week of "power marathoning" during the last week of April.

The email continued in what I would learn to accept as typical Larry fashion without much concern for spelling, punctuation or grammar.

> *you and 20 others are very curious as to the reality of this family and to be perfectly honest i am still in the same boat, only i am the one conducting diligence on them and we are spending some decent time on it but we only can find their city, a website of a lighting importer/exporter and a write up on Kolkata which is why i have more to be done on that.*

Had anyone of us read this paragraph closely, we might have cooled our jets. We were dealing with a guy who, acting as a broker, openly admitted he had not verified the reality of the funds and wanted empathy from those relying on him to provide funding for their dreams and aspirations because he was "in the same boat"!? If there was a condition that is more than naive it afflicted Larry and all of his clients as well

Then we soon discovered a more important paragraph which contained:

FUNDING DATE #1—MAY 5, 2003

> *Now from what i have been told because India has a banking holiday on Friday that they are planning to start signing the contracts and arrange for the releasing of funds this coming Monday to Wednesday or until they are done and the lengh of time is not certain on large transactions.*

> Holiday #1—banking

Whoa! Nelly! As Keith Jackson, the sportscaster would say during a spectacular college football play. Who cared about punctuation, spelling and grammar as the message needed no editor's pencil when it sent a shot of adrenaline from my tail bone to my brain stem.

Four days after getting involved with this group, I'm receiving email advising that within one to four more days MY FUNDS would be released!!! In the expressive words of the late, great Phil Rizzuto, former New York Yankees great shortstop and broadcaster—HOLY COW!!

I would read the rest of Larry's email without consulting E.B. White and his "Elements of Style" or Monsieur Roget. Let 'er rip!

> *Exactly when you will receive a signed contract this i do not know but i do know that you will not get any funds transferred without any banking information being submitted so this is between you and the lender not between you and me....*

> *As soon as these people release the first few allotments of capital then i am going to ask very adamantly if i have to but that maya not be necessary for some kind of proof of their bank and faxed confirmation of the funds being transferred even if it is only one bank slip or something. this is a minor detail but we will work it out.*

At this point I'm still trying to absorb the impact of the phrases "releasing of funds" "Monday or Wednesday" as they danced in my head. Larry's illogic had not penetrated. As soon as the first few clients got their funds he was going to ask for proof of funds from the investor's bank? Duh! The clients have the investor's money in their accounts. What more proof is needed?

Had Larry or Chris ascertained the existence of funds within the previous thirty days, this book would have never come into being. Jyeshtha, the Hindu god of bad luck, had other plans.

Next, Larry provided a suggestion that had I not experienced Madam Theodoritou and Clifford Newton, would have come as a surprise.

> *mostly everyone is submitting a bank and account number that has very little funds and can be shut down at any time and is simply going with what is requested if you want to do this as well tomorrow, then we can still send in on time your new but safe banking co-ordinates....*

As Larry's advice coincided with my approach to security with the Africans, I felt the need to forgive his inability to write a cohesive paragraph. His email concluded with the following two paragraphs.

anything further we can assist you with maybe chris is the one to ask as chris is in constant contact with the investor and the main agent for all the procedures.

If and when we get to the point of you supposedly receiving your capital (no matter if they pay off or not) you should receive another update from me on other verifiable funding sources as i am already working on other here in North America for everyone and should have that lined up completely in two weeks again with no cost upfront.

Had Larry the ability to edit himself, his credibility over the next eight months would have risen exponentially. Unfortunately, within one email on May 1, 2003 Larry unwittingly managed to erode his capacity to serve as someone who deserved his broker's fee. First he admitted his ignorance being in the "same boat" as the clients when it came to vetting the investor.

Next, in an attempt to prove to the clients that he was ever ready on the job working in their best interests he was determined to adamantly get confirmation slips from the bank <u>after</u> it had distributed funds.

For me, these were grievous sins: 1. Doubt that we'd get funded—"supposedly receiving your capital"; 2. Self promotion—whether they pay or not he was working on getting additional "verifiable funding sources" sometime in the future while at the same time failing to verify the current funding source! We all had enough self doubt without the guy we depended on getting weak in the knees at the crucial moment.

But, at the time all I focused on was my inability to get my documents through to Anamika's fax. Time was of the essence as I had to get my project accepted by her so that it could be funded, I thought, by Monday, May 5 at the outset. On Friday, Saturday and Sunday at the appropriate Indian Time I sent my fax, but nothing got through.

Certain that I'd missed my window of opportunity I received an email early Monday morning requesting that a non-circumvention, non-disclosure (NCND) agreement be provided to Anamika so that she could take it to the bank on Tuesday morning, which was my Monday night. Now I felt like an astronaut aboard Apollo 13 with one last chance to slide into the orbit that would take him home to safety.

May 5—2:02 EST Chris sent an email to all twenty two clients.

Here is a short attachment on some comments and information that we would like to share with you on this funding extravaganza.

one thing i would like to mention here is if you have not turned in your banking information for whatever reason then you are risking not getting your capital if this turns real.

if you wish to have a few funded before you turn this information in and then verify with the clients who have receive their capital then that can be arranged as well but please drop chris line if that is the case and i make no promises if you choose to take this route.

most of us have provide dummy account for this purpose and you could as well.

As all the rest of hat we need to mention is in the attached letter and we too have to wait for the results, we simply wish you all the vey best of luck.

#LATEST DEVELOPMENTS#
Now if you get this email the investor wants your project and to just reenforce your memory your investor is Anamka Biswas from A.B,. Exports expect a call from the RBI (Reserve Bank of India) as they are checking all the proposal letters and business plans that were submitted to anamika from you to make sure your biz is a legit one and not a dummy business.
Regards
Chris & Larry

Larry began the attachment with "Well twuz the night before christmas and all through the house...." Reexamining the entire episode over the eight-month spectrum, I realize that part of the reason for the frenzy of optimism that engulfed me and the others in the group was caused by Larry's utterly unfounded and puerile enthusiasm. While he admittedly had not verified the existence of funds, he was energized by the expectation of their imminent arrival! My position was cautious optimism, something akin to a kind of Reaganesque "trust but verify".

Yet. For months the "yets" deflected reality in the group seeking Anamika's investment like aluminum chaff acts to fool heat seeking missiles. Inside, my voice said "yet, suppose it is true; suppose Larry and Chris being closer to Anamika than you are, suppose they really, really know?!"

I started reading the rest of the three-page attachment.

I am not sure how you all feel after so many long hard fought years on your project but on mine and as real as i am hoping this all is for my family as well as yours, it surely does feel a bit like the night before christmas to me.

We simply want to touch bases to give you our latest findings and a deep sincere thank you for all of the effort that you all put in through out this short noticed affair and for that we apologize but it was sprang on us rather sudden as well.

We have been told that on monday morning (india time) Anamika and her father are heading to the Federal Reserve Bank of India to conduct all of the final discussions and the final approvals from these people on their investment choices.

So when we wake up over here tomorrow morning all of this will be over one way or the other.

Either the will be approved for these investments or they will not be and not even our investors can do anything about the government as far as i know.

Now many of you will find out before i or chris will as i am tied up all day and chris will be sleeping so some of you may get a faxed contract and a confirmation of funds tranfer slip although these will mostly be coming out as far as we know on Tuesday, Wednesday and if required on Thursday.

So please hold your patience as i know everyone needs this capital more than anything but rush things we cannot do as well as if this turns out to be a fake job, which it still might, then i do ask if you want to keep on searching for your capital through me, i will be within the next 30-60 days, arranging some serious amounts of financing through many different sources as we are also searching for lines of credit to finance not just projects but oil & gas, diamond, gold and bank instrument deals as well so we are constantly seeking new lenders and we always shoot for NO FEE 100% financing whenever we can get it so one never knows when we will get this accomplished.

This next time however i am heading soon directly to the arab oil money to see if i can tap into some of those groups which may or may not be difficult, this remains to be seen.

So that is all i need to mention except for those of you who do not know yet we have been told that these investors from india have made their investment capital in the following industries, but so far i can only verify one of these companies as being a real company although not much info was found.. just the name of the company she gave was found so far on one occasion.

They boast of the following
1. Assam Plywood
2. East Indian Plywood
3. Geat Indian Plywood
4. They have one other but i was not given the name
5. They apparently own AB Exports as you all know.
6. They are supposed to have (2) Coffee Plantations and from what i've seen on coffee plantations these are HUGE operations and exceptionally well run.
7. The own some larger real estate other as well as "50" homes that were mentioned but i am not sure what it all is.
8. Apparently they also own a garment manufacturing plant (maybe more than one not sure of that either) but no idea of the name or street address.

So that and the information of all her email address's and phone and fax numbers is all what we have been able to come up with so far and you know as well as i do that from all we've been through on our diligence on these peole that they have a 98.85% chance of being very real and us simply being the luckiest gals and guys in the universe and maybe that's all that this will proove ... that we got exceptionally lucky when we need it most....

And so we all prayed that Anamika and her father were 98.85% real. We had little choice but to believe the universe smiled down on us and we'd acquired exceptional luck at the very moment we needed it the most.

Why not? Why not all of us? But especially, why not me?

Larry concluded the attachment with "Hope these are the last days of us being poor." As he wrote those words, Larry and Chris stood to receive $10 <u>billion</u> dollars in investment funds from Anamika as well as commissions from the $23 <u>billion</u> the clients were to receive. By themselves they could banish poverty in Sierra Leone and Benin.

Months later I would learn that Larry, collecting unemployment from the Canadian government, was speaking more for himself than for the rest of the group. Over time I came to realize it was through Larry's personal filter that he strained the information coming from Anamika, repackaged and forwarded it to the clients in the group. We then interpreted it through the prism of our individual needs, wants, desires, expectations and fantasies, then lo and behold that dazzling substance before us was indeed gold. On May 5 at 11:06 PM in Los Angeles the fax went through without a hitch and I provided Anamika with all the documents she required. Whew!

May 6—1:51 EST—Chris sent out an email from Tasmania providing the "latest developments". He stated that Anamika required the NCND as well as a commitment letter from each of the clients.

Of greater interest was the fourth point in Chris' email.

> *4) The investor has had to apply for an American visa before the RBI (Reserve Bank of India) will approve the projects because of some rules in regards to share holder rights she is hoping for a quick turn around for getting this Visa.*

Later that morning—7:46 EST—he informed the clients that Anamika's fax had broken down after some of the NCND's had been transmitted. Chris assured the group the machine was being fixed and would be available beginning 10:15 AM India Time on Wednesday, May 7. Then, he provided seventeen of the clients with the time when they should send their fax. The slot for Thistle Productions was 11:35 AM India Time, which was approximately 11:05 PM in Los Angeles.

More importantly, Chris added "I have also been informed by Anamika that all Contracts and NCNDs will be signed and faxed back on her Thursday," meaning May 8. I quickly set about preparing the commitment letter and

NCND for Anamika anticipating her returning the signed documents in less than forty eight hours.

NON-CIRCUMVENTION/NON-DISCLOSURE AGREEMENT

KNOW ALL MEN BY THESE PRESENTS:

That we, **Thistle Productions, Inc. and A.B. Exports**, the undersigned principals, for good and valuable considerations and for the further consideration that one or more of us will have in the future introduced to one or more of the principal's parties who may advise, counsel, assist, negotiate and/or conclude some type of business transaction with one or more of us, do hereby covenant and agree that none of us will have any dealings present or future with any such parties or party so introduced to the other principal or principals hereof.

By way of illustration, but not by way of limitation, each of us understands and agrees that non-circumvention is to mean that none of us singly or in combination will ever, without the prior knowledge, consent and cooperation of the other principal or principals, approach, contact, solicit, discuss or negotiate with any such party or parties regarding any understanding, agreement, arrangement, undertaking or act by which profit, commission, income or other benefit would or might possibly result or accrue to anyone whomsoever, nor shall we permit anyone else in our behalf to perform any of the above acts of circumvention.

The term "such party or parties" includes, but not by way of limitation, any person or entity, (corporation, partnership,. associates or companies) and his or its alter egos, successors, assigns, substitutes, principals and agents who or which obtain his or its association, contact, information knowledge or introduction to a transaction through which we the principals, or any of us, for a time period of five (5) years.

Further, we the undersigned, covenant and agree to never disclose any information in regard to any business transaction conducted between ourselves and/or our principals.

This agreement shall be binding to each of us on all persons or entities with which we or any of us have non-circumvention/non-disclosure agreements and with all others whom we can prevent legally or by persuasion from circumventing others of us.

Legal jurisdiction is Los Angeles, California. Having read this agreement and as a sign of consent with all of its contents, we sign, accept and date below.

Vincent Panettiere   Date
President
Thistle Productions, Inc.

Anamika Biswas
A.B. Exports

May 5, 2003

Ms. Anamika Biswas
A.B. Exports
#84 Jatindra Mohan Avenue
Kolkatta, 700005 India

Dear Anamika;

Thistle Productions, Inc. is prepared to provide this Letter of Commitment showing that we are ready willing, and able to engage in the receipt of this funding for **Thistle Productions 3-Stage Growth Plan.** The President/CEO of our firm is capable, qualified, and authorized to act on behalf of Thistle Productions, Inc. to present, sign, and negotiate any loan terms and conditions for Thistle Productions, Inc.

1. **TOTAL AMOUNT**—$28.5 million (twenty eight million, five hundred thousand dollars USD)
2. **TERM**—five years from date each stage draw down completed at interest of 2% over libor per year.
3. **EQUITY** for AB Exports is 10% of revenue from films produced, with funds from this loan, by Thistle Productions, Inc. once the loan is paid.
4. No pre-payment penalty
5. **STRUCTURE**—three stages:
1. Stage 1—$8.5 million
2. Stage 2—$10 million
3. Stage 3—$10 million

There are no current loans or liens against Thistle Productions, Inc. and we are in good business standing with the State of California.

Thistle Productions provides this Letter of Commitment for a minimum of 30 days, at which time we can re-negotiate our position and extend this letter accordingly. It is further understood that upon receipt of this letter and acceptance of the terms hereof, a cooperative effort by A B Exports and the Reserve Bank of India will provide the necessary funds to fulfil the terms outlined in this letter along with the contract that has already been accepted by A B Exports.

Should you have any questions I, Vincent Panettiere, can be reached at (323) XXX-XXXX in Los Angeles, CA or by e-mail at thistleprods@netscape.net. We look forward to concluding this transaction with you and having a very profitable and lasting relationship. Again, thank you, for your assistance in providing funding for Thistle Productions, Inc.

Best regards,
Vincent Panettiere
President/CEO

My documents were prepared, but there was more difficulty getting a fax through to Anamika. We soon learned in dealing with her nothing would be easy. Technical problems would be the least difficult to over come.

May 7

Chris let us know he was on top of the problem in his 8:39 EST email.

> *Yes, I know you have all had problems faxing anamika at the time you were given it's because her business has there own power generator as do a lot of india businesses and the volate fluctuates and it burnt out the Fax Machine cable.* [*]
>
> *The fax will be on til "9pm India time" on her wednesday you can try your luck and see if you get through as I'm sure others will be trying to fax there documents through to her....*

---

[*]   We discovered the truth about the fax months later. Anamika didn't have a fax in her office. She was using the equivalent of an Indian Kinkos. Those answering the phone treated the clients with disdain and sarcasm. They could care less that our hopes, dreams and futures were riding on the documents we faxed to Anamika.

... now because the letters and NCND are being sent in late the meeting with the bank will be friday and contracts signed and *and ncnd signed and faxed back Mondya.*

Also I have been informed the RBI will only call you only if they have questions in relation to your project.

May 8

Chris advised the group that a two hour halt was placed on sending Anamika documents so that she could get fax "from her other busines dealings".
    Our investor seemed to be a very busy wheeler/dealer.

May 10

Saturday morning a curious "push me/pull me" email arrived from Chris—16:47:03

> *Hi*
> *How is everyone, some of you expected to see money in there bank account Friday when we clearly said that was not the case.*
>
> *Now all contracts as we have said before will be signed and faxed back to each business on the investors Monday, this has to be done before any money starts to flow which is an obvious thing we would think.*
>
> *The RBI (Reserve Bank of India) will be giving there decision from the meeting they had on Friday with the investor that went for four hours this decision will decide whether or not she is able to invest.*
>
> *Monday will be the deciding day for everything if all*
>
> *goes well and the contracts are sent back on Monday the investor will wire money Tuesday/Wednesday that sameweek.*
>
> *This is where things stand at the moment and this is where things will stand til her Monday when she contacts me.*

FUNDING DATES #2 & 3—MAY 13/14, 2003

Now some of you have be complaining about how long the investment process is taking now think to yourself how much longer other investment processes can take some of you may of had problems in the past with arranging funds but that's not my problem and if you want to complain talk to yourself as we will delete any complains that are not valid in our mind and not respond as we are not here to be harassed by clients.

That's it for now have a nice day.

Cheers,
Chris & Larry

Huh? The last paragraph was most perplexing. I'd been working with clients my entire professional career first in corporate public relations and later as a literary and sports agent. I'm sure clients irritated me on more than one occasion. However I'd never think to chastise them in print, let alone in public, mainly because I'd lose that client and its source of income. However by the time I'd finished Chris' offensive paragraph I had the answer.

I was providing a **service** to my clients and needed to be in their good graces. Chris and Larry (ostensibly) were providing **money** and couldn't give a loon or a kiwi whether the clients liked their method of operation or not.

Once again I chose not to apply the business standards I'd valued and instead made myself focus on what was most important. In three to four days I could have my funds wired to me by Anamika!

May 12

Chris' email—8:35:39AM EDT—bore the subject "Brilliant NEWS!!!

Hi
Well what do you know I was online hanging around for Anamika and what do you know she turns up and guess what she says can you guess??? … Well I'll tell you THE RBI SAID YES YES YES BLOODY YES providing she goes in tomorrow with her VISA.

Now your going wow i'm sure your jumping around going mad, hanging off the roof with your ears.

Anyways this is how things look at the moment when the VISA is taken in she will then go and sign the contracts and the NCNDs then fax them back in your evening so i think they will hit your fax machines late monday night early tuesday morning if your in Canada or the US.

FUNDING DATES #4 & 5—MAY 14/15, 2003

We are saying that investments will flow Wendesday/Thursday and the investor will arrange with her bank for pre-clearance of funds so transfer of funds will happen rathe smoothly and quickly.

Email me with any questions.
Kind regards,
Chris & Larry

May 13

Tuesday afternoon, Larry sent a fax—1:35:28 PM EDT

sorry this is a bit late perhaps but it is still early morning my time. here is the latest update and any questions after you read it i will answer in the evening only sorry.

other than that if no questions you have a week or so to wait until you can access any funds and please do not exepct it any sooner.

Attached were two pages of details in support of Larry's email.

Here is an update on what is now taking place and i know it is not exactly today that you can spend money but this is the best news we have for anyone right yet.

1. The Lady's visa is in transit between New Delhi and Calcutta and is supposed to arrive in Calcutta tomorrow morning.
2. Then Anamika will be sending out all signed ncnd's plus signed contracts so it is asked that your fax machine be on and available from 2am eastern to 6pm eastern time tomorrow.
So from tonite at 2am until 6pm tomorrow afternoon gives a very big window.
3. Then on Thursday and Friday (India times) which is our thursday and Friday as well, the banks is supposed to be sending our all pre transfer faxes directly to your Banks to inform them of the incoming

allotments of capital and then they will also within these time frames begin to start wire transferring your capital.

So this MAY get placed into the following Monday or Tuesday as well but this we have no way of knowing yet as things may happen on schedule still yet

FUNDING DATES #6 & 7—MAY 19/20, 2003

You are being asked to make sure your fax machine is available from 2 am Thursday & Friday until 6pm Thursday and Friday afternoons (our Thursdays & Fridays) in order to receive the funds tranfer confirmation slips without any trouble

If the following Monday or Tuesday is required for this then please use the same time co-ordinates starting on Sunday evening at 9pm til monday afterrnoon at 6pm this time use your local time zones.

4. Then there will be atleast 6-9 business days of the funds travelling from clearing house in London (say 2-3 days there) to the clearing house in New York (another 2-3 days) and then once it is cleared there, directly on to your bank (another 2-3 days there).

So it is May 13th today and if all goes super smooth and the funds are finished being transferred on the 16th (this coming Friday) and there is only 2 days per station then you will receive access to your capital by say the 26th or 27th of May.

FUNDING DATES #8 & 9—MAY 26/27, 2003

If there is say 3 days per station which is most probably but one never knows then this will be around the 29th or 30th of May.

FUNDING DATES #10 & 11—MAY 29/30, 2003

Thank you for all your patience and please note that as we find out new things we will be sending out updates so if you do not hear from us that is because we have nothing new to tell you.
Chris & Larry

From May 1 to May 13 we'd been given ELEVEN dates for funding! Such a build up of excitement and anticipation might only be matched in the brothels of Calcutta, home to some 20,000 prostitutes.

At the time I don't remember counting the funding dates. I was willing to give Anamika and the RBI all the time they needed to do what was required and then wire the investment into my company. I remained cautiously optimistic but deep down a part of me was secretly smiling with the knowledge that this was real and this would happen. Basically I stayed calm. Anyone looking at me would never have guessed that soon I'd be collecting $28.5 million.

May 14—10:55 EST Larry sent an update.

> *This is the latest situation and i have asked repeatedly about some upfront PROOF of FUNDS but am constantly told that POF's are not available until everything is cleared up with the RBI including the VISA.*

> *So please again be patient, but you were sent that update yesterday that had deliberately extra time built into it just in case there was a further delay and YES we have a "2" day delay*

> *and one of those days is because tomorrow is a holiday in India so it is totally unavoidable.*

> **Holiday #2—religious**

> *So everything has been delayed til Thursday and Friday in the US and Canada....*

> *This is no ones fault as the VISA did not make it today to the Calcutta office of the US Embassy and there is a Religious holiday tomorrow leaving Friday being the day it will finally get there.*

> *This is how the current time frame looks with these delays this is worked out on US days as your a half day behind the investor.*

> *Thursday nite our time at say 9-11pm pacific time—*

> *1. Investor receives VISA show to RBI.*

2. Investor Signs Contracts/NCNDs and attaches Banker details and other various documents.

Friday nite at again 9pm pacific

1. Day partial day of Wiring Funds as their bank operates For ½ day on Saturday.

FUNDING DATES #12 & 13—MAY 17/19, 2003

Sunday nite our time starting at around 9pm to 3am

1. Last day of Wiring Funds

In this email Larry indicated the wiring of funds had been moved up from Friday to Saturday with completion the following Monday. This would be two weeks after the first funding date we received on May 1. A delay of two weeks was a minor inconvenience. Larry continued.

We are expecting two different days in which the funds are wired, however they will use whatever they need to get the job done be it one, two or three days.

Please still keep your faxes open those time we arranged to give them lots of window opportunity for everyone and once you have received your contract and the ncnd i would seriously appreciate a short email to confirm you have received them so i can mark my list accordingly.

(When you send in confirmation of receipt also please inform me as to your total amount of capital expected and if you selected in traunches or in one lump sum. Then also tell me if you are from Stu and if you are honoring his agreement as i have not told Stu yet too much as i want to be able to confirm all this 100% first so anything he gets will be a surprise to him but i guess deserved as he did play his part by passing along your project and without that we would never have met so you decide and i will act accordingly.)

As well once you do get these papers back and the confirmed transfer slips, then i will also need to send you chris and my banking coordi-

*nates for separate transfers of our commissions and mostly i am split-
ting the 2% with Chris.*

*1/3 for me 2/3rds for him but on occasion i do split things with John
and not with Chris so i will tell you if there is a split and for how
much goes to whom when i send out the information.*

Thank you for your time today.
Chris and Larry

May 16

Twenty four of us in the group received an update from Larry at 4:53:25 AM
EDT.

*Well here is some decent new i hope.. some positive forward move-
ment anyways even though we never got everything we wanted at this
point in time.*

*Please be patient with this lady and her family ans they have tried
very had to reach this point in time and mean the best for you as well
as for themselves but there is nothing wrong with that.*

The email provided little information and I hoped there would be a more
fulsome explanation in Larry's attachment.

*Here is how things stand as of today and will most likely not change
too much in the near future. If anything the real times will be faster
than the times i have listed here below.*

*1. Anamika has confirmed from her Embassy that her letter of confir-
mation for her visa is in the couriers hands and enroute … estimated
time of arrival..up to next wednesday or thursday … most likely time
of arrival … next tuesday but thats only a wild guess at this point.*

---

*   Larry's May 13th email informed us the visa was due to arrive on May 14th. His
      May 16th email tells us the visa will arrive sometime during May 20-22. He gives
      no explanation how he divined the dates nor does he make the slightest effort to
      acknowledge or keep track of the shifting dates, either.

2. as of 5:30pm to 7:00 pm her time tonite, she is faxing back the signed contracts maybe the ncnd's as well.

3. estimated day for the pre-transfer slips if they still do them as well as the faxing of proof of funds ... wednesday to Friday of next week ... again a guess but i think a very close one.

4. estimated days of funds transfer ... anywheres from Thursday (May 22) next week to the following Tuesday (May 27) ... could be earlier ... this nobody knows yet.

FUNDING DATES #14 & 15—MAY 22/27, 2003

(In Larry's May 13 email he surmised we'd have **access** to our funds by May 27. Now he's saying the funds won't be **wired** until that date.)

5. estimated time of funds hitting your bank ... around the 25th to 27th Of May as was mentioned in your recent update.

Now he's saying the funds that will be "transferred" i.e. wired on the 27th could also be in our banks by the 27th. Confusion and desire was a narcotizing brew. But Larry wasn't finished.

6. estimated time for release of the funds by your banks ... between the 25th to the 29th ... could be earlier.

Thats ALL what we know as of tonite and i want you all to please simply relax if possible as a few things are very apparent.

1. We ALL need this capital so if you had to wait for 45 days for your money and it costs you nothing but a little bit of time i think that this is definatly well worth the wait. Especially to those getting the large sums of money and any other vc firm from over here would have taken 4-6 months for those types and amounts of deals and would have put you through so many hoops that mostly like not all of us would have been approved in the end.

2. ANAMIKA, HER FAMILY and the people from the RESERVE

BANK of India have done an outstanding job so far as have all Of you and chris as well ... everyone has done and still is doing their part.

Sure they too their time a little bit ok?? So what thats what smart intelligent people do on these investments so please do not dwell on the last 45 days too much ... please try to focus on the next 5-10 days (and not the next 3-4 as that will be too early to inquire ok.).

The rest of the attachment was information Larry had downloaded from the Internet on India's Foreign Investment Promotion Board, which promoted investment in India. Larry felt he could "imagine ... it is almost an identical procedure and review board for someone who wishes to invest OUTSIDE of India."

As for Larry at this juncture of the process he decided to "chill out completely for a week or two" so that things could happen "as they need to happen." He applauded the group for its "fine professionalism and patience so far."

I am convinced Larry meant well, but he was clueless when it came to the tone and tenor of his email which often sounded patronizing, was absent of concrete information and filled with guesses which represented Larry's fervent wishes and wild delusions of grandeur.

We in the group owned an equal share of complicity when we accepted his information without using our rational faculties.

Yet (another in a series of yets) here we were on May 16 anticipating we would be funded in approximately eleven days! Who couldn't wait? Who couldn't believe, when the dreams of a lifetime were less than two weeks from being realized? We all had hope. We had it bad and that ain't good. Though hope springs eternal, we would learn that "hope is the most treacherous of human fancies" (James Fennimore Cooper) and that "hope is independent of the apparatus of logic" (Norman Cousins). Six months would pass before we absorbed that lesson.

At 12:19 EST, Larry provided us with one of his philosophical emails.

Seems like this family as hard as they try and as rich as they seems to be or claim to be are an ordinary family after all.

We are depending on Larry and he continues to inform us that he has yet to determine within a mile of absolute certainty that Anamika Biswas and her family have the funds which he has advised us will be wired/transferred within the next two weeks.

things life health issues, fires, and acts of god, have no distinction betwee rich or poor and this family has had their share of downsides recently.

Geez!

Her father just went into the hospital last night for emergency surgery for a gall bladder operations so she will be on schedule but slower by 2-4 days for the contracts.

DELAY #1—father sick

so what you read in the attachment still stands but the contracts may not be out til next week. Her movement on these will depend on how her father fares in the hospital as being the head of the family this is serious stuff for them (maybe for anyone).

However this will move them that much closer to the actual visa bring delivered so we have to wait for that anyways,.

PLEASE DO NOT CALL HER ok, at least not until after the operation if you are discussing business but if you wish to call her with best wishes, that is up to you.

personally i am moving on to other lenders and my gold deals as this is my business, locating different lenders and not counting on any one of them.

WHAT! Larry leads us into the forest and now decides there are too many trees. The rest of his email was a commercial for all the services he could provide. There must be a personality flaw in him waiting to be identified— grandiosity, delusion. As with his inability to write a coherent email, my job was not to heal his psyche. I promised to repeat "it's the money stupid" one hundred times the next moment I let some distorted sense of missionary zeal deflect me from my goal.

At this juncture I had minimal contact with Anamika. We'd spoken once or twice on the phone as I tried to navigate the vagaries of the Indian Kinko's fax machine. She had reviewed my business plan, etc. However her father's illness presented an opportunity to connect on a more human level. I sent her a simple email.

> Dear Anamika
> I was distressed to learn of your father's operation.
> I wish him a complete and speedy recovery.
> Good luck

At the very early stage of our relationship, Larry advised that I sign up with Yahoo Instant Messenger so that, though hundreds of miles apart, we all could communicate in real time. On the evening of May 16th I learned from Chris on Yahoo Instant Messenger (IM) that the "company directors" would be visiting North America beginning May 27. He said the purpose of their trip was to sign contracts.

Up to this point the majority of email signed "Larry and Chris" were unmistakably written by Larry. Even engaging Chris in IM chat was difficult. Long pauses occurred between his responses which often were the equivalent of yeps and nopes. I thought of him, perhaps, as a reticent Aussie—Tasmania being an Australian island state like Hawaii—reaching out to the world through the miracle of the Internet.

Reticent or not, I endured the frustration and dissatisfaction which resulted from "communicating" with Chris because I believed he was close to and in direct communication with Anamika. Besides, I reminded myself, what was my goal?

May 17

At 11 AM I queried Chris regarding the purpose of the directors' visit scheduled for May 27th. Were they planning to sign contracts and/or wire funds? Were they from Anamika's bank or AB Exports, Anamika's company? Will the directors be "signing a contract with you (Chris) as the expediting head of this operation or will they be signing contracts for each of the projects under your umbrella?

Chris' reply was not complete but satisfactory enough as my reply to him at 11:42:03 PM Eastern Daylight Time indicates:

> Chris
> Thanks for e-mail regarding Toronto.
>
> Sounds very positive. I'll be away on business May 27-30th and can plan to be in Toronto the first or second week of June. Have already

checked plane fares and hotel rooms and can get reasonable rates for both.

Let's coordinate schedules for maximum impact.

As you know, I've been very positive and supportive through this process; but I admit to being as anxious and antsy as everyone else.

Having said that, I recall two recent experiences regarding possible investors. I signed papers with him and her. Investment funds were sent to Europe and I was instructed in the one instance that to get my "investment" I had to pay $8,000 to the courier. The second time I had to pay $21,500 in VAT to get my investment. Needless to say I didn't pay.

I raise this experience so that in case this aspect has not been raised with the Indian group, it might be. I don't think anyone wants to spend money to go all the way to Toronto just to be told they have to fork over big bucks to get their investment. I'm not suggesting or implying anything unscrupulous to the Indians, this is just FYI.

Unless I hear from you to the contrary, I will look forward to going to Toronto and hopefully meeting you and the Biswas family et al.

Thanks for everything.

I had resisted the entreaties of Madam Theodoritou, Chris Brown, Clifford and Agnes Newton, Barry Goldman et al and was not about to visit Toronto, then in the midst of a SARS crisis, to be pilfered by another third world Ponzi scheme. I re-read Chris' message and sent him another email within the hour at 12:54:48 AM Eastern Daylight Time.

Chris
In re-reading the e-mail, I conclude that the Biswas investments/loans are dependent on the outcome of our presentations in Toronto.

If my conclusion is correct, I/we will need to know what to prepare for i.e. what questions they may ask, what documents we'll need to bring—not only business plans (number of copies etc.) but articles of incorporation, resolutions from our board of directors etc. etc. to do a proper presentation that will result in funding.

Guess all this will come in due course, but I wanted you to know I've been thinking about this.

Let me know what you think about the above as well as about the earlier email.
Thanks

Several hours earlier—9:09:36 PM EDT—Larry sent the group an email with attachment which furthered our collective belief that funding was rapidly approaching.

Well here is the email most of you have been waiting so patiently for and i now am a real believer in the Biswas's however everone must decide for themselves.

Everything is in the attachment that we know presently …

Larry's attachment was eight pages of which I will provide here the salient excerpts as follows:

… we now have some great new developments that allows us … to ensure you that we are only ONE or TWO more emails and say 12-15 days away from actually MEETING with the BISWAS family on our funding capital and opportrnities …

Larry's calculation now brought us to

FUNDING DATES #16 & 17—MAY 29/JUNE 2, 2003

… through some good connections that Chris nurtured, * *he was able to bring to you all the Biswas family and their kind and genrous offer of 100% funding …*

---

*   We learned months later that the connections Chris nurtured was a guy named Reghu who worked in an Internet café in Kerala a State in the far southwestern tip of India. He "discovered" Anamika in some online chat room and passed her funding interest along to his "client" in Toronto, who munificently allowed Reghu to introduce Anamika to Chris, thus turning Anamika into some kind of virtual blow-up doll to satisfy their financial lust.

... WHAT IS ALSO The MOST IMPORTANT aspects of all of this is you people are GAINING some incredible PARTNERS and ALLIES in the BISWAS family and they are just as interested in your CAPABILITIES, TALENTS, SKILLS, TEAMS, GOALS, PLANS, STRATEGIC ALLIANCES, HARD WORK ETHICS, HOPNESTY and ACCOMPLISHMENTS as they are in providing the necessary capital for your projects.

So when you meet them please concentrate more on telling about your story as past present and future scenarios than the capital ok is all i want to mention then you will or should do just fine.

AS WELL NO CUSSING of any kind as these people are highly religious so lets respect their space and really do our best.

Now by now i guess you can figure out that soon you will be in direct person to person meeting with the board of directors of the Biswas Empire to discuss your project and their investment into your companies ...

... As when 23 people all ask the same question that we are not able to answer yet it really messes up my time schedule, not that i mind you inquiring but if we have the answers to something we will inform you ok so please wait like we have to.

AND FROM THIS MOMENT ON PLEASE DO NOT CONTACT Anamika or any member of her family ok as we will be sending you the contact info as we get it but right now it appears that

Anamika's father is going through some rough times with medical issues so Anamika is going to be assisting him and her mother and has, for now, nothing more directly to do with the funding of the projects.

This has been turned over to her Uncle and some of the rest of the Board of Directors of the Biswas Family and Bankers.

... the meetings are all going to take place in TORONTO Canada and we know they so far plan (firmly plan) on arriving in Toronto on the 27th of this month and then within a few days starting to meet with people and discussing issues and if they are pleased with the outcome of the conversation and personal diligence, then they will immediately release to you your funding....

HOLY COW! says it all—in more ways than one.

In case there was any doubt, Larry provided a transcript of an IM conversation between one of the clients, who he did not identify, Anamika and her Uncle Niraj.

The client, who it seemed to me was Kevin, "talked" with Anamika about her father's condition at approximately ten thirty in the morning (India Time) when she surprisingly told Kevin that her uncle wanted to talk to him.

After the usual pleasantries Anamika's uncle said "*u may not know me. i am niraj, one of the senior directors of the biswas empire ... we are a company of high return in india. We never invested abroad. We tried but always been cheated.*"

What follows is the essence of their on line conversation.

> *Kevin—Sorry to hear Sir!*
> *Niraj—thats why we had a fear to deal but recently we found that our most junior director anamika choose to invest abroad. As per business plans we received, we liked it all and even the banks liked it. But, there is a prob that to make a big investment we need to meet each other becoz u understand that investing a large amount is not so easy without knowing each other so as we had completed all the citeria of the bank leaving her visa we thought that we would visit to your place and see ever thing and settle the deal on the spot.*

This reasoning made perfect sense to Kevin and all of us as well once we read Larry's attachment. Kevin assured Niraj he had nothing to hide and would be pleased to meet with him and anyone else from Niraj's group.

> *Niraj—so for that reason we all total 9 directors and all our bank relationship managers will arrive with us so u could have all idea what our company potentially is and we would also have a look on the deal all will signed and finalize on the spot. i hope u agree.*

Kevin—All sounds good to me. I would expect then, you will formally sign these deals here and instruct the bank to wire the funds once you feel comfortable with whom you are dealing with. I have great teams lined up to make this happen and looking forward to doing this.

Niraj—i am agreed to wot decision she has taken wot i only like to do is come on the spot and meet u all and give your investment to u.

Kevin—That is TOTALLY understandable and I would want the same being in your shoes.

Niraj—ok so we are arriving on 27th of this month with the total group … ok so done.

Kevin—I can have a few companies meet you here in Toronto. I will coordinate this with Anamika and have these companies here for a day of meetings.

Niraj told Kevin he would be in Toronto a month or more, staying with his niece. He also emphasized that "… we are coming full prepared. we will not waste even a single min of yours trust me."

Kevin—Okay. very well then Sir. thank you and I do not want to waste a moment of your time or the families time.

Niraj—it is our pride that we are dealing with u.

Kevin—me too Sir, look forward to a long and great relationship with you and your family … as a working partnership!

Niraj—yes even we too.

Kevin—You have here an honest and hard working business man who needs someone to fund his good ideas and let me work hard to achieve what we see we can for us all!

Niraj—yes even we require a hard partner who will fulfill our dream as a friend. i am disappointed as are u for the delays but i am helpless.

i am trying to say u must be with us and the delays are here we must deal with them together.

Kevin—I totally understand and I believe you are being honest and want to invest in good businesses that will show you a return and pay-back your money and with all that has been going on ... I thought there was more people involved than anamika. I am right and if we can make this happen on the 27th I will be impressed and honored to work with honest and truthful people like your family!

Kevin appended a note to the transcript of the IM conversation.

"... we are set to meet them starting the 27th and this gives everyone time to make some presentation to the board of directors and Anamika's sister lives here already so her Uncle will stay there and i am not sure about the rest. I would like your company heads to take this time to get their collective data together and be prepared to make your case to them. It seemed to me that they are coming to want to get to know the people they are going to invest in. Nothing sinister about this ... just a fact!

"This is very real and no one asking me for flight money!

"So for myself, I set up with Narij to meet them May 28th here, once they have settled in and he stated he will not waste a minute of my time. I agreed right away to meet them! Have a good weekend guys and best of luck to you all."

May 18

Larry set about trying to coordinate the plans for those clients who were preparing to meet with Niraj and the directors in Toronto in his 12:12 EST email. Considering the Niraj/Anamika party was scheduled to arrive on May 27th, it was understandable that they should be given a day or two to erase jet lag and get organized.

Larry provided us with dates between May 29th and June 9th and told us he was trying to arrange a group hotel rate during the next two days.

May 20

At 00:55:26–0700, Larry and Chris sent us an attachment with information they felt we'd like better than the aforementioned meeting in Toronto.

Larry had received some new information from the Biswas group regarding their travel itinerary. He didn't reveal from whom he had received this info, but presented it as fait accompli.

"It seems they wish to travel more extensively to the United States than we first thought they might as they have just recently asked Chris and I to make up a list for them that would allow them to visit each of you in your local or preferred area."

Well and fine, but all was now diffuse and confusing. And far too egalitarian. We were the supplicants. It was proper for all of us to make the pilgrimage to Toronto, meet the Biswas group, state our case and wait for the verdict—funded or not funded.

This was the beginning of the end for Chris and Larry. Their inability to present cohesive thought led to fuzzy and muddled thinking when it came to email, relationships and meetings. Had they a shred of a scintilla of business experience, they might have suggested that after a preliminary meeting in Toronto, Anamika's group would then visit the cities of those approved companies.

Our group had been whipsawed emotionally by Chris and Larry with seventeen funding dates within the first twenty days of May. Our heads were reeling and we needed a firm footing. Meeting the group in Toronto would enable us to press the flesh, put a face with a name and cherish the humanity of those who would provide us with the fuel to implement our dreams.

I replied to Chris and Larry, fully prepared to fly to Toronto unafraid of SARS, make my presentation during a lunch or dinner meeting—not that money was no object, but there is less formality when sharing a meal. I hoped Indian businessmen and woman would feel the same. I placed a rush order for one dozen Thistle Productions logo shirts with the Queensboro Shirt Company of Wilmington, North Carolina, a company I have used for years because of their excellent service. I also had a dozen copies of my business plan duplicated. All was ready.

Not everybody was ready.

Allen, a financial adviser from Philadelphia, expected to raise $750,000,000 from Anamika for his "start up" investment banking firm. He wrote to Chris concerned that none of the clients had received a signed contract or the NCND as Larry had indicated on at least two previous occasions. While we had received a verbal agreement and verbal confirmation of funding "they are no substitute for a written contract. Nor can they be a substitute for a written contract," he wrote.

Allen wanted Chris to impress on the investor the importance of having a signed contract in place <u>before</u> the Toronto meeting. "By signing a contract," he continued, "the cake is baked (cementing and consummating our deal and newly formed relationship) and the meeting will be icing on the cake, furthering our partnership." He also opted for a central meeting in Toronto.

Next Bob representing his company America's Choice, Inc. made his contribution later in the day on May 20th. He wanted a letter of intent for the funding and signed contracts sent by email to all the clients. He also informed Chris and Larry that his Internet search under India Business Listings did not reveal the name of Anamika's company AB Exports, though he did find two Biswas in Kolkata who sold guns and ammunition and one who was an engineer.

> *Please understand the reason behind this. It is called "Due Diligence of our investor." They have asked for all our information and when I ask, well all I got was another change of plans, and more forms to fill out.*
> *I have acted in good faith, as I suspect the others have also.*
> *I have been told by Chris that I copped an attitude when I ask questions. I think that both Chris and Larry should remember that the Biswas may be the investors, but without the projects, and those that can see them work and become profitable, well Chris and Larry, you wont make that commission, and if that is copping an attitude, well I call it solid business sense.*
> *I think it is time the Biswas showed good faith.*
> *A reply is expected, and Chris don't cop an attitude. WE all need each other, and so far all I have gotten from you two and the Biswas have been excuses, delays, more forms and half truths.*

When it came to being criticized, Larry, a burly guy who weighed over two hundred pounds, had a particularly thin skin. The first example of this came from the correspondence from Allen and Bob.

Larry's initial salvo came in an email at 6:51:05 PM EDT, in which in provided the group with an update, then added "if you like what you read then that is fine and if you don't there is nothing more I can do at this point for you on proof of funds that is not already being attempted."

Larry's critics, and at this early date I was not one of them, had some valid points. My quibble with them was their timing. In a perfect world … there is no such thing as a perfect world … it makes no sense to continue. However, some people, Larry's critics included, believe in a perfect world like some five-year-olds believe in Santa.

No one with any business experience or sophistication would deny that Chris and Larry, mostly Chris since he made the initial contact with Anamika, <u>should</u> have verified her ability to fund the projects before they ever contacted any clients. In their unbridled enthusiasm—Chris' boyish enthusiasm, months later we learned he was twenty one years old, and Larry's delusional enthusiasm, in his fifties he had no venture capital or finance experience apart from what he conjured up searching the Internet—they contacted clients too early.

Theirs was a case of the worst kind of premature ejaculation; a combo of sugar plums holding dollar signs dancing in their heads coupled with adolescent wet dreams of power and glory. Remember as clients, they were to receive $10 billion as well as at least 2% of $23 billion as brokers!

My position during the eight-month experience was to drop the past and keep moving forward. By May 20 we were twelve days from the latest date to be funded (June 2) and seven days from when Anamika, Niraj and the nine directors would arrive in Toronto. Climbing on Larry's back at this point was both counter productive and bad sport. Better that energy was used doing whatever was necessary to bring about the conclusion we all hoped and prayed to experience.

However, I was not pleased with Larry's attitude. He was our "broker", who we looked to for information and guidance regarding the authenticity of the investor. His was a big responsibility which he could not shirk lightly without serious damage to his credibility. When two out of twenty four clients suggested things be done differently he copped an attitude. Perhaps in a previous life he had been Henry VIII and accustomed to getting his way.

No matter. Larry's petulant response was inappropriate, upsetting and cracked the control he had on clients.

Naturally, Larry's email had an attachment. The first was to the clients and the second was to Anamika regarding proof of funds.

Three days before Larry provided the group with the Kevin/Niraj IM exchange which added a new and positive dimension. Now, out of thin skinned insecurity, he was about to dissipate the glow of good will and optimism energizing the group, me included.

To The Clients

I have listened very seriously to all of your requests for more information on the proof of this funding affair from the Biswas family and I have come to the conclusion that YES you all are very correct and

proper in your information requests for REAL PROOOF of these peo-
ple and their intentions.

However it is against my better judgement to send this out simply
because they seem to be very touchy about discussing their money and
we only have like 7 more days to wait and see if they are going to per-
form so what i did here in the hopes of satisfying everyones coure-
ousity as well as my own is I made up an introductory message that
you can read below and then a letter that is attached requesting some
form of concrete proof of their existence to show you and alls we can
do now is wait and see if they reply.

This letter has already gone out to Anamikas email addresses so there
is no turning back and if the whole deal goes up in smoke i don't want
to hear one word of how i blew it from anyone....

I had to remind myself that I wanted to acquire non-traditional funding.
However I expected some semblance of intelligence and clear thinking. The
balance of Larry's attachment to the clients alternated between defensive
whining. "… at no time have we ever said to anyone yet that FUNDING IS
GUARANTEED 100%. We said we believe we have located 100% FUNDING
for your project and we are getting your project reviewed and analyzed" and
disrespectful patronizing "… if you think you would have EVER gotten past
the RBI's approval without having some excellent projects then you are simply
fooling yourselves … so you can feel very proud you made it with flying colors
past those people."

What was most damning and damaging was Larry's vacillation. "… if you
think of how many people have spoken to this family and all that has transpired has taken place in the last 45 days and IF this is real as i now think it
really is, you are all sitting on the very threshold of your funding …" We were
left to believe how we wished, but mostly held our breath.

Then I read Larry's <u>introduction</u> **to Anamika's** attachment.

As you know Anamika, i was seriously involved in the providing of the
projects that your family has been shown for the purpose of invest-
ment here overseas.

Now i do not wish to have you or anyone else take this attachment let-
ter wrong but i have been getting some very serious inquiries from the

clients as i am sure you have heard about before and these people are very needful for some information from you and group as they have serious plans to make and serious time schedules to consider and they are requesting very simply a nice formal letter from you and your board of directors to state that you indeed plan on making a trip here soon to North America to discuss their projects issues in person....

Anamika's Attachment

... I have been getting a fair number of questions in regards to whether or not you fine folks are really going to come over to North America. I guess working at such a great distance from each other is not eay for you nor for them and the clients will no longer simply take our word (me or Chris's) any longer on the reality of your family.

They are requesting as politely as possible some form of proof as to who you are, what companys can you show them? Can you supply any websites or information for them to review?

Is it possible that you can either call each client directly to introduce yourself or send them a letter as an attachment by email with your company letterhead stating who all is coming with you and their positions....

Bob kept pressing Larry in his 19:05 EST email, taking the extreme position that "... it might be best to get Interpol involved and have them do due diligence on the Investor."

He also used the negotiating ploy of deferring to the highest power when he indicated to Larry "... I have many of my own people, real-estate people, suppliers, contractors, and such asking questions everyday, and questioning my abilities to obtain the funding, and its source, and if this is some kind of game or joke."

I could not understand why the need for pressure when we were less than two weeks away from the latest funding date of June 2. Later I learned that Bob made or was going to make real estate option deals using money he had not yet received from Anamika. Spending money or promising to spend it before having it is not a brilliant idea and flies in the face of Bob's assessment of the Biswas group "... I am also sure that I would not want to do business with business people who do not know good business sense...." There must not be any mirrors in Bob's house.

Larry responded to Bob with regret and contrition in his email of 19:26:18–0700. He'd written the letter to Anamika in anger trying to redress "a big mistake", which was not getting proof of funds "… the instant or so that they (investor) indicated they had a desire to fund the projects."

Next he made a startling admission. His only contact with the investment group was "… once for a brief half hour til I upset Anamika been in direct contact with this investment group so I have no clout whatsoever and never will have. So it doesn't take very much to click/her them off at all. Apparently to them if you have to ask you are not thinking straight or something"

Larry conceded "… how unprofessionally this is being delivered but in reality its been only a short 45 days through it all so far, maybe less and we are only 7 days or so away from finding out if this is all real … a regular group from over here would still have 2-3 months worth of diligence left but who's comparing.…" Then he asked Bob to be patient until May 28th when he felt they would have confirmation "… of this all for you guys one way or the other."

In Larry's letter to Anamika he asked her, at my insistence, if there were any fees to be paid prior to funding. As I was involved with the Effexbank boys I tried to anticipate a similar scenario with Anamika.

Bob picked up on Larry's request about fees and laid him out.

> *Exactly what Fees are we talking about?*
> *No fees were ever mentioned, prior to this agreement, and now the words FEES appear in a letter to the Investor? You might want to address this issue, and if there is a fee, there best be proof that the funds exist, they are real, contracts signed and delivered and if a fee is to be paid, after the funds have been transferred, and deposited into the account. This issue will require major amount of information from them, prior to our meeting and investigated by the proper authorities.*
>
> *Larry, in all due respect a very large Red Flag popped up in my head. Pre-paid fees is usually used in a major money scam. You know my feelings about pre-paying anything. Please clarify, and please no double talk, or change of issues here.*

One of my favorite lines from Shakespeare is "methinks the lady doth protest too much." Hundreds of years later the essence of that quote can be applied to scoundrels of all stripes. Which is why I have never believed those who pound their breasts to tell the world how good, honest and righteous they are or how much sex they get, from religious leaders on down to politicians and businessmen. Deeds, not words.

I was fairly new to the group, coming aboard in the last week of April. By then, many of the other companies had been involved with Larry and Chris for four or five weeks. Consequently, I was not familiar with the group dynamic or individual relationships. My connection was blatantly self serving. I wanted my investment—over and out—nothing more and would participate to the extent that it furthered my desire.

While I was appalled at Larry's lack of communication skill, not to mention, grammar, spelling, punctuation—clearly English language usage—I supported him for the efforts he put forth for the group and my funding. This support was buttressed by the fifty dollars I sent him by Western Union the morning he revealed he did not have food money for him and his daughter.

Bob's tone, and what I perceived to be a self-destructive streak, so close to the funding caused me to respond to him by an email at 21:11 EST.

> I've read your recent email to Chris and Larry. While many of your concerns are valid, I believe your tendency toward hysteria is not helpful to you, Larry and Chris and most personally to me—since I am more concerned about getting my funding than about anyone else.

> Selfish, absolutely. Self involved—without a doubt. Which is the way we all should be—within reason.

> Putting all of this into perspective, I'm aware that the process for me will be three weeks old tomorrow.

> Consider—three weeks and we are several days away from actually meeting with potential investors. If they were American VC firms, I doubt we'd be this close this quickly.

> You are right about up front fees and their implication. What you don't know is that I ASKED CHRIS AND LARRY TO ASK THAT QUESTION.

> Your conclusion that somehow this mention of fees is another curve in the journey is an incorrect one.

I share your concern about upfront fees and wanted to avoid being sandbagged at the time of the meeting, or shortly thereafter—as in "we love your project but we need X dollars before we can release funds," etc.

I requested that question about fees be added to protect all of us and I resent your insinuations in this email and whining in the previous ones without putting this whole process into perspective.

Very simply, if this bothers you so much, you should seek funding elsewhere and play nervous Nelly with Dean Witter.

A positive, helpful constructive attitude would help all of us immensely. See if you can contribute that at least.

Bob responded to me with a haughty, rambling lecture on how he was in law enforcement, the threat of front end scams, etc. which I ignored as the pompous rants of a blow hard. Larry advised me on the QT that Bob's boorish behavior may have annoyed Anamika to the extent that she would not fund him.

Apparently, Bob's two trillion dollar presentation to build housing on the moon made him the cause of much humor and ill will. It seemed to all involved that he was a sardonic gadfly with a ready monkey wrench to derail progress, while at the same time having his hand out for funding. To create legitimacy he purportedly claimed that his project had ten thousand employees in four hundred companies waiting for him to be funded so they could start work.

We would learn that Bob allegedly stole the concept from some woman and then asked her to keep quiet and become his partner.

May 21

Larry provided the group with the first draft of clients' itinerary he planned to send Anamika so her group could organize their trip to the U.S. and Canada. Of the fifteen who responded seven wanted to meet in Toronto, five in Las Vegas and the others chose not to move from their cities—Atlanta, Orlando and Christchurch, New Zealand.

If the investors were going to meet the clients in the U.S. or Canada, I decided to separate myself from the herd by establishing my own direct line of communication with Anamika. At least when we met she would know me as an individual with some presence rather than just a face in the crowd. I inquired again about her father's health in my 14:37–0400 email.

> Dear Anamika
> I hope your father's health has improved considerably in the days since I last wrote to you. I'm looking forward to meeting you and the members of your family and company when you visit Canada and the U.S. Most likely my meeting will be in Las Vegas. Please let me know if there is anything I can do for you. Until then, have a safe and pleasant journey.

May 22

Chris advised us all in his email—6:46 EST—that he would be writing the updates instead of Larry. This was not the best news. Larry at least was accessible by phone to anyone in North America, where the bulk of the clients resided. He may have trouble expressing himself, but at least he was in a time zone no more than three hours away. Chris was down under more than 12 hours ahead and whenever I engaged him on Yahoo IM had less to say than the Sphinx, if he wasn't too tired to communicate at all.

He quickly reviewed the group's status.

> *- To begin with business projects are submitted to Anamika for review she accepts most of the business projects and some are rejects.*
> *- Accepted projects then submitted contracts. -RBI (Reserve Bank of India) authorize the investment by the Biswas family to proceed.*
> *- Father gets sick who is the head of the Biswas family business and control is turned over to Anamika's uncle Niraj*
> *- Niraj now wants to meet each business now before investment to say hello and sign contracts and wire funds on the spot hence the current situation.*
> *- 9 directors that include Niraj + there banker will fly to Canada on the 27th of this month and once the have visited with various businesses there they will then fly to the US.*

> *It's doubtful that they will send out any letters of confirmation proof of funds and such because they will be in Canada within 6 days and they are also taking there banker with them removing the need for proof of funds in there mind. Also the meetings that take place there will be no presentations needed.*

If you don't like this situation I understand but seriously the speed things are moving you haven't really got anything to complain about and as for these half truths and such well that's very untrue as all the information has been disclosed that the investor has said.

In the future if you have a problem u address it to me and not tell the entire group as we have seen today with the out burst from a certain client (Bob K) *that showed how unprofessional and unreasonable it is for a client to invade everyone else's space and fill up their email box with emails that truly have nothing to do with them.*

Now if you have had any problems with larries letters as some of you have expressed worrying that they may effect the funding I can not really foresee any problems from the emails and if there is I will sort them out Larry was just trying to help me out so I think some of you have been a bit hard on him.

I should hopefully finalize with the investor today or tomorrow times for them to visit with you when they go to the US and Canada.

This was better than I imagined coming from Chris. He needed a refresher course in the English language as well, but at least his approach was direct and updated the entire group in a clear manner. What we didn't know then was Chris' relationship with Anamika was eroding. He called her a bitch during IM chat and she learned that he was twenty one years old and not the thirty seven he claimed.

May 23

Anamika responded to my email regarding her father's health—1:30:19 AM EDT

Hello Sir
Thanks for the quiry formy father's health, he is much fine from before, his conditions are improving, as per our previous discussion we are travelling with our 9 directors and few bank personnals with whome we hold our accounts. We are likely to make our travels on 27th of this month but now as per Political conditions there is likely to be a strike on 27th so we are planning to travel one day latter that is on 29th of this month.

Hope that this sound ok to you. we look foward for your reply and cooperation.

WITH BEST REGARDS
ANAMIKA BISWAS

DELAY #2—transport strike

For all that an English teacher might fault her email at least she **did** confirm that she and nine directors would be traveling on May 29th. And, she gave us hope as well as our second **crisis** that would cause a two delay in their departure. I responded—2:05:26 AM EDT:

Dear Ms. Biswas:
I am pleased to hear that your father's medical condition has improved.
I wish him a full and fast recovery.
I am very much looking forward to meeting with you, your directors and bankers. I understand your group plans to visit the U.S. either in Las Vegas or somewhere in California. Los Angeles perhaps?
I could meet with you in Las Vegas or in my home city of Los Angeles or any other city in California you plan to visit. I look forward to receiving your itinerary in the States so that I can make appropriate arrangements for our meeting as soon as possible. In that way, our meeting can be used to the best mutual benefit.
Whatever information you can provide will be most appreciated.
Thank you for responding. My continued best wishes for your father as well as my wishes for a pleasant and safe journey.

Best regards,

Vincent Panettiere
Thistle Productions, Inc.
P.S. I am on Yahoo Messenger as thistleent. Perhaps we can communicate in real time at some point nearer to your departure.

Later that night I found Anamika on IM chat.

thistleent: one quick question
sarara_2001_in: YES
thistleent: I'm planning a luncheon meeting

thistleent: what kind of food would the group prefer
sarara_2001_in: I THINK THAT WILL BE A GREAT TROUBLE FOR U
sarara_2001_in: PLZ DONT DO SO
thistleent: in Los Angeles we have a wide variety from Italian to seafood, to Indian, etc
thistleent: no trouble at all
sarara_2001_in: OK THEY TAKE EVERY TYPE EXCEPT BEEF
thistleent: yes, I would not suggest a steak restaurant
thistleent: but, Italian, seafood, English
sarara_2001_in: ANYTHING OF YOUR CHOICE
thistleent: do you know if Los Angeles is on the itinerary?
sarara_2001_in: THEY HAVE ALL
sarara_2001_in: BECOZ WE DONT WANT TO TROUBLE THE CLIENTS
thistleent: I don't understand
thistleent: you will be coming to Los Angeles?
sarara_2001_in: YES
thistleent: GREAT
thistleent: I will plan for a luncheon meeting for no more than 15,
thistleent: now I can go to sleep without questions spinning in my head
thistleent: any idea of the date in Los Angeles
thistleent: or range of dates?
sarara_2001_in: i will prefer your choice
thistleent: my choice of date?
thistleent: or my choice of restaurant
thistleent: I've got plans for a restaurant in Hollywood with a view of the Hollywood sign, etc.
sarara_2001_in: of your choice of date
thistleent: Sometime in early June—June 4 to 14? something like that
sarara_2001_in: ok
thistleent: that date range is ok—good
sarara_2001_in: tell chris i asked him to call all the clients and ask the date of their choice
sarara_2001_in: so that they dont have problem
thistleent: we can pick a specific date once your group gets to Canada
sarara_2001_in: yes
sarara_2001_in: is all your choice
thistleent: I will let Chris know, but I think he already has put together a list of clients and dates to send you
sarara_2001_in: ok

sarara_2001_in: we will meet all of u as per your convenience
thistleent: that is very considerate
thistleent: I will plan to meet your group in Los Angeles on some date between June 4-14
sarara_2001_in: ok

I marked my calendar for a meeting with the directors of the Biswas group and their bankers some time in the first two weeks of June.

May 24

Larry wrote—10:02:37 EDT—"to share what i know as of today ok ... to take the edge off those of you who are not in the front lines."

> *... the general consensus after a few people have spoken to them* (Biswas group) *is they are raring to go full speed ahead only, they are just as committed as they were before and excited at meeting all of you, if not even more so and quietly behind the scenes they have been conducting their business taking care of their end of things so that they will be (and already are) ready for you fine people shortly after they land. Only they can not make the days go faster.*
>
> *I do not think that ANYONE will ever understand why they do not just come right out and place in a document form their intentions ok but possibly it is because they have spoken to enough of you and e have all been reassured many many times over the last month that all is well on their end and maybe its because some of you do not understand one VERY IMPORTANT FACT*
>
> *This is that the RBI or Reserve Bank of India MONITORS AND CONTROLS EVERY SINGLE BANK ACCOUNT IN INDIA and is VERY VERY STRICT AND PROFESSIONAL in their committee duties and regulations and we may well have very solid proof of (SOON) that they DO ALLOW INVESTMENTS both INSIDE and OUTSIDE of their country if all things are done the way they wish them to be done.*
>
> *So if they (the RBI) give the go ahead you should all have been reassured at that very moment that funding was all real....*

And as far as we have been told they have booked their flights and the meetings in Canada are to start on the 28th like scheduled in Toronto and as to where exactly i guess this too will be soon forthcoming.

What Larry didn't know was that Anamika told me they would leave on May 29th due to an impending strike. If he did not have information readily gained from the investor, how could he know that the RBI (similar to the Federal Reserve Bank) "controls every single bank account in India"?

I didn't question anything in Larry's email and waited for the clock to run down and reach June 2. I took comfort in knowing that if the RBI approved a large disbursement of funds outside of the country, then indeed the funds were real, but preferred to see the Biswas investment in my account before I started to spend it.

May 25

Larry provided the group with a message from Kevin who related that he had most recently spoken to Anamika on her cel phone. Kevin, a contractor, was building Anamika a house in Toronto.

She has never lied to me and was on her way back from the dropping them off I guess because she said one group of 6 directors will be in Singapore today and then Korea and then one to Toronto for Tuesday arrival.

She was 175 kilometers from home … so she was not going to be able to give any more info over the phone!

I am saying they will be here for Wednesday meetings!

We will get my time agreed to … might be 9am Wednesday after all and then once i know what the score is when i get a few minutes I will inform all of you to let you know
- how casual or stressful it was/is
- what type of info they are seeking
- what type of dress code they have
- exactly what may be expected as well as to confirm FUNDS

Also I am getting a meeting room everyone can use for there meetings.

Pass that on ... we are trying to find a meeting room in Etobicoke that is close to where they are.

Funds Transfer #1—Money in Toronto

Tell them the money is here in Toronto already and that they (6 directors) are on there way here to Toronto and 4 directors are on the way to New Zealand and then to the United States and she will inform us tomorrow of the itinerary.

Larry provided us with a list of the directors and bankers. Where he got it was not revealed. Whether or not it was completely accurate, we could never ascertain. At the time we were pleased to meet a group of serious investors, which included:

- Niraj Biswas—Anamika's uncle, now leader of the group
- Ashit Kumar Biswas—Anamika's father, who would not be coming
- Ajit Biswas
- Kunal Biswas
- Amar Biswas
- Akash Biswas
- Rajiv Biswas
- Sahil Biswas
- Pankaj Biswas

as well as Mr. Sanyal from the Bank of Boroda, Kamal Sood from United Bank of India and Govind Kumar from State Bank of India.

After that encouraging news—the investors are coming and the funds were already in Toronto—we did not need to get a message from Chris.

May 26—4:40:22AM EDT

His email was entitled "STOP!!!!!!!!!!". In typical fashion he wrote "Do not I repeat do not fly to Canada until the investor contacts u." No reason was given nor was there any indication Chris was aware of the logistical and financial impact this would have on the clients.

We all had lives apart from the funding process. I was scheduled to go to Arizona on business right after Memorial Day weekend. Since I planned to drive, my schedule would not be thrown off too much. But what about those who planned to fly in economy class who would be charged a fee for changing flights?

Craig, who lived in Toronto, responded to Chris' email—7:04:13 AM EDT—to assure those planning to meet in Toronto that the city was safe despite the SARS epidemic which was very much in the news. "At this time there is a greater chance that you will be hit by lightning in Toronto than you will be infested by SARS."

Just when we thought Chris would be providing all the updates, Larry was back to recap the latest events—14:50EST.

> *1. Niraj and his entourage ws headed for Singapore and Korea and now apparently are in Korea conducting business with a client.*
> *2. Apparently the client in Korea is giving them a bit of a slow down so they have no choice but to spend an extra day maybe even two getting things in order there before moving on to Toronto as planned.*
> *3. This will result in a delay of possibly 24 hurs maybe a bit more but everyone must wait until Niraj informs Chris or Kevin on the actual expected new time frames.*
> *4. At least one of the clients is heading up to Toronto still as we speak and he will be in contact with Niraj himself by tomorrow afternoon at the latest so we will forward on anything further that we learn.*
> *5. One fellow asked Niraj if all is still well with our funding group affairs and has been reassured that all is just fine only they need to deal with situation in Korea first....*
>
> *So okay these folks are not anywhere's near as professional as they could be that is for certain but everything is in a serious forward motion and if these people are real as they do seem to be there will be NO STOPPING them from attempting to fund those projects unless it is our attitudes, lack of patience at this point or simply you drop out all together.*
>
> *I say please give the devil his due as delays are a normal part of the business world....*

As if.

With the Biswas group seemingly mired in Korea, I decided to complete my plans and keep my business appointment in Arizona. I'd stay in contact with any developments through email. Since the investors may arrive in Toronto later than expected, I'd still have plenty of time to schedule a visit with them in Canada or later in Las Vegas.

As I nervously waited for funding I knew the rest of my life had to continue or I'd be in a perpetual state of suspended animation.

May 27—3:11:52 AM EDT

I received the following email with the subject—THIS IS VERY URGENT, PLZ, HAVE A LOOK THROUGH—as I was about to leave for Arizona.

HELLO SIR,
HI| I AM SOMNATH BISWAS UNCLE OF ANAMIKA BISWAS YOUR WOULD BE INVESTOR'S COMPANIES ONE OF THE DIRECTORS. EARLIER OUR OTHER DIRECTORS TALKED TO ALL OF U MOST PROBABLY (MR NIRAJ BISWAS), NOW, AT PRESENT HE AND OUR OTHER DIRECTORS ARE IN SEOUL FOR A VERY IMPOTANT AGENDA WHERE WE HAVE BEEN FRAUDED BY OTHER COMPANIES, AND WE FACED A LOSE OF MORE THAT 21/2 BILLION USD$. SO TO US IT IS MORE IMPORTANT TO DEAL THAT, WELL YOU ALL CLIENTS ARE ALSO IMPORTANT TO US NODOUBT IN THAT BUT AFTER HAPPENING OF THIS CASE WE ARE NOW FORCED TO GET A ENTITLE APPLICATION TO BE FILED IN THE COURT TO PREVENT OUR COMPANY FROM ANY FURTHER LOSE LIKE THIS KIND OF INVESTMENT.
SIR, WE REALLY OBLIGED FOR THE DELAY BUT WE ARE HELPLESS, BECOZ WE FELL IF THE MAIN SOURCE GETS EMPTY ALL THE COMPANY TO WHOME WE ARE THE INVESTOR OR ABOUT TO INVEST WILL TAKE US AS A PUPET WHICH IS OF NO USE.
WELL WE ARE PLANNING TO REACH U AT EARLIEST BY 4TH OF JUNE 2003 AND WE ALSO REQUEST U NOT TO MAKE TRAVEL WE WILL COME TO EACH OF U PERSONALLY IN ORDER TO STOP YOUR BAD INVESTMENT IN TRAVELLING.
HOPE THAT WE WILL RECIEVE A FULL COOPERATION FROM U
WITH BEST REGARDS
SOMNATH BISWAS
(SENIOR DIRECTOR OF THE COMPANY)

DELAY #3—defrauded in Korea

No one could have imagined this turn of events. Larry told us one of their clients was "giving them a slow down"—whatever that means, a considerable difference from defrauding US$2.5 billion. How does one respond to that, except with patience and support (and fingers crossed that the miscreants will be dealt with quickly so our funding can be accomplished)?

At 9:13:28 AM EDT I replied to Somnath Biswas

Dear Mr. Biswas
Thank you for your email. I am sorry for your troubles and hope they are improved quickly. I very much look forward to concluding a business arrangement with your family and your company.

Next I forwarded Somnath's email to Larry—9:10:48 AM EDT—, with the following note:

> Am forwarding this to you in case you didn't get. Surprised to get this kind of letter. Spoke with Chris and he knew about it. I asked him why he didn't give us a "heads up", he took a "not to worry mate" approach. Not bad, all in all, but somewhat alarming to begin with. However alls well when we get the $. Am going out of town on biz for few days.

Somnath Biswas replied soon after I got to Arizona.
Later that morning of May 27th I engaged Anamika, awake though late, on Yahoo chat.

thistleent: Anamika—received your uncle's email
sarara_2001_in: will u wait for a moment
sarara_2001_in: plz
thistleent: k
sarara_2001_in: well i like to talk to u frakly
sarara_2001_in: that we are a investor company wot u think we should always look after the benefit of the company
sarara_2001_in: not our self
sarara_2001_in: wot u think which is right
sarara_2001_in: did u under stand the mail wot my uncle wrote
thistleent: sorry
thistleent: getting a cup of coffee
thistleent: yes I did understand
sarara_2001_in: its alright

thistleent: all right

thistleent: am sorry for your troubles

sarara_2001_in: see hhe had asked for entitlement

sarara_2001_in: right

sarara_2001_in: which chris misunderstood

thistleent: what do you mean by entitlement

thistleent: is that a legal term in Korea

sarara_2001_in: he aske that for our safety from your side before dealing

sarara_2001_in: no it is alegal term in india where we draft a contract as per jurisdictioon of the investor country and get it signd by the company

sarara_2001_in: but since over here in india courts are all closed due to summer vacation they had to do it from their

thistleent: which provides what to you and company which received your investment?

thistleent: or, I should ask

thistleent: what does the entitlement do

thistleent: what does it require of you

thistleent: and what does it require of the company that received your investment

thistleent: hope thats clearer

sarara_2001_in: it is required that incase any of us do breech of contract it helps to get the things settled

thistleent: ok, understood

thistleent: so your uncle and the directors are in Korea getting their entitlement?

sarara_2001_in: because at first we thought we would do the dealing without entitlement but after the incident of korea we are force to do it

sarara_2001_in: i know it sounds bad that we cannot trust anyone but u can understand how important it is for a investor and as well as for a company

thistleent: by entitlement do you mean guarantee of repayment

sarara_2001_in: we fell that prevention is better thancure

thistleent: what does this mean for Chris investors

thistleent: and specifically, what does it mean for me and my company?

thistleent: or is the entitement specific only to Korea

sarara_2001_in: nothing

thistleent: and your troubles there

thistleent: ok, so for me to understand this correctly

thistleent: the entitlement your company seeks is specific only to your Korea problem

thistleent: am I correct in concluding that?
sarara_2001_in: yes
sarara_2001_in: but we are now taking thios for every investment
thistleent: so, I will be getting this kind of contract
sarara_2001_in: yes
sarara_2001_in: they will carry with them to u
thistleent: will I get a chance to review the contract before they arrive
sarara_2001_in: no u will have them on the spot yes u will have the ti me to review
thistleent: when I meet with your directors, they will give me this contract
thistleent: and time to review it
thistleent: how much time
thistleent: how extensive is it
thistleent: some contracts are ten-20 pages long
sarara_2001_in: nono
sarara_2001_in: not more than 10pages
thistleent: k
thistleent: am going out of town on business
sarara_2001_in: ok
thistleent: back in 2 days
sarara_2001_in: willbe back when
sarara_2001_in: or i will send u the mesage as they reach
sarara_2001_in: ok
thistleent: since June 4 is your earliest arrival date
thistleent: there is nothing for me to do until then
thistleent: but I will keep in touch somehow
thistleent: thank you for your help
thistleent: bye
sarara_2001_in: bye

I also mentioned this to Larry during Yahoo chat. He knew nothing of the entitlement plan, remarking "u know more than i i think." He revealed that Kevin had written a letter to Anamika, which he called "a big mistake." Kevin told Anamika "his banker said he needed more information on them (investors) because of money laundering and scams and could niraj please provide him with some form of verification."

May 28—9:25:42 AM E DT

Somnath replied

HELLO SIR,
WELL THANKS FOR YOUR KINDNESS AND FRIENDLYNESS. WELL I KNOW THAT WE REALLY HEART U FOR THIS DELAY BUT WE ARE HELPLESS BECAUSE OUR COMPANY WAS NOT USED TO THIS KIND OF INVESTMENT BEFORE BUT DUE TO ANAMIKA'S REQUEST WE WERE TRYING TO DO ITFOR LAST TWO YEARS AND WE WERE FACING A LOT OF LOSE AFTER THAT WE DECIDED TO STOP BUT ANMIKA MEANTIME TALKED WITH YOU ALL AND SHE DECIDED TO TAKE THE RISK AND THAT IS WHY SHE TOOK OUT THE LICENCE IN HER COMPANIES NAME KOWING THAT IT WOULD HARM HER EXPORT TO GREAT EXTENT, WE TRIED TO TELL HER BUT SHE IS VERY STUBBORN, BUT RECENTLY DUE TO HER FATHERS HEALTH SHE GOT A BIG PUSH BACK AND NOW THIS KOREAN GROUP MADE AGAIN DELAYED I KNOW AND ALSO UNDERSTAND WHAT YOU PEOPLE ARE FEELING ABOUT HER, BUT BELIEVEME IT IS NOT HER FAULT, SHE ID TRYINH HER LEVEL BEST, WE ALSO TRYING, BUT DELAYED HAPPEN WHEN ONE DAY SHE SUSPECTED THE FINDERS CHRIS AND SWAN BY THEIR CONVERSATION SHE ASKED US TO TRAVEL TO ALL THE CLIENTS TO ENSURE WHAT IS HAPPENING AND WHY IT IS HAPPENING ALSO FINALIZING THE DEAL ON THE SPOT.
BUT ON A CONTRARY I APPERICIATE YOUR PATIENCE AND REALLY APPOLOGISE FOR THE DELAY ON BEHALF OF ALL THE DIRECTORS.
HOPE THAT U WILL KEEP YOUR COOPERATION WITH US AS U WILL UNDERSTAND THAT NO ONE DELAYS LIKE THIS SINCE WE ARE IN THE FIELD OF BUSINESS AND HOW IMPORTANT THIS DEALS WILL BE TO US AS WE ARE GOING TO GAIN A VERY HIGH POSITION IN THE BUSINESS MARKET AFTER THIS DEALS GET COMPLETED.
HOPE THAT U WILL KEEP YOUR COPRATION WE WILL REACH U VERY SOON.
SEND U THE UPDATE AS EARLY AS POSSIBLE.
WITH BEST REGARDS
SOMNATH BISWAS
(SENIOR DIRECTOR)

Rather than question why Anamika wasn't writing this email, all I could do was to accept Somnath's sincerity, which carried more weight coming from a Senior Director. It seemed obvious that the investment group turned the problem over to a top member of management so that he could deal with us as respected entrepreneurs rather than some associates of their strong willed niece. I continued with my business in Arizona, but determined to send Somnath a reply in a few days.

During another IM chat session with Larry on May 28 he confirmed that a ten page contract was coming from Anamika, just as she'd told me. He also revealed that the Biswas group had been "verified as bona fide investors in a large company from singapore and korea who was in the newpapers recently for bilking their investors out of billions." He concluded "that proves they are NOT lying to us." Cool news to me in Phoenix, where it was 107 degrees.

May 29

Then, in his inimitable ham-handed style, Larry sent what he called "an informative letter on the funding situation"—1:32:46 PM EDT.

He advised the 23 companies involved that "many of us have conducted and are still conducting a lot of diligence on the Biswas family ... trying to locate some REAL evidence that the Biswas are REAL INVESTORS and seriously have the means to fund us all."

The whipsaw was at work again. Three days earlier he wrote there would be a twenty four hour delay before the directors would be coming to Toronto. Three days later he's trying to impress the group with his dedication to performing a task that was nearly eight weeks overdue.

Though Larry acknowledged it was not his "place" to send out updates, he said he saw a trend developing "that could easily damage the funding if they (Investors) are real." He suggested that a spokesperson be selected from the group to deal directly with the Biswas, nominating Kevin who lived in Toronto so that the future relationship could proceed "in an orderly manner."

It may seem that I have a particular grudge against Larry, but as he was the principal source of information at this period my responses can only be to what he put forth. Constant in his approach was to "make nice" with everyone. Occasionally when my frustration meter reached over boil, I "screamed" at him during IM chat. Either he could not take confrontation or he was a master manipulator. Whatever, he wasn't a major fund raiser.

The May 29th email was one such "make nice" effort. He wanted 23 different companies spread out across the world to "all get along" without any awareness that he was trying to get a bag of cats to settle down for the night. He also made pronunciamentos without any support and without I'm sure any expert knowledge. For example:

... Now i think you will find the Biswas's very appreciative of all of your concerns for their family as they really like you guys ...

Huh? This is the guy who admitted having almost no contact with the Biswas after alienating Anamika.

... and you will find the whole deal from the beginning was not as perfectly set up as it could have been (for procedures) but either way this family (and nation) takes as an insult the slightest thing that we would not possibly even worry about and whether that is a culture thing or a long distance thing I am not sure but I know i made even a simply suggestion and got them upset and it sure doesn't take much.

Finally, Larry got to the point. Some unidentified members of the group had gotten particularly offensive toward Anamika et al in their quest for information. This was uncalled for and potentially could put the entire funding operation at risk. We were all supplicants and needed to be in the good graces of those who would fund us. Yet, some had decided they were first class hard charging U.S. businessmen—miniatures of their President—who would not be thwarted by lesser, third world folks.

Somnath Biswas email to an unidentified member of the group indicates the beginning of a rift.

SIR WE ALSO FOUND THAT YOU LIKE TO TALK TO US, YOU MOST WELCOME TO DO SO, AT THE NUMBERS OF ANAMIKA BISWAS, BECAUSE SHE TALKED TO YOU AND WE ALWAYS APPRECIATE HER DECISION WHAT EVER SHE TAKES. BUT, WE ARE VERY SHOCKED AND SURPRISED TO KNOW THAT WHEN WE ARE COMMUNICATING WITH YOU PEOPLE YOUR ATTITUDE OF CONCERN TOWARDS US IS REALLY TO BE APPRECIATED BUT WHEN THIS THINGS ARE BEEN SHARED BY YOUR FINDER MR. CHRIS CATLIN THEIR ATTITUDE ALWAYS TERRIBLE AND TROUBLESOME AND THEY ALWAYS THREAT US TO TELL THAT WHETHER WE WILL DEAL WITH YOU AND OTHER CLIENTS OR NOT WHICH IS VERY HORRI-BLE AND INSULTING.

WE WOULD LIKE YOU TO CLARIFY IF ANY SUCH INTENSIVE QUESTIONS YOU HAVE FOR US OR YOU WANT TO KNOW

SIR, WE ARE GLAD THAT YOU ARE STILL CONSIDERED TO DEAL WITH US WELL i AM (SOMNATH BISWAS) IS IN INDIA DUE TO A LEGAL WORKINGS HE HAS TO MOVE TO INDIA, WELL IF YOU WANT WE CAN SEND YOU A NOTORY ATTESTED DECLARATION STATING THAT WE WILL FUND YOU AND REASON WHY DELAY IS HAPPENING, IF YOU LIKE US TO DO THIS THEN LET US KNOW.

WELL WE ARE TRYING TO REACH YOU BY THE FIRST WEEK OF THE MONTH OF JUNE.

HOPE THIS WONT GET DELAYED
BYE

I still don't know who insulted the Biswas group, or if any one in our group requested a notarized document in which the Biswas declare they would fund us. As long as the Investors held out the hope of meeting, I imagine no one wanted to rock the boat.

May 30

That approach was underscored by Chris' email—8:18 EST.

I was having a chat with Anamika trying to get the latest information out of her for the investors travel arrangements and such. The current unconfirmed date for the directors to fly out is the 4th or 5th of June now Anamika informed me that there will be an update coming out on the 2nd of June from the directors going directly to you the client, this email from what I understand will relate to there movements and to confirm arrival date in Canada and such.

So, to sum things up look out for an email on the 2nd of June I think that's the 1st of June if your on the other half of the world.

Once during IM chat, Larry offered "they like your deal so far." Feeling like one of the masses, several rungs below those who dealt with Anamika et al, I was pleasantly surprised, but I had to ask how he knew. "… because you have been approved so far by me, Chris, Anamika, her father, the entire committee from the RBI and the entire board of directors of the Biswas' family." Still, I needed more and again asked how that approval was demonstrated.

He replied, "… they would have rejected you immediately. There was a lot more diligence than you may realize, but you passed everyone so no worries. Those Indians are freaking smart ok so do not under estimate them. They will be like the Rockefeller family."

I had no more questions. The only question I could ask was Why not me? And so, with one month gone, I waited to see what June would bring.

MAY SCORE CARD

Funding dates	17	Next funding date—June 2
Funds Transferred	1	Money in Toronto
Delays	3	(illness, transport strike, fraud)
Holidays	2	(banking, religious)

5. JUNE, 2003

SIGNS OF LIFE, LITTLE MOVEMENT

I responded to Somnath Biswas upon my return from Arizona.

June 1–5:40:49 PM EDT
To: Somnath Biswas
From: Vincent Panettiere—Thistle Productions, Inc.—Los Angeles
Thank you for your reply of May 28. I apologize for not responding sooner as I have been traveling on business and only returned late yesterday.

Be assured that we sympathize with your difficulty in Korea. If it involves SK Global, etc. I am aware of that circumstance through reading the financial news of the past week. We wish you a speedy and just conclusion to your efforts in Korea.

Rest assured that we continue to have a strong and sincere interest in meeting Anamika and the directors of your company and executives of the bank(s).

I am encouraged by your intention of "finalizing the deal on the spot" and hope the directors continue to be so inclined. That is our intention as well.

Would you kindly advise me how many will be attending the meeting as I wish to make appropriate preparations?

Also, would you let me know if the group will travel to Los Angeles?

I look forward to your response and to a very successful business relationship with Anamika and her associates.

It was my surmise that the Biswas group may have been victimized by the $1.2 billion accounting fraud discovered at the trading firm SK Global in March. Global was a subsidiary of SK Group, Korea's third largest conglomerate. Restructuring between the Korean companies and their creditors had been proceeding since March, with debt service payments deferred to mid-June. Perhaps the Biswas group needed to act to protect their claim in the event SK Global filed for bankruptcy.

I spoke with Anamika on IM. As the SK Group scandal was in the business news almost daily, my primary concern was to determine if the Biswas contingent was on schedule. She told me the group would go to Toronto first and that I'd receive a "declaration", which I took to mean itinerary.

Anamika also indicated the group would go to New York and Las Vegas and finally to Los Angeles. "… that will be told to you in the letter you will receive from the directors where it is stated when they are coming and entire itinerary." Most probably the letter would come from Niraj, she added.

Larry was enthralled by the thick due diligence report he'd sent the clients. But, as it was a compendium of any reference to Biswas extant on the Internet, it was worthless, in my opinion. Not once in Larry's volume was there a paragraph answering the central and burning question—could Anamika Biswas by herself, with a company, with a consortium, with family members, or friends and the Marching and Chowder Society of Kolkata have enough funds to cover an investment of $33 billion in 24 companies located in the U.S., The Bahamas, Canada and New Zealand?

He remarked on IM "do you realize the Biswas' and Kumars are some of THE most influential people in India?" A superficial reading of Larry's "diligence" report caused me to conclude the name of Biswas was somewhat common.

"I wonder if Kumar isn't like Jones or Smith, though," I responded trying to inject an iota of sobriety. "But either way, you can't prove they are not related either," Larry replied.

Oy. Once again I was reminded that my goal was not to involve myself in anything more than raising financing.

June 2nd came and went without any funds reaching our banks as Larry calculated it would in his May 17 email "… 12-15 days away from actually MEETING with the BISWAS family on our funding capital and opportunities." Then "… if they are pleased with the outcome of the conversation and personal diligence, then they will immediately release to you your funding …"

Maybe we'd been inundated with so much email and IM chat that no one recalled our "great come and get it day", to quote a line from a song in the classic Broadway musical *Finnian's Rainbow*, had come and gone.

June 3

The *Asia Times* reported that the Korea Development Bank, one of the largest lenders for SK Global, parent of SK Group, was taking a positive view of the bail out plan.

Later that day I saw Anamika was online in Yahoo chat. When I greeted her I was in for a surprise.

sarara_2001_in: GOODEVENING BUT I AM NOT ANAMIKA
sarara_2001_in: I AM AKANSHA

sarara_2001_in: HER ELDERSISTER
sarara_2001_in: SHE IS NOT ONLINE DUE TO POWERFALIURE

DELAY #4—Storm and Power Failure

thistleent: I hope it is fixed soon
thistleent: sorry I didn't know you weren't Anamika
sarara_2001_in: IT WILL BE AS SOON AS POWERCOMES IT IS A CABLE FAULT AND
TRANSFORMER BUSTEDOUT FROM YESTERDAY
thistleent: what happened yesterday?
thistleent: was it rain or an electrical storm
sarara_2001_in: IT WAS STROMAND RAIN
sarara_2001_in: AND ALSOA BIGTREE FELL DOWN
thistleent: that will do it! are you talking with Chris?
thistleent: are you aware of the itinerary for the meetings?
sarara_2001_in: NOSIR
sarara_2001_in: I AM TALKING TO MR CHRIS
sarara_2001_in: BUT NOT AWARE OF ITINERY
thistleent: do you know when Niraj and his group will be in the States
sarara_2001_in: MY FATHER WILL BE THERE ON TIME
thistleent: has your father recovered fully?
sarara_2001_in: I AM DAUGHTER OF MR NIRAJ BISWAS
sarara_2001_in: HE IS IN SEOUL NOW
thistleent: Oh—sorry
sarara_2001_in: ITS ALRIGHT
thistleent: Do you know the date of your arrival
thistleent: I mean his arrival
sarara_2001_in: MY ARRIVAL?
sarara_2001_in: YES IN THE STATED TIME
thistleent: which is what? I do not have an exact date
sarara_2001_in: 4THOR 5THOF JUNE
thistleent: in Toronto?
sarara_2001_in: YES
thistleent: thank you

June 3

I relayed my conversation with Akansha to Larry when we chatted later the morning of June 3. He was confused by Akansha calling herself Anamika's "elder sister". He asked "so you're saying Anamika is Niraj's daughter?" I couldn't reconcile the two—unless I wanted to apply the logic of "Chinatown" where Faye Dunaway is both the sister <u>and</u> the daughter. But, I had to offer my explanation "… that designation must be more like an older cousin who feels like an older sister since Niraj is her father." Larry concluded "who can figure that out."

A bigger surprise awaited a few hours later when Larry told me the Biswas group would be delayed until they arranged "for investment approval from the US and Canadian governments" before they could come to North America.

"They lost their case in Korea's courts because they never applied for an investment certificate," he said. "So, they were basically alien investors and want to make sure it doesnt happen with us. The positive side is if they have us working this late on this, means a super much more positive future. Lesser people would have called it right off. So that means it might take a week but once approved we're done. Say by June 15th with money in the bank."

FUNDING DATE #18—JUNE 15, 2003

No one received the Biswas group itinerary on June 3 because the power outage continued. Chris advised that the power would be restored by noon India time, which was after midnight in Los Angeles. Nothing more to do but wait for another day.

June 4

Chris told me the group had a "hiccup" in the form of "foreign investment laws" that they'd be "fixing in the next twenty four hours." When I asked Chris if the foreign investment law would prevent further investment by the Biswas group, he signed off Yahoo and disappeared into the ether.

The latest hurdle all the clients had to face seemed logical on the surface. Since 9/11 the whole world, including India, knew that the U.S. Government was checking funds entering and leaving the country. For at least the next two days Anamika had every client scurrying to find out the U.S. and state requirements for foreign investment.

I was trying to determine with Larry what we could do to satisfy Anamika's request when he blurted out without provocation "we are in a word SO GOD DAMN FREAKING FILTHY STINKING RICH I CAN'T COUNT IT ALL." The explanation for this outburst was that "we (with Chris) are to get up front money soon, while they go around finalizing deals and regulations with each client. I even have an east Indian interpreter, he added."

The reason for Larry's jubilation was an email he'd just received from Anamika, one he advised she sent me as well. I checked and there it was.

June 5

The subject of her email at 9:49:02 AM EDT was: PLEASE VIEW IT AND LET ME KNOW BY TODAY.

HELLO SIR
WELL DUE TO BAD HEALTH CONDITION AND SUROUNDING SITU-TATIONS WE ARE NOT ABLE TO KEEP OUR WORDS SO NOW I AM SENDING YOU THE BOTH COMPENSATION AND NONDISCLOSURE AGREEMENTS AFTER U GET THEM IF U AGREE TO IT THEN PLZ LET ME KNOW BY EMAIL SO THAT I CAN SEND U THAT NOTORIZED. YOU ALSO HADA COMPLETE FREEDOM TO CHANGE THE POINTS IF U WISH. BUT, I NEED THE REPLY AS EARLY BY TODAY INORDER TO SEND YOU NOTORIZED. WELL OUR DEPARTURE IS NOT CONFIRMED BUT WE ARE REACHING WITHIN 9TH TO 13TH OF JUNE 2003. HOPE THAT U PEOPLE WILL UNDERSTAND US AND TAKE IT AS GRANTED THAT WE WILL INVEST YOUR COMPANY BUT IT WILL TAKE TIME AND IF U NEED ANY MONEY INBETWEEN TIME THENPLZ LET US KNOW WE WILL DISCUSS AMONG THE DIRECTORS AND LET U KNOW AS EARLY AS POSSIBLE.
WITH BEST REGARDS
ANAMIKA BISWAS

DELAY #5—Anamika illness

Her email continued with the following:

AGREEMENT OF COMPENSATION

THIS AGREEMENT IS MADE IN THIS 05THDAY OF JUNE 2003[DATE], BETWEEN THISTLE PRODUCTION, INCORPORATION GROUP LASVE-GAS REFFERED AS A COMPANY AND A.B EXPORTS OF INDIA REF-FERED TO AS INVESTORS.

IN CONSIDERATION OFTHE PREMISES AND OF MUTUAL COVENANTS SETH FORTH, PARTIES AGREES AS FOLLOWS

(1) THE PARTIES HAVE ENGAGED INAGREEMENT IN REALESTATE SOLUTION&INVESTMENTS COMPANY TO REPRESENT AS SOLE INVESTORS AND BUSINESSPLAN SUBMITTED IN DETAILS AND ACT ON BEHALF OF NEGOTIATIONGIVING THE BEST POSIBBLE ADVISE AND HELP WHEN ASKED BY THE COMPANY.

(2) THE TERMS OF THIS AGREEMENT STANDS EFFICTIVE ONCE-SIGNED, COMMENCING THAT DAY, THE TERMS ANDCONDITION ARE TO BE COMPILED AND CONSTRUED SIMPLE BASED UPON THIS AGREEMENT.

(3) THE TERRITORY COVERED BYTHIS AGENCY IS 'CANADA'REF-FERED TO AS' ABOVE TERRITORY'

(4) THE CLIENTS PROPOSALS IS ALREADY BEEN DISCUSSED AND NEGOTIATED AS TO CUT THROUGH ALL THE REDTAPE THERE FORE MAKING IT PLAIN AND SIMPLE THERE TO BRING THE CLINT BEST POSSIBLE DEAL FROM HIS SUBMITTED PROJECT WHICH WILL ALOW HIM/HER TO DEAL MORE CONFIDENTALY BUT THE ACCEPTANCE OF THIS AGREEMENT ALSO INCLUDES THAT ALL CONTACTS MADE TO THE CEO OF THIS PROJECTS SHOULD BE MADE PRIOR TO THE INVESTOR.

(5) THE ASSIGNMENT OF THIS CONTRACT WILL CLOSE HEREBY ALL THE CONTACT OF BOTH PARTIES DIRECTLY OR INDIRECTLY TO PUB-LIC WITHOUT THE PROIOR CONSENT AND NOTICE TO THE EITHER PARIES BOTH DIRECTLY OR INDIRECTLY.

(6) AFTER AGREEING TO ALL THIS SCHEDULES IF EITHERORNEITH-ERNOR BOTH THE PARTIES IF INDULGE IN COMPENSATION IT WILL BE HIGHLY RECOMMENDED.

(7) NO NEGOTIATION OR PRIVATE OFFERS SHALL BE MADE OTHER THAN 10%. BUT UNLESS OR UNTIL BOTH THE CLIENTS FELLS IT UNSUITABLE TO DEAL FURTHER.

(a) Being now stated I Miss ANAMIKA BISWAS have engaged into an agreem-net where as binds this dealconcerning the business plan being submitted to the client this involves a gurantee that both parties shall be benefitand be conducted in aprofessional businessmanner any breach of the agreement shall be the resource and settled by arbitation borad of either state of the parties.

(b) The setting of meetings shall be arranged, contact by phone, anything to constitute a clean understanding any party must comply within 24hrs.

(c) The assgnment will means that parties had decided to conduct without any breach of contact in this deal which will stand as a strong hold only disolves f disaster occured due to natual calamity.

AGREEMENT OF NONDISCLOSURE

THIS AGREEMENT CONFIRMS THAT THE NAMED INTRODUCING (SIGNATORYAND BOUND SIGNATORIES), AS AN INDIVIDUAL OR ENTITYAND THEIR COMPANIES, ASSOCIATES, AGENTS, CONSUL-TANTSAND/OR ANY RELATED PARTIES AGRES TO KEEP COMPLETELY CONFIDENTIAL AND NOT TO BYPASS, CIRCUMVENT, OR INANYWAY ATTEMPT TO DIVULGE ANY INFORMATION DISCLOSED TO THEM BY THE INTRODUCING SIGNATORY REGARDING THE ASSOCIATION OF THE SIGNATORIES TO ANY PARTIES NOT A PARTICIPANT OF THIS AGREEMENT WITHOUT THE EXPRESS, INWRITING PERMISSIONOF THE INTRODUCING SIGNATORY. THE AGREEMENT IS BINDING UPON THE SIGNATORIES, THEIR HEIRS, ASSIGNEES, AND DESIGNEES. BY THE SIGNATURE BELOW AND EXECUTION OF THIS AGREEMENT THEREBY, EACH OF THE SIGNATORIES, SEPERATELY AND INDIVIDU-ALY OF WHICH SIGNATORY IS PART TO OR OF MEMBER F, PRINCI-PALOR AGENTS FOR SAID ASSOCIATES IS BOUND HEREBY. ANY CONTROVERSY OR CLAIM ARISING OUT OF OR RELATION TO THIS AGREEMENT ORTHE BREACH THERE OF WHICH IS NOT SETTLE BETWEEN THE SIGNATORIES THEMSELVES SHALL BE SUBMITTED TO THE COMMONLAW COURT OF COMPETENT JURISDICTION. JUDGE-MENT UPON THE AWARD RENDEREDBY THE SAID COURT SHALL INCLUDETOTAL REMUNERATION RECIEVED AS A RESULT OF BUSI-NESS CONDUCTED WITHAND BY THE PARTIES COVERED UNDE THIS AGREMENT.

I cringe, having re-read the above, and question my sanity and intelligence. I am almost too embarrassed to continue writing this book. Maybe its better to shut this down early and not expose the world, or the few who may read this book, to such inane drivel and in the process leave me standing naked before the world. Not a pretty picture.

Upon reflection, I will continue and finish what I've begun, in the interests of completing the journey, a phrase I prefer to the ubiquitous "closure".

Al, one of the group from Atlanta, responded first at 10:36AM EDT and most likely expressed the reaction of all who received the same email from Anamika.

> *Anamika*
> *Your letter does not specifically refer to our business proposal and does not detail the terms of funding which we had requested on 5/27/03 from Somnath. In addition, it is full of typos and incomplete statements rendering it useless.*
> *I am not sure who you are and what this is all about, but if you want to fund our project then fax a signed letter of intent on your company letterhead … specifically detailing your investment terms and timing. Also include documentation of your company and financial capability to fund our project. If you want to be the exclusive funding investor, then you will need to wire $100,000 to our bank account by Friday, June 6, 2003 as a good faith retainer. If we do not receive documents and funds by then we will consider you only as a potential source of funds and will continue business discussions with other interested investors. This process has gone on too long without you providing legitimate due diligence on you and your company as requested many times by multiple parties.*

My response took a different tone.

Dear Anamika
I greatly appreciate your kind email. Let me assure you that I sympathize with the discomfort that you and your investor group have endured both physically and financially during the last few weeks.

It is a testament to the character of your group, as individuals and collectively, that you continue to show concern for us—your clients—and wish to continue to invest.

I agree to the compensation and non-disclosure sections of your email and look forward to receiving the notarized version.

FOR THE RECORD—the company name is Thistle Productions, Inc., Los Angeles.

If possible, I wish to receive 5% of your investment now so that I can prepare for the first film. I'm seeking $28.5 million and 5% of that is $1,425,000.

You are very generous and honorable. I look forward to a very successful working relationship and hope to meet with you and your group in Los Angeles in the very near future.

Larry was outraged at Al's email to Anamika and called it "a major mistake. He just insulted Anamika big time." Larry sent me a copy of the email and I read it.

thistleent: read it. I share his frustration and similar concerns. Yet
elusiveconnections: why didnt he stop to talk about uit first
thistleent: it was a poorly written and worded document to be sure, but there was a genuine effort to satisfy the group
elusiveconnections: anamika will be totally freaking pissed
thistleent: and the offer of money was there as well
elusiveconnections: they realy need to to do this right
elusiveconnections: if u were doing it
thistleent: they meaning anamika?
thistleent: I agree
elusiveconnections: would u do it with ANY output of cash from your end of things?
thistleent: in some ways she sounds like a kid who has no business experience
elusiveconnections: right
thistleent: yet you cant deny that she is spearheading the group, it seems
elusiveconnections: i tried to wisen her up
elusiveconnections: look what happened to me
elusiveconnections: anyways damage is done
thistleent: I agree, but it is better to get the $ than argue about grammar
elusiveconnections: and i am sure all other letter will be well written and polite
elusiveconnections: no doubt on the grammer
thistleent: for her sake, I hope so
elusiveconnections: who cares about grammer
thistleent: all we need is to have her get cheesed off at the whole group

elusiveconnections: just send the contracts and cash
thistleent: as a former literary agent, you can't say who cares about grammar to me
thistleent: all contracts have legal implications
elusiveconnections: not with everyone writing nice letters i do not think so
thistleent: maybe that's why they had problems in Korea
elusiveconnections: not professional enough
thistleent: who knows? all I want is the advance $, a meeting and total funding

Meanwhile, according to Chris the Biswas Group would not be arriving in Canada until sometime during the period of June 9-13. As a result of the Korean problem they would have to return to India and "activate their license", he said.

I told Chris what I'd learned about the investment documents.

thistleent: essentially—they don't have to file anything federal unless have more than 10% voting share
thistleent: and state filing is just to make sure they have legitimacy should there be a legal claim
thistleent: re: patriot act and money laundering, onus on me more than them
thistleent: I have to make sure they provide me with clean funds and I know who they are with passpot numbers, etc.
thistleent: how is anamika doing?
thistleent: interest strong?
thistleent: got her email, positive development
thistleent: so, where are we now?
flamethrower51: yeah shes apparently bee working to hard
thistleent: and?
flamethrower51: thats it
thistleent: any idea next steps
thistleent: do you expect to hear from her today?
flamethrower51: no doc told her to stay off someone got her on the phone
thistleent: what do you mean someone got her on the phone
flamethrower51: someone called her
flamethrower51: and talked to her
flamethrower51: someone else who is bringing her projects
flamethrower51: she's not very well
thistleent: how serious is this

flamethrower51: just from majorly over working she had to take a few days rest

DELAY#6—Anamika over working

The response of Larry and Chris was in yet another direction—7:44:59 PM EDT.

> *We are replying in regards to your very wonderful letter of commitment and notarized declaration of funding intent that we received this morning.*

> *We are very pleased to find out that you are as a world class investment group, still willing to fund our ventures....*

> *Now as for your supremely kind and genrous offer of interm financial support before the larger funding is secured, we are very humble and grateful and we know exactly what a fantastic partner- ship we are going to have with your family as only really truly great people would have offered such a kind but sometimes very necessary generous offer.*

> *We will be forever in your debt and will do well by your investment dollars intrusted to us.*

Larry then asked for $4.0 million up front should his $10 billion dollar investment arrive in more than thirty one but less than ninety days. He concluded by assuring Anamika and the Biswas Group.

> *... that in regards to outside investors, if we receive our full funding of $10.0 billion as we and your family/board of directors have decided upon that we shall not need any other investors that we know of this particular moment in time for at least a period of ten ("10") years*

What a pal!

Not everyone shared the concerns of the Atlanta client. A client on the East Coast told Anamika that his bank would write a letter of "acceptance/approval" stating they are ready to accept her funding transaction. His attorney, he said, found her email "sufficient for your purpose."

Meanwhile we all tried to gather as much information on federal and state investment regulations.

June 8—3:31:47 PM EDT

Dear Anamika

A thorough check with the California Secretary of State's office, the California Office of Corporations and the California Department of Commerce revealed that no documents were needed for foreign investment in a California company.

In actual fact, there are no general restrictions for foreign investment in the U.S. Quite the contrary. The trend is towards facilitating investment in the U.S.

However there are exceptions—mostly having to do with national or commercial security. The exceptions are in the following areas: Radio/TV; Satellite; Telephone/Telegraph; Aviation; Maritime Industries and Fisheries; Energy; Mineral Leases; Banking; Insurance; Real Property.

As you know, Thistle Productions is a feature film production company, which is not part of the above categories.

We have proposed an interest rate of 2 points over libor for sharing pari passu with the production company until 115% of loan/investment is recouped by you. After recoupment of the 115% you will receive 25% of the profits in perpetuity.

I intend to send you the following documents tonight, which I believe should give you a comfort level with regard to me and my company:
1. Statement and Designation By Foreign Corporation—this is a California State document; giving you right to sue in case of non performance by Thistle.
2. Thistle's articles of incorporation dated and signed by the Secretary of State of California.
3. Action of Sole Incorporator—indicating the company approves and adopts the California Corporation Code.
4. Resolution by Thistle's Board of Directors authorizing me to discuss and negotiate with you for the purpose of obtaining financing for a joint venture between our companies.
5. Email from Dave Snyder of the California Office of Business Investment indication no specific filings are required.

Please let me know if you have any questions with the above.

Unless I hear from you to the contrary, I will fax the above documents to you tonight (Monday morning in India).

Thank you for all of your efforts. I look forward to a long and successful relationship with you and your company.

Sincerely,
Vincent Panettiere

June 9

In Larry's 3:26:29 PM EDT email he advised clients that the investment papers Anamika requested were not required. In part he wrote:

> *"So the BOTTOM LINE is ... THEY CAN LEGALLY DEPOSIT THE FUNDS ANY TIME that they choose to from this moment on and hopefully this is what will happen soon after they get one last letter from each of you and off their declaration of funding intent."*

The East Coast client, after speaking with Anamika, was more direct. "I explained to her that these investment papers DO NOT exist." None of the people he spoke with at the U.S. Treasury Department had ever heard of them. As a result of his call, Anamika agreed that all she required was a simple letter on company letterhead stating that each client would take full responsibility in the event of default.

Later in the week, Larry sent out one of his typical updates regarding what he called "the Biswas funding extravaganza," which at first take seems like a strange word to use—until one consults the dictionary, which in truth I don't think he did.

American Heritage defines extravaganza as "1. A light orchestral composition marked by freedom and diversity of form, often with burlesque elements; 2. Any elaborate, spectacular entertainment." Maybe Larry was partially correct. The Biswas funding process certainly had "diversity of form" and often seemed like a burlesque. It was also elaborate in scope and temerity.

But, it was not entertaining. Not to me. Not when every day either brought elation or disappointment, mostly the latter. Not when every weekend was lived with inhaled breath, waiting and hoping that I would awaken on Monday morning to fabulous news.

June 12

We now must return to Larry's update—2:52:32 PM EDT

> *"I do not think you will like this update very much, but as like you, I am helpless to do anything but simply report the movements and directions that I have been given …*
>
> *"… And I will be the very FIRST to admit that my own lack of operating capital really has been a serious drawback as once funded to even the tune of $100,000 I would have been able to have a lot more diligence done better but I did the best I could with what I have to work with as did many others.*

Lack of funds is not a crime. But, it is abysmally stupid to reveal that fact to clients who are relying on their "broker". It places him in an entirely different frame of reference and drastically reduces respect. Larry thought his ersatz humble pie would win him friends and influence, but it did the opposite. He was tolerated and exploited as long as there was the slightest possibility that through dumb luck and divine intervention he might have found the mother lode in Anamika.

> *"… so we plan on staying with this one until the last day it bombs, then if necessary I know I will instigate some serious litigation for compensation for the damage done by the Biswas to my company."*

Who was he kidding? The guy just admitted not having a penny and he is bursting with bravado to take on a woman he never met, in a culture far more strange than British Columbia, through an international law suit.

His rationalization had the effect of pulling me, and the group back under the umbrella phrase "everything is possible." A concept we all wanted to believe.

> *"… as far as I'm concerned they could have simply stopped this a long time ago if it was not real so if it turns out that it is not real then they will deserve everything they will get."*

Larry reminded us once again that he and others had "checked them out at Citibank level and they come through smiling and getting TOP bankers of Citibank excited is not an easy task but excited they seem to be."

> *"... We've located a fascinating amount of TOP executives with the Biswas name in every possibly industry ... and some poor Biswas with nothing more than a coffee plantation worker's existence."*

> *"So what the heck is real we can't tell and will not be able to tell unless we do more diligence on them which I now refuse to as I have put in more than enough time ..."*

This from a guy who presented himself as our "broker", who brought us into the process and who was going to collect at least two percent of $23 billion! Hard to follow a leader who runs away soon as a shot is fired.

From this point on, it was clearly apparent that I, and I'm sure some of the others, recognized the need to have our own direct line of communication with Anamika. We learned she wanted that as well since she no longer wanted to work with Larry or Chris, who had cursed, and insulted her.

Larry co-opted his anticipated negative response to the email with "... if you are going to bail please let us know so that we can arrange for a replacement project ..." But he couldn't leave it there.

> *"... if anyone wishes to start litigation against my company for bringing them into this affair please note that I have an excellent lawyer who can handle all inquiries or law suits ..."*

My big brother can beat up your big brother. Yeah.

Chris's attitude was similar. At the end of a heated exchange with Allen during Yahoo chat, Chris' response was "u stay or you bail simple." Two nice dependable chaps, Chris and Larry.

As I stayed focused, the attitude of Chris and Larry was of little consequence since we were approaching the end of the June 9-13 window Chris gave us on June 5th when the directors would arrive in Toronto.

June 13

We had another set back in the form of an email from India with the subject

SOLICITORS INFORMATIONS at 9:57:42 AM EDT

MR VINCENT PANETTIERE
THISTLE PRODUCTIONS, INC

HOW ARE YOU, WELL I AM THE SOLICITER OF BISWAS GROUP, WELL I THINK THIS IS OUR FIRST MAIL AND INTRODUCTION AS WELL BEFORE WE MEET FACE TO FACE, WELL, AS OUR CLIENT THE BISWAS GROUP WAS ABOUT TO REACH YOU FOR INVESTMENT ON 13TH OF JUNE 2003, AS PREVIOUS THIS COMMITMENT ALSO FAILED BECAUSE THE MOST IMPORTANT DIRECTOR WHO WOULD BE LEADING THE GROUP ON THE TABLE OF INVESTMENT HAS LOST HIS WIFE ON 11TH MORNING AT ABOUT 5:00AM AS PER INDIAN TIME AND WHO WAS AT THAT TIME IN SEOUL WITH ME AND MOST OF OUR MEMBERS DEALING ON PAPER WORKS AS HOW TO PROCEDE WITH YOU ON 13TH AND ALSO WAITING FOR THE LICENCE

DELAY #7—death of Niraj's wife

TO GET THE PROVISON AND FUTHERED ISSUE AS IT GOT FREEZE DUE TO FOUR CONSECUTIVE LOSE IN A YEAR AFTER IT GOT ISSUED I PRESUME THAT YOU ARE AWARE OF IT AS I THINK OUR DIRECTOR ANAMIKA BISWAS TOLD YOU THAT WELL MR NIRAJ BISWAS HAD TO COMEBACK AS HIS WIFE PASSED AWAY DUE TO HEART ATTACK.
WELL AS A LAWYER OF THE FIRM I GURENTEE THAT THIS COMPANY IS NODOUBT IS CAPABLE TO FUND YOU ALONG WITH MANY PEOPLE TO WHOME WE HAVE ALREADY GOING TO AS YOU KNOW, BUT, AS A LAWYER I HAVE SOMTHING TO TELL YOU AND AFTER YOU TAKE THE DECISION AS IN WHICH WAY YOU WILL PROCEDE WE WILL FOLLOW THAT PATH:-
(1) WE CAN SEND YOU THE DHL AS WE ALREADY TOLD YOU ALONG WITH THE DRAFT OF 10%TO START THE WORK WITH AS THE DIRECTOR REACHES YOU.
(2) WE CAN OFFER YOU MOST WELLKNOWN GROUPS OF INDIA LIKE AMBANI, GOENKA. GODREJ AND MANY OTHERS IF YOU THINK THAT YOU HAVE DOUBT OF DEALING WITH BISWAS COMPANY, AND THIS COMPANIES CAN PROVIDE YOU FUNDS AS WELL AS PROOF ON THE FIRST MEETING WHICH BISWAS GROUP IS INCAPABLE OF AT THIS MOMENT.
(3) WE CAN OFFER YOU A COMPENSATION OF 50%OF THE TOTAL AMOUNT OF INVESTMENT WITHIN SEVEN DAYS AS CMPENSATION AND YOU FIND SOME ONE ELSE AS INVESTOR BECAUSE I THINK THIS IS THE FOURTH TIME BISWAS FAMILY ARE NOT CAPABLE OF KEEPING THEIR COMMITMENT, AND, I BELIEVE TO YOU PEOPLE BUSINESS

IS MORE IMPORTANT THAN ANYTHING AS IT SHOULD BE BUT TO BISWAS FAMILY THEY THINK LIFE IS MORE IMPORTANT THAN ANYTHING WELL I APOLOGISE FOR THEIR THJOUGHT I KNOW THIS FEELINGS HAS NO MEANING IN TODAYS WORLD WHICH THEY ARE NOT AWARE OFF AND THIS IS WHY BEING WEALTHY THEY ARE AWAY FROM LIMELIGHT OF THE WORLD.

SO AS A LAWYER I LEAVE THIS DECISION TO YOU AS WHICH ONE YOU WILL CHOOSE BECAUSE I KNOW THE FAILING OF COMMITMENT IS VERY BAD AND IT EFFECT THE REPUTATION AS I ALSO KNOW THE SITUTATION THAT MAKE THEM DO SO WAS NOT IN THEIR CONTROL BUT STILL AS A LAWYER IN GENERAL I DONT WANT THAT YOU PEOPLE SUFFER FOR THIS SO I SUGGEST YOU THE THREEWAYS AND IN MY OPINION IF YOU TAKE THE LAST WAY YOU WILL BE SAVED FROM THIS DELAYS.

WELL I WILL WAITE FOR YOUR REPLY BY TOMORROW IF YOU REPLY ME AS WHICH ONE YOU CHOOSE I WILL SEND YOU THE AMOUNT AS PER YOUR SUGGESTION WELL FOR YOUR INFORMATION LET ME TELL YOU THAT THEY ARE TRANSFERING IS ABOUT TO GET COMPLETE BY MONDAY TO ROYAL

Funds Transfer #2 (it was supposed to have been in Toronto May 25)

CANADIAN BANK SO IF YOU CHOOSE THE THIRD ONE IT WONT TAKE MUCH TIME TO GIVE YOU THE MONEY AND ALSO THEY WILL GET THEIR LICENCE WORKABLE 0N 16TH OF JUNE AFTER WHICH IF YOU DECIDE TO DEAL WITH THEM THEN THEY WILL FLY FROM HERE ON 17TH OR 19TH OF JUNE IN BRITISH AIRWAYS TO TORONTO VIA LONDON WHERE THEY WILL MEET THE CLIENTS AS PER THEIR PLANS BUT IN THE MEANTIME AS A LAWYER THE ABOVE MENTIONED POINTS ARE MY SUUGESSION TO AGREE OR DISAGREE IS COMPLETELY YOUR DECISION.

WILL WAIT FOR YOUR REPLY AND DECISION BY TOMORROW TO WORK FASTER.

WITH BEST REGARDS

ANIL MITRA

(M.COM LAW)

As much as I had regret for the death of Niraj's wife, the inability to get my documents to Anamika by fax was causing me to die an inch at a time. If it wasn't power outages, it was burnt out cables, the solution of which would take hours and even days. At 1:27:40 AM EDT, I contacted Anamika

Dear Anamika
Once again I've tried to fax you a one page revision of the 7 pages I sent you on Monday and once again I've been told to fax another day—because the fax is not working.

This is the same document I sent you via email in html.

I am very distressed at the delay in getting this to you and hope it does not prevent me from receiving the DHL package you plan to send to the clients.

Please advise what to do. When to try to send this again, etc.

Would also appreciate if you can tell me when the itinerary will arrive, etc.

I appreciate your assistance and look forward to a very successful and profitable relationship.
Sincerely, Vincent Panettiere

I also responded to Anil Mitra, Anamika's Solicitor later that morning

To: Anil Mitra
From: Vincent Panettiere—Thistle Productions, Inc.

Thank you for your email.

1. PERSONAL—I am saddened to learn of the death of Niraj Biswas' wife and share the Biswas' belief that "life is more important than anything." While I cannot directly experience his pain, I know how I would feel if my wife—God forbid—should die suddenly. Under such circumstances all else must become secondary. Please express my profound sorrow to Niraj, Anamika and the entire group.

During my brief experience dealing with Anamika, Somnath and now you I have been constantly reminded of your honesty and openness. While delay is always frustrating—under the variety of circumstances the Biswas family has experienced in the last few weeks, the delay is understandable. What is amazing is how the family continues to carry on despite such adversity—from Anamika's father's illness to Korea and now Niraj's wife.

I appreciate and accept the sincere apology in your email, but considering the family's troubles, it is not necessary.

I will be proud to be associated with such a resilient and honest family.

2. BUSINESS—I accept offer #1. Please send me the DHL package along with the draft of 10% so that I can begin work before the Directors meet with me in Los Angeles. As you know, my proposal is for $28.5 million to produce a series of feature films. Should you prefer, you can wire the funds into my account with Bank of America. In that case please advise and I will send you banking coordinates.

I am pleased the directors still plan to visit Toronto in mid June. Please advise if they will also visit Los Angeles, where I live, and on what date. If not please advise where and when I can meet the directors.

I look forward to meeting you, Anamika and all the directors. And, most especially I look forward to a long, cordial and profitable business relationship. God bless you all.

Sincerely,
Vincent Panettiere
Thistle Productions, Inc.

My response to Anil Mitra was heartfelt and sincere. It did not differ from the reactions of the other clients. Who couldn't be moved, particularly when it seemed like there was a Job-like quality to the calamities befalling the Biswas family. Months later we would feel _we_ were jobbed more than _they_ were Job.

Shockingly, Larry's response to Anil Mitra did not contain one word of sympathy or condolence. I accept that everyone handles death differently and has dissimilar standards of empathy, but his callous disregard and ignorance of basic human courtesy made me even more determined to put distance between us while strengthening my relationship with Anamika. From that point I would exploit Larry for whatever limited useful information he had to offer, but not confide in him.

Another change that occurred at this time involved various clients interacting with each other more frequently while purposely bypassing the ineffective gatekeepers, Larry and Chris. A complete break was nearly three months away.

Larry claimed that Anil Mitra was the son of the Director of the Industry Trade and Commerce of India. However, he never called India to verify his claim. Instead he called one of the clients who had some contacts in India "who says he knows the Biswas's, confirmes for us they are REAL PLAYERS but to what extent we don't know yet, but REAL PLAYERS none the less." That's like saying Harry Jones of Parsippany, N.J must be related to Jerry Jones, who owns the Dallas Cowboys, based on finding Harry in front of a TV set some Sunday in October!

June 16

Larry's next pronunciamento at 3:42:14 PM EDT referred to the aforementioned client providing Larry with the name Bose & Mitra, a law firm in Calcutta, along with address, phone/fax numbers, web URL and email address. "Recommend you, call these people direct," the client appended to the information. Rather than make the call (lack of funds prevented it we learned later) Larry concluded the information

> "... *confirms beyond any show of doubt so far anyways that the Biswas lawyers are conversing to us FROM A CONFIRMED LAW OFFICE IN INDIA ...*"

This is not something I can easily make up.

> "... *if this is true then i think this has an excellent chance of turning all very real ... very very soon ... if its not real at least we'll get some form of capital as compensation. If they are penniless fools playing us for a bunch of suckers, then we cant get anything from them.*

> "*I happen to think they are exactly who we found some very hard working very wealthy highly talented East Indians and Associates who indeed are seeking serious out of country investments....*

> "... *payday is only 8 or 9 days away or sooner we are going to know about it really soon.*

FUNDING DATE #19–20—JUNE 24-25, 2003

"so far i have $225.0 mil in commissions coming and $10,000,000,000.00 (Billion they say) and within 2 weeks say $500.0 mil minimum should be in my bank account.

I responded to Anil, (10:54:07 AM EDT) not knowing who he was, as a matter of course—determined to take each step down the garden path until Nirvana came into focus.

To: Anil Mitra
From: Vincent Panettiere—Thistle Productions, Inc.

I hope by now you've received my reply to your email of last week and my intention of accepting a 10% advance from the Biswas investment group.

Would you kindly advise me of next steps. Specifically:

1. Are the directors still scheduled to arrive in Toronto by the 19th of this week?
2. Will they be travelling to Los Angeles? On what date?
3. When might I anticipate receiving the 10% advance?
4. In what form would the advance be sent—i.e. by wire or bank check?

I realize the entire family must still be in mourning and don't mean to be offensive by the above.

However, for planning purposes I'd appreciate some indication to the above.

Thank you for your assistance.
Sincerely,
Vincent Panettiere

To which he replied:

June 17

HELLO SIR
WELL AS PER YOUR QUESTIONS I ANSWER HERE, WELL THANKS FOR REPLYING TOO YOU WILL RECIEVETHE THINGS WITHIN A SHORT TIME BUT YOU WILL RECIEVETHE DRAFT NUMBER BY TOMORROW

EVENING OF OUR TIME OF 10% ALONG WITH THE DHL TRACKING NUMBER. WELL AS PER YOUR QUIRIES THE

Draft/Tracking Number Date #1—June 18

DIRECTORS ARRIVAL IS NOT YET BEEN CONFIRMED SO YOU ALSO HAD THIRD OPTION LEFT TO YOU IF U CHOOSE IT THEN LET US KNOW BECAUSE WE FEEL BESINES CANNOT STOP FOR ANYTHING AND BUSINES MEANS PROCEED NOT RETREAT SO IF U CHOOSE NO 3 OPTION THEN ALSO WE WILL BE APPRECIATED AND SEND YOU THE DETAILS BY TOMORROW.
ONCE AGAIN THANKS FOR THE COOPERATION
WITH BEST REGARDS
ANIL

Instead of wiring the funds into our accounts each of us would be receiving a bank draft (check) via the DHL courier, meaning I could deposit that check in my account after the two to three days it would take a courier to reach Los Angeles from Calcutta. While I knew wiring was instantaneous, I rationalized it might cost Anamika less to send a check by courier.

I expressed my pleasure to Anil at 2:34:33 AM EDT

To: Anil Mitra
From: Vincent Panettiere—Thistle Productions

Thank you for your reply. I look forward to receiving the draft number by tomorrow evening for the 10% advance along with the DHL tracking number.

You indicated I have the choice to take the third option.

It was my understanding that the Group liked my business plan and wanted to fund the entire proposal of $28.5 million. My intent has been and continues to be a desire to establish a long term business relationship with the Biswas Group.

I realize there have been delays and do not blame anyone with the Group for the delay. The advance is very generous and much appreciated. I hope the Biswas Group will fund the entire project.

Can you advise me of the following:

1. If I take the 10% will the remainder be funded?
2. Over what time period will it be funded?
3. Will I meet with the directors before the remainder is funded?

Thank you for your assistance. I look forward to your reply.

Vincent

Larry relayed an email he received from Anil, who he identified as a "BON A FIED Lawyer" at 12:37 EST.

> HELLO LARRY
> WELL WE ARE PLEASED TO HEAR FROM YOU.
>
> WELL I GURENTEE YOU THAT WITHIN SEVEN DAYS YOU WILL RECEIVE YOUR FUNDS AND ALSO CHRIS WILL RECEIVE HIS COMMSSION ON FULL, WELL BOTH OF YOU WILL RECEIVE FORM OF DRAFT WITHIN SEVEN DAYS AND ITS ENTIRE INSTRUCTION ALONG WITH DRAFT NUMBER AND DHL TRACKING NUMBER WILL BE DELIVER TO YOU BY EMAIL ON TOMORROW EARLY IN THE MORNING.
>
> PLEASE BE ASSURED THAT YOU WILL RECEIVE AND WE WILL NOT DIS HEARTEN YOU AS YOU HAD GIVEN US A VERY GOOD SUPPORT
>
> ONE MORE THING ANAMIKA TOLD THAT WILL YOU PLEASE DELIVER THE LETTER TO ALL THE CLIENTS WHO HAVE NOT RECIEVED THE OFFERS YET.
>
> BECAUSE I AM MOVING AWAY FROM TOWN FOR TWO DAYS I WILL BE BACK ON WEDNESDAY OF MY TIME AND THEN WE WILL DISCUSS IN THE MEAN TIME IF YOU DO THAT FOR US IT WILL HELP US A LOT.
>
> ONCE AGAIN WE THANKS ALL THREE OF YOU FOR YOUR COOPERATION AND PATIENCE.
> WITH BEST REGARDS—ANIL

Anil confirmed to me and then to Larry that the funding date—the date when we would actually receive our funds—would be by June 24.

June 19

Two days later, while Larry was wondering "… if she is actually going through with this affair …" I received an encouraging email from Anamika which underscored the value of direct communication. THIS TIME IT IS LAST was the subject of her email at 9:59:15 AM EDT

RESPECTED SIR,
THIS IS THE ULTIMATE MAILS THAT REACHING YOU BEFORE THE CLOSING OF THE DEALS AFTER WHICH YOU WILL RECIEVE THE ULTIMATE CONFIRMATION OVER FAX ABOUT DRAFTS NUMBERS & DHL TRACKING NUMBERS.

Draft/Tracking Number Date #2—sometime between June 19 and June 24

WE AS A INVESTOR CANNOT REACH TO YOUR DESTINATION DUE SOME PERSONNAL PROBLEMS AND THIS DELAY TOOK TIME PERIOD OF MORE THAN 2MONTHS AND SO WE ARE HELPLESS AND FOWARD-ING YOU OUR ULTIMATE CHOICE OF GIVING YOUR COMPANY 50% OF THE TOTAL INVESTMENT YOU ASKED FOR YOUR PROJECT WHICH I THINK AT THIS STAGE WILL SAVE YOUR TIME AND ALSO WILL SAVE YOUR COMPANY AS YOU HAD WASTED MUCH OF YOUR PRECIOUS TIME FOR US.
WELL SIR WE AFTER A LONG DISCUSSION WITH OUR SOLICITER AND BANKS AND ALSO FROM RBI (RESERVE BANK OF INDIA) FROM WHERE WE GOT OUR LICENCE WE CONCLUDED THAT WE WILL SEND YOU THE DRAFT 50% OF THE TOTAL AMOUNT THAT IS STATED IN THE PROJECT BY 23rd OF JUNE (MONDAY) 2003 WE TOOK THIS TIME FOR OUR BANK TO CALCULATE THE AMOUNT AND CONVERT IT AND MAKE THE DRAFTS.
WE ONCE AGAIN APOLOGISE AS WE TOLD PREVIOUSLY WE WILLSEND YOU WITHIN SEVENDAYS BUT WE COULDNT AS OUR MEETING WITH RBI CANNOT ABLE TO HAPPEN AND SINCE FROM THIS INVESTOR LICENCE WE WERE DEALING FIRST TIME WE HAD TO WAIT FOR THERE PERMISSION.
WELL I AGAIN APOLOGISE IF ANYONE COULDNT FOUND MY MAIL AS PER THEIR CHOICE PLEASE DONT MIND AFTER RECIEVING THIS

AMOUNTS IF YOU WANT TO ENGAGE WITH US WITH A FRESH CON-
TRACT WHICH WILL NOT HAVE A SINGLE LINE WITH THIS PAST YOU
ARE WELCOME TO DO SO. AND ALSO IF ANYONE DIDNT RECIEVE
THE PREVIOUS EMAILS FROM US WE ALSO REGREAT FOR THAT AND
HOPE THAT THIS MAIL WILL RELIEF U A LOT AND HELP TO SAVE
YOUR COMPANY.
LAST OF ALL WE AGAIN REGREAT TO WHAT LOSE WE CAUSE YOU FOR
OUR DELAYS AND OFFICIAL PROBLEMS WE HOPE THAT WITH TIME
YOU WILL FORGIVE US.
WITH BEST REGARDS
ON BEHALF OF ENTIRE MEMBERS OF OUR COMPANY
THIS IS ANAMIKABISWAS

Incredibly, Anamika was going to provide me with fifty percent of the
investment I'd requested because she and the Biswas Group had not kept their
word! At the core was her apology, a sense of empathy for discomfort the delay
caused the clients, as well an underlying morality which was foreign to us.

I wasted no time in responding to Anamika at 10:11:45 AM EDT

Dear Anamika
Thank you for your e-mail. I accept your 50% offer and look forward to receiving the DHL and draft information.

I regret your unfortunate troubles and hope we can work together in the
future. Nevertheless, I will keep you updated on how your funds are used.

Thank you for your honesty and courtesy.

I sent Larry a copy of Anamika's letter, which he used to inform the clients.
When the DHL tracking and bank draft numbers were not forthcoming within
four days of Anamika's email to me, the clients began to grumble.

June 23

One client wrote "… today is Monday the 23rd and my group is still waiting for
the DHL #, banking draft etc. please update us promptly as I need to let my
group know …"

Just as clients' impatience and anxiety whipped itself into a stampede,
Anamika fired a shot that stopped all movement. In an email to one of the
clients she stated that she could not send any funds to any clients "till 65 days

get completed." This meant that clients would get funded sixty five days after they made their initial deal with Anamika, a requirement that no one had anticipated, even if they were fully versed in the arcane workings of the Reserve Bank of India.

DELAY #8—65 day waiting period

Later on June 23rd, Larry advised Anamika that the clients "will not allow this to go further without serious proof of reality ... they are really upset today after not getting a fax like was promised."

I wanted this funding deal to be true and completed as much as Larry or anyone in the group. In the past every delay had a plausible explanation. I expected another would exist to support the 65 day rule. As we all remained supplicants with our hands out, I felt tact, humility and patience would be more effective than threats. I continued trying to establish lines of communication with Anamika via email at 10:16:33 AM EDT.

Dear Anamika
I did not receive a fax from you last night.

I hope there was nothing seriously wrong and that you and your family are well. Please advise when you might send out the fax again.

Additionally, if it is easier, you can send the information to this email address.

Which was followed at 1:10:27 PM EDT by

Dear Anamika:
I've been advised that the RBI requires the passage of 65 days from the date of the contract, before an investment draft can be issued.

If that is correct, I calculate that the 65th day from the date (April 30, 2003) I sent you the contract will be July 4.

Please advise if that date is verified in your records.

If we all were playing an actual game of poker with Anamika, instead of a virtual one, we could describe her next email as "see you and raise you."

June 24—3:42:13 AM Eastern Daylight Time

RESPECTED SIR
Well thanks for replying, well there is something that has to be cleared by you as early as possible, well as you know that we are closing the deals with your company as a investor, because we are not able to reach there on time and you people are also ina big hurry. so we thought that we will pay you people 50%of the total investment you asked for the company.
Well so you can understand that we made agood lose which is good for nothing, so in doing so as a investor and also since it was my first group of ventures after i got my licence I had to obey the RBI rules, since i dont know all the rules by heart I am facing the problems, well generally as company you people had to wait for three months because that is the time of negotiation the both company should get, but i understood that none of you will wait, and so since you are unable to do so then you have to wait for 65 days to get your contract. As i am much aware that from the begining our deals didnt run in a right track because we had a very tittle time to communicate as per situttation of indianeconomy and also due to our personnal problems we had verymuch littletime to cummunicate with each other so now it is your choice as we had made the commitment to send you the funds we will send you also i will fax you the same with the photocopy of the drafts on tomorrow but we cant send you till 65days get completed.
Hope that you as acompany will understand us and your promt anticepation is earnestly soliciated. As you can understand that 3months for a company who is making this great investment is very short but we take entire thing as our fault but still we keep infront of you our problem which is last barrier on the path of closing the deals i hope that you people will cooperate with us.

FUNDING DATE #21 & 22—JUNE 30-JULY 2

On the other hand we also found that most of your 65days are not been completed yet it will be in month of July so we also offering you that we can pay you full 100% in a negotiation date with you in around 30th of June to 2nd of July if you promise to put A.B. EXPORTS IN A FULL PUBLICITY WITHIN 48HRS AND ALSO ANAMIKA BISWAS NOT BISWAS COMPANY if you do so both you and i will be in a profit that in doing my publicity your fund will reach you more earlier and RBI won't able to put any barrier because after publicity no one can force us to delay that is what you will get profit and my profit is that i will geta wide range of market away from my family ties. Well this is my first offer to you as a client and hope that you will acept it and give me the chance to serve you in a right time and ina proper situation.

If you can do so i will grateful as i you need the funds to run the business without a delay well i also need investment project otherthan your company to get my licence running.

Hope that you will agree with this GIVE AND TAKE POLICY AS, THIS IS THE FIRST TIME I AM ASKING SOMETHING IN RETURN OF MY INVESTMENT WHICH I WILL MAKE IN YOUR COMPANY WITHOUT ASKING ANYRETURN

WITH BEST REGARDS

ANAMIKA BISWAS.

DELAY #9—Anamika Needs Publicity

Synthesized, Anamika wanted me and the rest of the clients to create publicity for her and her cmpany within 48 hours! For that assistance we'd receive 100% of the funds we requested and would not have to wait the full 65 days. She also suggested she would not want "any return"!

Her request mirrored the relationship with Anamika during the previous two months. On the surface it was a simple, but surprising task. There was great motivation—one hundred percent funding without any return. Yet, it would be difficult to accomplish in order to reach the June 30-July 2 time frame—less than six days away, including the weekend.

Based on the new 65-day waiting period, with my project accepted on May 5th, I was scheduled to be funded on July 10. Still, I was not too keen on overturning heaven and earth to comply with the bauble she held out. After two months, which I admit is not a very long time, of more than twenty funding dates that never materialized—not to mention various delays, I was not prepared to go any further and made that clear in my email to her.

> "… I promise to give full publicity to A.B. Exports and Anamika Biswas. Naturally, this publicity will not occur until after Thistle Productions is funded. You and your company will be fully recognized in the press announcements as the funder of Thistle Productions, Inc.…"

Anamika's response was off the mark and though addressed only to me seemed to be written for others in the group thereby tarring me with the same brush.

... AS FAR AS I KNOW I DIDNT ASK ANYTHING FROM YOU ABSERD I THOUGHT AS PER YOUR PROJECT YOU SHOULD HAVE SOME PUBLICITY BUT AS PER YOUR COMMENT I FOUND THAT YOUR DEAL WILL HAVE NO PUBLICITY FOR MY SELF ATLEAST SO THANK YOU. YOU WILL RECEIVE THE CLOSURE AMOUNT (WHICH IS 50% OF THE TOTAL INVESTMENT) ON 3RD JULY 2003 IN THIS DATE IT WILL REACH YOU....

FUNDING DATE #23—JULY 3

I ALSO NEED PUBLICITY WELL IT'S MY BAD LUCK THAT I CANNOT GET IT.

Geez! I'd known first hand Italian mother guilt. Now I was faced with third-world-woman guilt. What could it hurt? I'd written tons of press releases during the years when I was in the public relations business representing some Fortune 500 clients as well as television series and movies. So, I wrote one more

June 25

FOR IMMEDIATE RELEASE
THISTLE PRODUCTIONS ANNOUNCES
JOINT VENTURE WITH A.B. EXPORTS OF KOLKATA

Los Angeles, June 25, 2003—Thistle Productions, Inc., the feature film production company established by former literary agent Vincent Panettiere, today announced it had entered into a joint venture with Anamika Biswas and her company A.B. Exports of Kolkata.

"We are very pleased to be associated with Ms. Biswas," Panettiere said "and look forward to a very successful relationship."

Additionally, Thistle also revealed the first three films it will produce and co-produce. Ms. Biswas will serve as Executive Producer of all three films.

"The Agenda", a thriller written by David Cahill and Nicholas Ellis, will be directed by Mario Di Leo, who has directed episodes of such series as "Miami Vice", "Xena" "Babylon 5", "The Untouchables," etc. Di Leo also directed the feature film "The Final Alliance" starring David Hasselhoff.

The second film to be produced by Thistle will be a sexy romantic comedy "The Big Sizzle" written by Debbie Desideri and to be directed by UCLA grad Cameron Spencer.

Thistle will co-produce "The Caress" from the Liam O'Flaherty short story, with Irish writer/director Maurice O'Callaghan who has adapted the story and will direct. Picture will be shot in the rugged Aran Islands. O' Callaghan's previous film "Broken Harvest" was critically acclaimed internationally.

Contact: Vincent Panettiere (323) XXX-XXXX; thistleprods@net

Her response was:

"I AM REALLY GRATEFUL TO WHAT YOU HAVE DONE FOR ME PLEASE RELEASE THIS PUBLICLY SO THAT BARRIER GET REMOVED AS EARL AS POSSIBLE.
WITH BEST REGARDS
ANAMIKA BISWAS

My first inclination was to send the release to the entertainment industry trades—"Variety", "Hollywood Reporter," "Film Daily", etc. After I advised her where the first batch of releases were sent, she reminded me that she had as keen a nose for "ink" as anyone else in the business.

HELLO SIR
TOME WORK IS ALWAYS FIRST NOW WHEN I AM WRITING THIS LETTER TO YOU MY BODY TEMPERTURE IS MORE THAN 200DEGREE F, WELL SIR AFETR IT GET RELEASED AND I HOPE IT WILL ALSO GET RELEASED IN INDIAN PAPERS LIKE TELEGRAPH, STATEMAN, ECONOMISTIMES THEN OUR WORK WILL BE MORE USEFUL BUT YOU KNOW BETTER THAN ME HOW WILL IT MAKE MORE USE FUL.
I AM ALWAYS SNOBISH INFRONT OF YOU.
WITH BEST REGARDS
ANAMIKA BISWAS

DELAY #10—fever

It may seem callous to disregard someone's illness. Her excuses were wearing thin. Besides, if she had such a frail constitution, she was better off spending her fortune going for the cure in a Swiss clinic. Her temperature most likely was twenty degrees Celsius, with all the typos and misspellings I felt like I was learning a whole new language. Yet she knew what she wanted—publicity in The Telegraph, Statesman and Economic Times. The first two were local Kolkata papers and the last a national one.

When she learned that I had contacted a broader list she wrote back "… THANKS FOR WHAT YOU ARE DOING FOR ME. I WILL TRY EVERY-THING AND ANYTHING I CAN DO FOR YOU IN ANYWAYS TIL I LIVE. The words were mangled, but the sentiment clear.

I reminded her on June 25th that I was looking forward to getting the DHL tracking and bank draft numbers. A gentle nudge to remind her that I did my part, now it was up to her.

Her reply was "WELL I AM ALSO LOOKING TO GIVE YOU AT LEAST A VERY CHARMING AND FRUITFUL RETURN OF EFFORT YOU HAVE GIVEN FOR ME IN A VERY SHORT SPAN. HOPE I AM NOT DISSAP-POINTING YOU.

While I was trying to figure out how to pitch a story half way around the world to reporters in an unfamiliar culture regarding two people who were not international celebrities, nor household names, Larry was bombarding the clients with more effluvia—patronizing, demanding and on a human level down right disrespectful.

June 27

Larry forwarded the most recent email response from Anamika

WELL AS I ALREADY CONVEYED PREVIOUSLY THAT I WILL SEND YOU THE DRAFTS BUT WHEN I TALKED TO MY BANK THEY SAID THAT AFTER 65 DAYS GETS COMPLETED THE DRAFT WILL BE DEAPTACHED FROM HERE WHICH WILL TAKE 72HRS AS MINIMAL TIME AND THEN 15 DAYS FOR ENCASHMENT OF THE AMOUNT TOTAL.

FUNDING DATE #24 & 25—JULY 11-14

THIS ENTIRE DEALS WILL TAKE 18 DAYS, WHICH NOT ONLY YOU MAY HAD PROBLEM BUT FOR MYSELF I HAD A PROBLEM THAT IS I WILL BE MAKING A TRIP TO LAS VEGAS FOR VACATION WITH ME FRIENDS WHICH ILL GET POSPONED IF I CHOOSE THE DRAFT METHOD TO SEND YOU FUND, SO I ERNESTLY REQUEST YOU TO TAKE THE SWIFT CODE OPTION.

BELOW I STATE MY ACCOUNT DETAILS WHERE THE FUNDS WILL BE REMITTED AS YOUR 65 DAYS COMES CLOSURE.

NAME—MISS ANAMIKA BISWAS
ACCOUNT NO—S/B 176401
BANK—UNITED BANK OF INDIA
SWIFT CODE—UTB11NBBOVE

THIS PROCESS WILL TAKE 48 HRS AS REMITTENCE TIME.
WITH BEST REGARDS
ANAMIKA BISWAS

Meanwhile, the publicity machine was humming away. I finally reached the Metro Editor of The Telegraph, Sumit Das Gupta. He was a very enterprising journalist and immediately put me in touch with Nisha Lahiri. Within less than an hour they were prepared to interview Anamika in her home. Then Rahul Das of the Statesman agreed and I felt confident that I would meet Anamika's publicity deadline, which would remove any RBI barriers and lead to my receiving one hundred percent of the funds I requested.

The articles appeared in rapid succession: **June 30**—Screendaily.com; **July 1**—The Telegraph; **July 4**—IndiaWest, a weekly paper for the Indian community in California; **July 7**—Variety.com; **July 8**—Daily Variety; **July 19**—The Times of India; **July 21**—The Weekly Voice, the paper for the Indian community in Toronto and Ontario.

While The Statesman interviewed Anamika they chose not to run the story because The Telegraph story came out first and beat them to the streets.

As June ended I believed I had developed a trusting working relationship with Anamika that would place me toward the front of the line when funds would be dispersed.

Who knew?

JUNE SCORE CARD   **TOTALS**

		TOTALS
Funding Dates	8 (next funding date July 14)	25
Delays	7 (hard work, death, fever, etc.)	10
Funds Transfer Date	1	2
Draft/Tracking Numbers Sent	2	NA
Holidays	0	2

The Telegraph
calcutta, india

| Tuesday, July 01, 2003 |

Front Page > Story

IN TODAY'S PAPER

Front Page
Nation
Calcutta
Bengal
Opinion
International
Business
Sport
At Leisure

CITY NEWSLINES

Choose Region ▾

ARCHIVES

Since 1st March, 1999

THE TELEGRAPH

- About Us
- Advertise
- Feedback
- Contact Us

email this page   Print this page

To Hollywood, all alone
- Girl breaks family barrier, signs up to produce big-ticket films
NISHA LAHIRI

Anamika in her office. Picture by Aranya Sen

Calcutta, June 30: Actor Jeet is the *Champion* in the film of the same name, now playing at Radha cinema. But it's one of the daughters of the Biswas family, owners of the Hatibagan movie hall, who is busy scripting a story that is the stuff of celluloid dreams.

It's not in Tollywood or Bollywood where Anamika Biswas from Shyambazar is making a splash, but in Hollywood. She's been all the way to Los Angeles, from her conservative Jatindra Mohan Avenue home, but it's still the approval of the men in her family that she's keen to achieve as a businesswoman.

"They consider a working woman as an embarrassment, because it means the family needs the money. My father was furious when I started my own enterprise, and still threatens to cancel my licence if anything goes wrong."

She's only 24, but age is no obstacle to ambition for Anamika. This young woman has made it from Calcutta to California on her own steam. From textiles, marble and granite exports to executive producer of Hollywood films, she has come a long way, but has set a lot more goals to achieve.

"I just love doing business," she smiles, seated behind the massive desk in her home, which also doubles as her office. At the moment, apart from running the export side of her company, Anamika has her hands full with Hollywood offers. Having signed up with the LA-based Thistle Productions for a Rs 80-crore investment, she's now set to co-produce three films. On the table is another partnership, with the LA-based Silvertouch Pictures Ltd, on a film called *Gangster Wives*, and she's in talks with Timber Wolf Productions to make American television serials.

The first of the Thistle Productions projects is *The Agenda*, a thriller, to be directed by Mario Di Leo, the director of television serials like *Xena* and *Miami Vice*. *The Big Sizzle* is a romantic comedy, and *The Caress*, written and to be directed by Maurice 'Callaghan, of *Broken Harvest* fame, will be shot in Ireland with Peter 'Toole playing a "significant role" in the film. All three are slated for an end-2004 release.

The owner of AB Exports started off her company as an 18-year-old, in her first year as a B.Com student at Asutosh College, despite many an argument with her father, a firm believer in the woman's place at home. But with inspiration from her mother, Anamika took the plunge and hasn't looked back. Despite continuing resistance ("I'm not even allowed to roll down the windows of the car when we go on family drives"), she's travelled from Singapore to Toronto to establish her identity in the industry.

Anamika is not ready to buckle under the marriage pressure either, with business as her lone love in life. Building business relations is her one true passion. "Ever since I was a child, setting up my own company was my dream. After fighting with my father for years, I finally went ahead with it. But I didn't think it would last this long, let alone come such a long way, where I now earn Rs 3 crore a year."

It was one such relationship with a client that turned into a golden opportunity two years ago. Vincent Panettiere of Thistle Productions, a former executive with Twentieth Century Fox, sent her a proposal and she accepted. He wanted to branch out in collaborations in other countries and she wanted to shift base from exports, because "export will become *daal bhaat* in India soon, so I want to try something different".

Six months in the making, and the deal is almost sealed. She's off to Las Vegas in July, with father Asit in tow to "check things out", for tête-à-têtes with all her prospective partners. That's not all. She's ready to invest in a 97-acre studio that Thistle wants to build in California, and also has proposals from Riviera Resorts in Malta to invest in a hotel and spa complex on the island of Gozo.

So, what's next on her to-do list? Well, to make inroads into the Indian film industry, but not on her family's name — the owners of Radha Cinema and Co. "No one here has offered me anything so far, but I am really keen. I have started out on the top, in Hollywood, but I need strong roots, in the Indian film industry." As for help on that score, "I'd love to," says Panettiere, speaking from LA. "I have watched Indian films earlier, my favourite being *Bandit Queen*, and I really want to make an Indian film, in India. And I am open to scripts from writers there. All they have to do is get in touch."

email this page   Print this page

This article is reprinted with permission of The Telegraph, Calcutta

6. JULY, 2003

SOME GET CONTRACTS

July began with optimism, even though, up to then, we had received twenty five unfulfilled funding dates. Surely, this would be the month. We only had to wait another two weeks until July 14, which would be a piece of cake as we had survived the last eight. We could do the time standing on our heads; spoken like a bunch of veteran convicts, which psychologically we were becoming.

Jailed by our convictions, it was more comfortable being inside with our beliefs than outside with reality.

Some might say that denial is also a river in India, as well as Egypt, but for us it was more a trust in the positive, life affirming aspects of hope. We were actively engaging in the virtues of faith, hope and patience while awaiting Anamika's charity.

However, I continued to maintain constant communication with Anamika, under the "trust but verify" philosophy. My latest email inquired about her planned, as rumors had it, trip to Las Vegas. In July! Don't ask.

July 1—9:51PM EDT

Dear Anamika
I've been thinking about your planned trip to Las Vegas.

1. Do you plan to be in Las Vegas July 12-25?
If the date has changed, please let me know new date.

2. Do you know what hotel you will be staying in?
If you are staying with family/friends do you have a number where you can be reached.

3. Are the directors coming to Las Vegas, too?

4. Do I need to I meet with them?
If they are available I would like to meet with them.

5. I can come to Las Vegas the week of July 21.
Please select a date when we can meet.

I received an email early on July 2nd which buttressed my belief and answered my query.

July 2—2:08:47AM EDT

HELLO SIR
AS I ALREADY SAID YOU EARLIER THAT I AM GOING TO DO BUSINES
WITH YOU ALL ALONE, WELL I AM COMING WITH MY PAPENTS AND
DATES ARE STILL SAME IT HAS NOT YET BEEN CHANGED, I WILL LET
YOU KNOW THE HOTEL IN WHICH I WILL STAY BUT FIRST LET ME
TRANSFER THE FUND ON 5TH OF JULY TO YOU THEN I WILL COME.
WITH BEST REGARDS
ANAMIKA BISWAS

FUNDING DATE #26—JULY 5, 2003

At the time, I didn't chart the various dates from Anamika's email, but blithely
went from email to email in the belief that when a person tells you something
there is every reason to take them at their word. Inherent in this belief is awareness and acceptance that things change and life is full of accidental twists and
turns which need not be assigned a value judgment.

I also was not immune to flattery. She had singled me out. Was going to do
business with me "alone". No doubt she had seen me, through my email, as a
person of character and accomplishment. Heady stuff.

No wonder when she advised she would "transfer the fund on 5th of July",
shortening the previous time by nine days, I did not think the change was worthy of microscopic examination and simply prepared to receive the funds.

I replied graciously with appreciation for the new funding date and looked
forward to meeting her in Las Vegas. The next morning Anamika made us
aware of life in India during monsoon season.

July 3—1:18:56 AM EDT

HELLO SIR
… I CANNOT RESPOND YOU YESTERDAY EVENING AS I HAD WATER
LOGING ALL OVER HERE FOR HEAVY SHOWER FOR THREEHOURS
CONTI NOIUSLY.

DELAY # 11—Heavy rain and flooding

Had we been Buddhist monks, we would have spent the days by our prayer
wheels patiently Omming the time away.

Unfortunately, some in the group were the kind of Homo sapiens who
could not contain their childish impulses to foul up a straight line.

By July 3rd Larry was back to begging, exhibiting a lack of dignity no matter his dire circumstances. No awareness of his position within the group or his relationship to Anamika.

> *"… we need to have some operating capital very very soon or we may not all be able to hang on as long as we want to. Some of us are feeling the pinch of not having operating capital, say even 10% of our requested amounts would really help us out …"*

Larry continued to be more concerned about having Anamika prove that she and her family had the funds. Obviously, he never realized the time for proof of funds had long since passed. But, his key point was buried on page two. He told Anamika that the only time clients get upset was when "they are told they will be funded, then nothing happens."

To quote Gabby Hayes, "yer darn tootin". All the clients would agree to this central point. No one, no matter the circumstances or relationship wants to participate in a "push me/pull me" exercise. No sooner does one gear up for the fulfillment of expectation, than the bottom drops out. When this process recurs, patience stretches to the breaking point. This was a possibility Larry intimated to Anamika.

> *"… i know we need to have some results here soon or many of these clients may very well start law suits against me and chris and possible against you as well, as this is taking too long to complete for real conrete proof of funds.*
>
> *"AND ONLY proof of funds will satisfy most of them as in minimum 10% of the amounts requested transferred within a weeks time or sooner…."*

On the same day Larry was whining to Anamika, she and I exchanged thirteen emails!

Briefly, her emails advised me she:

> - would be sending me 50% of the investment amount, but if I needed more she would send it.

> - explained the reference to 80 Crore in the Telegraph article

- inquired if the article in the Weekly Voice of Toronto, slated for July 12, would run her picture.

- would be interviewed live by Tarabangla—a TV channel in Kolkata

Twice on July 3rd she was effusive in her email. "ITS MY PRIEVALAGE AND I AM HONURED THAT I AM WOKING WITH YOU" she wrote to me in one and "THANKS FOR UNDERSTANDING ME" in another. Both were such departures from her previous "strictly business" approach that I was sure my steady stream of email was having an effect.

All well and fine, but secondary to the relationship. I may not be immune to flattery, but I am not so impressed with myself that I would forget the central mission. Money. We needed to clear up a $14,250,000 discrepancy. I wrote to Anamika at 2:44:21 AM EDT

Dear Anamika
Prior to receiving your email of June 24, I was prepared to gladly and graciously accept your kind offer to fund 50%. However that email indicated you "can pay … full 100%" if I promised to put you and your company in publicity.

While I can certainly work with 50%—though it will not cover all the films in the business plan, nor the studio—I do believe your offer of 100% based on my performance changed the anticipated amount of your funding. In your email to me of June 24—the last paragraph reads as follows:

"On the other hand we also found that most of your 65days are not been completed yet it will be in month of July so we also offering you that we can pay you full 100% in a negotiation date with you in around 30th of June to 2nd of July if you promise to put A.B. EXPORTS IN A FULL PUBLICITY WITHIN 48HRS AND ALSO ANAMIKA BISWAS NOT BISWAS COMPANY if you do so both you and i will be in a profit that in doing my publicity your fund will reach you more earlier and RBI won't able to put any barrier because after publicity no one can force us to delay that is what you will get profit and my profit is that i will geta wide range of market away from my family ties. Well this is my first offer to you as a client and hope that you will accept it and give me the chance to serve you in a right time and ina proper situation.

"If you can do so i will grateful as i you need the funds to run the business without a delay well i also need investment project other than your company to get my licence running. Hope that you will agree with this GIVE AND TAKE POLICY AS, THIS IS THE FIRST TIME I AM ASKING SOMETHING IN RETURN OF MY INVESTMENT WHICH I WILL MAKE IN YOUR COMPANY WITHOUT ASKING ANY RETURN WITH BEST REGARDS ANAMIKA BISWAS."

As a result of the above, it was my understanding that if I promised to get publicity for you and A.B. Exports you would pay 100%.

Upon immediate receipt of the June 24 email, I wrote a press release, which you approved. Accordingly, over the next five days I contacted many newspapers in the U.S. and India.

You were interviewed by reporters for The Telegraph and Statesman. The Telegraph story appeared on June 30—within the June 30-July 2 window you requested—and it prominently featured publicity on you, with picture, and your company. A story in India West will be published in the July 4 edition.

As I responded faithfully and professionally to your request of June 24, and my efforts resulted in the publicity you desired within your time frame, I respectfully request the full amount of US$28.5 million.

Please let me know if this is a problem for you or if it imposes an undue burden, so then we can discuss an alternative.

Whatever the result, I remain very grateful to you and your company and look forward to a long and successful working relationship.

Her response was gratifying—3:34:51 AM EDT

HELLO SIR
I WILL SEND YOU 100% AS YOU NEEDED OR RATHER AS I COMMITTED, YOU WILL GET THIS ON 7TH OR 8TH OFJULY 2003AS I COMMITED.—ANAMIKA BISWAS

At the time I gave her high marks for keeping her word. Nevertheless, what we both didn't know at the time (who was counting) was she had provided me with

FUNDING DATES 27 & 28—JULY 7TH or 8TH, 2003

By this time, Larry's "begging" email surfaced and I wanted to preserve my hard fought direct communication with Anamika—2:59:14 PM EDT.

Dear Anamika:
I want you to know that I DO NOT agree with what Larry expressed in the email he sent you today.

As I've written to you previously—I am dealing directly with you. What I express to you, are my thoughts and needs for me and my company.

While Larry and Chris introduced me to you—and will receive a proper fee for doing so—they do not and cannot speak for me.

I have a very high opinion of you by the way you conduct business with me and I look forward to a long and successful business relationship.

In her reply of July 4th, Anamika seemed to appreciate the support.

> "... SIR I HAVE TO SAY YOU ONETHING THAT MOST OF THE CLIENT SAYING THAT LARRY IS MAILING EVERYONE AND TELLING THEM SOMETHING ABOUT ME SO DONT LISTEN TO HIM, HAVE FAITH ONME AND KEEP PATIENCE."

I assured I would "keep patience" with her and she advised me

> "... I WILL SEND YOU FUND ON 5TH SO THAT YOU GET IT ON 7TH OR 8TH IN YOUR ACCOUNT. YOU NOT AT ALL BOTHERED ME IT IS MY DUTY TO CALIFY ALL DETAILS TO YOU.

Here it is, July 4th and Anamika has informed me she will wire my funds the next day, July 5th so that I will have them in my account two to three days later! What's not to be believed?

I lost some of my exuberance when I learned from Larry that pompous Bob K had taken matters into his own hands and acted precipitously. In his mind I'm sure he considered the action was "prudent". Yet it may very well have obliterated any chance of funding the rest of us would have with Anamika.

He told Larry in his July 4th email—14:45:57–0400:

> *I sent request to the Regional Bank of India, The Bank of India and*
> *The Reserve Bank of India.*
> *This is the first response I got back.*
> *The account she sent was in the Bank of India.*
> *Nothing from them as yet.*
> *Neither from the Reserve Bank.*
> *I have sent them the information on the other person to contact.*
> *I have another broker who has connected me up with an Asian group*
> *that is funding Phase I, Phase II, Phase III and Phase IV, totaling $20*
> *billion.*

I don't think he ever stopped to think what <u>his</u> reaction would be if some-one called <u>his</u> banker to determine <u>his</u> solvency. It would take four days for the shock wave from BobK's clumsy attempt at due diligence to make its impact on the group and wobble its cohesiveness.

I was scheduled to leave July 9th for a trip to New York. As I had never been the recipient of nearly thirty million dollars before, I seriously considered can-celing the trip to deal with—who knew what? Forms to fill out. People to see. Plans to make. Not to mention the two anvils I'd have to purchase to tie around my ankles to keep my body from levitating.

Upon reflection, and considering all the funding dates we'd received, I decided to send Anamika my banking coordinates, go to New York and hope for the best. Her reaction was a complete surprise.

July 5—2:01:38 AM EDT

HELLO SIR
THANKS FOR THE REPLY YOUR EFFORT IS UNFORGETTABLE AND IF I TRY FOR MY WHOLE LIFE I CANNOT PUT THIS BURDEN DOWN FROM MY HEAD OF WHAT YOU HAVE FOR ME I AM IN DEBT TO YOU, SIR YOU WILL RECIEVE THE PAPERS ON FAX BY MONDAY 7TH JULY 2003.(CONFIRMATION SLIP)
WITH BEST REGARDS
ANAMIKA BISWAS

Confirmation Slip Date #1—July 7

Later on July 5th—8:03:58 AM EDT I received another email from Anamika

HELLO SIR
HOW ARE YOU, WELL I AM FINE, LET ME TELL YOU THAT I HAVE
DONE THE WIREING BUT IT WILL REACH YOU ON WEDNESDAY 10TH
OF JULY AND FOR

Anamika Has Wired Funds #1—July 5

FUNDING DATE 29—JULY 10th, 2003

THAT YOU WILL GET THE CONFIRMATION SLIP ON MONDAY

Confirmation Slip Date #2—July 7

While the date for receipt of the slip confirming Anamika had wired the funds
did not change, I was pleased neither did my plans to travel.

I informed Larry and Chris about Anamika's email and plans to wire funds
by July 7th.

July 7

Before anyone had received a confirmation slip or checked their bank balances,
Chris advised in email of 7:47:25 AM EDT:

> *"Well great news Anamika has wired the funds to each of you, confir-*
> *mation slips should be produced via fax on Tuesday in the US and*
> *wherever else clients are.*
> *The funds were wired on the 5th the funds then hit chase manhattan*
> *and then are transfered to the respective bank accounts of the clients.*
> *So just wait for a little longer and all this will be over.*
> *Cheers, Chris*

There was nothing to cheer about.

The next day Akansha once again wrote on behalf of Anamika. She needed
five minutes of my time she said for a long email.

July 8—8:52:55 AM EDT

HELLO SIR
WELL A VERY GOODEVENING TO YOU, WELL ON BEHALF OF ANAMIKA I AM ASKED TO WRITE A MAIL TO INFORM YOU THE INITIAL SITUTATION THAT HAS HAPPENED AFTER THE WIREING DONE ON 5TH OF JULY 2003 SATURDAY 10:45AM. SIR AS YOU WOULD BE KNOWING THAT OUR BRANCH MANAGER OF OUR BANK GOT CHANGED AND NEW BANK MANAGER HAS ARRIVED ON THE DATE OF HIS ARRIVAL THE WIRE WAS DONE,

DELAYS #12 & 13—New Bank Manager/Funds Sent to Wrong Bank

SO DUE TO LACK OF CROSSTABLE COVERSATION WE COULD NOT ABLE TO TELL HIM OUR ACTUAL PLAN OF CONDUCT. FOR WHICH AS USUAL AS FORMATED TO INDIAN BANK THE WIREING ARE USUALLY SEND TO ECONOMICAL METRO OF INDIA THAT IS BOMBAY WHICH WE NOW CALLED MUMBAI FROM WHERE IT TAKES THE HELP OF ITS COLLBORATED BANK AND GET SEND TO THE RECIEPENT BANK BUT IN OUR CASE WE DIDNT PLANNED OUT LIKED THAT OUR PLAN WAS OUR FUND FROM OUR OWNBRANCH IT WILL MOVING TO OUR NEW ACCOUNT BRANCH WHERE WE NEWLY MADE OUR ACCOUNT WHICH DETAILS IS GIVEN TO YOU WITH SWIFT CODE (UTB11NBBOVE) FROM WHICH WITHOUT SPENDING MUCH TIME IT WOULD BE REACHING YOUR ACCOUNT DIRECTLY FROM CALCUTTA ITSELF INSTEAD OF MOVING TO BOMBAY BUT OUR PLAN DIDNT WORKED OUT AND SO NOW ANAMIKA IS MOVING TO BOMBAY FROM

Anamika Travel #1—To Bombay AKA Mumbai

THERE THE FUND WILL BE RESEND TO CALCUTTA INTO HER SWIFT CODE ACCOUNT FROM WHERE IT WILL BE SEND IT TO YOU. WELL AS ANAMIKA TOLD WHAT SHE GOING TO DO BUT SHE DIDNT TOLD ME WHAT TIME IT WILL TOOK SO I LEFT THIS TO ANAMIKA AS SHE CALLED ME AND ALSO TOLD THAT SHE TALKED TO JACK, KEVIN AND KHOA FOR THIS AND HER LINE GOT CUT AS SHE WAS TALKING TO MARC,
SO FROM HER BEHALF I REQUEST ALL OF YOU TO WAIT FOR 36HRS TO GET THE FUND IN YOUR ACCOUNT.
HOPE THAT OUR REQUEST WILL BE GRANTED.

WITH BEST REGARDS
AKANSHA
NB:—TODAY IT FOUND THAT SOMEONE CONTACTED BANK OF CAL-CUTTA TO GET IT VERIFIED AS WHAT HAPPEN, WELL I DONT KNOW WHO HAD DONE THIS, BUT THIS SHOWS THAT YOU ARE NOT COM-FORTABLE WITH YOUR INVESTOR AND FOR WHICH YOU NEED THIRD PARTY TO STAND AS A GURANTEE, WELL THOUGH I AM NOT SO BIG BUSINESS PERSON BUT STILL I FEEL UNLESS YOU RECIEVE THE FUND IN YOUR ACCOUNT IT IS TAKEN THAT YOU AS A COM-PANY AND ANAMIKA AS A INVESTOR IS STILL UNDER CONTROL OF RBI AND IN THIS KIND OF SITUTATION RBI CAN CHANGE UP HIS MIND IF THIS NEWS OF ENQUIREY GOES DIRECT TO RBI, SO IT IS OUR EARNEST REQUEST THAT IF ANYONE OF YOU KNOWS THAT WHO HAD DONE IT PLEASE TRY TO STOP FROM DOING ALL THIS KIND OF THINK BECAUSE FOR ONE PERSON ENTIRE TEAM GOING TO SUFFER.

There is was! Because the self important BobK couldn't keep his willful, pomposity zippered we all might suffer the loss of funding.

Chris sent out an email to the entire group which translated the above, advising that funds should arrive in the U.S. by Friday, July 11.

FUNDING DATE #30—JULY 11th, 2003

He provided the following advice for the clients.

> *a) don't call the bank asking about her and her account because they won't tell u and if they do tell u something it won't be the truth its called privacy.*

> *b) some people have been calling her bank and the bank have been calling her complaining about this constant calling so again stop call-ing the bank*

> *c) sit back chill out and wait a bit longer as its not going to kill you.*

The last point was not exactly the advice Banker's Trust would provide its clients, but then we weren't Fortune 500 companies.

The impatience of the clients trying to verify Anamika's funds, and either mistrusting or disrespecting Larry and Chris as representatives of the group, created a major rift between clients, the brokers and Anamika. Cliques began to form and the daily business disintegrated from the search for funding to establishing primacy in the group.

Additional pompous blowhards began to emerge. Like sharks smelling blood, once they detected Chris and Larry were weak and ineffective, they started nipping around the edges. The latest to join the group was Steve, who hailed from New Zealand, Chris's ass end of the world. He responded to Chris' email the same day.

> *After our previous written assurance of funds transfer on Saturday 5th July to all, it's hard to believe instead of 23 remittances to project principals that only one was made to UBI Head Office Mumbai— WOW that is some mistake and amounts to nothing but culpable neglect on the part of ALL involved for such a US$ billion error!!*

These PBs (pompous blowhards) left no doubt in anyone's mind about how impressed they were with themselves. Commenting from the sidelines about a problem never solves it, yet to them self aggrandizement was paramount. Steve continued:

> *If your information is correct this time, it is pleasing to hear, however, that now 100% funding is being provided but until confirmation of remittance from UBI and funds are cleared into our respective bank accounts, without signed, sealed proof, there still is no level of comfort as we are in fact no further advanced than we were on day 1!*

What a remarkable grasp of the obvious.

It should be noted that the PBs mentioned above were in line to receive $3.7 million and $6.7 billion respectively.

Next, Kevin weighed in to the fray with an email that went to all of the clients as well as to Anamika.

July 11—7:35:10 AM EDT

Good morning and good day Ladies and Gentlemen!

PLEASE FOLLOW THE INSTRUCTIONS BELOW——if anyone calls and we find out who … you will be EXTREMELY SORRY!!!

Now, I spoke with Anamika an hour ago, 5am EDT.
She asked me to write this down ... due to bad info being thrown about.

Now, she is finishing things up but funds will not arrive until 4:30 PM her time so tomorrow she will go to the banks and do one set of wires and then back on monday morning she will complete the remaining wires and then fax us in her afternoon, the receipts.

She said she was sending to 24 clients and she had near 50 wires to do and one draft—guess who, so some saturday and the remaining monday morning. She says the funds should be in our accounts by tuesday. I am trying to call her back and confirm this but phone has been busy. It looks like she will send 50% and then the other 50% to those staying with her.

Have a great weekend everyone, she will leave for Vegas once all this is completed.. next week. I beg you all to just relax ... she is no scammer ... and she is trying very hard to make us all what we want to be.. top business men and women ... so go get happy and party all weekend.. as I believe we are a couple days away from this coming reality and we have stuck with this until now ... Anamika or anyone else has asked for a dime from us ... unlike ALL the rest we have dealt with, so again, I beg you all to relax over the weekend and Monday morning we will have our receipts by 9 am EDT.

All confirmed—She is sending the bank wires—Except for the DOC he still wants a draft.. and she will forward that. The Dr. is the only one of us not going further with Anamika.

She was told today when she got to the bank.. who has called- Shawn, we know, Dr. Khoa and Larry have contacted her bank.. So folks, these people recklessly played with our futures ... with no regard for us or even themselves.. and what you fellas think you could gain by calling someones bank ... blows my mind. IDIOTS the 3 of you and anyone else who called!!

So from here on out ... we have 5 days to wait for our funds to arrive. She is sending 2 wires and then will fax only one receipt to us. So I tell you all..
PLEASE for the love of God ... give her until wednesday next week.. money should be there tuesday ... but your bank will be able to see the transfer in transit.. once you send the receipt to them and also with the amounts coming.

Now I will contact her tomorrow and make sure all is moving forward.. and maybe leave her alone.. I will let you know if anything changes.. again, she will fax everything Monday morning our time.

HAVE a GREAT weekend everyone … trust me, trust her … all will be good to GO on tuesday!

Ms. Anamika is travelling to Vegas later in the week.

If any of you have a problem or question.. please call me 416-XXX-XXXX is my cell. As you can see, this went to Anamika as well … so she know what I am putting out so if anything is incorrect.. she will let me know.. but I called her back a few minutes ago to clarify what amounts and when.. all is good to GO!!

I want to thank you Anamika for your hard work, TENACITY (my favorite word) and dedication to completing these deals with us all. I am honoured to work with yourself and the family in the future and look forward to a long relationship that will only benifit all involved. Until monday, play and work safe please.

I know we all feel privileged to be on this train of success … with all players ready to go the distance with you except one.

Have a good relaxing weekend everyone.. cuz once you have the funds.. the real work begins!! Making money to pay for all this and pay the Biswas' back with profits … so get ready to be successful!

Bye for now folks … please take it easy.. everything happens when it is suppose to!

Your information man of the week.

   Kevin had passion and tenacity and courage. He also had a lot to gain and lose—building a house for Anamika and her family plus $1.35 billion in investment funds. Yet, I'd rather be on the team with Kevin than with all the PBers in the world. Kevin put all he had on the line, rather than sit on the side-lines and grouse. If, through his approach he preserved the Biswas funding deal we all would benefit.

The narrow minded, short sighted, self important PBers could not bear for Kevin to succeed. Those captains of industry, who strode the world in seven-league boots snapped back by the end of the day with email from BobK—9:24:48 PM EDT—to Chris and Larry.

> *I do not like the fact that an individual, (Kevin O) who I do not know nor have I elected to have them (sic) represent me, should be involved in my transactions with the Biswas, nor should he have information about me and my business. That is in direct violation of the original confidentiality agree- ment.*

> *By the way. Anyone who feels that a business or person who wants to have acknowledgement (cq) of funding, to which none has been shown or actually took place is far from being an idiot....*

> *As far as Kevin O is concerned, who appointed him as God?*

BobK went on to complain about the delays over the four months he was involved with the Biswas project. His "Promises, yes fulfillment no." was an appropriate summation of what all the clients experienced. Yet, where Kevin was involved proactively, BobK carped from behind the safety of his computer screen.

The most telling part of his email, that which described to me his character and philosophy of life—"... if the money is transferred by Wednesday of this next week I will write an apology to the Biswas and you," proving he didn't have the courage of his convictions, nor intestinal fortitude. Had he been so wronged and ill treated, there always remained the option of dropping out of the group. The money was too important to BobK and he was too much of a child to stop whining. He stayed in the group, unfortunately for us.

Though I was in the New York area, I continuously tried to stay in contact with Anamika, even when there was no movement for the first few days. My email informed her I was away on business and asked if she could email me the confirmation number from the bank. I also asked for an update on her Las Vegas itinerary.

Beyond maintaining contact, I felt this approach would remind her of an obligation to send the wire confirmation number, enable me to verify the funds had been sent once I had that number and also let her know I wanted to meet her, not just her money, in person.

The approach seemed to work, as Anamika continued to keep me informed.

July 14—8:17:15 AM EDT

HELLO SIR
WELL I HAVE DONE PART WIRE OF 50%TODAY AND TOMORROW I
WILL DO NEST PART OF 50%WHICH WILL MAKE TOTAL 100%AND
WILL SEND YOU THE CONFIMATON SLIP BY EMAILL
WITH BEST REGARDS
ANAMIKA BISWAS

Anamika Has Wired Funds #2—July 14

Confirmation Slip Date #3—July 15 (maybe)

July 14th, the same day I received email from Anamika; Larry circulated a similar email that had been sent to another client. Larry also wanted to "set the record straight" regarding the calls to Anamika's bank.

> *i and Dr. Kilgallon have NOT MADE EVEN ONE PHONE call to
> ANY BANK nor would we.*

[What's not being said here is that neither could afford to call India which is why they relied on email.]

> *We did however write a letter to the RBI*

[that's like writing to the Federal Reserve Bank in Washington]

> *(AND ONLY WAS AFTER DAY 100 WITH NO PROOF) but that
> was to conduct diligence on the lender and anyone who tells me i can't
> conduct diligence can go to blazes.*

Larry apologized in some fashion for "jumping the gun by a week" with his letter, but conveniently called it "water under the bridge." Larry had a way with clichés, if not with logic. The act of the RBI contacting Anamika about Larry's letter "PROOVES beyond ANY SHADOW of a doubt to me that they are indeed dealing with the Biswas's and all this funding is very very real."

What Larry didn't mention is the mere fact of "dealing with" a client does not of itself prove that the client has $33 billion to fund 24 companies.

He also officially informed the group that he and Chris had appointed Kevin as the spokesperson because of his rapport with Anamika. This was a good idea since both Larry and Chris were becoming increasingly ineffective.

Ostensibly the move was for Kevin to interface with Anamika and give her some breathing room to get her job done without constant calls from clients. Kevin would be responsible for the flow of communication back to the clients.

The subtext of this move was purely and simply an abdication—only without the pomp and circumstance—of Chris' and Larry's responsibilities as so-called brokers for the group. They bailed.

By the next day, Larry and Chris were still the ones communicating, but I was more interested in what Anamika was writing me.

July 15—10:40:34 AM EDT

HELLO SIR
THANKS FOR REPLYING, YES I WILL SEND YOU THE EMAIL VERSION OF IT SO THAT YOU COULD HAVE A TRACE OF IT.

WELL I SHOULD SAY THANKS TO YOU OTHERTHAN YOU SAYING TO ME.I WILL REMAIN GREATFUL TO YOU THROUGHT OUT MY LIKE TILL DATE I BREATH THE ITINERY WILL BE EMAILED TO YOU SOON.

WITH BEST REGARDS—ANAMIKA BISWAS

How could I distrust her, when she was responsive to my queries and was pledging undying gratitude? True she hadn't sent one dime my way. But, that was a minor matter to my thinking. It could be explained away. We were dealing with a third world country, with different systems, culture, etc. For example we learned banks usually open at about mid-day. We also didn't know how far Anamika lived from the bank or the efficiency of the transportation system. There were a myriad of factors unknown to us living in the comfort of the Western world.

As long as it seemed that I was dealing with a sincere, determined woman who was open and communicative, I decided to give her the benefit of all doubts.

Larry continued to be defensive about contacting the Reserve Bank of India in his email to many of the group—9:26:47AM EDT.

> *"I wrote the RBI a week ago to get confirmation from then on the Biswas's. They went directly to Anamika.*

So the RBI "knows her" and "is dealing with her" FOR SURE 100% thats all we can really confirm so far, other than her television interview and her 4 newspaper interviews seem to be very very real, so many of us are very relaxed and hopeful at this point in time and we think it's safe to say something concrete is up so far....

Basically we simply wait until she decides to show us what she feels like sending out and if it takes another day well then so be it.

IF there is NO FORTH COMING proof or NO CONFIRMED wire transfers by the end of this week well then we have to all decide what is the best option at that point in time and we do ask so that no one simply goes off on their own to start things without consulting the rest of us.

This reveals another aspect of the dynamic of the group. Larry and Chris felt they could present us as a solid bloc when in reality we were all individuals, separate companies with far ranging areas of expertise. They never faced the glaring reality they had no control over any of us since losing our respect. Therefore, asking us to not go off on our own, should the funding not be realized, was naïve and unrealistic.

But Anamika's latest email did not allay any insecurities or fears at 9:59:58 AM EDT.

HELLO SIR
WELL LET ME TELL YOU THAT I DONT KNOW WHAT YOU ALL FELL ABOUT ME BUT I JUST WANT TO TELL YOU SOMETHING THAT AFTER WORKING WITH ALL ODDS SITUATION BOTH FROM FAMILY AND GOVERNMENT IF SOME OF YOU STILL SUSPECT ME THEN I HAVE NOTHING TO SAY, BE REST ASSURED THAT I WILL NOT CLIAM ANY AMOUNT OF INTEREST OR PROFIT RATIO OR RETURN OF THE MONEY I AM GIVING YOU, SO YOU DONT HAVE TO WORRY AND QUIRIEY ME FOR WHAT I DONT TODAY OR HOW I AM DOING, WELL FOR YOUR INFORMATION LET ME TELL YOU SECOND WIRE IS ALSO DONE BUT I DIDNT GOT THE

Anamika Has Wired Funds #3—July 15

Confirmation Slip Date #4—July 16

DELAY #14—Power failure at bank

CONFIRMATIONSLIP BECAUSE THE BANK HAD GOT POWER FALIURE AND FOR THAT REASON CONFIRMATION SLIP WILL BE GIVEN TO ME ON TOMORROW WHICH I WILL FAX YOU ALL RESPECTIVLY AND ALSO I WIL SEND THIS COPIES TO RBI (RESERVE BANK OF INDIA) AS IT WILL SHOW THAT CLOSED THE DEAL WITH ALL OF YOU AND I AM NOT ENTITTLED WITH ANYONE OF YOU IN ANY WAYS WELL IF AFTER RECIEVEING YOU STILL WANT TO DEAL WITH ME I WILL BE GRATEFUL AND ALSO LET YOU KNOW WHAT IS MY LASVEGAS ITINERY BUT THIS CHOICE IS COMPLETELY YOURS WHETHER YOU WANT ME TO BE INCOLLBORATED WITH YOU OR NOT.
I HOPE THAT BY TOMORROW AFTER RECIEVING THE FAX YOU PEOPLE WILL GET VERIFIED THAT I AM NOT FROWADING YOU
WITH BEST REGARDS
ANAMIKA BISWAS

Poor me Anamika #1

This was a part of Anamika's character that we would see more of during the next four months. It was all variations of the same theme of "poor me, third world woman controlled by men", blah, blah. That immediately played into the political correct sensibilities of the group, in which there were only two women.

Maybe the men were mature, sensitive human beings who saw in Anamika their own daughters or female relatives. Possibly the men in the group had become "womenslimpified" as a result of the steady social drum beat over the last three decades and automatically gave favor to any woman so they wouldn't be accused of being sexist, tipping the playing field, etc.

At this point, it didn't matter. She got my, and our, empathy.

July 16

Chris advised the group that "Anamika will be faxing the confirmation slips today as she will have the slips in the next few hours, the wires have gone and we should be able to see the wires today."

Chris never revealed the source of that information. What should our reaction be—over the top elation or stomach churning dread that his info would become another disappointment? Push/pull. Up/down. Swing right/swing left. Backwards/Forwards. Elation/despair.

July 17

And, the next morning Chris told us:

> *I hope this is the last update i need to send you all but here is the latest situation.*
>
> *Everyone will have there confirmations by 6:00pm India time tomorrow because that is the deadline that is imposed by the RBI and she said they will meet the deadline.*
>
> *She's very calm and collected and also offered to fax it direct to our bank if we wish, all we have to do is email her the fax no, and name of bank officer of our bank. I hope this email pleases you all some what. Chris*

To which Larry added his "words of encouragement" feeling "very strongly" that we were in one of "the very last days of this funding affair with Anamika Biswas."

That day I received an email from Anamika—9:20:40 AM EDT—indicating vanity stops at no geographical or cultural borders.

HELLO SIR
WELL THE THINGS (CONFIRMATION SLIP) WILL REACH YOU SOON BY 18TH OF JULY 2003 WELL I PRESSUME THAT THE PAPERS WILL HAVE MY PHOTOGRAPH.
WITH BEST REGARDS
ANAMIKA BISWAS

Confirmation Slip Date #5—July 18

While I was in the New York area I called the Bank of America wire department to get a sense of time frame for funds being wired from India. One of the staff told me they usually expect to receive wires in up to three weeks. I was told this is what "they train their new bankers to say to customers" awaiting funds wired from India. Larry passed this information to the clients.

Before returning to California on July 18th I sent Larry an email advising him that I "did not get my confirmation number by email as Anamika said she would." By the time I returned home and checked I learned that no one had received an email with the number confirming she had wired the funds.

Larry threw his bravado into the wind, by sending "Anamika a nice letter ... requesting some answers. If she cancels my funding or tells me off then the heck with her. I am tired of these freaking games. Sorry I dragged you into this...." A lot of good that did any of us.

Clearly, the cohesiveness of the group was fraying around the edges and seemed on the verge of unraveling. Kevin and BobK slung accusations at each other through cyberspace. Kevin wrote to PB#1

> *You mentioned in your email that you have not received your fax from Anamika and that you are glad you are not relying on Anamika.*
>
> *And you should get nothing ... why does everyone consider something a scam when you have not been asked for anything but some more time ... as this is her first try and she has tripped up a few times ... and being a woman in India ... I'm sure it takes longer because you are a woman.*
>
> *So I will pray that she had the good sense to cancel your amount as you seem to have something else going for you. I would say GO because when the funds arrive I want to know what you people, who Feel you are being scammed have to say???*
>
> *No scam afoot ... just someone trying to get money out of India. So go and do whatever you are doing and forget Anamika and your amount ... that way we do not have to listen to more negative attitude ...*
>
> *Then tell Anamika that you do not need her investment ... so I will make sure I mention it to her tomorrow and see if she cannot stop one or more transfers.*

BobK began his response to Kevin as "Dear self proclaimed God" and pomposity oozed down the page, along with the sound and fury which signified less than nothing.

> *... If you feel that you have total control over Anamika and that you can make her cancel our agreement and the funds do not arrive, then I hope that you will have enough money to cover a $5 + Billion Dollar litigation, not excluding court costs, attorney fees, any loses to Chris,*

Larry and to Anamika that would of been compensated to her in agreement to our Limited Partnership.

Figure 30% of $30 Billion for 10 years as just a starting point....

... Your actions represent an irrational behavior, and lack of professionalism and does not best represent Anamika the entire group, that of myself or the corporation, but rather that of a self centered individual seeking fame and glory and what ever power that he may think he has.

I hope you understand the consequence of your letters and statements.

I could care less what Kevin and PB#1 did to each other. My concern was more with how their feud would impinge on Anamika's willingness to fund ME. Suppose all the delays and problems were the result of the inexperienced, but sincere, efforts of a young woman with large goals, as Kevin suggested. And, suppose she became aware that as she was doing her best to pull off the biggest deal of her life, some of the beneficiaries of her largess placed a ten ton rock on her back and forced her to walk up the side of a pyramid.

At some point she might ask herself "why am I going through all this trouble?" Then it would be bye, bye funding. If I had an extra $33 billion in my pocket I'd never get involved with Larry, Chris and the PBers to begin with as I have a low tolerance for whiners.

When I did not receive the confirmation number by email as Anamika indicated, I contacted her about my concern. Later that morning I heard from her.

July 19—8:11:25 AM EDT

HELLO SIR
WELL MY BANK TECHNICAL PROBLEMS GOT SOLVED AND I AM
SENDING YOU

DELAY #15—bank technical problems

Confirmation Slip Date #6—July 21

ON MONDAY BECAUSE TODAY IS SATURDAY AND MY BANK HAD
GREAT RUSH AND IT ALSO GOT CLOSED ON 12:00PM SO I COULDN;T
MAKE IT BUT I WILL SEND YOU ON MONDAY EVENING OF MY TIME
IN THE MEANTIME I WANT YOU TO CONTACT MR KEVINBECAUSE I

EMAILED HIM JUST NOW AND I ASKED HIM FEW QUESTIONES AS PER ATTITUDE OF THE CLIENTS SO I PLEASE REQUEST YOU TO GET BACK TO HIM SO THAT I ALSO CAN GET TO KNOW WHAT YOU FELL WITH BEST REGARDS
ANAMIKA BISWAS

Had I kept track that Anamika had given us six dates when the confirmation slips were going to be sent, I most likely would not have sent her the following—9:30:07 AM EDT.

Dear Anamika
I regret there were technical difficulties with your bank.

However, as far as my attitude toward you is concerned, please note

I hold you in high regard
I believe in you
I believe your word is to be trusted
I respect you
I am grateful for how you are helping me and my company.

With all that, when you say you've wired the money—I believe you.
When you say there are technical difficulties—I believe you.

I was willing to wait. And she was willing to let us wait. But her reply was disarming—10:15:13 AM EDT

HELLO SIR
I ALSO LIKE YOUR ATTITUDE AND WAY YOU MAKE ME FEEL NOW, WELL I ALSO WANT TO KEEP THIS RELATION EVEN AFTER WIRE REACHES TO YOU
ANAMIKA BISWAS

I wrote to Larry and Chris, with a copy to Anamika. Coincidentally, that day was the feast day of St. Vincent de Paul, my namesake, who is the patron saint of little children. Oh, to be a little child again.

A brief note to let you know that I continue to believe in and support Anamika Biswas.

I believe the technical and personal difficulties she has experienced during the more than 75 days since I've been involved were absolutely unavoidable.

[Time to get the salt and pepper so I can eat my words.]

Please do not do anything on my behalf that in any way would jeopardize the establishment of her investment in my company or a future working relationship with her.

I am very certain that we all will benefit from our relationship with Anamika. We need to stick to belief +trust and patience.

I made my bed and would lie in it for the next four months.

Anamika told us she wired funds on two days—July 14th and 15th.·· From the Bank of America I learned wires from India, which it considered a "slow pay" country, took three weeks to arrive at the Bank. Therefore, I did not expect much to happen before August eleventh.

Rather than fret and pace and create doomsday scenarios, I decided to use the time for preparation. Once the funds reached my account, I wanted to hit the ground running. This would mean building a company and production entity from scratch. Starting with renting production office space and including office equipment, staff, permits, locations, casting, etc.; I had lists for everything and timetables for each list.

The boys had other plans. Larry forwarded email on July 20th from two of the clients and advised us that Anamika was having trouble with her bank— The United Bank of India.

Kevin reiterated the crises—new Bank Manager, wrong transfers, and power outages—and reminded us that the traffic in Calcutta was as bad as in New York, etc. He counseled patience "in the last few remaining weeks as this funding scenario winds to a conclusion and with all the luck of the Gods, it will also mean the bright beginning of all our companies.

"… she swears she has done the deed and the bank told her Friday to come pick up the slips … so we should have them Monday.… Please remember … scammers do not go for press coverage and ALWAYS ask for fee money … we have none of that in this deal … just problems of dealing with the issues and people responsible for making this so hard for her … and I think the bank is doing this on purpose to make some quick money," Kevin concluded.

Many of us shared the same opinion. No third world country wants to see billions of dollars in hard currency leave its national treasury. We all thought the RBI was manipulating the float for as long as it was able to make itself thousands of additional rupees or crore or whatever.

Anamika had no idea the can of curry powder she opened by asking for the attitudes of the clients toward her. Kevin gently pressed her for a letter from her bank to the clients describing the difficulties and providing specific date when funds, confirmation slips, etc. would actually arrive.

But he also intimated that there would be "bad press" if the wires were not sent. Then, he opened the door for the last and most contentious of the PB (i.e. pompous blowhard) triumvirate to arrive on the scene.

Craig was brought to the group by Kevin and was to receive $7.1 billion from Anamika for some trash disposal process he was exporting throughout the world. Craig's comments regarding Anamika to his benefactor Kevin, who would also get a "finder's" fee from Craig, not only were patronizing toward Anamika but revealed subconscious jealousy toward my relationship with her.

> *Kevin*
> *One additional point.*
>
> *As hard as Anamika is trying, her youth and lack of experience make her an easy target for the banks to take a lazy approach to her business operations. Since she listens to you, the following suggestions may help her.*
>
> *The pressure Anamika is getting from some of the 23 recipients is understood and false commitments and non- performance is not tolerated in business let alone multiple times by the same party.* **The India media has glorified Anamika for her new Hollywood status through her investment in Thistle Productions, etc.**

WHAT INVESTMENT!? Thistle is my company. I wrote the release. I pitched the Indian press and my bank account was shy of the $30 million dollar investment PB#2 Craig presumed. The subtext of that paragraph was most revealing. Mommy wasn't paying enough attention to Craigywaigy. Ahh.

> *If Thistle retracts this media release, there will be a media frenzy that will dwarf the raves and reviews that Anamika received over*

*the past few weeks. Her name and business will be dragged through
the Mumbai gutter.*

If this wasn't subliminal wishful thinking on his part, it certainly was presumption. I was not contemplating even the vaguest notion of retracting anything I'd sent or said to the Indian press. Besides, since the stories ran in early July there had been some logical reasons for delay in funding.

In addition, Craig had gotten his Kolkata confused with his Mumbai. Anamika lived and worked in Kolkata, the new name for Calcutta; while Mumbai was the new name for Bombay. Might seem like harmless confusion, but the rest of Craig's letter in tone fell a hair short of expressing his contempt for the third world "wog".

> *However, if you've done your job in business, and a third party has the potential to destroy you and your company, you have to know how to divert the nastiness directly to the responsible party.*

> *Anamika needs to tell the UBI (President, VP or Senior Manager) that if any media releases are retracted, she will issue a media release of her own pointing out that it was the UBI and banking industry in India that not only caused her to lose her investment opportunity with the Hollywood movie industry but they have likely damaged the entire film industry in India.*

With that kind of hyperbole, he should have been writing screenplays instead of memos.

> *She can tell the UBI that her own media release will not only be issued to the media in India but also to the media in the United States, particularly California. In other words, she can tell the UBI that "If I go down, I'm taking the UBI and the banking industry in India with me."*

Sounds like he's instigating blackmail. At that time, he seemed just the kind of guy, the U.S. needed to negotiate with the Taliban and Saddam Hussein.

> *I will tell the United States not to invest in India and not to invest in the India film industry because our banks will jeopardize your funding and will not co-operate with you.*

Is this passive aggressive portion of this letter in effect telling me to retract my release or he will try to destabilize my funding? Get a grip! Quit admiring your visage in the mirror. "Mirror, mirror on the wall, who's the Mr. Macho of them all?"

> *I will tell everyone about my banking experiences in India and suggest that all foreign companies keep their money out of India's banks. If you don't think I'll do it, just watch me.*

> *She needs to get tough with UBI and move the pressure off of her back and right onto the shoulder's of the bank.*

> *Kevin, I think Anamika needs some direction and assistance in dealing with the UBI.*

Kevin added a coda to the email: "Monday is our D-Day and the bank stated to you Anamika that they effected ALL transfers … so by their own word … no reason not to have the slips waiting for you when you arrive tomorrow. Thank you again Ms. Anamika for your determined efforts!!"

Jack, a client who had not voiced any opinion up to now, was moved to comment. "… I am impressed with the latest attempt by all of you to proof up a bankable funding commitment on this deal … I personally believe that Anamika will have this transaction complete within the next couple of days. Let's hope things work out with the confirmation slips soon."

I was angered by the presumption in Craig's email that I needed to retract my release, if that were possible. First, it was based on sheer stupidity and lack of knowledge of how the press functions. Next, was the absurdity of just what I was going to say? Did he imagine I would call up the reporter and say:

"You remember the person I said was going to fund me three weeks ago, well she's not. Waaaaa! Waaaaa! Waaaaa!"

What did he expect would happen next—the Senate Banking Committee would launch a world wide investigation?

Clearly, the issue of Anamika was not equal to, for example, raising money to feed starving orphans and then running off with the funds.

July 20

I had to respond and sent an email to the group with the subject—I SUPPORT ANAMIKA.

I am very pleased to have initiated the publicity for Anamika Biswas, AB Exports and my company Thistle Productions, Inc.

To date articles have appeared in Daily Variety, Film Daily, The Telegraph in Kolkata, The Times of India, India West (of California) and The Weekly Voice (Canada).

[Take that, you incompetents!]

With 20 years experience, earlier in my career, as a PR professional with Exxon and Bristol-Myers as clients, I consider the above to be my most satisfying and important achievements.

If I did not have the utmost faith, respect and gratitude, in and for Anamika I would not have undertaken the considerable and expensive efforts required to help her.

Naturally, it also helps Thistle. But without funding from Anamika Thistle might easily succumb due to a mountain of egg on its reputation.
It was/is a risk I took willingly. It is a risk I know will pay off.

Thistle and I SUPPORT Anamika without hesitation or reservation.

Thistle WILL NOT RETRACT any of the publicity (as if that would ever be considered let alone a remote possibility).

Thistle WILL NOT REPUDIATE its intended, future business association with Anamika and AB Exports.

Kevin was the only client to reply, assuring me they were all "prepared to go the distance" with Anamika. Unfortunately, he added, "some of the group have taken other liberties with her and she is trying to get the bank to move on this … and as she said, they are at the bank waiting for her … we all hope."

July 21

The next crisis came Monday morning, the twenty first of July—2:13:03 AM EDT.

DELAY#16—Anamika gets conjunctivitis

HELLO SIR
WELL THIS LETTER ANAMIKA IS NOT WRITING AS SHE HAD A BAD TYPE OF CONJUNCTIVITIES SHE IS DICTATING, WELL SIR SHE IS SAYING LIKE YOU IF EVERYONE COULD HAVE UNDERSTND HER THEN SHE WOULD HAVE BEEN A MOST HAPPY PERSON INTHE WORLD. YOU KNOW TODAY SHE WENT TO THE BANK WITH ME FROM THERE SHE IS BEEN THROWN AWAY BY THE MANAGER TELLING THAT SHE SHOULDNOT COME TO THE BANK LIKE THIS BECAUSE ALL PEOPLE SHOULD HAVE SAME DISEASE FROM HER AND HE ALSO TOLD US THAT THEY WILL SEND THE WIRING AND ALSO SEND HER THE FAX OF CONFIRMATION SLIPS AND THAT SHE MUST NOT COME TO THE BANK UNLESS SHE GETS WELL.
ON BEHALF OF ANAMIKA BISWAS
NISHITA

What to do? Hard to imagine getting thrown out of the bank due to an eye infection. Just a bit of an over reaction. But, then, who knew about the customs in India. Didn't make any logical sense, the germs were not exactly going to leap from Anamika's eye across the desk to the Bank Manager as Anamika was signing papers. She was banished until she recovered. Who could tell how long that would be?

As much as I supported and wanted to believe Anamika, the frequency of excuses was gradually going beyond the beyond for me. Who but the most callous humans could not understand delay caused by illness, bankruptcy and death? But then there were floods, electricity outages and now an eye infection.

I wrote her a letter of support—8:35:57 AM EDT—but also advised her that she was rapidly expending her "get out of jail free" cards, though not exactly with that metaphor.

Dear Nishita
Please tell Anamika I wish her a speedy recovery.

While no one wishes her to be ill, I'm afraid this latest delay does not help her reputation with the group.

Though I am pleased Anamika is made happy by my support, she needs to understand that the accumulation of delays has not caused much happiness in the group.

No one is blaming her, but it is reality just the same.

In part of your email you say—regarding the bank manager "HE ALSO TOLD US THAT THEY WILL SEND THE WIRING AND ALSO SEND HER THE FAX OF CONFIRMATION SLIPS …"

Using the words "will send" indicates to me that the wires have not yet been sent. All along I've been given to understand that they were sent either on July 12 or July 14.

Please have Anamika clarify. Have the wires been sent, or WILL they be sent by the bank manager in the future? It is very important that we know the answer.

Some of the clients envisioned themselves as burly football linemen, like pulling guards and tackles, who would brush aside all obstacles in Anamika's path. I felt strongly that she needed a keeper.

For some reason BobK, the numero uno PBer, sent me a copy of a recent email from Anamika—10:20:24 AM EDT.

DEAR DR KILGALLON

Poor me Anamika #2

WELL LET ME TELL YOU SOMETHING THAT THOUGH WE ARE FAR AWAY FROM EACH OTHER MY RESPECT FOR ALL OF YOU REMAINS SAME NO MATTER HOW I GET A RETURN TREATMENT FROM YOUR SIDE, WELL AS PER YOUR CONCERNED I MUST TELL YOU THAT I ALWAYS WANTED TO DO SOMETHING IN MY LIFE AND FOR THAT REASON I WENT TO DO THE BUSINESS MY EDUCATIONAL QUALIFI-CATION IS NOT SO HIGH AS COMPARED TO YOUR'S BUT MY INTUTA-TION TOWARDS WAS VERY HIGH AND IT STILL REMAINS HIGH THAT FORCED ME TO GO OUT AND DO BUSINESS INSPITE OF UNWILLING-NESS SHOWN FROM MY FAMILY AS YOU SHOULD BE KNOWING A

RECENTLY I GOT A EMAIL FROM LARRY HE ASKED MY FATHER'S DECISION TO DO BUSINESS WITH ME I TOLD HIM MY FATHER WILL NEVER ALLOW ME TO DO ALL THIS DEALS BECAUSE AFTER TWO GREAT MISHAP IN MY FAMILY MY FAMILY MEMBER STARTED TAKING THAT THIS DEALS ARE PROOVED TO BE UNLUCKY FOR US AND THAT WE WILL BE IN LOSS IF WE DO SO BUT I DIDNT AGREE TO THEM AND STILL DOING BY JOB AND FIGHTING ALL THE ODDS ONES OUT EVEN TODAY THIS LETTER THAT YOU WILL READ IS NOT WRITTENBY ME AS I AM HAVING A VERY BAD KIND OF CONJUNCTIVITIES WHICH CAN TAKE AWAY MY LEFT EYE AND CAN MAKE ME BLIND SO I TOOK HELP OF ONE OF MY FRIEND TO WRITE THIS LETTER TO ALL OF YOU, PLEASE BELIEVE IN ME THAT I AM TRYING MY LEVEL BEST AND THAT I AM SENDING YOU 100% OF FUNDING YOU ASKED NOT 50% IT IS UPTO YOU HOW YOU TAKE IT BUT MY FEELING TOWARDS ALL OF YOU NEITHER WAS BAD; NOR IT IS BAD AND NEITHER IT WILL BAD BUT I AGREE THAT I AM TAKING TIME BUT AT THE SAME TIME IF YOU KEEP YOUR SELF IN MY PLACE AS A GIRL YOU WOULD HAVE UNDERSTNAD WHAT HUMALITATION I HAD TO GO THROUGH BOTH FROM FAMILY AND SOCIAL OUT LOOKS TO DO THIS DEALING AND I ALSO LIKE TO TELL YOU I AGREE THAT YOU PEOPLE WORKING POWER IS VERY FASTER BUT BEING IN INDIA WHAT TIME I AM TAKING IS VERY SMALL BUT I ALSO KNOW THAT I DEALING WITH YOU ALL IN ABROAD AND THAT I SHOULD BUCK UP MY SPEED OF WORKING BUT BY BUCKING UP OF MY SPEED THIS WORK WONT DO BECAUSE STILL I AM IN ANYHOW DEPENDABLE TO OTHERS WHO WILL NOT BUCK UP THERE SPEED AND ALSO WHO DIDINOT BOTHER TO DO WHAT I WANT AS THEY CONSIDER GIRLS AS A VERY INEFFICIENT MACHIEN IN THE WORLD THIS ALL I AM WRITING TO YOU BECAUSE JUST NOW DUE TO MY CONJUNCTIVITIES I WAS THROWN OUT OF BANK MY MANAGER AS HE TOLD ME THAT HE DONT WANT TO GET INFECTED BY ME AND I SHOULD STAY AWAY FROM BANK AND HE WILL FAX ME THE CONFIRMATION SLIP AFTER HE SENDS THE WIRES SO FROM HERE YOU CAN UNDERSTAND THAT HOW UNFAIR HAPPENS TO A GIRL IN THE INDIAN SOCIETY AND AFTER THAT IF YOU PEOPLE ALSO START UP AND START ABUSING ME THEN I HAVE NOTHING TO DO JUST WAIT FOR GOD GRACEWHEN YOU WILL ALL NDERSTNAD THAT I AM NOT JOCKING WITH YOU OR NEITHER I AM PLAYING WITH YOU I WILL BE HIGHLY

GRATEFUL IF YOU CONVEY MY FEELINS AND EXACT CONTENT OF
THIS LETTER TO REST OF THE CLIENTS TO WHOME YOU KNOW.
WITH BEST REGARDS
ON BEHALF OF
ANAMIKA BISWAS

Bottom line—no confirmation slips were received by any one in the group on July 21st. This meant either that the slips were available, but not sent or, more importantly, that wires had not been sent to the clients.

More clients jumped into the cyberspace fray. Everyone had an opinion. However, there remained a constant belief in Anamika and desire to forgive and understand her inexperience all the while keeping fingers and toes crossed.

Craig of Toronto sent me an email of explanation, "… I used Thistle as an example only with no disrespect intended … I trust the above explanation clarifies the unauthorized distribution of my e—mail communication…." We remained on opposite sides of whatever issue was up for consideration by the group from that moment on.

A group dynamic began to develop, though not apparent at the time, which flowed out of common need as well as fluctuating and changing emotions. I started communicating by phone, email and Yahoo chat with many of the clients who only days before were part of the blur of email addresses at the top of a page. Gradually, we became living, feeling individuals who learned to trust each other until we discovered the trust was betrayed.

Email, which before was a one way correspondence from Larry or Chris to either the group or one individual, was now shared widely, further chipping away at any control Larry and Chris had over the clients.

Messages such as:

"High stress today, please does anyone know what is going on?"

"I beseeech thee bretheren to be patient and wait on your funding." began circulating.

And suggestions to bring the process to a successful conclusion were offered. One client offered that a group go over to help her, another wanted to pressure the bank by threatening to withdraw from current deals in India, another wanted to write directly to the President of the United Bank of India. All had the common purpose of trying to reduce the already costly delay in funding.

Through all the complaints and offers of help, many remained very supportive of Anamika and were not reticent about expressing their positions. There was support for her tenacity and criticism of the Indian banking system for what a client believed was its unkind and sexist treatment of Anamika. Another cautioned that we not "rush to judgement." Someone else advised that "if you stand strong you will succeed."

The sum total of the group's reaction and responses to the situation was typically American, in the best sense of that phrase. Americans are known for banding together in the face of calamity—whether national, local or international. There may be various disagreements regarding method, but unity when a common goal must be reached.

While all requested different amounts of funding for a variety of enterprises, we came together from these disparate backgrounds to keep the center from collapsing and maintain our dreams.

July 22

I spoke with Kevin who had spoken to Anamika earlier that morning. She requested the clients send her a letter advising that if the funds are delayed any longer they, the clients, will have to charge Anamika interest. The idea was to use the irate client letters to brandish at the bank. Whether or not the letters would cause the UBI and Indian banking system to quake in their boots was another story.

I sent Anamika the following, not knowing that less than a year later I'd be keeping a more accurate score of the delays.

July 22, 2003

Ms. Anamika Biswas
A.B. Exports
#84 Jatindra Mohan Avenue
Kolkata, 700005 India

Dear Anamika

I am distressed and very concerned about the delay in the wire transfer of your investment in Thistle Productions. Let me remind you of the delays that occurred during the last two weeks.

1. July 5—The funds were transferred by the Bank in Kolkata to Mumbai instead of to our banks.

2. July 14—Your email said you did part of the wiring on July 14 and the rest would be done on July 15.

3. July 17—You told me in an email the confirmation slip would reach me by July 18.

4. July 19—You said technical problems were solved and you would send me the confirmation number on Monday July 21.

5. July 21—The Bank Manager refused to deal with you and give you the confirmation slips because you had conjunctivitis. I hope the Manager is a better banker than he is a doctor. More importantly the Manager said "they will send the wiring and also send the fax of confirmation slips." **This means that as of July 21, one week later, the bank had not yet wired the funds!**

While I believe the United Bank of India is solely to blame for these unconscionable delays, nevertheless it is my fiduciary duty to my company Thistle Productions to advise you that if the funds are delayed any longer, I will have no option but to demand a penalty fee from you for non-performance.

Considering that this inexcusable delay is costing me money and soiling my reputation in the film community, I have no recourse but to demand a 25% penalty fee, above and beyond your investment, approximately $7 million additional, if I am not notified—with a confirmation number—that the funds have been transferred by close of business on Thursday July 24. This fee will not be included in your return on investment.

I regret having to take this position, but the banking delays leave me no other option.

Sincerely,

Vincent Panettiere

President

VP/srs

If the letters to the bank did any good, we never heard. The effort was akin to a tree falling in the forest when no human is present.

Along came Larry with a seven page attachment. Once again he raised hopes in those who may have believed him by stating "… we are now getting to the final moments of this funding affair with Anamika…." I know there are sixty seconds in a minute and sixty minutes in an hour, but I was never able to determine how many final moments were in a second, hour or day.

Larry made the following points:

1."We have simply lost control of this situation because Anamika wishes to be polite and deal direct with each client personally."

2. Despite what he admitted to being "short comings", the wait for funding "has ONLY BEEN 3/12 MONTHS.

3. He felt the clients expected "way too much too soon from this lady and from us and it has caused some real tension...."

4. He thought it would be "really nice if we could simply all go back to being friends and associates as we were when this started as we meant only the best for you all and tried hard to assist you through this."

5. But ultimately Larry had to conclude "... we have pieced together what seems to still yet be a supurb and great 100% funding opportunity from a foreign investor into our businesses."

6. He suggested we "SHOULD BE TREATING HER (Anamika) WITH A LOT OF RESPECT as we would THE PRINCESS of the SAUDI ROYAL FAMILY. She HAS THAT STATURE IN REALITY were she not a woman in India who really seem to be frowned upon in business."

Next, Larry appended a note from Mike, one of the clients who had been a Vice President of security with Deutsche Bank. Mike advised us as follows:

> *My opinion on this matter is that Anamika is being jerked around by the United Bank of India—a notorious custom in India is floating of remittances while the financial institutions play the currency market. I've heard of cases in Mumbai where local banks would float the remittances for 30 days or longer— while claiming government interference....*

Mike suggested someone with a friendly relationship with Anamika's banker should initiate a trace on the wired funds. He also advised that:

> *... financial institutions normally will not even acknowledge this procedure is in existence since it causes huge waves throughout the financial markets when such a trace call is effected and becomes public....*

Mike at least confirmed what up to then had only been a group surmise.

Next, Larry made a startling revelation—not something for the National Enquirer, but amazing nevertheless. He claimed that someone in the group had sent an associate, possibly a lawyer to "put eyes on the ground" as it were and learn whatever they could first hand about Anamika and her capability to fund the projects.

Such action Larry made clear was not authorized. Naturally Larry failed to recognize that such authority was not in his or Chris' possession and that any client with the financial means was free to visit Kolkata and discover whatever he or she could. He also didn't reveal where or how he got this "scoop".

Larry's sense of outrage {here I picture Larry looking and acting like the actor Jack Black in *School of Rock*} was overflowing.

> *... the fellow just blatantly walked up to Anamika's house last night and knocked on her door stating most of our names and how he was representing us as a group and he DEMANDED TO BE TAKEN TO HER BANK so that he could see who was holding up the sire transfers.*
>
> *Now I am not sure what any of you think of this and its a great idea to do this but to have serious blatant freaking disrespect ... not even a nice dinner out ... not any real introduction ... nothing ... just to start in on the wire transfers and HOW MUCH MONEY IS IN YOUR ACCOUNT Miss Biswas ... shows a serious lack of intelligence and respect as far as I am concerned ...*

Larry DEMANDED to know "who the heck sent this fellow" and he felt that the action taken "insulted us after months of incredibly hard darn work to really treat this lady as a great lady of great means."

Larry noted that "Anamika has weathered and dealt with this already ... and the good part of it was that she answered her door, was home at the address provided which is a very nice thing to see but was not treated like this situation calls for." Then Larry announced that he and Chris had asked that only Kevin and Brian were to deal directly with Anamika. Together, the new spokesmen requested more than $8 billion in funding from Anamika.

Before July twenty second was over, Dave, one of the clients who had emerged during the last few days, admonished Larry for his "unnecessary exaggeration" with regard to the duration of the funding process. Dave said he had spoken to Anamika that morning "... and she was in very good spirits. I would prefer that she stays that way.

"There have been too many occasions where these updates come out and have not been accurate. This causes Anamika to have to explain herself to multiple clients," which disrupts the process he wrote. Ultimately Dave proved that he should be regarded as Pompous Blowhard #4.

Steve weighed in to Larry from down under. While he stood to receive about $6 billion in funding from Anamika he said he had not authorized "anyone visiting India regarding our funding." While I have always considered

PB#3 more a part of the problem than the solution, he did provide a concise appraisal of the situation.

> *Yours and other intermediaries continued efforts in this protracted funding option is most appreciated but with all due respect it must be strongly pointed out that all of the projects being funded ARE INDE-PENDENT. The funding HAS NOT BEEN syndicated and each project has an individual legal contract between themselves and AB Exports. As such, each project principal has a legal right for direct communication with Anamika as she too has a moral obligation to communicate direct with the principal. Irrespective of who is doing this for the first time it is NO EXCUSE for ignorance of the most simple and basics of funding fundamentals nor to berate any principal for taking whatever course of action they deem necessary to protect their own interests....*
>
> *Hiding behind spokespersons or other excuses does not move each project funding forward and only creates a bureaucracy which should never have been there once contact was made between the principal and Anamika.*

On a lighter note, Larry informed Anamika that if he was not funded, per her request, by July 27th or 28th, he would charge her ten million dollars per day. That works out, he said, to one half of one percent per day on the $10 Billion she was supposed to invest in his company.

Next, BobK informed Anamika that if his $5 Billion was not transmitted within eighteen hours from the date of his July 22nd email he would charge her interest of six percent per day. He claimed to have sent a copy of his letter to the U.S. Treasury Department.

With his parting shot he proclaimed:

"These delays will no longer be tolerated or accepted and the World Banking industry will know how India Banks operate."

You mean to say, BobK that for all the decades banks around the world have dealt with banks in India they <u>never</u> knew how those banks operated? Which means those banks have been waiting patiently for the moment you would reveal all to them?

July 23

That morning Anamika sent me the following email:

HELLO SIR
IN THE MEANTIME I ALSO LIKE TO SEND A LETTER TO YOU IN MY
LETTER HEAD SEALED AND SIGNED BY YOU WHICH WILL CONTAIN
THE AMOUNT I WIRED FROM WHERE I WIRED AND WHICH DATE
WIRED HOW MANY DAYS WILL IT TAKE TO REACH YOU AND IN
WHICH ACCOUNT IT WILL BE REMITTED ALL SORTS OF DETAILS SO
THAT YOU CAN PRECEDE YOUR WITHOUT DELAY AS FUND REACHES
YOU.
WITH BEST REGARDS
ANAMIKA BISWAS

No matter what was going on with other members in the group, it was grat-ifying that Anamika and I were communicating. In reality, her intention to send me a letter with all the wire information was not date specific—so what else was new?

Later that day, Mike relayed an update from Kevin. In it he confirmed that Anamika had chosen Kevin as spokesman to reduce the rumors and misinfor-mation that had been circulating (through Larry I might add).

Anamika also revealed that "no one had showed up at her door" (wrong again Larry). But it was Craig who had called.

In addition, Anamika told Kevin she would be sending a letter on July 24th "around 10:30 AM her time" to each client on her letterhead detailing how they will be funded by her. Individual bank remittance slips will accompany each letter.

Confirmation Slip Date #7—July 24

Kevin related that in a conversation with Anamika she had sent a letter to one of the clients fully detailing where she had obtained the $33 Billion to be invested in the twenty four companies. Typically, no one knew who had the let-ter. Either Kevin had been so overwhelmed by the existence of such a docu-ment, which would prove unequivocally Anamika's financial substance, that he forgot to ask or Anamika by accident on purpose forgot to tell him.

Finally, Kevin informed the group through Mike that "It appears the United Bank of India is the controlling power now. Anamika relayed that she's done everything possible to live up to her agreements."

July 24

Encouraged by the free spirited communication newly developed in the group, Jack sent Anamika his suggestions—15:33 EDT. He asked her to provide:

> 1. Letter of Commitment by fax to him by 5:30pm July 25
> 2. Copy of documentation signed with the bank authorizing transmission of wire by fax.
> 3. Copy of the SWIFT confirmation slip
> 4. If SWIFT confirmation slips are not available he wanted a letter from her bank permitting his banker to receive Electronic Proof of Funds

Jack then advised Anamika that "failure to complete this transaction is not an option.... Simply provide the necessary documentation to support your statements."

Along came Steve from down under with "... the longer this frustrating, protracted, incredulous saga drags on, the more unlikely it is to come to a positive conclusion...." He was frustrated—as were we all—by the difficulty in communicating with Anamika, with the time difference being the least of it.

But this whiner, who stood to receive nearly $7 Billion for some thatch-roofed resort south of Pago Pago, seemed to think that he was so superior he had to be treated extra special nice with a cherry on top. All the while he had his hand out!

His email concluded:

> *I might add that over a six weeks ago, I was directed by one of the intermediaries that I had to call Anamika and after wasting two days trying to call, when I finally got her, instead of her being appreciative and friendly, she too was MOST rude, arrogant and demonstrated a most unprofessional and atrocious attitude. I have wasted many hours and thousands of dollars over the duration of this saga and loath being treated rudely by Anamika or anyone associated with her. Although I have serious doubts and am sick and tired of the excuses, deception, and broken promises, I am still in until the end if for no other reason than to see what transpires.*

Yeah, sure! What he means is that his grubby, little hand was stuck out palm up and ready to be filled by the arrogant, rude, unprofessional woman with the atrocious attitude.

Several months later the group learned that Steve had falsified his military record, but that is a story for another chapter.

For both expediency and psychological relief, I started insinuating myself deeper into the group discussions. PB#2 was particularly galling with his superior and smarmy approach. What follows is my email to the group, including Anamika.

July 25—7:34 EDT

Dear Mutineers or Mousketeers (hard to tell)
Last time I looked there were no Fortune 500 members in the group.

If the process of funding by Anamika is too complex, your concentration span too adolescent, your ego too inflated—do yourselves and all of us a favor and call Morgan Stanley. Please let them fund you.

This constant carping, whining and foot stamping will not get funding any quicker and creates a negative atmosphere that benefits no one except those who need to reveal the superficiality of their character.

As I said in an earlier email—I continue to support Anamika.

It's your choice if you don't support her. If so, quit trying to play both ends against the middle and go away.

Vince Panettiere
Thistle Productions

Then I sent a separate email to Anamika—11:29:09 AM EDT

Dear Anamika
I'm getting very annoyed at those who refuse to believe in you.

My feeling is those who are disrespectful or rude to you or who threaten you with legal action or make unreasonable demands on you should not be funded by you.

I'm not telling you what to do. Just expressing my contempt for those who are acting stupidly and childishly toward you.

As you know, you continue to have my support.

Later on that morning I spoke with Kevin who related that Brian had spoken with Anamika the previous evening. The third hand information I received indicated—Anamika was still upbeat and believed all would be okay; she had a long meeting at the bank with her lawyer; the assistant bank manager told her all would be completed in 48 hours; Anamika felt the bank was being cooperative and the money was out of her account; Anamika wanted to get the transactions completed so that she could reschedule her postponed trip to Las Vegas.

Confirmation Slip Dates #8—July 27

Anamika Has Wired Funds #4—July 27

Funding Date #31—July 27

We were now, as we had been thirty times before (since the first of May) only forty eight hours away from funding. If the money was out of Anamika's account, as Kevin relayed, all must be true.

As I thought of Anamika's billions being released, I wondered if it felt strange to know that money she once possessed, but no longer controlled, was drifting around in the cosmos doing nothing but making more money on the float for the bank which had been instructed to distribute her investment to twenty four companies.

Even forty eight hours could be too late for some of the clients who desperately needed either a proof of funds letter or a funding letter of intent to salvage projects with option dates.

Later in the day on July 25th, Mike provided clarification on some of the information Kevin learned—i.e. the reason Anamika spoke with "a bank assistant" was that the manager was away at

DELAY #17—Bank manager away

a UBI function for two days. She planned to return to her office and fax the "individual bank packages" which included the "letter of funding" and remittance slips.

As banks in India are open only half a day on Saturday, my calculations predicted Anamika's fax to me would arrive about ten in the evening.

However the most interesting part of Mike's email was the attachment of a letter from Anamika in which she documented where her funds orginated.

HELLO SIR
WELL LET ME TELL YOU THAT EVEN I AM TOO VERY MUCH OVER-WHEMLED BY THE THOUGHT YOU HAVE FOR ME, AT THE AGE I CAME TO THE BUSINESS THAT IS 18YRS OLD I GOT NOTHING WITH ME BUT ONLY THE MONEY 2,50,000/-RS WHICH I GOT AFTER I SOLD MY JEWELLERY WHICH I GOT ON MY BIRTHDAYS AND OTHER OCCA-SIONS FROM MY PARENTS AND GRANDPARENTS AND STARTED TO TRAV! EL IN THE WORLD OF WOMANISER WHERE WOMEN ARE TAKEN ONLY AS A SLAVE OR SOMETHING ELSE WHO HAS NO DIG-NITY OF ITS OWN OTHER THAN A SHOWPIECE IN THE SHOWCASE BUT I TOOK MY JOURNEY ALL ALONE WITHOUT EVEN THE HELP OF MY PAPRENTS AS MY FATHER ALSO BELIEVES THAT I NO POWER AND I CANNOT WORK AS PER QUALIFICATION WHICH IS NOT ONLY A MEDIOCARE BUT ALSO INFRONT OF MY OTHER SISTERS AND BROTHERS QUALIFICATION MY QUALIFICATION HAS NO VALUE FOR WHICH I WAS VERY MUCH HUMALIATED IN MY HOUSE AFTER I STARTED MY BUSINESS I HAD ALSO STARTED FACING HUMALIATION BOTH FROM MY HOUSE AND FROM THE PLACE WITH WHOME OR ASSOCIATES THAT JOINED ME DOING THE EXPORTS.

Poor me Anamika—#3

YOU WONT BELIEVE THAT EVEN TODAY I STILL FACE ALL THIS AND EVEN I FAMILY ALSO DON'T WANT TO HELP ME BECASUE THEY FEEL THAT GIRLS CANNOT DO BUSINESS, YOU WONT BELIEVE THAT IN THIS INVESTMENT I GIVING MY ENTIRE ENRRINGS ALONG WITH ALL THE MONEY I GOT AFTER SELLING MY ALL FIXED ASSESTS! I GIV-ING YOU XXXX THOUSANDS CRORES ONLY RUPEES AND AFTER THAT I WILL LEFT WITH ONLY XXX CRORESRS TO START ANY BUSI-NESS IN INDIA AND FLOURISH AT THE SAME TIME WITH YOUR BUSI-NESS.

SO YOU COULD UNDERSTAND THAT HOW IMPORTANT IT IS FOR ME TO MAKE THIS DEAL HAPPEN BECAUSE WITH IT I HAVE ENTIRE LIFE DEPENDING ON IT. I KNOW SHAWN, CHRIS OR LARRY WONT UNDERSTAND THIS BUT AT FIRST ALL THIS DELAY HAPPENED BECAUSE FIRST MY FATHER ANDOTHER MENBERS OF MY FAMILY

AGREED TO HELP ME WITH MONEY BUT WHEN SUDDENLY NIRAJ LOST HIS WIFR EVERYONE STARTED SAYING THAT THIS DEALING WAS NOT GOOD FOR US AND EVERYONE STEPPED OUT FROM THIS BUT I SINCE I MADE COMMITMENT I STOOD BACK TO HELP YOU ALL AND STARTED SELLING MY WHATEVER PROPERTIES I HAVE IN ALL OVER INDIA GIFTED TO ME BY MY GRANDFATHER AND GATHERED THE MONEY AND WHATEVER MONEY WAS LEFT OUT I GATHERED AFTER I SELL OUT ALL MY SHARES IN MY FAMILY BUSINESS, SOLD OUT ALL MY SHARES TO MYFAMILY MEMBERS AND TOOK MONEY FROM THEM AND ALSO I LEFT AWAY MY HERIDITERY RIGHT FROM MY FAMILY BUSINESS IN ORDER TO INVESTYOU, SO I HOPE THAT NOW YOU CAN UNDERSTAND THAT HOW IMPORTANT IT IS FOR ME TO DO THIS DEALINGS BECAUSE WITHOUT THIS DEALINGS HAP-PENS I WILL TURNED TO A STREET BEGER AND IF THIS DEALING HAPPENS I CAN TURN MYSELF TO A MULTIBILLIONAIE IN INDIA AND INA NEXT FEW YEARS IN THE WORLD.

I CONVEYED YOU MY HISTORY BECAUSE I THINK YOU, KEVIN, BRIAN AND JACK AS FAMILY MEMBER SO I TOLD YOU WHAT I HAVE DONE AND TOO ME THIS INVESTMENT IS VERY IMPORTANT BECAUSE IF THIS INVESTMENT DOESNT HAPPEN RBI WILL FORFEIT THIS FUND I WILL BE TURNED INTO STREET BEGER. BECAUSE I LOST MY RIGHT IN MY HOUSE ALSO IN WHICH I LIVE, SO YOU CAN UNDERSTAND THAT HOW HOW IMPORTANT AND ESSENTIL FOR ME TO DO THIS DEAL.
WITH BEST REGARDS
ANAMIKA BISWAS

"She sold all she owned to help faceless people she never met?" was a question that repeated itself over and over in my head. The only person I faintly remembered doing something vaguely similar was Buddha, though I was not a witness. The concept of limitless charity was not even in the embryonic stage in the U.S. where robbing from the poor/middle class and giving to the obscenely rich through so-called tax cuts was more the order of the day

Before long Steve set everybody straight from his comfy confines down under.

"The copy of Anamika's personal email is appreciated. Although it is touching and the embryo of a unbelievable story, bearing in mind that Indian Rupees 1,000 crore equates to approximate US$216,872 mil-

lion, it is very hard to understand where an amount of US$20-US$33 billion comes from for investment. If this sort of wealth is genuine then it places Anamika in the same league as Warren E Buffett, who with a wealth of US$30.5 billion, is the second richest person on the globe! Wow what a feat for such a young entrepreneur!! I continue to watch what unfolds with GREAT interest and anticipation.

I was pleased that he would finally have something to do with himself at night.

With our funding date Sunday, July 27th based on Kevin's report that Anamika spoke to the assistant bank manager on the 25th who told her basically all would be well in forty eight hours; we knew the earliest we would hear from Anamika would be Monday morning, July 28th.

Larry sent us an email on Sunday, the contents of which he apologized for before he even spilled them. Breathlessly he exclaimed:

"1. We now fully believe that Anamika is very very real, very very wealthy and is GOING to VERY SOON fund all of our projects."

With that build up he started his spiel, the core of which was that Brian was planning a trip to India and needed to raise $1,000 from the group for expenses so that he could meet with Anamika and prove that she was as "very, very real and very, very wealthy" as Larry proclaimed.

Ever the gentleman, Larry limited his fund raising to the men in the group. "The ladies in our group are not being asked for obvious reasons," of which I was oblivious. Chivalry was not dead, but it was misplaced.

I prepared to send Brian one hundred dollars, not thinking that if—let me repeat if—Anamika funded the group within the next twenty four hours, his trip would be unnecessary. As with the entire experience, no one connected the dots in real time.

Naturally Craig, from his lofty sideline perch, disagreed with Larry. He didn't think Brian's trip to India "was warranted at this time." Instead, he offered to "prioritize the following steps as the appropriate sequential course of action in this matter:"

a) If Anamika needs assistance, she should retain the legal services of a top law firm in India. The appropriate law firm may have close links with the UBI or have a senior partner on the Board of Directors of the bank. If one of the top law firms in India can't assist her then the following steps may not be successful either.

b) If assistance is needed via resources outside of India, Then the intermediaries representing some or all of the 23 corporate recipients in this funding transaction should provide whatever administrative or referral services they can that have appropriate experience in the banking industry in India.

c) If the intermediaries involved in this transaction do not have any sources of assistance, they should solicit the 23 corporate recipients to ascertain if there is professional and knowledgeable help in the group that can provide Anamika with some definitive direction

d) As a last resort, someone from the group should go to India to provide assistance providing their attendance is specifically requested by Anamika whereby their travel and expenses will be paid for by Anamika.

I think the best solution for all parties at this time is continue to wait.

Waiting is the raison d'etre of pompous blowhards, who would prefer to do nothing more than pontificate, noses high in the air, so they do not even get a whiff of the fray. Do nothing but remain ever vigilant to be critical of those who, unlike them, had the courage to act.

Then

Like the first drops of rain after a ten year drought.

A miracle happened. The first client got a fax from Anamika within forty eight hours. Just as she told Kevin. Just as the assistant or assistant bank manager told her.

We all had hope again. More importantly one of the clients had his letter of commitment and funding from Anamika.

Brian, who was planning the trip to India, was the first client. Anamika told him that the other clients would be getting their confirmation letters July 28th or 29th.

Soon after we heard that Kevin had received his confirmation letter. Then Jack and even Dave. I started getting very annoyed. Of that group, I was the only one to get Anamika the publicity she required. Not only had she been grateful for my help, she indicated a desire to continue in a close working relationship.

I know I am whining, but I was pissed off! When that condition occurs, steam needs to be released. The frat brothers in "Animal House" had a road trip. I had email. I wrote to Anamika

July 28—1:11:22 PM EDT

Dear Anamika

I understand Brian Gordon received a confirmation fax from you. That is very good news.

However, I have provided you with a great service in the form of publicity. I acted immediately after you asked for help and I was very successful—you were interviewed by two newspapers and a TV station; articles appeared in newspapers in India, Canada and the U.S. They are: Kolkata Telegraph, Times of India, Variety, Film International, India West and Weekly Voice.

I have been very supportive and very respectful, while other clients have not.

Surely, you can demonstrate your appreciation by making a determined effort that I be among the first to receive a confirmation fax from you.

I look forward to meeting you and doing business with you, but I cannot explain why you have treated me this way.

Best regards,
Vincent Panettiere

When all else fails, I depended on guilt to win the day. The next morning I received her reply.

July 29—1:40:17 AM EDT

HELLO SIR
DONT WORRY I WILL REMEMBER WHAT YOU HAVE DONE TO ME TILL THE LAST MINUTE OF MY LIFE BUT YESTERDAY MOST OF THE FAX DIDINT WENT THROUGH AND I GOT TENSED SO THIS THINGS HAPPENED SO DONT WORRY I WILL SEND YOU TODAY YOU WERE IN MY FIRST PREFERENCE CLIENTS LISTS ALONG WITH KEVIN, RN MANSFIELD, JACK, ALAN, BRIANBUT I CANT GET THROUGH WITH ALAN, RNMANSFIELD AND JACK SO I GOT TENSED THATS WHY I WAS INCAPABLE FOR FAXING.
WITH BEST REGARDS
ANAMIKA BISWAS

In fact, both Brian and Chris advised the group the same day that Anamika was having trouble sending her fax to several of the clients. Chris also advised she was trying to "wrap this whole deal up with each client...." Even though Brian had received his commitment letter he still planned on going to India, meet with Anamika and help the process, along with himself.

Craig was still not getting enough attention from mommy. The "individuals who have been designated as the Anamika spokesmen" were not sharing information with him. "... if those that know information are not prepared to share it with the rest of the group then please allow us to initiate our own direct communications with Anamika again."

Nothing had ever stopped him but his own inertia, laziness and misguided sense of his exalted stature.

Not to be out done, Steve from down under provided his own request. "It would be appreciated if those individuals who have been designated as the Anamika spokespersons for the group would communicate DAILY with the rest of us." Daily? As if they had nothing else to do but keep His Lordship informed.

There was an eerie similarity between the email from PB#3 and PB#2. "... if those that know information are not prepared to share it with the rest of the group then please allow us to initiate our own communications with Anamika again." Hmmmm? Yet, his activity prior to his July 29th email belied his request. He had sent Anamika half a dozen emails over the preceding week. Is there any wonder why she didn't respond to them?

Then the true nature of this latest message became clear. He was in as much of a frenzy over funding as we all were. If only he had been mature enough to admit it instead of hiding behind his transparent facade of propriety, professionalism, etc. We all wanted to be funded. We all needed to be funded. Anamika's intent to fund all of us represented the potential culmination of our wildest hopes and dreams. We all knew wishing doesn't make it so. Therefore it was very important that funding occur so that we could leave the fantasy world of wishes and enter reality.

Steve continued.

Several principals have received faxes from Anamika but nobody has advised, even in sanitised format, what the contents are. In view of all this unprofessionalism, mismanagement and lack of reliable information, can you confirm if the funds are now coming from UBI or another bank? If not UBI, which bank is Anamika now using for the transfer of funds? When is it likely funds will be transferred? What is contained in the fax that is being sent out? If the fax does not contain a copy of the confirmation slip of funds remittance, it will have no significance or credibility with our banks, vendors and project contractor who have lost patience with this protracted process.

It is hoped that commonsense and professionalism prevail and this most unsatisfactory situation can be resolved forthwith.

If it was so unprofessional and unsatisfactory, why did he stick around? All together, now
M-O-N-E-Y.

July 30

Larry's email—11:20:77AM EDT—informed the group that four hundred and fifty dollars had been donated towards Brian's trip to India, which he understood "will really make a big difference at India prices."

He also explained: "Brian was going over to represent himself and some others of us anyways and we were simply trying to offer everyone the chance at some representation in a professional manner."

About an hour later we heard from Craig. He sounded like the quintessential, stereotypical nagging wife. To the PCers who disapprove of such a description I say—if there weren't such persons in real life they couldn't be stereotyped. Moving on to his specific email.

What is the purpose of Brian's visit to India? For those that support Brian's trip and seek his representation on their behalf, is there an expectation that their funding will be released first and those that do not support Brian's trip can wait? Will this trip interfere with Anamika's funding schedule such that due process will be replaced with a priority list of companies that support this trip?

[There is a wellspring of unmitigated gall in his first paragraph. Beyond that I've found that those who are willing to suspect the worst in others usually intend to do the worst to others. Psychobabble, perhaps. Nevertheless it remains an often used stratagem to undermine the value and intent of others before one's own gets discovered.]

Brian and Kevin have received their fax letters. Of the remaining 21 companies in the funding group, how many others have received a fax from Anamika? Do you know if the balance of the faxes will be sent out prior to Brian's trip to India or will they be sent out after his arrival?

There has been no update on the bank confirmation slips. What is the status on the transfer of funds? Are the funds still being sent from the UBI? If not, which bank is Anamika now using? Are the transfers on 'hold' for any reason?

It would be appreciated if someone in the group could answer some or all of the above questions.

Larry admitted his failings as a"broker" for the group in his reply.

"… i was taken out of the 'Click' so to speak in week 3 by anamika herself when i gave her a few suggestions and have never been nor will i ever be placed in any position of authority since. She really dislikes critisism no matter if she is wrong or not.…

I felt sorry for those who chose to put their faith in Larry and Chris, yet it was their choice to sit back to be fed information, rather than mucking about in the scrum. I tried to be helpful and responsive to anyone who asked but didn't rely on Larry, Chris, Brian, and Kevin et al to feed me.

Craig was not satisfied with Larry's admission of impotence as his paranoia and distrust continued to brew.

… I wonder if Brian has now told Anamika not to send out any more faxes until he comes over to 'organize the paperwork'. She can't be having problems sending faxes to all of the other 20 members of the group

(Brian, Kevin and Scott had received commitment faxes at this point)

My key issue with Brian's trip to India is that he's stepping outside of the group and saying 'me first'. Brian was selected as one of the spokesmen for the group. I believe he is using this 'power' to prioritize his own agenda and gain ahead of everyone else.

(I have my doubts Craig would've have done anything different given the chance or the initiative. He was too old to be so naive. And if he wasn't naive he had to be disingenuous.)

> *If he's going to represent the group then he should provide fair and equal representation for everyone regardless of whether they support his trip to India or not.*
>
> *Kevin advised me yesterday that the transfers would be completed by Saturday August 2. Now it looks as if Brian has interfered and told Anamika not to send out the transfers until he gets to India.*
>
> *I may be wrong on the above assumptions, but that is the perception that is being portrayed right now. Since neither Brian nor Kevin will respond to my up-front and fair questions, they are only fueling speculation on some game-playing in this transaction.*
>
> *If Biotron doesn't receive a fax from Anamika within the next 24-48 hours, then it would appear that someone is interfering with the process. If the fax doesn't arrive until after Brian arrives in India then any speculation may prove to be reality.*
>
> *I think it is also safe to say that if all the faxes and transfers are not completed before Brian goes to India then someone has given Anamika direction to hold off.*
>
> *We'll see what the next few days brings.*

There was enough insecurity to go around the world as PB#3 from down under provided his opinion.

> *On the funding option I'm sure most of us, like you, are keen to know the answers and why only a select few are being corresponded with whilst the rest of 'we mortals' have to beg for information and still are in the dark.*

Maybe he should take the hint. NO BODY LIKES YOU BECAUSE YOU ARE A WHINING, SMARMY, MANIPULATIVE PHONEY. How's that for an answer?

Before long, another precinct was heard from. Myke, not to be confused with Mike, sent Anamika an email which he graciously shared with the group. He was to receive more than one billion dollars from Anamika.

Dear Anamika
I am not enjoying reading the cc'd email from our other clients

(what he meant to say was *your* other clients—it gets better)

They say you have changed your phone numbers and email. This is no laughing matter I assure you I have seen newspaper exclusives and media coverage with mentioning my film company name without our consent, then we are told to instruct our bank you are sending funding and nothing comes in from you.

We are now being discredited with our own bankers and have been used for your publicity. How do you expect us to feel or react in conjunction to this.

I have questions.

1. HOW DID YOU MEET MR. CATLIN?
2. WHO IS YOUR BANK MANAGER?
3. WHAT IS YOUR BANKS PHONE NUMBER
4. WHAT IS THE LAST DATE YOU GUARANTEE FUNDS TO BE WITH US BY
5. WHAT IS THE AMOUNT?
6. WHAT IS YOUR AD MR. CATLINS HOME PHONE NUMBER

FAILURE TO REPLY COULD RESULT IN A MULTIMILLION DOLLAR LAW SUITE SUEING FOR WIRE FRAUD UNLICENSED FINACIAL LENDING, SLANDER OUR ATTORNEY SAID 77 CHARGES COULD BE BROUGHT. SUPINAS AND BAILIFES AND COURT ORDERS CAN BE BROUGHT TO YOUR DOOR BY POLICE AND MR CALINS

The rest of this email for some unexplained reason he addressed to

SIR

(I wondered if he thought Anamika was a man, even though he had seen her picture in the Kolkata Telegraph. Yikes.)

> *UNLESS I HAVE A FULL WRITTEN EXPLANATION WITHING 36 HOURS WE WILL APPROCH THE SUPREME COURT WITH THIS AND YOUR OTHER 19 CASES*

> *IT IS AN INSULT TO HEAR FROM MR CATLIN TOMORROW TOMORROW ATFER IT COST US MONEY AND OUR PRO-FESINAL TIME TO MEET YOUR CRITERIA.*

> *TO BE USED AND DISCREDITED AFTER 36 HOURS IF YOU DO NOT PROVIDE OR MR. CATLIN PROVIDE A FULL REALISTIC EXSPLANATION WE WILL WIRE THREE MILLION DOLLARS TO OURNEW YORK ATTORNEY ON WALL STEET TO PRESS CHARGE AND LAUNCH A FULLFEDERAL PRIVATE INVESTI-GATION INTO YOUR ENTIRE FAMILY AD MR. CATLIN.*

In addition to not being able to spell or construct a coherent thought Myke, upon further investigation on Internet fraud sites, turned out to be a bit of a shifty character as well. Good grammar does pay.

At this point I continued to believe in Anamika and was determined to protect her—don't ask me why—from the bullies in the group. I wasn't alone. Not everyone who defended Anamika thus far had received their funding fax either. There was Alan in Texas and Miss Jody, along with Allen and Allen from Philadelphia and Phoenix respectively. By adding Brian, Kevin and Jack we represented one third of the group while outnumbering the vocal critics two to one.

I decided to drop Myke an email—7:53:04 PM EDT—with copies to the group and a blind copy to Anamika.

July 31

Your email this morning to Anamika was a great disservice to the group and to yourself.

When the anxiety level is at an all time high among those who have been getting closer and patiently waiting for much-needed funding—you decide to throw a grenade into a gasoline tank.

While your childish rant may have vented your spleen and may have given you short term relief, in the long run you may have ruined the opportunity we have for financing with Anamika.

I certainly hope that is not the case.

I'm sure you don't care. Your letter was all about you, self involved, childish, 'I want what I want when I want it', immature you—and I don't care how old you are. Your letter was adolescent.

And, your poor syntax, grammar and mis-spellings revealed your lack of professionalism.

More importantly—YOUR THREAT IS EMPTY—A JOKE!

If you had a shred of a scintilla of an idea about how the U.S. Supreme Court works you'd know such a suit as you propose would never get passed a lower court.

And your baseless claim that Anamika mentioned your (Fortune 500 isn't it) in a news story. Such a crime!!! Like she has no right to speak. And, I'm sure you have no contract with her embargoing that speech until some future date.

But on the bright side.

I WANT TO PLAY POKER WITH YOU! Your bluffs are so transparent I'd clean up and I can't tell a full house from an empty one.

My suggestion to you—and those who agree with you—is leave the group. Get financing elsewhere, Morgan Stanley, the Bank of England, etc. I will be glad to oblige your whims.

If you care to stay, keep your insecurities and cancerous negativity in check—like big boys.

If I got that letter from you, I'd cut off your funding in half a heartbeat.

I continue to believe in, support and trust Anamika who is a very generous and courageous woman.

If you don't—tough. Bite your tongue and act like a man.

Sincerely,
Vincent Panettiere

Myke's response to me was to suggest that I perform a biologically impossible act.

Even though I sent Anamika a blind copy of my letter to Myke, I felt she needed to hear further clarification from me. Beyond that, I wanted to maintain contact with her as five clients were in receipt of her funding letter and I was determined to get mine—10:03:49 AM EDT.

Dear Anamika
I am disturbed by the email some of the clients have sent you, particularly the one today by Myke Macino of Silvertouch.

It not only was disrespectful, but not truthful as well. What I see as a big bluff—like in the game of poker when you have a poor hand of cards and try to get the other guy to commit first.

Please give me some information that I will distribute to the clients to calm them down.

I'm aware of the thunderstorms and phone difficulties. I've tried calling you and gotten a message that all circuits in the country are busy, etc.

I believe in you, trust you and support you.

Let me help.

Best regards,
Vincent Panettiere

Craig, with a remarkable grasp of the obvious decided to ride to the rescue in his email late in the evening of July 31st.

> *Frustrations are running high which, in my opinion, have been caused by:*

a) No commitments have been fulfilled....
b) No scheduled dates have been met....
c) No communication from those who have assumed responsibility to speak directly with Anamika and report back to the rest of the group....

Blah, blah, blah went the rest of his letter. In the end he appointed Steve, the wonder from down under, to be the new spokesperson and barked orders to Kevin and Brian to have Anamika "arrange to have this bank letter issued and faxed by August 1 or August 2, 2003 to each member of the group."

He was taking over? After others had expended time, energy and money while he sat on the sideline pontificating with his joystick, he was taking over? Not bloody likely as we say in Brooklyn.

Larry sent the group another of his "make nice" emails—10:34:37 PM EDT—in which he asked all to "settle down give her the time. She has not asked anyone for money or anything but some papers ... Monday she is to have the slips ... and if she even says she has them ... we should be able to see it through our banks ... So lets just settle down and have a good weekend ... all should be coming to an end Monday ... Tuesday."

According to the report from my machine, while I slept I got two fax late on July 31, 2003—so late it was almost August. At 23:29 I received one page. And, at 23:32 I received the other.

But I would not become aware of these documents until the morning of August 1.

JULY SCORE CARD		TOTALS
Funding Dates	6	31
(next funding date July 27)		
Delays	7	17
Funds Transfer Date	0	2
Draft/Tracking Numbers Sent	0	2
Holidays	0	2
Confirmation Slip Dates	8	8
Anamika Has Wired Funds	4	4
Anamika Travels	1	1
Poor Me Anamika	3	3

7. AUGUST, 2003

MY PRAYERS TO LAKSHMI ARE ANSWERED?

Christmas came the morning of August 1, 2003.

I GOT MY LETTER OF INTENT AND INVESTOR CONFIRMATION!

After all those unmet funding dates, crises and excuses, delays, unanswered email, late nights spent trying to out maneuver the Indian phone and electrical systems and on and on and on.

Indeed, my prayers to Lakshmi, the Hindu goddess of fortune, had been answered—along with those to martyred saints, extra terrestrials and my Aunt Josephine—couldn't hurt.

At the very least Anamika not only believed in my project, but—by funding me early—acknowledged that I had been helpful to her. Ego gratification, like Master Card is priceless. It was a feeling I was pleased to luxuriate in that morning.

Now came the time to actually read what she sent on her letterhead addressed to me and dated the first of August, 2003.

SUB: LETTER OF INTENT ALONG WITH INVESTOR CONFIRMA-TION LETTER RESPECTED SIR

THIS IS TO INFORM YOU THAT I ANAMIKA BISWAS DAUGHTER OF ASHIT KUMAR BISWAS RESIDING AT 84 JATINDRA MOHAN AVENUE KOLKATTA-700005 INDIA BY PREOFESSION EXPORTER, HA RECENTLY GOT THE OFFER ON 29TH OF APRIL 2003 FROM YOU THROUGH CHRIS CATLIN THAT YOUR COMPANY NEED THE INVESTMENT OF 1.035 BILLION (ONE BILLION THIRTY-FIVE MILLION USD), AND THAT IF YOUR INVESTMENT ARE MADE BETWEEN ONE YEAR YOU WILL REPAY ME IN 20 YEARS IN THE TERM OF 25% UNTIL EXCEEDING THE PRINCIPAL AMOUNT OF FUNDING IF THE AMOUNT IS PAID IN RIGHT TIME THE 25% OF COMPANIES COMMON STOCK WILL ENSURED TO AB EXPORTS SO AFTER ACEPTING YOUR CAUSE I AS THE CEO AND CHIRMAN OF MY COMPANY I AGREES TO INVEST IN YOUR COMPANY, AND ON THIS RESPECT THE FUND WAS INI-TIALISED FROM MY ACCOUNT THORUGH UNITED BANK OF INDIA SAVINGS ACCOUNT NO 178401 ON 14TH OF JULY 2003, BUT DUE TO SOME TECHNICAL PROBLEM IN BANKING SYSTEM THE FUND HAS NOT BEEN ABLE TO DELIEVER AND NOW THE ENTIRE THING WILL BE DONE THROUGH DIFFERENT INDIAN BANK PRESCRIBED BY UNITED BANK WITHIN TUESDAY 29TH OF JULY.... THIS LETTER WILL ALSO INCLUDE YOUR LETTER OF INTENT AS ANNEXTURE AND

AFTER THE RECEIPT OF THIS FAX YOU ARE REQUESTED TO HOLD THE SAME TILL THE DATE WITHOUT ANT FURTHER QUESTIONS AND ALSO YOU ARE REQUESTED TO TELL ALL THE REST OF THE CLIENT THAT THIS KIND OF FORMATED LETTER WILL FORWARD TO THEM ALSO BY TODAY OR TOMORROW HOPEING THAT YOU WILL HOLD PATIENCE AS I AM STILL UNDER CLAUSE OF YOUR TIME PERIOD.
WITH BEST REGARDS
ANAMIKA BISWAS
CEO OF THE COMPANY

She was sending me what? One Billion, Thirty Five Million U.S. Dollars?

Could this be? I was helpful to her, but still a Billion more than I'd requested? Now, that is real gratitude. Much more than a hearty handshake or beautifully framed certificate, a Billion dollars is what one sends when one cares to send the very best. Yowee!

But, could it really be true? I re-read the letter and my bubble lost some air. This was not exactly the kind of letter one expects to receive. True there was no doubt it was from Anamika—the misspelled words and poor grammar were consistent with all her other communication.

Nevertheless, it did express her intent—even if the standard legal language was missing.

Then came the old balloon deflator worming its way into my adult consciousness—"if it sounds too good to be true, it usually is."

"Why should that be so", my Hopeful Persona asked, "just because so-called 'conventional wisdom' and old wives tales says so?"

"If I accept that premise," HP argued, "then, is it true every single time something seems TGTBT it actually is TGTBT? Do any records exist showing that in even a small percentage of cases an opportunity that seems TGTBT actually is REAL?"

Adult Consciousness was silent on the matter. It didn't know if there actually were any records kept in this area. But it was certain that conventional wisdom could be relied upon.

HP dismissed AC with a hearty "WHY NOT ME?"

The lack of response to that question enabled HP to move forward. I planned how the $1.35 Billion would be used. Extensive charts that expanded the initial goal of six films were created. New opportunities and ventures were added including ownership of a baseball team. Three to four hundred million could snag an under performing major league team; much less for a top minor league operation. Vision was expanded. Nothing seemed impossible to achieve. How wonderful to feel so good and be so lucky.

Trying to contain a self confident grin, I sent Anamika an email of appreciation. "You are very generous. I am grateful."

August 2

The next morning an email from Anamika was waiting in my mailbox

HELLO SIR
HOW ARE YOU WELL EVEN IT IS MY PLEASURE OF HAVING A FRIEND LIKE YOU, I AM GRATEFUL TO GOD FOR HAVING YOU AS AFRIEND, BUT AT THE SAME TIME I AM SORRY FOR SENDING YOU THE FAX IN DELAY FOR WHICH I KNOW I HAVE HURT YOU, WELL THERE IS ONE MORE FAVOUR I NEED FROM YOU THAT IS I HAVE STARTED NEGOTIATION WITH HINDI FILMS SO CALLED BOLLYWOOD BUT NEED YOUR ASSOCIATION AS APATNER TO DO BUSINESS WITH ME ONT WORRY YOUR FUNDING WILL NOT REQUIRED IN IT BUT I WANT YOU TO STAY WITH ME. SECOND THING I NEED YOU TO DECLARE IN THE PRESS THAT FUNDING IS BEEN DONE ON WEDNESDAY THAT IS 6TH OR 7TH OF AUGUST.
THIRDLY I NEED HELP MORE YOU TO INTRODUCE MYSELF TO US ENDOWMENT COUNCIL FOR DOCUMENTRY WHICH I WILL SUPPLY THEM FROM INDIA.
WITH BEST REGARDS

ANAMIKA BISWAS

Funding Dates #32 & 33—August 6 or 7

Five days after the last funding date of July 27th (provided by Kevin after speaking with Anamika) passed without anyone receiving funds she provided new funding dates five days hence. As Letters of Intent appeared in the fax machines of seven clients, the group was more focused on when more letters would appear than on the fact that July 27th, the thirty first date given for funding passed without the transfer of one rupee.

I advised Anamika that we could partner in her negotiations with Hindi Films but decided "NOT to release anything to the press about funding until the funds are in my bank account in Los Angeles." One month had passed since Anamika received a deluge of publicity from my efforts. During that interval I had not received any funds, nor had anyone else. It was time for Anamika to "put up or shut up," or something more vulgar.

As some primitive tribes believe a photograph steals the soul, we were beginning to believe that Anamika was extracting some unknown substance from her so-called clients rather than deliver funding. This belief would become solidified and more specific in days ahead.

Yet, ever hedging my bets, I sent Anamika a conciliatory email on August 5th in which I reminded her of my intention to send out a release upon funding, but to sweeten the deal I would also take out "large advertisements in the entertainment trade papers—Variety and Hollywood Reporter."

For the next few days communication between clients centered on the same, familiar theme—no communication from Anamika. Two of the pompous blowhards in the group were particularly active. One injected the first divisive seed into the group. According to Steve, Anamika was "not going to communicate with the majority of the principals, other than the few 'chosen' ones who have her contact coordinates and speak with her daily ..." To further state his little boy jealousy, he added: "The situation doesn't appear too promising as still there is no proof of anything, particularly those of us who have received not even the faxes that the 6 principals have received (not surprisingly 3 of those principals being Anamika's 'chosen ones')."

Knowing the temperature of the group, I tried to reasonably appeal for Anamika to save her reputation by responding to all the clients in a manner that would be acceptable by Western standards of business.

August 6—10:55:56 PM EDT

Dear Anamika:
Over the last few weeks I have written to you and expressed my deep and sincere belief and trust in you; my continued support and everlasting gratitude.

I truly understand what a stressful and frustrating time this must be for you. I've tried to explain that to my colleagues in the group, to get them to understand what you are going through.

Some do, but many do not agree with me. Those who don't agree with me have become crazed with worry and fear and paranoia. There is talk of lawsuits from some—which makes me very angry.

It upsets me that they do not see in you what I see—a very strong, courageous and generous young woman who is doing all of us a great service.

Information needs to be forthcoming in the very near future. I suggest, as one who believes in you, that you find a more effective and efficient way to distribute the routing numbers from the bank to our individual accounts.

If you want to send them to me by DHL courier you can charge it to my account.

For your own well being and credibility please let me help you.

I can keep confidence and will distribute to all by fax from here if that is the direction you take.

I hope you give this serious consideration.

Best regards—Vincent Panettiere

Soon after my advisory was sent to Anamika, BobK could no longer keep his ego in his pants and nearly exploded the entire deal, for yet another time. In this instance his email was most offensive—though I'm sure in his puerile pea of a brain he thought it hilarious.

We were also shocked because among the recipients were Anamika, her father and uncle! We felt that email was another example of ugly American insensitivity and poor judgment.

All of us in the group received a multi-colored, animated email from PB#1 on August 6th at 7:32 PM.

Against a black background we read and see the following:

(The body of the letter was preceded by three skeletons wearing pink top hats and dancing like Rockettes. The first paragraph contained yellow print.)

Attention is requested for those involved in the funding.
It is now 7:20 pm. Eastern Standard Time Wednesday 06 August 2003 in the United States.

(The next line was in apple green print.)

There seems to be a problem, that needs to be addressed.

(The following paragraph was in aqua blue print.)

A few chosen individuals have received a Fax from Anamika while the rest of us have nothing, and we all sit and wait. (Why?) A few chosen individuals have open communications with Anamika while the rest of us have been banned from communicating with our investor. (bad idea) However it seems evident through all of this, that none of us have received any funds. (Why is That?)

(An opening and closing cell door preceded the next paragraph in white print)

I think that someone should open the door of communications and ask the question that everyone is to afraid to ask. No more delays, no more threats of loosing funding because we offend someone. Where is the funding?

There I asked it, and I think everyone agrees. PLEASE GET CLOSURE WITHIN 24 HOURS. With my and others sincere thanks.

(At the very end was a wad of twenty dollar bills being riffled.)

It was an appalling display of bad taste—not surprising considering from whence it came. However, more than anything the email and assorted graphics put the lie to PB#1's contention that he was a sober, reasonable businessman.

When I queried him on his shocking bad taste, his response was simply "got your attention, didn't it?"

August 8

Alan, from England, and one of the more sensible members of the group conveyed it best in his email of August. 8:

> *On the one hand everyone is trying to conclude this deal by assuring Anamika we are all supportive. With BS like this is it any wonder she decided to restrict her communications?*
>
> *I am sure if this was viewed by her uncle or Father I can only imagine their thoughts and responses. A lot of people in this group have remained quiet and patient and have a lot to gain from this if it is concluded in a satisfactory manner, if it falls through from BS like this*

I expect that any lawsuits better be aimed at people who pull tricks like this.

Within a day of sending that email to Anamika, I was very surprised to suddenly become her conduit with the group. Her fax to me was addressed:

RESPECTED SIR
SORRY FOR THE INCONVENIENCE BUT I AM HELPLESS ... DELAYED HAPPENED BECAUSE I HAD A DISPUT WITH MY FATHER FOR WHICH I AM THROWN AWAY FROM THE HOUSE, AND I ALSO HAD A TROUBLE WITH FAX AS IN

DELAY #18—Anamika is thrown out of her father's house

INDIA 31ST OF JULY IS THE DATE OF FILLING RETURN IN WHICH ALL OF YOUR INVESTMENT WAS KICKED OUT BY MY FATHER FOR WHICH I HAD TO PAY LARGE AMOUNT OF TAX AND FOR THAT I AM DELAYED BUT ON 13TH OF AUGUST 2003

Funding Date #34—August 13

ALL OF YOUR FUND WILL BE IN YOUR BANK I TRANSFER MY BANK IT NOW WENT TO STATE BANK OFINDIA INSTEAD OF UNITED BANK OF INDIA.

WELL I ALSO FOUND THAT THERE IS A FAX CAME TO MY BANK HEAD OFFICE YESTERDAY AROUND 4:00PM BUT I DON'T KNOW WHO SEND IT BUT IF YOU CAN TELL ME THAT I WILL BE HELPFULL VERY SOON I WILL GIVE MY DIFFERENT LAND LINE NUMBER WHERE I AM ... NOW AND ALSO MY NEW OFFICE NUMBER TIL;THEN MEANS TILL MONDAY 11TH OF AUGUST 2003 YOU CAN CONTACT ME OVER FAX AT 2351891 AFTER THAT I WILL GIVE YOU MY NEW NUMBER WHERE YOU GET 24HRS IN 7DAYS IN A WEEK.

TODAY I AM SENDING THE FAXES OF ALL THE CLIENTS NDA AND LETTER OF INTENT BUT I WANT THEM TO SEND TO YOU TO THOSE I CANNONT REACH IF YOU DON'T HAVE ANY PROBLEM CAN I FORWARD YOU THAT.

IN THIS FAX I AM SENDING YOU THE LIST OF ALL THE CLIENTS TO HOM THE FUND WILL REACH BY 13TH OF AUGUST 2003 SO I HAVE STATED THEIR NAMES, COMPANIES NAME, DATE OF GETTING PROPLSAL DATE OF SENDING THE FUND TIME PERIOD TAKEN TO COM-

PLETE THE DEAL AND AMOUNT THAT WILL REACH THEM. SOME ARE CONTACTING MY FATHER INSTEAD OF ME AND THEY WANT TO COME BUT I WONT MEET THEM.

I KNOW I AM TROUBLING YOU BUT PLEASE, PLEASE STAY WITH ME I NEED YOUR SUPPORT. THIS LIST I AM SENDING TO FEW OF THE CLIENTS ALONG WITH YOU AND IF YOU ALSO SUGGEST ME THAT TO WHOM I WILL SEND THOSE FAX AS I CANT REACH EVERYONE I WILL BE GREATFUL PLEASE INFORM THIS TO ALL CLIENTS.
WITH BEST REGARDS
ANAMIKA BISWAS.

The second part of the fax contained the categories as Anamika described them—list of companies, name of contact person, date of first contact, date contract with Anamika was completed, total time taken to complete the deal and amount of investment. The following list, which I have edited, only shows name of company and amount of investment.

KO GROUP—$1.35 Billion
Biotron International Limited—$7.1 Million (PB#2)
Thistle Productions Inc.—$30 Million
Timberwolf Productions—$1 Billion
Image Entertainment—$30 Million
Globalstar Inc.—$7 Billion
Tri-State Medical Services—$100 Million
Farrel Aviation—$750 Million
America's Choice, Inc.—$37.5 Million (PB#1)
Maximus Tiger—$105 Million
Reserve Oil & Gas—not specified
R. Allen Associates—$650 Million
Magick World Ltd.—not specified
Curo Interactive, Inc—$10 Million
JJ Concept and Design—$10 Billion (Larry's company)
Armada Holdings—$4.672 Billion (PB#3)
Enhanced Telecommunications—$3 Million
Macino Organization—$1 Billion
JA LAD—$1 Billion
Gisser Automotive—$50 million
Genesis Staffing—$3 Million
Stressless—$4 Million

Two companies were not included but later received Letters of Intent.
I contacted the group as Anamika instructed at 4:05:00 AM EDT.

To All
I received a fax last night from Anamika and she asked me to inform as many clients as I can. Some other clients will also receive the same fax as I received.

She indicated that she had family problems and tax problems which delayed her contacting us.
She said the funds will be in our accounts by Aug. 13. Her account is now in the State Bank of India rather than the United Bank of India.

The reason for the delay she said was because she had to pay a "large amount of tax."

On Monday Aug. 11 she will have a new land line. Until then you can contact her on her fax line—9133 2354 1891. The new number will be open 24/7.

I also received from her a list of 22 clients and the amounts they will receive on Aug. 13.

Please contact me with any questions.

Best regards,

Vincent Panettiere
Thistle Productions

Craig, AKA PB #2 was the first to respond—6:42:30 AM EDT unable to believe anyone but he could get results.

Vincent:
I have not copied the rest of the world on this particular e-mail.

If the funds are expected to be in our accounts by Wednesday, August 13, that would indicate that the transfers will be done on Monday, August 11. Has Anamika confirmed that the transfers will be done on Monday?

Previously, the UBI used Chase as their corresponding bank. Do you know which corresponding U.S. bank the State Bank of India uses?

I think that in light of all of the past delays and false dates that have been given, Anamika should obtain a 1-page letter from the Bank Manager at the State Bank of India confirming to her that "all the SWIFT transfers, as per the amounts noted for each company on the attached list, will be completed on Monday, August 11, 2003 and the State Bank of India will fax the confirmation slips directly to the recipient's bank and to the recipient company's principal as provided by Ms. Biswas." This letter could be faxed to you and anyone else she can send a fax to and those that receive the fax can forward it on to the others in the group. Ideally, this letter should be issued today or tomorrow at the latest. Otherwise, this latest update could be perceived as just another story for further delays.

If you can pursue these issues with Anamika it would be greatly appreciated as there hasn't been any direct updates for the past week from either Brian or Kevin.

Regards,

An hour later that morning Craig contacted the rest of the group.

Fellow Members of the Group:

Further to my correspondence yesterday regarding my early discussions with a senior manager at the United Bank of India, I did not receive a fax overnight from the bank and I have been unable to reach the bank by phone as an operator's recorded message states that there are "technical problems" with the phone lines. I will continue to pursue this matter to see if they can confirm that Anamika no longer has an account with the UBI.

Although Anamika's fax provides further optimistic hope that this transaction will come to a favourable conclusion, in light of Anamika's past history of promises and excuses (most of which come at the end of each week), this latest update should not be taken too seriously. Just four days ago we were told that the transfers were done and she had the confirmation slips in hand.

A letter from the State Bank of India confirming that the transfers will be completed on Monday, August 11, 2003 and that the State Bank of India will fax the confirmation slip to each recipient and their receiving bank would Certainly add credibility to this latest update. Perhaps Brian and/or Kevin (or anyone else that has access to Anamika) can get Anamika to have this letter faxed to some or all members of the group today (unlikely) or tomorrow.

I will provide the group with further updated information as it becomes available.

Mr. Generosity! He had not one clue that, with self-serving rationalization, he almost queered the deal by contacting Anamika's bank. All in the name of prudent due diligence. Hah!

I forwarded his email to Anamika telling her directly it was Craig who had called her bank. I also advised her to "be aware of the handful of clients who have been disloyal to you over the last month or so and who even with the email I sent last night continue to doubt you. You might want to reconsider the safety of your funds with such people."

By this time many in the group were losing patience with the delays, no matter how much they wanted to believe in Anamika or how illogical such belief seemed. When she informed us that she was moving her account from the United Bank of India to the State Bank of India some of us felt it would expedite the transfer if we moved our business accounts to SBI as well. There was a branch in Los Angeles and one in Chicago. For a few days we discussed the feasibility, ultimately concluding the change would cause more confusion and delay. We stayed put. But Anamika's email to me on August 9th advised of her move.

August 9

HELLO SIR
WELL I ALSO APPRECIATE THAT YOU GOT MY FAX I HOPE THAT YOU WILL FOWARD THAT TO EVERYONE, EVEN IN MY LETTER I ASKED THAT CAN I FAX EVERYONE'SNDA AND LETTER OF INTENT TO YOU OR NOT BUT YOU DIDINT REPLY THAT TO ME YET. WELL TODAY I WILL OPEN MY ACCOUNT IN SBI WHERE I WILL TRANSFER MY FUND ON MONAY AFTER WHICH I WILL GIVE YOU MY ENTIRE DETAILS

OVER MAIL IN THE MEANTIME I AM OPENING MY ACCOUNT IN FED-
ERATIONSTREET BRANCH IN KOLKATA.

WITH BEST REGARDS
ANAMIKA BISWAS

DELAY #19—Moved Account to another Bank

As SBI is a much larger bank it had a well sourced website. A check did not
reveal any branch on Federation Street. Though there was one on the same
street—Jatindra Mohan Ave.—as where she lived. Could be the branch was
known by its cross street. Yet the address was on Jatindra Mohan. Another discrepancy we chose to ignore.

Soon thereafter Mike informed the group that Anamika was using a commercial fax facility, like Kinko's, to contact us. We in turn were sending our
information to some hourly worker who could care less. No wonder many of
us encountered surliness whenever we called to complain about each succes-
sive delay in transmission. Oh, well....

More than three months into the ... process or fantasy no one was sure ...
and I began to feel as if I was experiencing the Indian version of the Helsinki
syndrome—i.e. when the captives start identifying with their captors. Call it
the Kolkata syndrome.

Under the spell of the Kolkata syndrome, I took it upon myself to advise
Anamika like a Dutch uncle—if that is not mixing cultures as well as alienating
the PC crowd. So be it. By any other definition, I was not minding my own
business.

However, my quotient of charity was running on empty when it came to
those in the group who did nothing but carp and criticize. No effort or development was ever good enough. If Anamika didn't communicate, they complained and when she did the content was never sufficient.

I sent her an email in which I asked her to reconsider some of her investments. I have no doubt that my motives were conflicted, ambiguous and less
than pure. I sent it.

Dear Anamika
THE FOLLOWING IS CONFIDENTIAL BETWEEN YOU AND ME

After reviewing the list of clients and your intended investments for each, I
began to worry about the safety and security of your funds.

It may not be my business—so please forgive me as I have only what is best for you in my heart—but as your friend and someone who is older and more exposed to many unpleasant aspects of the world I would not be honest with you if I did not strongly suggest that you reconsider the size of some of your investments to some of the clients.

Let me add that I am not alone in the above feeling. Others who are close to you, who I will not mention here to let them speak for themselves, agree with me.

A billion dollars is a lot of money and 10 billion dollars is a huge amount of money to spend on projects that are not realistic in the market place.

I don't know who is advising you and how you selected the projects, but before all your money leaves your hands you might want to reduce some of the funds you invest with clients who have been critical or disloyal until they prove capable through early stage performance of properly and efficiently using the balance. or you might simply and finally reduce it.

I know this is a late time to reconsider, but I'd hate to see you be taken advantage of and lose so much money. I fear that will happen.

I recall emails from you in late June expressing your hurt at how some of the clients treated you and spoke to you in their letters.

I also think you shouldn't fund at all those who have been very critical, disloyal or disrespectful to you and your family.

I believe the way they treat you now, is the way they will treat you and your money in the future—in a disloyal and disrespectful way, which will not bring a return or a profit.

Since those I refer to anonymously are ones who DO NOT have signed contracts with you—the letter of intent—I believe the amounts can be legally and ethically changed.

You have a right to reconsider and change your agreement before it becomes binding.

I hope you will give thought to the above.

I will support you no matter what decision you make, I just felt in my heart I had to express my concern.
With great respect, admiration and gratitude, I send you

Best regards,

August 10

Larry contacted some members of the group about what he called his "backup group." He described them as a "SUPER HUGE CONGLOMORATE and … one of the RICHEST FAMILIES IN INDIA" which he claimed had a total value of $485 Billion.

A check of Tata Groups website revealed it consisted of more than eighty companies and was involved in such industries as automotive, metals, hotels, power, chemicals, insurance, tea, publishing, engineering and information technology. Like many of Larry's suggestions, including Anamika, Tata was never a viable option.

Larry told us he was making a presentation to the group and requested we send him two pages to summarize our companies and their needs.

I declined to participate as I felt it was a "slap in the face" of Anamika. Specifically I told Larry that such an action would be saying to Anamika "… we don't trust her and we regard her so lightly that we would go around her back to others. As we are so close to a positive conclusion with Anamika, I will not engage in anything that is so blatantly unethical and self destructive. But, what irritates me more is that you stand to gain more billions from Anamika than anyone else in the group and you're the one instigating such a despicable action against her."

Larry, obviously, took umbrage, characterizing his email as an attempt to provide his clients with alternative sources of financing. "… i run a venture capital connection service so i have access to well over 20,000 lenders in over 50 countries … i simply present the options …" he informed me.

August 11

By now, Anamika was becoming more concerned about the clients who were calling her bank and creating potential embarrassment. She responded to that issue as well as to Larry in her email to me.

HELLO SIR
THANKYOU, WELL LIKE LARRY HE ONLY TOLD YOU BUT THERE IS SOMEONE WHO DIRECTLY STARTED ASKING BANK WITH FAX AS WHAT POTENTIALITY I HAD WHICH ALSO A BIG REASON OF TRANSFERING MY BANK FROM UBI TO SBI I WILL ALSO LIKE TO HAVE YOUR FAX OPEN SO THAT I CAN SEND EVERYONES PAPERS TO YOU AND ALAN SO THAT EVERYONE CAN HAVE THERE NDA AND LETTER OF INTENT. I ALSO LIKE TO SEND ALAN AN DAVE FAX TO YOU.
WITH BEST REGARDS
ANAMIKA

Thirty minutes later—2:45:24 AM EDT—Anamika also reached out to Brian, enlisting his help to prevent clients from calling her banks.

HELLO SIR
I LIKE YOLU ALL TO BE WITH ME AND ALSO I WANT YOU ALL TO SAY MR CRIAGE THAT SINCE I AM NOT DEALING FROM THAT BANK HE SHOULD TELL THEM THAT IT WAS A MISUNDERSTANDING HAPPENED BETWEEN INVESTOR AND CLIENTS THAT HE FAXED THEM INSTEAD OF ME. SO THAT INFUTURE MY DEALINGS WITH MY BANK REMAINS NORMAL BECAUSE YOU ALL WILL AGREE THAT I AM ALSO AN EXPORTER SO AFTER YOUR BUSINESS INVESTMENT MADE I NEED TO DO BUSINESS IN INDIA AND FOR THAT I NEED INDIAN BANKS WITH WHOME I CAN DO BUSINESS AND THAT LIST TGHIS BANK IS ALSO THERE FOR WHICH THIS LETTER WHICH BIOTRON GIVE CAN PUT REPUTATION IN STAKE TO BANK SO PLEASE FOR GOD SAKE ASK MR CRIAGE TO RESEND A FAX BY GIVING A POSITIVE IMPREESION OVER INVESTOR SO THAT THIS SITUATION GETS NORMALISED AS EARLY AS POSSIBLE. BECASU IF THIS LETTER ALSO GOES TO RBI THERE WILL BE AGAIN SOME PROBLEM WHICH MIGHT CAN ARISE. HOPE THAT ALL OF YOU WILL AGREE WITH ME SINCE THERE IS NO FORCE FOR OPINION.
WITH BEST REGARDS
ANAMIKA BISWAS

I received yet another email from Anamika on the same theme at 3:05:30 AM EDT.

HELLO SIR
WELL ITAKE YOU AS MY BEST FRIEND, PHILOSOPHER AND GUIDE SO
YOU CAN TELL ME WITHOUT ANY HIDE AND SEEK AS I WILL TAKE
YOUR WORDS AS HIGHEST PRIORITY. SIR I AM SHOCKED TODAY BY A
BEHAVIOUR OF MR CRIAGE S. FIELD OF BIOTRON INTERNATIONAL
WHO NOT ONLY PUT MY REPUTATION AT STAKE IN BANK BUT ALSO
PUT ME IN AEMBRASSED POSITIONBECAUSE OTHER THAN
INVESTOR I AM ALSO A EXPORTER WHO DO BUSINESS THROUGH
INDIAN BANKS FOR WHICH I NEED TO MAINTAIN A GOOD RELA-
TION WITH THEM BUT THIS LETTER LOST ALL MY REPUTATION. I
DON'T KNOW WHAT TO DO.

WITH BEST REGARDS

ANAMIKA BISWAS

WAITING FOR YOUR SUGGESTIONS

Anamika considered me her "best friend, philosopher and guide" and she was
waiting for my suggestions. Very flattering. It wasn't exactly the position to
which I currently aspired—a combo big brother and father confessor. I'd
already given at the office as a literary and baseball agent. By changing direc-
tions, I wanted to leave my years of advising in the past. Happily I saw that
Brian was willing to also help Anamika.

Brian forwarded Anamika's letter to Craig—AKA PB#2. Forcefully he told
Craig to follow Anamika's request and contact the bank stating his earlier letter
was a mistake. "By you sending this letter to UBI you almost ruined it for all of
us," Brian told Craig. "You are jeopardizing a project of mine that the funding
is 7 Billion USD, and I will not allow anyone to mess this up including YOU."

Those willing to assist and defend Anamika continued to grow. This time
Alan, who was another client with a written Letter of Intent from Anamika,
once again stepped forward at 12:07:07 PM EDT.

Dear Anamika
I spoke to Vince this morning privately regarding the mess that Craig Field
seems to keep generating. Both I and Vince have been settling everyone down
to give you breathing space so he usually refers to me to state it clearly and
diplomatically as he does not have the tolerance for the grief they are causing
you. I can say without hesitation Vince is definitely one of your best friends
and most loyal advocate for what you are trying to achieve.

I wanted to contact you as soon as I found out about the problems you are getting over UBI. After everyone is clear on what is going on I once again apologise that one or two seem to be obsessed with making this a mess again.

I have been updated on the whole time frame of the situation and now know that you were never really guided by Larry, Shawn or Chris. Indeed, I think they basically let you organize this and sat back as they were simply not competent enough to negotiate or administer something of this magnitude.

If it is acceptable to you I would on behalf of all members of the group, with the exception of the Dr. and Craig send a personal letter to your father, uncle and UBI which states categorically that down to unprofessionalism and the lack of cultural understanding that you were placed in such difficult circumstances.

While this is entirely your undertaking I feel obligated to offer my apologies to all members of the Biswas family for the complete failure of the "brokers" and the mistreatment you received due to this.

It seems apparent that certain members of this Group are under the impression that you are there to fund them with no regard for the fact that you have a business of your own to run.

Please do not allow them to cause you worry or anxiety I assure you that this matter will be resolved.

With best regards,
Alan
World Business Web, Inc.

Later on that evening—8:41:49 PM EDT—I responded to Anamika's "best friend," email.

Dear Anamika
I value your friendship and generosity. The following "suggestions" below will be direct, but for you to decide as I am not TELLING merely OFFERING suggestions.

While it is easy to offer suggestions, I also want to give you a direction.

Since you haven't sent contracts to those below as yet, you might inform them that their investments are on hold pending due diligence by your attorneys. Let your attorneys in India or Canada thoroughly investigate the business plans of those below and the reality of their proposals returning at least your initial investment.

Attorneys will cost less in the long run than what could be at minimum a $25 Billion investment.

These are the people whose investment I suggest you reconsider.

Larry—he will make plenty of money from commissions and $10 Billion is far too much to invest in a fantasy project without sufficient due diligence; and his emails have been disrespectful and poorly written, indicating an inability to think properly, in my opinion, as well.
Dr. Kilgallon—his emails have been constantly disrespectful with the last one—the one with the dancing skeletons—particularly offensive; he sent it to your family, which was an attempt to embarrass and discredit you.

Craig—I hope he sent his apology, but after reading his emails and the way he insists he is right after jeopardizing your reputation, how can he expect to be rewarded when he has almost ruined it for the group.

Steve Stinson—his emails to you have been disrespectful—talking down to a child like he was a father figure, not to mention critical and disloyal.

Myke Macino—I have email from him that said "there will be no (curse word) money, don't you (same curse word) get it?"

The above represent nearly $25 Billion in investments which you might reconsider.

I have no animosity towards any of the above, in my conscience I cannot stand to see someone as generous and open hearted as yourself—even though it is your money at risk—made to look foolish and taken advantage of.

Let me know if I can do anything else for you.

Best regards,

About two hours later, I sent Anamika suggested language she might send to those she decided not to fund.

> *Dear Sir*
> *After careful thinking, I have decide to reconsider the investment*
>
> *of AB Exports in your company until after complete, accurate due diligence conducted by my attorney and other representatives.*
>
> *You have choice to be funded by ot her. If you not wish my company to fund you please tell me.*
> *Until that time please wait til our looking closely at your project is complete.*
> *My advisors say this is right thing to do.*
>
> *With best regards,*
> *Anamika Biswas*

Re-reading this I am embarrassed for writing my suggested letter using the same rhythms and poor grammar to approximate Anamika's style of writing. As I figured she wouldn't be able to tell the difference, I was engaging in my own form of disrespect to her.

August 13

This was the thirty fourth funding date we'd been given by Anamika. It came and went without incident—and without funds. When next we heard from her on August 14th, she presented us with yet another surprise, but one that was more troublesome.

Someone in the United States was threatening to send Anamika to jail!

August 14

HELLO SIR
WELL I AGREE THAT I NEED TO LOOK TOWARDS THE FUNDING OF SOME PEOPLE BUT AT HIS MOMENT I CAN DO BEHIND THE BAR BY A PEOPLE OF YOUR COUNTRY HIS NAME IS MR GARY DEAN CHILDER.

HE IS THE OWNER OF REALESTATE SOLUTION AND INVESTMENT COMPANY HE STAYS IN MORGANTON, AFTER I GOT YOUR DEALING HE WAS INTRODUCED TO ME BY SHAWN A FRIEND OF CHRIS CATLIN BUT THE DEALING COULD NOT GO BUT RECENTLY AROUND MONTHS OR TWO AGO ANOTHER PERSON CALLED REGHU GAVE ME THE CONTACT OF GARY DEAN CHILDER FIRSTLY I COULDNOT RECOLLECT HIM BUT LATER ON I DID ABLE TO RECOLLECT HIM HE BROUGHT ME A PROPOSAL OF A MINE CALLED JM CARD RESOURCES BUT SINCE I COMMITTED YOU PEOPLE FIRST I THOUGHT THAT I MUST COMPLETE YOUR DEAL FIRST SO I LINGERED HE ALSO GAVE ME PROPOSAL OF SOME FUND BUSINESS FOR WHICH HE SEND ME POWER OF ATTORNEY BUT SINCE I DIDNT SEND HIM FUND I KEPT THAT POWER OF ATTNORNEY WITH ME. NOW HE HAD FILED A CASE ON ME AND NOW HE IS SAYING THAT IF I DON'T PAY HIM BY FRIDAY WHICH IS TOMORROW HE WILL PUT ME BEHIND BARS WHICH AS YOU UNDERSTAND WILL BE VERY DIFFICULT FOR US TO DEAL.
WHAT I WANT FROM YOU IS THAT YOU PLEASE CONTACT HIM AS I WILL GIVE YOU HIS NUMBER AND TALK TO HIM AND ASK HIM TO GIVE ME 10DAYS TIME WHICH I ALREADY ASK FROM HIM SO THAT I CAN COMPLETET YOUR DEAL AND AND THEN PAY HIM AND AFTER THAT IF HE WANTS ME TO PUT BEHIND THE BAR I WONT HAVE ANY REGREATS FOR THIS AS I WILL BE HAPPY THAT I HAVE DONE YOUR DEALS AND THAT YOU PEOPLE WILL NOT SUFFER FOR ME. I HOPE YOU WILL DO THAT.
WITH BEST REGARDS
ANAMIKA BISWAS

I immediately contacted Brian and some of the others who were loyal to and concerned about Anamika's welfare. Over the weeks, it was apparent to me that Brian had the closest relationship with Anamika. However, he was so intent and focused on getting his $7 Billion in funding from her that the dynamics of the group held little interest for him. My feeling was that until we had the money in the bank we had to be aware of potential and real problems.

Later that evening I found Anamika on Yahoo chat. Anamika told me she was being threatened by a man named Gary Dean Childers. In her email she said he lived in Morganton, which initially I felt she had misspelled until I learned she was not referring to Morgantown, West Virginia, but Morganton, North Carolina. The town was located in the northwest part of the state between Hickory and Asheville.

As we chatted, Anamika told me Gary Dean accused her of defrauding him. She wanted more time to gather the financing for our group. What intrigued me was that Gary Dean had only threatened Anamika by email. He had not served her with any legal papers.

I tried to allay Anamika's fears and told her "we will do a search of his character to see if he is trying to trick you." To my surprise she told me that Gary Dean knew Chris. Soon it was plain that Anamika had been handed down from one so-called "broker" to the other like a cyberspace blow up doll.

Anamika, for whatever her grasp of reality, was being used by those who only wanted to exploit her. She didn't want me to contact Chris "because he will make it a big issue … chris has a hobby of making things go big in shape … when they can be small".

Instead she wanted me to talk to Gary Dean and gave me his Yahoo chat ID which she thought was "investment5000 or investment 3000."

Earlier in my chat with Anamika I'd contacted Chris and asked if he knew Gary Dean. He responded while I was "talking" with Anamika. "Hi Vince, Good question who is Gary Dean Childer where did you hear about him? Chris". It was his usual cheeky evasion.

I assured Anamika I would not tell Chris that she gave me the information "you can tell him some one has told you to contact him," she said.

Moving on to a subject that we all cared much more about, I inquired about her new banking arrangement. She told me "it is fine. They are working well and they are cooperative too." And, the wiring? "Wireing will be completetd by saturday as tomorrow is our independence day so everything will be closed."

Funding Date #35—August 16

Holiday # 3—Independence Day

thistleent: I just want you to know that there are many of us who support you
thistleent: that we are not all the craig and Stinson's
eximp_group_pioneer: yes
thistleent: we appreciate what you are trying to do and are grateful
eximp_group_pioneer: i know that why i discuss my happines and sadness both with you all
thistleent: I look forward to us having a very successful relationship
thistleent: and look forward to meeting you in the near future
eximp_group_pioneer: i consider you all as my power to work
thistleent: good
thistleent: I am signing off

eximp_group_pioneer: ok
thistleent: night
eximp_group_pioneer: have a very releaxed night sleep.

But sleep did not come easily as I pondered the ramifications of Gary Dean's potential legal actions, assuming, of course, that he was totally legitimate. There was a glimmer of hope in the whole affair. Anamika had been threatened by email, but not received any legal papers. IF, and this is elitist but so what, someone living in the boonies of Morgonton, North Carolina could figure out how to file legal proceedings in Kolkata, formerly Calcutta, India IF he could even locate the giant subcontinent on a map, I'd have more cause for concern. For mine, and our, sakes I hoped Gary Dean stayed on his turnip truck.

I went back onto Yahoo chat.

In this second session of the night I was pleased to learn that Larry was not involved with Gary Dean. "GARY WAS INTRODUCED TO ME BY SHAWN", Anamika told me. Shawn was an Indian living in Northern California and the "broker" for two of Anamika's clients who were among the seven who had received contracts and Letters of Intent.

Here is where it starts to get very complicated—as if up to now all was straight as a string.

"AFTER WARDS," Anamika continued, "REGHU INTRODUCED ME THROUGH ID CALLED INVESMENT5000."

Reghu was a young man who worked at an Internet café in Kerala state which is located on the southwestern tip of India. Reghu trolled the Internet in search of those seeking financing and tried to match them with his money sources. Initially, he found Anamika for a client in Canada and got permission to pass her on to Chris. Pretty soon Anamika became the cyberspace version of a five dollar hooker.

I asked her what happened after Reghu made his introduction. She told me "I STARTED TALKING TO HIM AND I REALISED MUCH LATTER THAT HE WAS INTRODUCED TO ME FIRST BY SHAWN. THEN HE TOLD ME THAT HE WILL DO A FIND BUSINESS IN WHICH IF YOU SPEND I BIL-LION U WILL EARN ONE TRILLION IN 30 DAYS."

I wanted Anamika to know that Shawn had not taken very good care of his clients Alan and Dave. He would often call me for the latest information, instead of obtaining it from Anamika, as a reputable and real broker would. Her latest revelation elicited from me "OH NO!"

Anamika did not react to my outburst and continued with her reason for entertaining Gary Dean's proposal. "WHICH I THOUGHT WILL BE FINE TO DO AS I CAN MAKE MONEY MORE FASTER. BUT HE FOR THAT SEND ME A POWER OF ATTORNEY THAT AFTER YOU MAKE INVEST-MENT YOU CAN EARN THE MONEY FROM HIS ACCOUNT. BUT SINCE I WAS BUSY WITH YOU ALL I DIDNT DONE THAT. SO I DIDINT TOOK HIS ATTORNEY. BUT NOW HE S SUDDENLY TOLD ME TO SEND MONEY I ASK HIM TO GIVE ME SOME TIME AS I TOLD HIM THAT MY MENTAL CONDITION IS NOT AT ALL GOOD SO I NEED SOME TIME BUT SUDDENLY HE TOLD ME THAT HE WILL ... PUT ME BEHIND BARS...."

I assured Anamika as best I could that she would not be arrested. By now the outrageous attempt at extortion was becoming apparent. I also advised her not to deal with him, but deep inside knew she might not listen. Throughout the nearly four month process communicating with her, I became convinced that Anamika was a strong willed woman. It wasn't a compliment. I meant she was stubborn as a child and as willful. She would do what she wanted when she wanted and no one could penetrate that wall.

Yet, now that she appeared to be in serious trouble she wanted help. Maybe that was the means to convince her that a new and improved business approach was needed ...

She explained "EVEN I MAILED HIM DAY BEFORE YESTERDAY AND ASKED TEN DAYS TIME BUT TODAY WHEN I AM CHECKING MY MAIL I FOUND HE GAVE ME ONLY 4 DAYS TIME WHICH IS COMPLETING BY TOMORROW BUT I CANT DO IT."

I asked for his phone number and address and she said she would send it later by email. In the morning I would begin tracking down Gary Dean. The following gives some indication of the frustrating way we communicated.

thistleent: DO NOT SEND HIM ANY MONEY!!!!!!!!!!!!!!
eximp_group_pioneer: I AM NOT DENYING THAT I WILL NOT PAY HIM
eximp_group_pioneer: BUT I NEED TIME
eximp_group_pioneer: OK
thistleent: You will pay or you wont pay
thistleent: tell me
eximp_group_pioneer: I HEARD FROM MR LOUIS THE OWNER JMCARD RESOURCES
thistleent: and?
eximp_group_pioneer: THAT HE HAD FIVE FRAUD CASES

eximp_group_pioneer: AND THEY INFORMED ME NOT TO DEAL WITH HIM

thistleent: who had five fraud cases—Gary or Mr. Louis

thistleent: DO NOT PAY GARY DEAN ANY MONEY

thistleent: DO YOU UNDERSTAND?!!!!!!!!

eximp_group_pioneer: THAT WHY IN THE END FOR ONE OR TWO WEEKS I KEPT AWAY FROM HIM (GARY DEAN)

eximp_group_pioneer: YES

thistleent: Tell me you won't pay him any money

thistleent: write it out so I can understand

eximp_group_pioneer: WHEN MR LOUIS TOLD HIM THAT HE DONT WANT TO DEAL WITH GARY THEN ONLY I STOOPED TALKING WITH HIM

eximp_group_pioneer: I WILL WRITE OUT EVERYTHING EVEN I WILL RESEND THOSE EMAILS TO YOUR ID

eximp_group_pioneer: SO THAT YOU CAN VIEW IT

thistleent: ok

thistleent: One more thing

eximp_group_pioneer: THE EMAILS SEND TO ME MY MR LOUIS THAT HE DONT ANT TO DEAL WITH GARY

eximp_group_pioneer: AND ALSO GARY'S EMAILS

eximp_group_pioneer: THAT HE HAD FILED CASE AGAINST ME

thistleent: this you'll forward to me by email?

eximp_group_pioneer: YES

thistleent: excellent

eximp_group_pioneer: IT WILL HELP YOU TO VIEW

thistleent: good

thistleent: Remember this, many people want to be successful with you

thistleent: Brian and I and Kevin and Jody and others

eximp_group_pioneer: THAT I KNOW

thistleent: let us help you

eximp_group_pioneer: YES

thistleent: please reconsider some of your investments as I mentioned

thistleent: in an earlier email

thistleent: you can't be spending 23 billion on those who do not respect you

eximp_group_pioneer: I KNOW

thistleent: do you understand what I'm saying

eximp_group_pioneer: YES I DID

thistleent: do you have a financial advisor in India that you trust

eximp_group_pioneer: AND I RESPECT YOUR FEELINGS
thistleent: thank you
eximp_group_pioneer: AND I WILL OBEY THEM
eximp_group_pioneer: SPECIALLY OF SJ STINSON
eximp_group_pioneer: YES
thistleent: I am not your father, just a friend who wants to help
eximp_group_pioneer: KHOA NEUGUN
thistleent: what do you mean by SJ Stinson?
thistleent: I see those are the ones you do not want to fund
eximp_group_pioneer: BUT IN THE AGE OF MY FATHER THOUGH YOU ARE FRIEND BUT I RESPECT YOU AS I SHOULD DO TO MY FATHER
eximp_group_pioneer: YES
eximp_group_pioneer: BECAUSE STINSON WAS VERY RUDE
thistleent: he was
eximp_group_pioneer: OLD NOT BY AGE BUT BY EXPRIENCE WHICH IS VERY IMPORTANT
thistleent: May I suggest you fund those who have been loyal and supportive
eximp_group_pioneer: YES
eximp_group_pioneer: YOU CAN
thistleent: and then re-examine the others by asking for more due diligence
eximp_group_pioneer: YOU CAN SEND THOSE BY EMAIL
thistleent: I sent you a list of five names by email
eximp_group_pioneer: AS I AM MOVING NOW TO GET XEROX AND ALSO TO BANK
thistleent: ok, will sign off
eximp_group_pioneer: I WILL GET BACK TO YOU LATTER ON
eximp_group_pioneer: OK
thistleent: am going to sleep
eximp_group_pioneer: BYE
thistleent: bye
eximp_group_pioneer: REMEBER I HAVE 24 CLIENTS
eximp_group_pioneer: FROM WHICH LEAVING YOU 5 YOU HAVE CHOSSE
thistleent: I will chose
thistleent: night
eximp_group_pioneer: OK
eximp_group_pioneer: NIGHT

We ended our session on Yahoo chat. Anamika went off to take care of business and I tried to get some sleep, knowing there was a challenge I'd never faced before waiting for me when I woke up on the morning of August 14th.

Eventually, Shawn realized it was in his best interest and that of his two clients who had agreements with Anamika to provide me with the information I needed about Gary Dean. Mr. Childers did business under the name Professional Acquisition Investor, with the address of 5435 Blumie Carswell Dr, Morgonton, NC 28655. When I called the two numbers Shawn gave me, both were "not in service or disconnected."

Later in the day Shawn sent me a copy of a letter from someone named Ramzi to Anamika regarding a High Yield Investment Program. HYIPs, have been used over the years to scam the unsuspecting. As Shawn said Ramzi was a friend of Gary Dean's no doubt the two clearly regarded Anamika as a clueless pigeon.

Ramzi's letter had been sent to Anamika April 16, 2003 just about the time Larry and Chris were putting their group together and two weeks before I got involved. No wonder Gary Dean wrote such a threatening letter to her. He and Ramzi had their hooks in her for a long time and must have discovered via Reghu or Chris or Shawn that there were twenty four clients, with viable and more credible projects than a HYIP, ready to feed at the trough.

I called the office number on the letterhead for Ramzi's company "Structure Finance Group, A Subsidiary of Hollywoodland Films" and learned that there was no such company at that number or at the address provided. In fact, the address was for a complex where offices where rented and had a receptionist to answer all the phones. Nothing intrinsically wrong with that but it indicates his company had the ability to fold its tent at will. That is what it did between April and August. A check of the phone company came up empty, as well.

I sent Anamika information on HYIPs, which was complex but still hoped she would understand enough to realize Ramzi and Gary Dean were scamming her. Next I tried contacting the Morgonton Sheriff's Department only to learn that the investigating officer, Lt. John Suttle was away until the following week.

More than anything I wanted Anamika to shift her focus away from the "threat" and direct it toward the group of us who were most supportive—Brian, Kevin, Allen, Alan, Jody and me. I asked her to "please concentrate your energies on those businessmen and women in the group who are loyal, honest and hard working; people who support you, value you and your investment and want nothing more from you than to share in successful business ventures."

I informed Anamika of what I'd found in just one day of searching and asked her to realize that if Gary Dean could not pay his phone bill, he certainly could not afford to retain a lawyer and pay his professional fee plus expenses for a trip to India and all the other costs involved with filing legal documents in Kolkata, Mumbai or wherever such matters were adjudicated.

At this same time, I would learn months later, Reghuraj contacted Anamika regarding Gary Dean. In his email to her on August 15th he wrote "Dear if u give me Garys details, may be I can solve it, or make him silent, I will tell him, I will share the commission with him and no more troubles at you, that's what Im doing with others now ..."

This certainly was proof that Gary Dean was a product of Reghu's Internet surfing. Instead of finding a few minnows he landed a more threatening species.

But, Reghu also had other problems. He initially found Anamika for Jerry of Toronto. Now eight months had passed and Jerry had not been funded. Reghu was frantic, a condition most of our group would not experience for a few more months.

August 15

When I checked email on the morning of August 15th I found one from Anamika at 2:04:43 AM EDT that once again threatened to destroy what we all had been working toward.

HELLO SIR
THIS IS TO INFORM THAT IF ANYONE NOW AS I CAME TO KNOW PLANNING TO CALL SBI TO CALLS SBI THEN THIS DEAL WILL CLOSE HERE AND I WILL NOT PAY ANY ONE EVEN A SINGLE PENNY. SO I HOPE THAT YOU WILL UNDERSTAND THAT EVERY INSULTING HAS AN END AND IT HAD TO BE ENDED SOMEWHERE, BECAUSE I CAME TO FUND YOU BY GIVING ALL MY ASSESTS TO GO TO SELL SO THAT YOU PEOPLE GET GOOD FUTURE OF BUSINESS AND AS WELL AS ME, BUT IF YOU PEOPLE KEEPS ON ABUSING ME THEN I HAVE NOTHING TO DO OTHERTHANSTOPPING THE DEAL. HOPE THAT YOU PEOPLE I KNOE WAITED FOR YEARS NOT FOR ME BUT YOU DIDNT GOT ANY-OFFER AND NOW WHEN I AM OFFERING YOU AND TRYING MY LEV-ELBEST YOU PEOPLE ARE PLAYING FUN OF ME BY ABUSING ME, BY INVESTIGATING AT THE BACK OF ME. THIS IS NOT EXPECTED FROM PEOPLE LIVING IN CIVILIZED WORLD. IT IS REDICULOUS TO SAY THAT THOUGH WE CONSIDER YOUR COUNTRY AS MODERN COUN-

TRY BUT PEOPLE LIVING THERE ARE FAR BEHIND MODERN CIVI-
LIZATION.
SORRY TO SAY THIS. I HOPE SOMEONE REPENT TO THIS ATTITUDE.
ANAMIKA BISWAS

This was the most anger we had ever read coming from Anamika. At about 6:15 AM Los Angeles time I forwarded the email to the group suggesting that anyone who disagreed with Anamika should contact her directly. She was close to the breaking point and I hoped the group would be smart enough to understand what we all risked. They weren't.

I received an email less than an hour later from Craig in Toronto.

> *Dear Vincent*
> *Thank you for the message from Anamika. I think it would be beneficial if Anamika would send her email correspondence to all members of the group so that everyone is equally informed at the same time. Anamika's fax letter issued on August 8th stated that the funds would be in all of the principal's accounts by August 13th. There has been no update, correction or retraction of this information since August 8th. Accordingly, I'm sure many members of the group informed their respective bank (again) of the pending incoming funds only to find out on August 13th and 14th that nothing arrived. If the funds had arrived as per her stipulated date of August 13, then it is unlikely that anybody would have contacted the SBI. Again, the failure of those that are in frequent contact with Anamika to provide the rest of the group with daily updates and accurate informate is the main source of the problems and tensions. Also inaccurate dates being provided directly to the group by Anamika herself are not being corrected either.*
>
> *Anamika's letter dated August 8th also stated that she would provide all members of the group with a phone number that would allow all the principals to contact her directly. She also stated that the balance of the NDA and agreements would be faxed out to the respective principals. Unfortunately, Anamika has not done anything that she specifically stipulated within her own August 8th correspondence.*
> *Anamika has told Brian Gordon that the transfers will be done on Saturday, August 16th without fail. I personally don't think that the transfers will be completed on August 16th and I have asked all mem-*

bers of the group to wait for the bank documentation to arrive by the end of the business day on Monday August 18, 2003 in India.

I have tried to provide ALL members of the group with transparent communication. It would be appreciated if Anamika and those that are in frequent contact with her would do the same.

Most importantly, we are looking forward to receiving her committed funding so that we can move forward with our respective corporate agendas relative to her investment.

Here was another example. The pompous ones complained when there was no information and they complained when there was information. I ignored Craig but forwarded his letter to Anamika and those in her "support group."

Allen, a businessman from Arizona, replied to me "… it sounds like extortion to me. I believe this might be a blessing in disguise for Anamika. She can rid the problems and avoid investing money in the likes. What a shame. I hope it doesn't ruin it for all. She certainly has my support."

Once again I advised Anamika to drop seven of the clients and provided her with a draft of the letter she might consider sending each. Vindictive? You better believe it!

Saturday morning, Los Angeles time, I received an update from Anamika. "… I AM MOVING TO BANK TO DO WIREING SINCE MY BANKING HOUR IS TILL 12:00PM SINCE TODAY IS SATURDAY BUT IF I CANT ABLE TO SUCCEEED TO DO WIRIEING TODAY I WILL COMPLETE IT ON MONDAY MORNING BOTH WIRENG AND FAX TO ALL OF YOU WHICH WILL BE YOUR SUNDAY EVENING. SO PLEASE DON'T WORRY …"

Less than two days earlier Anamika told me during Yahoo chat that she would wire the funds on Saturday. Now she was doing what she—promised may be too strong a word to use considering all the dates when funding was missed, instead I'll use—indicated. That was all any of us in the group, including the pompous blowhards, wanted—for Anamika to do what she said she would do. And so it seemed funding would be speeding through the banking system to some of us by Saturday and at the very latest Monday. We might all see a change in our bank balances within the next seven to ten days. We had come this far (fill in the blank).

But then … Those of us who were veterans of this pursuit knew intuitively that every silver lining must have a black cloud. Ours came in the form of Gary Dean Childers' email to Anamika at 9:212: 22 AM EDT. Now we knew why Anamika was so upset. The email was titled "Pease".

"Animeka may God Bless you this Day A new beginning can arise water is considered under the bridge.

"There is a Gentleman trying to contact you concerning your Banking Static. I informed him that you was a true honest and responsible citizen. As soon as your able to travel you and I shall meet him he may send you mail within 30 Day's this person wants to help you grow. I will expecting as you promised the sum of $950.095.00 Nine Hundred Thousand Thirty Five Dollars. per your letter. If you will ask your Bank to expiate these Funds.

"Recorded this day Mr. Buyers and Mr. Brown are in your town waiting to hear from me. If you Funded as noted in your letter. They are meeting with cabinet members in your jurisdiction and Finical institution on Monday. This is just a PRE-CAUTION STEP if you are represented by Legal advisors email me there names and I will forward this …"

Upon close examination it doesn't seem like this email could cause much trepidation. Ignoring spelling, grammar and punctuation errors, I wondered if the expiation of funds was a new banking product much like home loans. The numerical amount of funds and the written are not the same, etc.

Following his "Pease" email Gary Dean instructed that Anamika have the funds sent to his account at the B.B&T—Bank Branch & Trust Company in Morganton, N.C. He requested "Nine Hundred Fifty Thousand Ninety Five Dollars Exactly united States Dollars" be wired into his account "Investment Opportunities of N.C.; Gary Dean Childers, Routing Number 053101121; Account number 5290109460.

However, on the third of the eight page email seemed to be the part that spooked Anamika. With a heading "INTENT TO WAVE ADDITIONAL COST AQUIRED PER YOU FULFILLING YOUR AGREEMENT AS NOTED BELOW" Gary Dean made his threat.

From: The Investor

Date: Thursday, August 14, 2003 06:42:56
To: syndralla_2003_star@yahoo.co.in
Subject: BUISNESS
Animeka your time expired per 8 hurs as reviewed By My Attorneys these forth from this letter your time EXPIRES no later than Monday your time Tuesday my Time. Really I gave you in accordance to your Sovern Country Laws the minimum time to give Entente. I will this day over-ride my Attorneys advice. I have spent in preparation and Attorney Fees as of Friday $127,425.00 My Attorneys will be here on Monday we will leave here Tuesday for your 14 hr flight 3290 on Airtrain and Canada and have several stops at 5:19 from Charlotte N.C into your country.

I will grant you this request. In accordance to your Deadline Monday & Tuesday is final. I mean you no harm and don't want you to get upset. I don't think you fully understand what yo put me through. My reputation is shot with some of the finest Attorneys & Bankers in the World. (((((Otherworlds you made me look like a fool)))))))). Perhaps not meaning to. I had 2 Attorneys Fly into Canada and do all the research L.L.C. and communications with the Mining Board. Jim is mad as hell. To be honest I caused that man a Sale he held off other clients. That hurts me very much you write 10 days 10 days10 days 10 days 10 days. Your time frame needs to be met in accordance to all Internet Laws look in volume 12 of the Laws Black Book in your country Due the fact that I have a Diplomatic Account granted by 15 Foreign Nations 101 Common Law Attorneys supersede and Laws known to man. Therefore by your Commitments you are Liable for the cost of exactly $600.250.00 Six Million Two Hundred Fifty Thousand Dollars this is forgotten if you do as you promise this time. Plus if JM Card exercises that option I signed with him I am in some deep uncalled for LITIGATION. The structure I had arranged and will show evidence no party could have ever put this together no less than $18 million Dollars. I after all this am willing to Extend you Tuesday no later but I have Attorney fees NOW THESE NEED TO BE PAID.

Admittedly, Gary Dean's email is an incoherent mess. But more importantly to us it had rattled Anamika. The more I read her response on August 11th to Gary Dean's "Notice of Breach of Contract" letter it was clear how deeply she felt threatened.

HELLO SIR

WELL BEING SERIOUSLY BREAKDOWN OF BOTH PHYSICALLY AND MENTALLY I COUNT NOT ABLE TO CONTACT YOU, WELL IN THE MEAN TIME AS PER JM CARD RESOURCES I FOUND A LETTER THEY SENT IT TO ME WHICH PUT A QUESTION MARK ON YOUR CREDENTIAL WHICH I ALSO CAME TO KNOW TODAY AS ALONG WITH YOUR NOTICE. WELL I LIKE TO HOW MUCH I HAVE TO PAY YOU TO STOP THE DEAL AS PER MAIL OF JM CARD RESOURCES THAT THEY NOT GOING TO DEAL WITH YOU SO SINCE I DON'T KNOW ANYONE OTHER THAN YOU I ALSO LIKE TO STOPO THE DEAL BUT LIKE TO PAY YOU THE AMOUNT YOU ASKED FOR SO I ASK FROM YOU A TIME LIMIT OF 10DAYS WITHIN WHICH AS PER YOUR PREVIOUS BANKING INSTRUCTION YOU GAVE IT TO ME I WILL SEND YOU THE MONEY. ON THE OTHER HAND I ALSO GOT A MAIL OF YOUR SON WHO ASKED ME WHY ARE YOU DREPRESSED WHICH AGAIN I THINK YOU CAN STATE BETTER THAN ME.
DUE TO MY MENTAL AND PHYSICAL CONDITION I AVOID PHONE CALL OF ALL THE CLIENTS SINCE I NEED SOME REST SO I PREFFER TO STAY AWAY FROM HOME. IN THE MEANTIME I FOUND THAT YOU HAVE CONCLUDED THE DEAL AND ALSO THE JM CARD AS THEY DON'T WANT TO DO THE DEAL SO I ASK THE TIME LIMIT OF 10DAYS TO PAY YOUR MONEY THAT YOU HAVE SPEND ON DOING THE WORKS FOR ME.
WELL I HOPE THAT AT LEAST NOT IN WAY OF BUSINESS BUT WE CAN BE FRIENDS IN THE RELATION OF HUMANITY, WELL AS YOU ACUSED ME THAT I BETRAYED LET ME TELL YOU THAT GOD KNOWS THAT I HAVE DONE NOTHING OF THAT SORT TO YOU BUT I HOPE YOU WILL AGREED THAT WE DON'T HAVE ANYCONTROL OVER SITUATIONS WHICH ACTUALLY HAPPENS TO ME BECAUSE THINGS OVER HERE WENT OUT OF MY CONTROL BOTH FINANCIALLY AND MENTALLY
WITH BEST REGARDS
ANAMIKA BISWAS
THERE IS NEVER TOO LATE WHEN YOU START AND FROM WHERE YOU START IT CONSIDERED TO BE THE BEGINING

Just as we were absorbing the implication of the Gary Dean/Anamika relationship, Brian received another email which threatened Anamika.

THIS IS HENRY

ME THE MAN BEHIND OF DEAL THAT U CANCELED, MAY BE YOU DON'T REMEMBER ME, BECAUSE YOU DUSCUSSED WITH MY PARTNER. IM THE CEO OF THIS COMPANY …

NOW WE WANT 5 BILLIONS AS COMPENSATION

WE HAVE MADE ALL THE PAPERS IN ORDER TO DO THE COURT PROCEGURES, IF YOU CAN'T PAY ME, I WILL START THINGS TO WORK WITH MY LAWYER AND FOR MINIMUM FOR 1 YEAR YOU CAN'T DEAL ANY OF THE DEALS OR CONTINUE THE EXISTING BUSINESS THAT YOU ARE GOING TO ESTABLISH HERE. WE ALSO PLANNING TO WRITE INDIAN CONSULATES TO KEEP A EYE ON YOU AND ROGHU. THE AMERICAN GOVT WILL STUDY ABOUT HE REPORTS THAT WE MADED. ME AND MY ASSOCIATES ARE LOSSING A BIG AMOUNT, WE HAVE ALSO REPORTED ABOUT YOU AND ROGHU TO THE CAMBER OF COMMERCE, IN MY CITY IN UNITED STATES OF AMERICA, I HAVE YOUR EMAILS, FAXES AND CHAT CONVERSATION, INCLUDING THE 1ST CONVERSATION WITH YOUR SECRETARY …

WE BELIEVED YOUR SECRETARY (ROGHY ROJ) WORDS MADE ME TO DEAL WITH YOU. AND THE INITIAL PROMISSES OF YOURS MADE US TO WAIT FOR A 2 MONTHS AND AT THE MEAN TIME I CANCELED THE OTHER INVESTORS BY BELIEVING YOUR WORDS.…

WE SEND PEOPLE TO CONTACT YOUR SECRETARY IN SOUTH INDIA. BUT HIS CONTACTS IS STARTING FROM WORLWIDE MAFIA TO AMERICAN AND OTHER COUNTRIES MINISTRIES. SO WE MADE A MEETING WITH HIS PEOPLE. AND THEY SAYS THAT HE DON'T KNOW ANYTHING ABOUT THE MISTAKES YOU MADED, AND ALSO TOLD ME THAT HE IS FACING A LOT OF TROUBLES BY DOING A HONEST JOB WITH U, HIS LOSS IS BILLIONS.…

HE HAD TRIED TO SOLVE THIS PROBLEM WITH YOU AND YOU DIDN'T REPLIED FOR HIS EMAILS NEITHER PHONE CALLS. HE IS LIEING AT ME THAT YOU AND HIM ARE NOT IN CONTACT NOW …

SO NOW THE THINGS ARE IN UR HAND, NOTHING WE GET FROM THAT IDIOT, HE IS VERY CLEVERLY PLAYING WITH EVERYONE. HIS FRIENDS CALLING ME FROM THE AROUND THE WORLD BY THREATS, NOW I CHANGED MY BUSINESS MOBILE NUMBER AND THEY SAYS THAT, HE CAN'T DO NOTHING WITH ME, BECAUSE THE DEAL IS BETWEEN YOU AND ME … AND THEY ARE NOT RESPONSIBLE FOR THE LOSSES YOU HAD. AND ALSO TOLD ME IF SOMEONE MAKES TROUBLES WITH ROGHU THAT PERSON WON'T BE LIVE FOR LONG …

ALREADY SOMEONE BURNED MY CAR, NOW I ALSO GOT AN ANONY-
MOUS LETTER THAT THEY WILL KIDNAP MY WIFE AND MY BABY
GIRL … I BELIEVE/DOUBT THESE WORKS ARE DONE BY ROGHU'S
PEOPLE … NO PROOFS TO SHOW HE IS THE PERSON BEHIND IT. AT
LAST I MADE COMPROMISE WITH HIS PEOPLE. NOW YOU JUSS CAL-
CULATE BY DOING BUSINESS WITH YOU … WHAT MY LOSS??…. ITS
ALL BECAUSE OF YOU.
NOW I WANT MONEY … YOU CAN SEND IT TO MY PEOPLE IN MUMB-
HAI OR SEND IT TO MY ACCOUNT … IM ALSO GOING TO CONTACT
MR. ROGHU, WOTS HIS OPINION ABOT THIS COMPENSATION …
ALSO EMAIL ME HIS EMAIL ADDRESS, STILL HE IS NO MORE INTER-
ESTED OR READY FOR A COMPROMISE WITH ME. TAKE A DECISION
AND REPLY ME….!!!
HENRY THOMAS

Quite a double whammy. At least we knew Gary Dean existed in reality with
an address and phone number. But, Henry Thomas, whose letter did not
sound like an illiterate American, but also not like an Indian struggling with
English either.

As it was the weekend we were not able to determine Henry Thomas' true
identification. Gary Dean and the Sheriff would take care of itself once the
next week started. We put those issues aside and decided it was best to send
Anamika supportive email.

I continued to provide Anamika with my support and gratitude, looking
forward to meeting her in Las Vegas once the funding was completed. Jody, a
generous and sincere client from South Carolina, advised Anamika to "stand
strong, have faith and be strong. We are here for you." Others sent similar letters of support and encouragement.

Friday, August 15th was a holiday. Saturday, when banks were open for half
a day, the bank managers Anamika needed to see were unavailable since they
were meeting at the main branch on the new interest rates. This we all learned
from an email Anamika sent us from a cyber

DELAY #20—Bank managers away at a meeting

café on Monday, August eighteenth. She was trying to complete filling out all
the forms and hoped all would be completed by Wednesday, the nineteenth.
Why not by Tuesday?

Holiday #3—Lord Krishna's Birthday

On Wednesday Anamika intended to fax all the confirmation slips to Kevin's number by noon so that we'd receive them as we woke up across North America.

Confirmation Slip Date #9

Anamika hoped once we received the confirmation slips our days would go well "because after that," she said "I will behind bars" and would not be able to contact us.

Her last paragraph brought forth again, the "poor me" Anamika side of her personality. She asked that if she were imprisoned we, the group, should set up a bank account for her in the U.S. If after a period of time we didn't hear from her, Anamika instructed us to give the money to UNICEF or the Red Cross "so that people gets benefitted from me." Anamika revealed she had troubled "people like from childhood I troubled my parents". She felt that through the donation to a noble cause she could make amends for her troublesome past. OY!

Poor Me Anamika #4

A few days later I finally spoke to Lt. Suttle of the Morganton Sheriff's Department. Then I let Gary Dean, and Anamika, know what I learned.

August 19—4:56:41 PM EDT

Gary Dean
This is what I know about you:
August 17—you became a suspect of the Morganton, NC Police Department in a forgery case. May—You were evicted from your house because you couldnt make payments.
May 30—You were served with papers on behalf of City Financial, suing you in civil court.
That suit is just one of many law suits against you.
Both of your phones are "no longer in service."
Your friend Ramzi's office phone is not working, either. No one knows him or his company at the "office suites" with the Beverly Hills address.
You have a record for forgery and are considered "one of the local punks" in Morganton, NC.
Supposedly you are a construction worker working in N.Y.
Your wife is connected with a small real estate development.

Lastly, you are considered a drunk who mismanages (obviously) his money.

You couldn't buy a bus ticket to Pumpkin Center or Magnolia, NC and you are not able to employ lawyers and transport them and yourself to visit my business associate on the 17th of next month or any other month during the next millennium.

Get into your hole and go back to your bottle.

The next time you make a terrorist threat or bother our business associate and friend in the slightest way, you won't have to worry about food, clothing or shelter for a long time, because the state will be very happy to provide all your necessities.

That's the good news. The bad news is you wont be able to get a drink while you're a guest of the state.

Have a great day.

Gary Dean's reply later that night was terse, but graphic "you a very stupid muther fucker and got your information incorrect keep digging."

Kevin's response to the Gary Dean email was "Horray for Vince!", but his post script was distressing. "I hear nothing will come until Thursday now? I am really tired of this tomorrow … she needs to deliver."

I was also tired of yet another tomorrow, being reminded of the famous quote "… tomorrow and tomorrow and tomorrow creeps this petty pace filled with sound and fury signifying nothing." Good ol' Will Shakespeare had a reaction for all situations even if the breadth of his imagination never conjured up the Internet.

My response to Kevin was "… as much as I still believe in her the fuel tank is past the 3/4 mark."

At this time I thought it might help Anamika to contact her lawyer and others to express our support for her.

Dear Sirs:

We have not communicated in several months. However, I thought you should know that a group of us remain steadfast in our support of Anamika Biswas as a person and business woman.

We are fortunate that she has shown an interest in funding our projects.

I had the privilege of arranging the publicity that Anamika received in India, California and Toronto. It was a pleasure working with her.

I have come to respect Anamika for her honesty, generosity and hard work. I hope I will continue working with her for many years.

During these last few months my belief in and respect for Amanika has been shared by several members of the original group.

We are determined and committed to making our projects the most professional and profitable that we can so that we do not diminish the faith Anamika has shown in us.

We are pleased that Anamika has shown much wisdom in here review and assessment of all the projects. Accordingly, we understand that she has reduced the number of companies she will fund. In the process she has shown a discriminating eye toward working with the most sincere clients whose projects have the most realistic chance of being successful.

I thought you would want to know how we feel about her and that all is proceeding toward a very successful conclusion.

I appreciate your time and look forward to keeping you updated on our progress

Neither Anamika, who had been copied, nor any of her advisors responded.

Brian, who anticipated receiving a $7 Billion investment from Anamika, tried to establish contact with her the day before our latest funding date of August twenty first. He was concerned because he couldn't contact her by phone anymore and wanted to know the status of "our funding … I trust that we are still on for Thursday as you have indicated to me. Saying my check would be good on Thursday … it would be nice to hear from you that we can move forward there is so much at stake … You indicated to me the other night on Yahoo Chat that you were 200% sure that I would get funded soon … my reputation is weighing in the balance."

Most of us had similar concerns. Only a few imprudently committed themselves to deals without having any funds available. Those were the ones complaining the loudest, crowing about their extensive business acumen. However it seems none of them ever learned not to spend money they didn't have.

I gave little attention to them and focused instead on Anamika's latest email of August twentieth. It was in answer to several questions I asked earlier. First, she said she was not able to send dismissal letters to those clients she planned not to fund, but she did add the additional companies we suggested receive her investment. She continued to worry about Gary Dean's threat and then confirmed she had the same reservation for her trip to Las Vegas. That concluded old business.

She did provide the welcome news "by today I think I will complete my job." We all took this to mean she would be wiring funds on Thursday, August 21st as indicated earlier.

None of us knew at the time that Anamika had written a long email of explanation to the chief pompous blowhard. Only four—the three pompous ones and Larry—members of the group got to read it until Larry sent it to Brian and he sent it to me. This secrecy was suggested by PB#2 who advised "I'm not sure that her email should be shared with the others at this time." Yet, he was the one who wanted us to immediately share all we knew, which we did, with him. Then he found fault with the substance of the information.

This is her reply to BobK. It presents a side of her we had not seen before as well as a glimpse into her thinking.

HELLO DR KILGALON
WELL HOPE THAT YOU ARE FINE, WELL LET ME CLEAR YOU SOMETHING WHCH I THINK THAT AFTER THIS EMAIL YOU WONT HAVE OBLIGAT8ION FROM YOUR SIDE TO ME.
WELL IF YOU TAKE ME AS A PREFESSIONAL I WILL LIKE TO TELL YOU THAT I NEVER DIFFERENTIATE ANY OF YOU WITH ANY ONE I HATE TO PLAY THE CONCEPT OF DIVIDE AND RULE POLICY BECAUSE AS A BUSINESSWOMAN I FEEL THAT I SHOULD BE BALANCE TO EVERY ONE SO THAT NONE OF MY CLIENTS FELL INSCURED FROM THEIR ASPECT OF THINKING
WELL LET ME ALSO TELL YOU THAT I STARTED MY EXPORT BUSINESS UNDER NAME OF AB EXPORT AT THE AGE OF 18YRS WITH THE PRINCIPAL AMOUNT OF 250,000 RS WHICH I GOT AFTER SELLING A FEW OF MY JEWELLERY WHICH I PREFERED THE BEST WAY OF GETTING MONEY OTHER THAN PUTTING MY HAND IN FRONT OF MY FATHER FOR MONEY.
NOW AFTER 7YRS MY COMPANY TURNOVER IS 160 CRORES USD FOR WHICH I DON'T GIVE CREDIT TO ANYONE OTHER THAN MY SELF BECAUSE I WORKED DAY AND NIGHT TO MAKE THIS MONEY, EVEN I GOT PROPERTY OF BULK VALUATION AND I COULD NOT EVEN BOTHER TO INVEST YOU ALL AND SIT BACK IN INDIA AND ENJOY THE COMFORTS OF LIFE MOST LAVISHLY WITH PROPERTY GIVEN TO ME BY MY BOTH MATERNAL AND PATERNAL GRANDPARENTS WHICH WILL WORTH NOWADAYS MORE THAN 300 MILLION USD BUT I DIDNT CHOOSE THAT IN SPITE I SOLD OUT ALL THIS PROPERTY OF MINE AND EVEN I SOLD OUT MY PORTION OF MY HOUSE TO MY FATHER AND OFFICE SO THAT I CAN HAVE MONEY TO SPEND ON YOUR PROJECTS I TOOK OUT ALL MY BANK BALANCE, BROKEN ALL MY FIXED DEPOSITS FROM WHICH I USED TO EARN APPROX 80

CRORES USD IN A YEAR BY WHICH I COULD HAVE SLEPT IN MY HOUSE AND EAT BECAUSE WITH THAT MONEY WHICH I EARN EVEN MY GRAND CHILDREN COULD HAVE SPEND THEIR LIVE LAVISHLY BUT I DIDNT CHOOSE THAT INSTEAD I TOOK EVERY PENNY I HAD TO SPEND IN YOU PEOPLE BUSINESS BECAUSE I BELIEVE IF YOU WILL SUCCCEED IN YOUR DREAMS WHO KNOWS LATER ON EVEN I CAN SUCCEED IN MY DREAMS AND CAN AFFORD TO SEE MUCH BIGGER DREAM.

I CAN UNDERSTAND THAT SOME PEOPLE ARE PLAYING POLITICS AT THE BACK OF ME BUT THEY WONT BE A LE TO AS SOON AS BY WEDNESDAY CONFIRMATION SLIPS REACHES YOU ALL I WILL BRING THAT MAN IN DISGUISE DOING ALL THIS POLITICS OR YELLOW JOURNALISM AGAINST ME IN LIME LIGHT.

I CAN UNDERSTAND YOUR FEELING OF INSECURITY THIS CAN ALSO HAPPEN TO ME BUT IF YOU ALSO THINK ME AS NORMAL PERSON THEN ALSO YOU WILL FIND I CONSIDER ALL OF YOU AS MY FAMILY MEMBER SO IF YOU FEEL THAT I CHOOSE COUPLE OF PEOPLE AS MY SPOKESPERSON THEN I MUST SAY THAT YOU ARE WRONG BECAUSE FOR EXAMPLE I LIKE TO TELL YOU ALL OF YOU KNOW JA LAD INVESTMENT COMPANY FROM THERE JODY LAD SENDS ME EMAIL EVERY DAY BUT WHEN I GIVE HER REPLY FROM SAME MAIL IT COMES BACK TO ME ... BUT THAT DOESN'T MEAN I CHOOSE COUPLE PEOPLE AND THROLWED AWAY REST OF THEM. BY SAYING THIS YOU ONLY HURT MY FEELING AND NOTHING ELSE.

ARE YOU ALSO AWARE THAT SOME PEOPLE ARE GOING TO COURT TO PUT ME BEHIND BARS BECAUSE THOUGH I DIDNT DEAL WITH THEM BECAUSE THEY ARE ONLY AGENT AND THE DEAL THEY BROUGHT FOR ME DIDNT WORK OUT YET ITS ON THE WAY BUT I HAD TO PAY THEM MONEY IF I DON'T DO IT THEY WILL PUT ME BEHIND BARS THERE ARE ALSO SOME INCIDENCE HAPPENING THAT I DONT KNOW THAT PERSON WHO IS CLAIMING MONEY FORM ME OR OTHERWISE HE WILL PUT ME BEHIND BARS. YOU KNOW THIS KINDS OF INCIDENCE BREAKS ME AND I AM NOW VERY MUCH TENSED THAT WHAT WILL HAPPEN TO YOU ALL IF I GO BEHIND BARS.

BUT I AM SHOCKED THAT FOR WHOM I AM WAKING UP NIGHTS IN NIGHT MARES THAT IF ANYTHING HAPPENS TO ME ALL THIS 24 PEOPLES DREAMS THEIR FAMILY AND THEIR EVERYTHING WILL SHATTERED BECAUSE I FEEL WHEN I CANNOT GIVE ANY ONE A

WONDERFUL LIFE I DON'T HAVE THE RIGHT TO TAKE HIS LIFE AWAY. BUT WHEN I CANT SLEEP NIGHT AND THINKING OF YOU ALL AT THAT TIME YOU PEOPLE WRITE ME A MAIL TELLING ME THAT I AM BECOMING PARTIAL TO SOME PEOPLE.
WELL THERE IS NO LIMIT OR CONTROL OVER WORDS SO I CANT STOP YOU PEOPLE FROM THINKING LIKE THIS BUT CAN ONLY BEG YOU TO BE WITH ME.

WITH BEST REGARDS
ANAMIKA BISWAS

Sounded like the kids in the group whined to mommy that she wasn't paying them enough attention. These are adults! I think.

Craig admitted in his August 19th sub rosa cyberspace tete-a-tete that Anamika confirmed to him in an email she would send the confirmation slips on August twentieth. But even putting his hand in the wound of Jesus wouldn't satisfy him. "She could easily erase any speculation regarding these ongoing delays and excuses by having the SBI issue a simple, one-page letter confirming when the transfers will be completed. We also don't know what information she is being fed by Brian, Kevin and Vincent as they continue to ignore the rest of the group and will not issue updates." We, as plainly indicated elsewhere in this text, did not ignore the group. Craig actually was saying that unless information was passed directly from his lips it had no value and <u>he</u> chose to ignore, trivialize and discredit whatever we sent. His last pronunciamento in the secret email was typical of his inflated ego.

"I will address the group," he began imperiously, "by 11:00 a.m. this morning and ask that everyone remain patient until we see what happens by 2:30 p.m. Eastern time on August 20." Then came the threat "... there has to be either performance or supporting documentation by SBI to confirm the status of the bank transfers. More excuses and delays on August 20 that lead into the weekend or next week may not be favourably received by some members in the group."

Brian, his wife Evalani, Jody and Jack all contacted Anamika providing an overlay of support and encouragement while trying to ferret out some nugget of information that would provide solace and a reason to keep the faith with her.

Anamika told Jack "everything is fine" on August twenty first. He would get his confirmation slip and money in his account "in this week ... so don't worry." Then she apologized for not being able to give an exact date the funds would be delivered.

That same night Jody spoke with Anamika in Kolkata. She told Jody her computer had a virus and had been shut down since August twentieth.

DELAY #21—computer virus

Jody also learned there had been a bank strike and that a transportation strike was scheduled within the next few days. However, Anamika told Jody she would complete her work

DELAYS #22 & 23—bank/transportation strikes

with the bank on Friday, August twenty second as she was anxious to come to the United States.

Alan warned Anamika that some of her clients, mostly the Pompous Blowhards, were preparing to distribute "negative publicity regarding the deal." It was the "if-I-can't-have-it-no-one-will" syndrome as best expressed when a jealous child breaks the toy of a sibling. Alan hoped "the funding can be concluded to allow those you intend to fund to strike first with positive publicity and thus counter anything they say."

Alan's email to her was the most direct and impassioned expression of support and understanding of Anamika. Because he was one of the seven with contracts from Anamika he declined another funding source "... money may be money but it does not buy honour, honesty or true friendships."

Those who supported Anamika often expressed their desire to maintain a friendly relationship with her, not because we were lonely or in need but out of a desire to let her know we were not interested in exploiting her money or her generous nature. I had many conversations with our group and all, except one, who became PB#4, were of like mind.

Alan concluded his email with a caution. "... it is very close to becoming a situation where those who have demonstrated their lack of ethics and professionalism will throw off the gloves and do what they can to drag you down through their own spiteful actions, whether they tarnish you, your business and family name is of no consequence to them ..."

Jody learned from Larry that negative press releases were being prepared for distribution on Monday the 25th and I so advised Anamika.

Meanwhile, one of the jealous children notified all the companies in the group, deigning to give it an "Update" at 1:07 PM. on August twenty third. Since he was not in direct or even infrequent contact with Anamika, we wondered what new and vital information would be provided. Soon we learned his email contained more of his bilious posturing.

Fellow Members of the Group:
As expected, and as per Anamika's past history, there have been no further NDA or contracts signed and returned, there have been no SWIFT bank wire transfer confirmations, no funds received and no letter from the SBI confirming Anamika's capability to fulfill her funding commitments.
Some members of the group received e-mail correspondence this past week from Anamika stating that the funding would be done this week and that faxes would be sent out. This, again, did not happen.
There were stories of strikes and computer viruses in India but the banks were open and the fax machines were likely working.
It is quite possible that Anamika does not have the funds to fulfill some or all of her commitments. A letter from the SBI confirming the status of the transfer of funds would certainly help to clarify the true status of this transaction. However, this has been requested over two weeks ago and Anamika has not yet accommodated this request.
As stated in my update on August 20, 2003, this is my final update to the entire group. Each member of the group should now follow the direction and interests of their respective Board, shareholders, partners, legal counsel and/or other advisors at this time and proceed accordingly. Some will stay with this uncertain situation until there is some form of closure. Some will seek their 50% compensation and pursue alternative funding options. Some will seek litigation against those that they feel have been irresponsible in this transaction. Whatever option or route you choose, you may wish to advise Anamika of your company's intentions from this point on. She still responds from the e-mail address eximp_group_pioneer@yahoo.co.in.
To each of you, good luck with your projects.
Regards,
Craig AKA PB#2

This was the beginning of dueling emails with Larry, who responded about three hours later. It was his attempt at a mea culpa, which all the clients justly deserved, while at the same time washing his hands.

Hello
Well i guess the waiting for Anamika is over for some of you, maybe for many of you.

I am not going to take long today so please bear with me. As an agent that was part of bringing you to her table i have said before and i will say again … at no time was i or am i going to be responsible for some one elses actions or LACK OF ACTION and that includes Anamika Biswas as nice as we all think of her.

She has tried very hard and she is a very shrewed lady but what exactly she is all about is yet to be determined and before things get way out of hand due to a lack of gorup control please let me state here that if anyone is thinking of bringing forth any type of immediate litigation towards Anamika then they could very easily blow this entire deal for the rest of us who are simply patiently biding out time while we wait for her to conlude her business if indeed our incoming data is correct and that is what she is doing.

This we are gong to be determining this coming week and the following 2 weeks after that so i think lots of control and thought should go into things before anyone goes flying off the handle.

simple.. lets wait her out as most of us are doing other lenders at the same time anyways and this was never supposed to be such a stressed out affair. As well we are confiming, but i do believe this will happens soon, that Brian Gordon will be leaving very soon for India so i for one will wait for his full report before doing anything and if anyone else wishes to set a certain date to drop out of this affair then so be it but please try to be considerate by a few weeks on any action as nobody is running anway or hidiing anything from anyone despite what anyone thinks. We simply have never had the funds or resources to fully explore the full diligence on this lady and every time we have tried we have been threatened with the loss of our funding as well as told to stop all diligence (in her words).

So this is a very rough deal at best and i basically quit counting on it three weeks ago already but i would certianly not do anything to jeordize anyone elses funding becuase i choose to no longer believe in her and alls i am saying is please have the very same courteousy in return from everyone else. From now on i think group funding is completly out as far as my company is concerned as it was tried on a group effort to see what all could be done and was started in great spirits but has become a huge dissappointment in many ways. However because Anamaika thinks it is a group funding I feel that it is better left alone until we get some more answers.

Thank you kindly for you time today and i for one would vote for atleast one solid group laison person if anyone wants the task. Larry

Less than an hour later, PB#2 responded.

Larry:

Just for the record, I haven't gone anywhere. The reason I have removed myself from providing updates to the entire group is due to the fact that there is no information to provide a meaningful update. Anamika responds to e-mail enquiries on a selective basis and the information she provides is continuous excuses for delays.

Those that are in communication with Anamika on a daily basis seem to have entered into a joint code of silence so there is no written update from them. This is a story that never ends and the story has no words.

I wouldn't be too concerned about anyone undertaking immediate litigation as it will likely take a few weeks to prepare the court documents. From a Canadian legal perspective, Anamika and her family will have to be located in order for them to be served with a copy of the statement of claim against them after which they will have 30 days to file a defence.

Now, the India media, police or a local law firm could likely assist in locating Anamika and her family or the statement of claim could be published in the India newspapers which is usually accepted by the courts if a person cannot be located.

Assuming Anamika and her family do not file a defence, and a summary judgement is awarded, this judgement would have to be filed with the courts in India whereby they would have to agree to honour the Canadian court's judgement under the laws of India (which is highly likely as Canada and India follow British law).

Upon receiving judgement in India, you would then have to try and collect the amount awarded which could be more difficult and a longer process than the original court process itself. If it turns out that Anamika, A. B. Exports and Anamika's family have no money, the court judgement isn't worth the paper it's written on.

Criminal proceedings against Anamika would involve a thorough investigation by the local police in India. Enough said about that option. So, litigation by some members of the group is possible but don't panic on the immediacy of the event. However, the local media in India would likely enjoy a feast of potential scandal though.

Regards,

I forwarded both to Anamika so that she would be aware of PB#2's threat.

The next day Larry and Craig were dueling again. Larry continued to defend and rationalize his efforts to provide information and "due diligence" to the group about Anamika. "Well over 2000-3000 combined man hours of research went into our diligence efforts."

We should pause here to wonder why, after thousands of hours conducting due diligence on Anamika Biswas, her company and family to verify the existence of $33 Billion that would be used to invest in 24 companies, THERE WAS NO PROOF OF FUNDS! That he should have the lack of intelligence to make such an assertion was galling. Yet I had to remember my goal. It was not jousting with the semi-literate Larry.

Craig tipped his hand by revealing "… the media in India may be contacted August 28/29 if the funds aren't transferred by August 27…." When understanding, human kindness and honest discussion failed the pompous ones could always rely on blackmail. He also "understood" that in early September a "formal request for a government enquiry will be submitted to the Government of India to Investigate the RBI's transaction with the Biswas on the premise that Anamika Biswas may have falsely used our investment proposals to free up funds for alternative self-serving business reasons with no intention of funding the group at all … she'll likely face some interesting music," if she doesn't perform, he concluded.

We heard from Anamika on Monday.

August 25

HELLOMR VINCENT, JODY, MR BRIAN, MR KEVIN, MR ALAN
WELL I HAVE DONE MY ALL THE WORKS THAT I HAD TO DO AND THAT I ALSO CONFIRMED JODY WHEN SHE CALLED ME UP ON FRIDAY MORNING AND I TOLD HER THE EXACT POSITION OF THE BANKING I ALSO TOLD HER THAT I WILL ALSO GO TO THE BANK TODAY BUT SINCE THERE WASA PROBLEM OCCURED INTHE CLEARENCE OF THE BANK I COULD NOT ABLE TO MAKE MY WORK OUT BUT ON SATURDAY I DONE MY WORK BUT DUE TO BANKING HOURS WAS TILL 12:00PM I WAS NOT BEEN ABLE TO COMPLETE THE ENTIRE CITERIA OF THE PROCEDURE, AND FROM TODAY EVENING THE STRIKE STARTS BUT I TODAY I AM GOING TO THE BANK AGAIN BUT ENTIRE SITUATION OF THE CITY IS VERY CHAIOTIC EVERYWHERE THERE PROTEST PRECESSION WHICH IAM DOUBT FUL REGARDING REACHING THE BANK IN RIGHT TIME BUT FROM TODAY EVENING 72 HRS STRIKE GETS STARTED WHICH WILL AGAIN SHATTERED THE CITY, SO SINCE I HAVE COMPLETED MY WORK I HAVE TO NOW WAIT FOR 72 HRS TO GET OVER OR INMEANTIME IF STRIKE GETS WITHDRAWN I WILL SEND ALL OF YOU YOUR

REQUIRED FUND IF I GET A GOOD WORKING CONDITION OF THE BANK FOR 6HRS I WILL SEND YOU THE FUND AND GIVE YOU THE WIRESLIP. FAXED.

SO THIS EARNEST REQUEST TO ALL OF YOU TO PLEASE TAKE THIS AS OUR LAST DELAY AND BE PATIENT BECAUSE AFTER THAT YOU WONT FIND ANY MAIL FROM ANAMIKA STATING THAT THE DELAY HAPPENED FOR THIS REASON.I COULD NOT ABLE TO CONTACT YOU BECAUSE I HAVE NO MONEY WITH ME NOW

Poor Me Anamika #5—no funds to maintain cel phone

AS I HAVE GIVEN ALL MY PENNY TO YOU ALL SO I COULDNOT ABLE TO MAINTAIN MY CELL PHONES AND WHERE I STAY AWAY FROM MY PARENTS I DONT HAVE LANDLINE TO CONTACT YOU. SO I AM CONTACTING YOU NOW WILL CONTACT YOU THROUGH EMAIL GAAIN ON TOMORROW AS U KNOW SINCE SHORTAGE OF FUND I COULD NOT ABLE TO MAINTAIN MY COMPUTER.

Poor Me Anamika #6—no funds to maintain computer (a few days earlier she told Jody the computer had a virus)

I WOULD LIKE IF YOU CONVEY THIS TO EVERYONE.

WITH BEST REGARDS

ANAMIKA BISWAS

A SMALL NOTE FOR MR BRIAN

I KNOW I AM YOUR BURDEN BUT PLEASE DONT THINK THAT I WILL BE ON YOUR SHOULDER FOR THE LIFE I WILL NOW AFTER THIS STRIKE LIKE YOU AND YOU WIFE TO STAY ON TOP OF MY SHOULDER AND I WILL CARRY YOU IN REST OF MY LIFE, HOPE YOUR SON IS FINE I GOT YOUR WIFE MAIL BUT DONT THINK THAT I AM UNSOCIAL BUT DUE TO LACK OF FUND AFTER INVESTING YOU FOR A YEAR I HAVE TO BE MISER TO BRING BACK MY STATUS. THATS WHY I DIDINT REPLY HER BECAUSE NOW EVERYDAY I CANNOT AFFORD TO DO SURFING.

It took us some time to learn that she, and maybe many Indians, did not have home computers, as we know them, and used those at Internet Cafes. This should have been a major insight but it wasn't.

TO MR GRIAGE—I KNOW SINCE YOU ARE NOW IN A VERY GOOD POSITION AND WILL BE IN A BETTER POSITION AFTER 72HRS CAN TREAT EVERYONE LIKE DOG BUT PLEASE REMEMBER THAT YOU ALSO CAN BE INA NEED OF DOG, BECAUSE YOU NEVER KNOW WHEN YOU NEED SOME ONE. YOU CANNOT LEAD A LIFE ALONE BECAUSE ECONOMICS OESNT RUN SINGLE HANDED.
ANANMIKA

What to make of this? We knew, by checking the Kolkata newspapers on line that a transportation strike was imminent and would most likely last for three days. If, as she indicated, this would be the last delay—we'd come this far, another seventy two hours of waiting would be easy.

Then, I let my ego get in the way. My frustration with the pompous ones and the potential damage they could cause which would impede or destroy the funds I needed, spilled over into a late night email to Anamika at 3:13:56 AM EDT

Dear Anamika:
We were very pleased to receive your email after so many days of being out of communication with you.

The image you send of not having any money hurts me. This is not what we want for you.

Reduce the amount you plan to send me and take funds you need to live, pay your phone bill and restore your computer.

How will you get to Vegas.

You have sent contracts to only 7 companies and we ask that you fund four more. That will total $10billion.

If you insist on funding those who are disloyal to you, at least be sensible and reduce the amount you provide to some or eliminate them all together.

It is foolish to fund those like Craig, Stinson, Kilgallon who would conspire to hurt the reputation of you and your family.

Call me and reverse the charges so we can discuss this further (323) XXX-XXXX. If you call in your evening 6pm, I will be able to talk to you in my morning.

You can give me the wire numbers on the phone and I will forward them.

Let us help you.

Unfortunately, bleary eyed, I sent that letter to the <u>entire group</u>, including the Pompous Blowhards. I was sure I'd just made a catastrophic mistake, the basis for law suits from those I'd advised Anamika not to fund. Steve was the first to comment.

Vincent,
Your communiquéé to Anamika is acknowledged but not being privy to what you are responding to is a little confusing. Your comment to Anamika: Quote … If you insist on funding those who are disloyal to you, at least be sensible and reduce the amount you provide to some or eliminate them all together. It is foolish to fund those like Craig, Stinson, Kilgallon who would conspire to hurt the reputation of you and your family…. Unquote, is not only completely incorrect and false but is malicious, mischievous, misleading and damaging and as such it would be remiss of me not to immediately correct you on it. At no stage has Armada's Holdings International Pty Ltd (AHI) or its principals been anything but fully supportive of Anamika, the Biswas family and any of their employees or professionals on retainer. Our communication has ALWAYS been very courteous, most professional, correct and made genuine offers of assistance as well as furnishing much work to expedite matters have been made on many occasions. As such it is expected that you will correct this false allegation to Anamika forthwith, afford all principals the courtesy of a copy and ensure that you do not issue such inflammatory misleading state-ments again. I eagerly await your immediate corrective action. Thank you. Most sincerely yours in hospitality, Steve

I ignored him. There was no corrective action taken by me, as the wonder from down under was a paper marsupial. He also fudged his military back-ground and medals, but that is part of another chapter.

Next, we were witness to another set of dueling emails. This time between Craig aka PB#2 and Kevin, who through the kindness of his heart had brought him into the deal he now tried to sabotage.

From: kevino@peaksgci.com>
To: biotron@on.aibn.com.>

Hello Craig!
This is my new addy for now as my account seems to be under attack! I have been SKED BY BRIAN AND vINCE FOR YOU TO STOP NOW BEFORE ANY DAMAGE IS DONE. Whom ever is planning on bring ing this forward will only cause us more time and lost business. As far as we know, she is trying to complete this deal Friday, last week. So let's see what m onday brings and right now no one can call her so no one has privy to info.. like we never controlled this as well. So please chill out yourself or who ever wants to cause us ALL more grief.. once we get a hold of her.. we can discuss future action. Brian is headed for India as soon as he can speak to her and let her know he is on the way. I told him to go and we will let her know. Craig, Brian ha sthe US ambassador involved, his congressman and is well aware of this transaction and he is trying to get them to help him once over there.. again, please stand down andall the other as well.. wait this week and then see what happens by Sept 2nd. I do not like to wait eithr..but she may be done!
Kevin

My responses will be in italic.

Kevin:
You have not been copied on any of the recent e-mail communications as you asked to be removed from my list. However, it appears that Brian and Vincent have informed you of the content of my e-mail correspondence that was issued yesterday.

First of all, let me make it very clear that Biotron HAS NOT initiated

> *Initiated does not mean he didn't advise or was not part of those who did—weasel word*

any litigation, investigations or other actions against Anamika Biswas, A.B. Exports or the Biswas Group of Companies. Biotron continues to sit and wait for the arrival of funds as per Anamika's commitment. The information noted in my e-mail correspondence on Sunday, August 24, 2003 was provided for knowledge of Larry, Vincent and Brian as to the POSSIBLE forthcoming actions of others.

> *Possible forthcoming, which he was privy to and most likely a partici-pant.*

The information provided also indicated that these actions MAY take place,

> *Backtracking with more weasel words.*

Although I have stopped providing updates to the entire group due to the lack of worthwhile information to report, I do receive correspondence from many members of the group who feel they have been abandoned and left to attend to their own matters due to the lack of leadership and effective communications by those self-imposed spokesmen of the group.
abandoned and left to attend to their own matters due to the

> *If anyone was "self imposed" it was Craig, who took no initiative but criticized those who did.*

You are asking for people to 'chill out' and yet nobody knows that Brian is going to India or that he has his Congressman and the U.S. Ambassador look-ing into the matter. So, it appears that it is OK for Brian to conduct his own investigation but other members of the group cannot. It is likely that Brian's actions are self-serving and not for the benefit of the entire group otherwise he would have kept everyone informed of these activities.

> *No one stopped Craig or anyone else to join forces with Brian and go to India or to journey alone. Yet not one of the PBers volunteered to go, mainly because they did not have the funds or the courage.*

There are 23 independent companies involved in this transaction and each one has received specific, individual commitments from Anamika Biswas and from the legal counsel for the Biswas Group of Companies for both investment funding and for compensation. You, Brian and Vincent cannot dictate the operative activities and remedial actions that each of these companies may or may not undertake or are entitled to pursue on the advice of their Board, shareholders,

> *Clearly, no one was dictating. We were appealing to common sense notions—not to rock the boat or bite the hand that might be feeding us.*

partners, legal counsel or other advisors. What each company does is totally at their own discretion.

I see Vincent has now asked Anamika not to fund the projects of Biotron, Steve Stinson and Bob Kilgallon. It appears that the information I have provided to Vincent and Brian has been misrepresented and they have now provided incorrect and improper advice to Anamika. This will be addressed accordingly.

> *Am still waiting to be "addressed accordingly". Another empty sack.*

In the future, I will ensure that any new information I receive on the activities of other members of the group will be kept strictly confidential with the party from whom it has been received.

Please do not misread my correspondence and undertake to disparage Biotron.
Regards,
Craig

Next, Craig responded to my "Please Be Sensible" email.

Vincent:

It appears that you have provided Anamika with legal and investment advice for which you have no authority to do so.

> *In truth, Craig had no idea what authority I had or did not have. We never spoke on the phone, as I had with many others. His ego trip would not allow such condescension.*

You have clearly advised her to fund only 11 of the 23 companies that she has issued commitments to.

If he'd read the email I asked her to omit four companies from the 24, leaving 20, not 11. Simple arithmetic.

Perhaps you could provide us with a list of those companies that you have told her to fund and those companies that you have told her not to fund.

Once again, he did not read the email. Only four on the list.

If Anamika does not have the funds to honour her commitments to all 23 companies, then she should certainly seek good legal advice at this time. Most members of the group agreed a few weeks ago that, should a shortfall of funds occur, a pro-rata distribution of the available funds would be a satisfactory solution. This would likely be the most fair and equitable solution to all parties. It appears from your third sentence whereby you ask Anamika to "send me" a reduced amount of funding, that you have a self-serving agenda and have not put forth a solution to the benefit of all 23 members of the group.

My "self-serving agenda" was to reduce Anamika's stress, if, as Craig assumes, she did not have all the funds.

I will not comment on your specific notation to Anamika; "It would be foolish to fund those like Craig, Stinson and Kilgallon who would conspire to hurt you and your family."

Mighty big of him not to comment.

Craig AKA PB#2

And now, a word from the dancing skeleton man himself. None other than BobK.

Hello Everyone
I had gotten this email this morning, after returning home from the hospital … Vincent, I do not know where you are coming from, or the fact that you represent the best interest of Ms. Anamika Biswas or other members of the group. I will not even stoop down to your low level of corrupt self importance ego, by responding to you comments since none of it makes sense.

Thank God. It hurts to see a pompous blowhard stoop.

Alan, When I agreed with Anamika on the 50% settlement and finding our own financing, I had found that financing, through a group in Asia. However, when Anamika told me that she wanted to finance the entire amount, I informed the other investors, out of professional courtesy to Anamika, to look at other phases of projects to fund, which they have.

This guy could give a course in gross rationalization.

I think many of the people have the same feeling and because Anamika asks for our faith and trust in her, in doing what she said she would do, that we have stood by her and trusted in her.
I have taken this opportunity to forward an email to everyone that I had gotten from Anamika this morning. There is an old saying "Go to the source and not the rumors or speculations." I still have other funding sources that have been notified, and are looking at many of our projects and as I speak the funding is being accomplished. I also believe that it is only the person who is doing what they do, that truly knows what they do and not someone that has no concept or idea, of what that person is doing or attempting to do, and should make no irrational comments as to what they feel about that person, or their business, no matter how important they feel about themselves..
Sincerely
Dr. Kilgallon
From: "akansha agarwal" <eximp_group_pioneer@yahoo.co.in>
To: "Americas Choice" <americas@alltel.net>
Subject: Re: Press Release for approval
Date: Monday, August 25, 2003 1:39 AM

HELLO DR KILGALON
WELL I LIKED YOUR PRESS RELEASE BUT DONT DO IT NOW AS YOUR FUND IS YET DELAY TO REACH YOU BECAUSE NOT FOR ME I DONE MY WORK THAT I HAVE TO DO:—PAYING TAXES, FILLING UP FORMS IN THE NAME OF EVERYINDIVIDUAL AND TRANSFERING FUNDS FROM UBI TO SBI BUT SINCE FROM TODAY EVRYTHING OF KOLKATA IS CLOSED FOR 72HRS I HAVE TO SIT AND WAIT TILL THE STRIKE GETS WITHDRAWN BECAUSE IN THIS STRIKE EVRYDAILY NECCES-SITY IS ALSO CLOSED LIKE PETROL PUMP, OIL TRANKERS AND MANY OTHERS SO PLEASE I PRAY YOU TO BE WITH ME.

ANAMIKA BISWAS

When the email stopped flying, I was unscathed. We were all more concerned with getting funded than feeding a feud. The transportation strike ended by August 27th, and we were eager for the latest information from Anamika. Only two days earlier she asked us all to be patient with her, all she needed was six hours working in the bank and the funds as well as the wire confirmation slips would be faxed to us.

I wrote her to say I was "… pleased that the funding process has begun …" Jack also wrote her, offering the services of his lawyer and banker "… if there is anything we can do to help…."

Just when we felt safe to go back into the water, another shark emerged. Surprisingly, he was one of the seven who had received contracts from Anamika. However, through his constant carping and booing from the bleachers Dave became Pompous Blowhard #4.

He spread the rumor that he had Anamika checked out and her "name came up on the U.S. State Department 'hot list'". But, he never explained its significance. His implication was that she was a bad character of some sort. This was a guy with a contract for funds trying to assassinate the character of his potential benefactress. Why?

Maybe he discovered Anamika was really Osama Bin Laden in a dress. Check that. OBL wears a dress—of sorts. Maybe he found Anamika was OBL with breasts!

Four days passed and we did not hear from Anamika. Her last email on the 25th was to PB#1 and me. I spent two of the last three days of August trying to contact her without success.

AUGUST SCORE CARD		TOTALS
Funding Dates	4	35
(next funding date, we think Sept. 1)		
Delays	6	23
Funds Transfer Date	0	2
Draft/Tracking Numbers Sent	0	2
Holidays	1	3
Confirmation Slip Dates	1	9
Anamika Has Wired Funds	0	4
Anamika Travels	0	1
Poor Me Anamika	3	6

8. SEPTEMBER, 2003

A GLIMMER OF HOPE

September began with mixed messages. Though hardly a surprise, considering the previous months, nonetheless they seemed more numerous.

September 1

During a phone conversation Brian told me, after speaking with Anamika, that she was unable to wire the funds because the bank manager was on vacation.

DELAY #24—bank manager on vacation.

However, he continued, the funds would be in our account by Thursday, September 4th and Anamika would arrive in Las Vegas on September ninth, the following Tuesday. He felt all would be resolved in the "next twenty four to forty eight hours."

Funding Date # 36 & 37—September 3rd & 4th

September 2

I was surprised to speak with Anamika on Tuesday, September second. She told me the funds would be in our account by Wednesday, the very next day. We concluded she was once again doing what she said she would and hoped that funding on this latest and thirty seventh date would actually be realized. While the funding dates caused confusion, Brian and I were pleased that we were back in contact with Anamika.

That same day, Larry concluded "… she has decided to 'close the doors' I think on all of us without so much as even a howdy or a good bye. Darn right disrespectful I'd say, but thats no surprise."

This is yet another example proving that the so-called "brokers" had not clue one about Anamika, living as they were in a parallel universe that sometimes took flight in various tangents. In fact, they never knew who she was and had never met except in cyberspace.

Larry suggested someone write her one last time "… BEFORE we set about blacklisting her as once we start there is no turning back from it the press releases will be nasty as hell I am sure."

Larry's delusions continued. Blacklisted from where, one might ask. She did not own a seat on the New York Stock Exchange. Who outside of the twenty four companies and her family knew she existed? As far as nasty press releases, not one person in the group was capable of getting any news printed in early July. What made them think they would be more successful in September?

Only a few could pay to have some self-serving tripe distributed over a publicity news wire.

I'd gotten the only significant press coverage for Anamika and I was not about to retract it or discredit her then or later, no matter the outcome. This need to be vindictive is the same ego-centric mentality that starts invasions of countries without provocation. The odor of self involvement was definitely in the air and highly contagious.

Larry asked for comments. I told him he was agitating the waters instead of calming them; reminded him of an earlier email in which he planned to give Anamika another week as well as the strike-caused delay. I voted to do nothing until Monday September eighth.

What we didn't know then, on September 2nd, was that BobK contacted Anamika by email with the beginning of an elaborate ruse to put fear into her heart and try to discredit me for my "PLEASE BE SENSIBLE" email to her of August 25th in which I suggested she not fund those who were disrespectful to her i.e. Steve, Craig and him.

Dear Anamika Biswas
The entire staff of Americas Choice Inc. are concerned about your health and well being.
Is evident that for some reason you feel it necessary to alienate those who have trusted in you, and gave all the faith they had.
I have responded to a news paper person, who for some reason had my email address, to which I never gave to them. If you like I would suggest that you find out from them how they got my Email address, because I did not know this person up to the time they contacted me.
This is the email I got from him/her:

Dr. Kilgallon,
Below is the purported email response to the phantom email sent from PB#1. He has removed the headers from her email. See full text below.

Dr. Kilgallon,
This is Nisha Lahiri, from The Telegraph newspaper. I need more details to pursue your allegation against Anamika Biswas. Could you provide me with names and addresses of some of the other businessmen? I also need to know what business you are in, how you came into contact with Ms Biswas and what you need the funding for, as well as what she has said in response to your asking for the money.

Please do let me know, so that I can take this up.
Thank you.
Nisha Lahiri,
The Telegraph,
Calcutta, India.
PS—this email address does not accept any attachments. If you need to send me any documents, you could cut and past it onto this email, or send me a mail to delirium1980@yahoo.com

End of Nisha Lahiri's purported email to Kilgallon. His letter follows

I said nothing to her about you, except praise for your courage, and willingness to succeed. I sent you my letter back to her, and to all those who you are funding. I feel that someone in the group wants you to feel that I have betrayed you. This is not true. When I first contact a person I use my full and complete name. Dr. Robert D. Kilgallon. There are 3 Robert Kilgallon in the US. One is my son and the other is a cousin. To separate me from them, in an initial letter, I use my complete name.
Since you feel that you have no need to talk to me, and let me know what is going on, or respond to my emails, then it is evident that you are either sick, in the hospital, upset, or regard our friendship as being over.

I had suggested several options for you. Because of what Vincent had written to everyone and you, about not funding ACI, Craig, and Steve. (see below email)
This is the same person that uses abusive filthy language with an intellectual and business level of someone who is physically and mentally immature, and not worthy of being in the same league as you, let alone give you sound business advice..

The very first email I received from him started with, Hey Dude!

Anamika, that is not business like, nor mature business behavior, and shows nothing more then an armature childish abilities. I do not want to get into telling you what you should or should not do. That's strictly your business.

However, ACI is my business and since the start of meeting with you, and placing our hopes and faith in you, it has costs this company several millions in security deposits, and loss of millions in revenue.

I had stopped funding from another source due to the fact that I put my trust in you and what you said. I hope that you understand that I do know what you have been going through there, however you must understand that I also have responsibilities to people here, and they are in the hundreds.

Everyday, I have people asking about the funding. Everyday, they think that I am a fool because I believe in you and that you will do what you say you will do.

I have tried to help you with ideas and suggestions and offered you every business curtsey and options that I could think of.

Vincent's email to everyone & you:

The Please Be Sensible email of 8/25—see Chapter 7

I know he has your address on it, and I hope you got this email, and that is the reason I sent the response to you.
If you can not afford to fund us, or not going to fund us, then let me know. I will go elsewhere for funding. I would also like to know why you are not funding us, if that is the case here.
S incerely
PB#1

September 4

Brian told me that he had again spoken with Anamika. "All went well at the bank … funds will hit before" he planned to leave for a two-week trip to India.

September 6

Anamika finally responded to my email about allegedly being on the State Department "hot list". She hoped the rumor could be stopped and that it didn't affect her business career in the near future. I hoped it wouldn't prevent me from getting funding. We all have our priorities, after all.

Later that day Anamika told Brian she planned to be in Las Vegas within the next four or five days. That was excellent news. I hoped her trip would indicate all the funds had been wired, at last. Brian was going to India while at the same time Anamika was going to Vegas? Confusing? You betcha.

Then came yet another "update on the Biswas Saga" from Larry in which he breathlessly cautioned the group—as if he had any control—"PLEASE DO

NOT YET DO ANYTHING AGAINST ANAMIKA OK????" Were the four question marks for emphasis or was he unsure of what he asked. We, and he, would never know.

He continued "… we have had FINAL CONFIRMATION THIS MORNING that BRIAN IS LEAVING IN '5' DAYS FOR INDIA." He advised that Brian would provide the group with an update once he "learns the score" and asked that no one "jump the gun and do anything ok please."

September 7

Anamika told Brian she was only talking to him and me and that she would be in Las Vegas within the next four to five days. Brian was willing to hold his travel plays in abeyance. If the funds arrived there was no need to go. If once again there were no funds he understood the trip was imperative.

We soon had another of those "Jaws" moments. Just when you think it's safe to go back into the water.…

Just when we thought, at last, funding was on its way and within five days we would actually meet Anamika in the flesh. BAM a bolt of lightning singed our expectations.

DELAY #25—FBI comes to arrest Anamika; case filed against her (we think)

Jody was the first to learn in an email from someone called Vikran Ahuja. Who? No one had heard of him before. His email indicated he knew Anamika and well enough to contact Jody via another of Anamika's email addresses. We gradually discovered Anamika had at least five!

September 9

HELLO MRS JODY
WELL I AM NOT ANAMIKA MY NAME IS VIKRAM AHUJA, I AM THE FRIEND OF ANAMIKA, WELL TODAY SHE FIRST TALK WITH MR BRIAN AT 9:00AM IN THE INDIAN MORNING WHERE SHE ASKED HIM TO CALL HER AFTER TWO HOURS AS THE BANKING HOUR HAD JUST STARTED THEN, WELL IN THISTWO SHE CANNOT ABLE TO COMPLETE THE WORK BUT SHE HAS DONE IT WITH IN FOUR HOURS THAT IS APPROX 3:00PM, AT THAT MOMENT SHE WAS ABOUT TO COME OUT OF THE BANK AND ABOUT TO ENTER HER CAR A FEW PEOPLE CAME AND INTRODUCED THEMSELVES AS PEOPLE OF FBI CAME TO ARREST HER ON THE COMPLAIN OF SOME OF THE CLIENTS FROM ABROAD SPECIALLY CANADA AND NEWZEALAND,

AND THEY WERE ABOUT TO TOOK HER I TOLD THEM THAT I CAN GIVE BELL FOR HER BUT THEY DIDINT AGREED AND THEY TOOK HER TO NIZAM PLACE OUR CITY HEAD QUARTER OF CBI FROMTHERE I TOOK HER AWAY ON BELL BUT SHE HAS GONE THROUGH COMPLETET NERVOUS BREAKDOWN AS SHE HAS NEVER HAD GONE THROUGH SUCH SITUATION BEFORE, WELL WE DIDINT MIND ANYTHING FOR THIS BUT AS HER CHILDHOOD FRIEND I NEVER SEEN HER SO DEPRESSED BEFORE NOT EVEN WHEN HER FATHER THROWED HER AWAY FROM HER HOUSE THAT TIME ALSO SHE WAS CONFIDENT BUT TODAY SHE HAS BROKEN LIKE GLASSES OF MIRROR, I LIKE TO BEG FROM ALL OF YOU AS WHO EVER HAS DONE TO TAKE REVENGE FOR THIS DELAY I AM BEGGING HIM THAT PLEASE DONT DO IT AS FOR BUSINESSMAN HIS/HER REPUTATION IS VERY IMPORTANT IN THE MARKET BEFORE ANYTHING ELSE AND I WILL ALSO BEG FROM ALL OF YOU TO PLEASE GIVE HER ONE MORE DAY, STRESSLESS DAY SO THAT SHE CAN OVER COME THIS SITUTA-TION,

I WILL SEND THIS MAIL TO EVERYONE ON TOMORROW MORNING BUT IF YOU CAN INFORM TO ALL 8 PERSON WHO SHE HAD COM-PLETETD THE PROCESS OF WIREING THEN I WOULD HAVE BEEN GLAD AND I ALSO REQUEST YOU ALL 8 PEOPLE TO KEEP THIS WORD WITH YOU ONLY AS WE FRIENDS OF ANAMIKA THOUGHT THAT WE WILL TAKE ACTION ON THIS INCIDENT ON BEHALF OF HER AND WE WILL FIND OUT WHO IS THIS PERSON AS SHE TOLD ME THAT YOU 8PEOPLE CANNOT BE BUT SHE IS SUSPECTION LARRY AS SHE TOLD THAT HE SAID TO SOMEONE THAT HE WILL NOT LEAVE HER SO WE WILL DEAL WITH IN OUR WAY WITHOUT ANY INTERFERENCE OF ANYOF YOU.
YOUR 8 PEOPLE WORKS ARE DONE, BUT GIVE US ONE DAY THAT IS TOMORROW WHOLE DAY ITS OUR REQUEST TO ALL OF YOU SO THAT WE CANBRING ANAMIKA TO NORMAL.
HOPE THAT YOU ALL WILL AGREE WITH US.
VIKRAM AHUJA

Brian also got email from Vikram the same day.

HELLO

WELL LET ME INTRODUCE MYSELF MY NAME IS VIKRAN AHUJA I AM ANAMIKA BISWAS'S FRIEND, WELL I WAS ENTIRE DAY WITH HER AND KNOW WHAT SHE HAD DONE AND HAD HAPPENED TO HER.

YESTERDAY WHEN YOU CALLED HER IN THE LAND LINE OF HER HOUSE SHE TOLD YOU TO CALL OVER CELL AND YOU DID SO AND SHE TOLD YOU TO CALLER BACK AFTER 2HRS AND YOU DID SO AND SHE TOLD YOU THAT NOW BANKING HOURS HAD JUST STARTED AND SO YOU PLEASE CALL HER AFTER 3HRS AND YOU MUST HAVE DONE SO BUT DIDINT GOT ANYREPLY THIS BECAUSE AS PER HER COMMITMENT SHE DONE HER WORK, AND BANK SAID THAT BY TODAY (9TH INSTEAD OF 8TH THE FUND WILL BE DISBURSED) AND IT

Funding Date # 38—September 9th

WILL REACH TO STATE BANK OF CANADA ON 12TH EVENING OF INDIAN TIME, AND THAT THIS DEAL FROM HER SIDE WILL GET CLOSED AFTER LONG DELAY HAD DONE TO COMPLETET THE WORK WHICH MOST OF YOU THINK THAT SHE DONE PURPOSELY AND YOU PEOPLE FILED THE CASE AGAGINST HER TO YOUR COUNTRY COURT THAT YESTERDAY PEOPLE FROM FBI CAME AND ARREST HER, THIS IS SUCH A SHAMEFUL INCIDENT HAPPENED THAT AS FRIEND I CAN NEVER THINK SO THAT ANAMIKA HAD DONE BAD TO ANYONE EVEN IN HER DREAMS, I KNOW HER WHEN SHE AND I WAS ONLY 5YRS OLD AND FROM THAT DATE TILL THIS DATE I NEVER KNOW OR I CANT REMEMBER ANYTHIN SHE HAD DONE IN LIFE THAT BROUGHT BAD TO ANYONE, BUT I HOPE THAT YOU ALL MUST BE AWARE THAT SHE STAYS AWAY FROM HER PARENTS ONLY BECAUSE OF YOU ALL AS NO ONE IN HER HOUSE LIKED THE IDEA OF FUNDING YOU PEOPLE SO SHE WAS THROWN OUT AND YOU PEOPLE TOOK THAT ADVANTAGE AND FILED CASE AGAINST HER.

DIDINT SHE TOLD THAT SHE WILL FUND ALL 8 PEOPLE OF YOU: MR VINCENT, MR BRIAN, THAT IS YOU, MR JACKFULTON, MR KEVIN, MR ALAN, MR MR DAVE BOWER AND MRS JODY. AND SHE ALSO TOLD THAT REST SHE WILL DO AFTER TALKING TO ALL OF YOU BUT SHE WILL NOT FUND LARRY AND MR KHOA NUGUN AND FOR THIS YOU PEOPLE FILED CASE AGAINST HER TELLING THAT SHE IS FRAUD.

SHE REAPETEDLY TOLD THAT SHE WILL FUND MR ALAN AND MR DAVE THEN HOW COME THEY ASKED SHUKWINDER DHALIWAL TO

FILE A CASE AGAINST HER, SHE SAID THAT SHE WILL DECIDE FOR
REST OF THEM ONLY BECAUSE SHE WANT 14DAYS MORE TIME TO DO
ALL THE FUNDING OF ALL THE CLIENTS BUT SINCE YOU PEOPLE
CANT WAIT SO LONG SHE SAID THAT SHE WILL SEND YOU PEOPLE
FIRST AND THEN REST OF THEM AFTER 14 DAYS IN BETWWEN SHE
WILL ALSO VISIT TO LASVEGAS AND MEET EVERYONE OF YOU PER-
SONALLY. BUT I AM SORRY TO SAY THAT NOW I THINK AFTER THIS
ATTITUDE OF YOU PEOPLE ANAMIKA'S FATEHR WAS RIGHT HE
ALWAYS USED TO SAY ANAMIKA THAT THIS PEOPLE CANNOT BE
GOOD FRIEND AND SO DON'T TRUST ON THEM BUT SHE USED TO
SAY THAT THEY (YOU PEOPLE ARE GOOD) LIKE GOD AND SO SHE
HAD NO PROBLEM WITH YOU ALL, BUT I THINK SHE WAS WRONG
AND SHE IS NOW COMPLETELY UNDER NERVOUS BREAKDOWN.

DELAY #26—Anamika has nervous breakdown

ONLY MY REQUEST TO ALL OF YOU IS THAT PLEASE BE SURE THAT
YOU ALL WILL GET THE FUNDING AFTER THE FIRST PHASE WITHIN
14DAYS REST OF YOU WILL GET BUT PLEASE WITHDRW THE CASE OR
OTHERWISE WE WILL TAKE ACTION AS WE ARE ALREADY UNDER
DESTRUCTION FOR THIS CASE BUT WE WILL DESTROY TO ALL OF
THEM ALONG WITH US.
I HOPE THAT YOU AS A GENTLEMEN WILL UNDERSTAND THIS AND
DO SOMETHIN OR GIVE US A WAY TO SOLVE IT.
WITH BEST WISHES
VIKRAM

I immediately called Anamika and spoke with her on September ninth
regarding her "arrest." The problem, she told me was not with the funding. The
funding was "done." She said Larry and Shawn had filed a suit. "They filed the
case in such a way I have to go to the U.S.", she said. I asked her to describe the
incident and she told me that two men who she said were "Americans" were
waiting to talk with her, but they showed her no papers.

I tried to reassure Anamika in an email that she was not in danger and the
core of her supporters was still by her side.

Dear Anamika
I was very pleased to speak with you this morning. However, I regret the experience you had the other day. Maybe the following can help.

THE "LAW SUIT"—I believe it is all a phony act. Because:

1. The FBI has no jurisdiction outside the US.
2. If the men you met at your house did not show you valid identification, I cannot believe they were from the FBI.
3. If they did not give you some kind of writ or subpoena detailing the nature of the complaint—they are bogus.
4. Shawn, Larry and Chris do not have five cents to split between them and therefore could not hire an attorney as far away as India. But they or someone else could try to make trouble and intimidate you.
DO NOT BE THREATENED OR INTIMIDATED. Brian and I and the others will stand by you.

DR. KILGALLON AND THE CALCUTTA TELEGRAPH

Dr. Kilgallon in his email claims that someone is trying to make trouble for you by contacting the Telegraph. I spoke this morning on the phone with Nisha, the reporter. She tells me the initial inquiry came from Kilgallon's computer, which he denied. Since he did not substantiate any of his claims she is not going any further and is not interested in doing a story on you.

DR. KILGALLON IS MAKING TROUBLE FOR YOU AND SHOULD NOT BE FUNDED.
HE MAY ALSO BE THE ONE BEHIND THE PHONY FBI AGENTS!!

Brian forwarded your email. I was very pleased to read that the funds will be in the Bank of Canada by September 12.

Will you email Brian or myself the confirmation numbers? I could also call you on the phone and you could read them to me so I can forward them to the clients. We are open to whatever is easiest for you.

I am feeling very positive about how all is progressing and look forward to meeting you in Las Vegas soon after Brian returns from India.

Hope your knee is better. Stay well.

Later that day I confronted Shawn with Anamika's allegation that he was behind the suit. "She's lying," he told me.

Re-examining Vikram's email, we had some reason to be suspicious, yet with all the strange turnings, as we approached the start of the fifth month, all of us in the support group chalked off this latest development as another twist in the journey.

I decided to also contact Vikram.

To: Vikram Ahuja
From: Vincent Panettiere—Thistle Productions

Jody Hussein forwarded your email to her. And I also read the email from Anamika to Brian Gordon. However, prior to all of this, I spoke this morning with Anamika and she gave me some of the details of what happened.

Your email to Jody was very helpful. The Canadian client who most likely tried to discredit Anamika is Craig Fields. The New Zealand client who is most likely his partner in this despicable act is Steve Stinson.

Both have complained loudly over the last few weeks, but lately have been silent—no emails of any kind—while they sneak around.

I dont believe Larry has the money or the experience needed to take such action.

However, until official documents are produced, Anamika should be cautious and quiet. This entire matter could easily be a fraud. If no official documents are produced, then it is clearly a fraud.

Only three people know of this—me, Jody and Brian. We do not want to expand it so that if action is taken against Craig and Stinson, they will be completely surprised. In the meantime it is most important that Anamika's wires of the funds be received by the 8 clients as soon as possible.

Once Brian arrives all will be handled to Anamika's satisfaction.

Thank you for the email. Advise Anamika to be strong and stay well.

We all look forward to meeting her and having a successful relationship.
Best regards,

Vikrum never responded.

September 11

Anamika sent a very friendly email to Jody on September eleventh, inquiring about her children and expressing her pleasure that Brian was coming to visit. Anamika hoped that as a result of Brian's visit "the clients doubt will be removed."

BobK, the pompous one who brought us the dancing skeletons, was up to his dirty tricks. Though Larry had tipped us off to the possibility of "nasty" press releases emanating from the jealous children in the group, PB#1 took a more under handed approach. He fabricated an email. But got caught.

I was the only one who had the email address of Nisha Lahiri, the reporter I spoke with at the Kolkata Telegraph who interviewed Anamika in late June. The story that appeared in the July 1st edition contained her byline but no direct email address. The only way anyone could contact her was to send an email to her at the "feedback" (see below) address for the newspaper and hope for a response. This is what BobK did and how he got caught trying to defame Anamika and sabotage those who she was to fund.

From: "Ambalika Lahiri" <ambalika@abpmail.com>
To: <americas@alltel.net>Sent: Tuesday, August 26, 2003 5:20 AM
Subject: Re: [Fwd: Feedback about the website: The Telegraph]

Dr. Kilgallon,
This is Nisha Lahiri, from The Telegraph newspaper. I need more details to pursue your allegation against Anamika Biswas. Could you provide me with names and addresses of some of the other businessmen? I also need to know what business you are in, how you came into contact with Ms Biswas and what you need the funding for, as well as what she has said in response to your asking for the money.
Please do let me know, so that I can take this up.
Thank you.
Nisha Lahiri,
The Telegraph,
Calcutta, India.

Rather than provide direct answers, he reacted with shock and horror as well as a broadside against the press. They were the usual denials and protestations of a scoundrel. Below is what he claims was his response to the email he incited.

Dear Nisha Lahiri
I do not know who had given you information that I was filing any allegations against Anamika Biswas. Who ever it was, they are not a reliable source.

She replied to his email and addressed him by name.
Who else was the source?

It is not the business practice of Americas Choice Inc to provide anyone, let alone the news media, with information that is in direct violation of a confidentiality agreement. This includes the names of businesses that are clients of Ms. Biswas.

The pompous and transparent "confidentiality defense" which is similar in
veracity to "executive privilege"

Americas Choice Inc. is a business development corporation listed with Dun and Brad.

Proves nothing. Almost anyone can be listed on D&B

If you want more information our web site is: www.alltel.net/~pres2000. Ms. Biswas is one of several Investors in Americas Choice Inc. and a valued Limited Partner.

Investor? She hadn't sent him any money.

It is a shame that a woman, of India, who wants to develop and expand her abilities professionally and increase her financial future has to face the daily abuse of her own country, just because she is a woman.

What me responsible? Pointing the finger at others

We at Americas Choice Inc. Applauded her efforts in doing the best she can, considering the circumstances and business ethics that she has to deal with from day to day.

I feel that a paper with your circulation would rather concentrate on the real issues of your country. Protests, riots, bombings of the financial districts, terrorists, and sexual discrimination.

Good offense is the best defense

I deal with several businesses in India. It is a nation with a proud past, and a great future, only if some of the prejudicial traditions would be dropped and allow the people, no matter their sex, to develop themselves and their country.

Ugly American always knows best

If you have any questions dealing with any investment issues of Ms. Anamika Biswas I would suggest that you contact her directly, and not go on a media feeding frenzy to destroy an individual, and those she is working with through side show tactics of making something out of nothing.

Aggrieved sanctimony when all else fails

I thank you for your time, and I will not ask who gave you my email address, at this time. I may request such information in the future for possible litigation of slander and defamation of character.

He knows because he wrote it; threat of litigation impotent as usual

A copy of your email and this one will be sent to Ms. Biswas and those concerned, or have a need to know.
Signed by BobK

Next, he covered his tracks with the group in the first of several "explanatory" email messages. The sum total of all his messages is the male version of "methinks the lady doth protest too much." Had he been totally innocent, no such explanation would be offered, as there would be no need for any defense. However, the ego that would send the "dancing skeletons" email desperately needed attention. He wanted everyone to know that he tried to defame Anamika through the Kolkata Telegraph. To do that he had to expose himself while also covered in "plausible deniability."

From: americas@alltel.net
To: (all clients plus Anamika)
Sent: Wednesday, September 03, 2003 5:47 PM
Subject: Please read this information
This is for your information!
As you know I had gotten an email from the Telegraph Newspaper of India. It was from a Nisha Lahiri. She requested information on the names and email addresses of the individuals and their businesses that were involved in Ms. Biswas funding.

But he doesn't admit he instigated her response

I sent a copy of the email to everyone, including Anamika.
I did not send this nor did anyone from ACI.

This doesn't mean it wasn't someone or some place else

So I asked Nisha Lahiri to send me the email she got telling her of the information. It has been copy and pasted below.

Note email lacks identity of email sender

It was sent from their own web site (The Telegraph) which I did not know they had one, and the person who wrote my name as Dr. Bob Kilgallon is an amateur child.

Point the finger at someone and four are pointing back at you

First of all I would never use a nickname in any business correspondence with a news paper or any media. Very unprofessional. That is like addressing a CEO of a Major Corporation with "Hey Dude!"

Such self-righteous indignation

Anyone could put my email address on it. because there is no properties to follow, on who originally sent it..

How convenient

Then there is no company name, address, phone numbers, only the country of US.
I had no knowledge of how many businesses, the total amount of funding, or what country these businesses are in.

Not true, he sent copies of his email to everyone

At this time I only knew of 6 businesses. I estimated that there was 36 being funded, and their actual names and what type of business they were in was irrelevant to me.. However, the person who submitted this would have access to all the names, and amounts being funded.

Another reference to the Please Be Sensible email

Being ex-military Intelligence I always put the day before the month followed by the year. I would of written 30 June 2003 not June 30,2003. Which would of been and is inaccurate, because I had contacted Anamika long before that month.

Military intelligence is a classic oxymoron

I do not capitalize a persons full name: example: NISHA LAHIRI is not my way of writing, only the person who submitted it. Very unprofessional and childish.

An expert in style who can't spell

On the 26th of August at 01:36 am I was asleep in bed. If it was in the afternoon I was in Pittsburgh, Pa. from 10:30 am till 5:00 pm looking over a couple pieces of property.

Me thinks the lady doth protest too much

The last comment. She has yet to perform. This would not be used by me. When someone does not know me. or who is not even close to my intellectual level, then you should not attempt to pretend to be me.

Aha! Superiority complex revealed at last

So to figure out who sent this, all I have to do is figure out who is not smart, an unprofessional business person, with amateur ideas, childish mannerisms, and would gain the most from the removal of me (and a few others) from Anamika's funding.

Meaning Moi

This would be done by spreading lies and telling her that I would cause damage to her and her family through submitting this article and telling her that I did it..

Proves he read my Please Be Sensible email

I wont say who did it "I know who it is," they know who they are, and now Anamika knows it, and many of you know their name. By the way our corporate attorney's know it now, you better pray that ACI gets funding.. For your Information. This is not a threat, it is a promise!

My knees are quaking

This is what I got from the Telegraph
Sincerely
Signed by PB#1
Nisha Lahiri's response to the email PB#1 instigated
This is the original message, sent to our feedback address for readers comments. It's all I have. Let me know if I can help.
Nisha Lahiri.
-----Original Message-----
Sent: 26 August 2003 01:36
To: ttfeedback@abpmail.com
Subject: Feedback about the website: The Telegraph
The Telegraph Feedback
Name: Dr. Bob Kilgallon
Address:
Country: US
Phone:
Fax:
e-Mail: americas@alltel.net
Comments

NISHA LAHIRI should check out the investment commitments of Ms. Anamika Biswas from story of June 30,2003. Since April, she has told 23 businesses in the US, Canada, New Zealand, and Australia that she will fund their business plans to the tune of $33 billion dollars. Since then, she has been telling everyone the money is being wired, but nothing happens! I am one of the 23 trying to get funded and would like to know if she is for real. She seems to like publicity, but has yet to perform after weeks and months of promises.

Notice that the "from" address in the email to the Telegraph is missing.

September 12

HI everyone
I had received this just now from Anamika. I thought that I would forward this to all of you.

I have responded to her questions about the newspaper with specific information that pertains to the situation and those involved. You all had gotten my previous emails about the Telegraph newspaper, the same that I sent to Anamika.

This is a very positive letter from Anamika and I will keep you posted as to when the funds will arrive.

Anamika can you give me any information as to date and time expected for the funding to arrive? You can fax it to 1-309-4130564 anytime.
Sincerely
Robert Kilgallon

Earlier that day Anamika responded to what PB#1 purported was a "follow up" email to him from the reporter at the Kolkata Telegraph who had interviewed her in June. As shown above, the email was concocted and sent by Kilgallon to defame Anamika and cause her harm.

What he didn't show the group was his initial email to Anamika which elicited her response. That email follows here:

Dear Anamika
I had never asked to have any news paper or media to inquier about you. Someone who does not like me, and requires that they get funded used the newspaper web site inquiery to make it look like that I did it.

Typical dirty trickster points finger away from self

Why would I do anything like that when I am and still ready to publish Nationally and International the pres release that I sent to you.

Yet unable to get any publicity in June

I do know who did this. However unlike him, I will not lower myself to his level and cause misstrust and hatred between him and you. I had even talked with Jody and told her that I was behind you and believed in you 100%

Would be appreciated if he learned how to spell

This act was done by a childish non profesional person who considers himself as the most important person in the world, he knows what is best, and looks out only for himself, and will promiss everything, and will stab you in the back the first chance he gets.

There he goes looking in the mirror again

This kind of person would give you bad advice and make like he is the only person you can trust. I have sent any email I got form you, and my response to everyone, and letting them know that I support you.

He also sent out the dancing skeletons

I am hurt that you would still consider that I was not your friend and future business partner. I was the third person that you had agreed to finance. I have been there since day one, praying for you, and supporting you.

A martyr, yet

We were sent an email from this person in which he specified that you did not have enoughh money to finance everyone, let alone to live on, and that you should not consider financing Me, Steve, and Craig.

Did he send her any money to live on?

I felt that something was wrong, becuase you did not respond to emails that I sent concerning your well being and what was going on over there. I was the one that told the group of the bombings rioting, and everything else that was going on in India. I sent you emails of my response to the India news paper, and what I had found out from them.

Your decision is your decision. I pray and hope that you will see that both you and I, and probably others, may have been a victim of a single persons childish and unprofesional behavior. I appolgize to you, for their actions and what has happened. I know they would never admit to it, or appologize to you, I, or those he has hurt..

Guess spelling is not a requirement for a PhD in molecular genetics?

I await your reply, and looking forward to a long and prosperious business partnership.

Sincerely
Robert Kilgallon

The email from Anamika was PB#1's trophy. His proof of her discomfort showed the group that retribution had been meted out to Anamika, all the while claiming innocence—wink, wink ...

MR BOB
I GOT YOUR MAIL. I KNOW THAT FOR MY DELAY ALL OF YOU HAD TO FACE A PROBLEM. WELL I HAVE DONE MY WORK AND YOUR FUND IS BEEN WIRED BUT IT WILL TAKE SOME TIME TO REACH YOU.
WELL CAN I ASK YOU A QUESTIONES? WELL I AM ASKING YOU WELL DO YOU PEOPLE THINK THAT I AM FRAUD THT YOU PEOPLE ARE QUIRING ABOUT ME TO PAPER LIKE TELEGRAPH, CAN U VISUALISE THE SITUTATION BY PUUTING YOUR SELF IN MY PLACE AND FEEL IF THIS KIND OF THINGS COMES OUT IN PAPERS OR THIS KIND OF THINGS GET IN NOTICE TO THE MEDIA WHAT BUSINESS TRANSAC-TION I CAN DO OVER HERE DIDI YOU EVER THOUGHT OF THIS.
I WILL WAIT FOR YOUR REPLY AND YUR OPINION AND AS PER YOUR OPINION I WILL DECIDE WHAT SHOULD I DO.
WITH BEST REGARDS
ANAMIKA BISWAS

Yet, Brian spoke with her on the tenth and told me she as in "good spirits." Next, Anamika contacted me.

HELLO VINCENT,
I HOPE THAT BY THIS INCIDENT MY REPUTATION OVER HERE IS LOST BECAUSE I CAN UNDERSTAND THAT IF ONCE YOU COME IN THE BAD NOTION OF MEDIA YOU ARE FINISHED, HOW WELL WE WILL WORK WE CANT COME IN GOOD EYES TO THEM THIS DR KILGALON DESTROYED ME, I DONT KNOW WHAT WILL HAPPEN.
WELL TAKE CARE
ANAMIKA BISWAS

Unlike BobK, I could afford to place a long distance call. I called the reporter at the Kolkata Telegraph and advised her that some of Anamika's clients were disgruntled and that she should not pay any attention if any of them contacted her.

Dear Anamika
Please do not worry.

Kilgallon TRIED to destroy you with a fake email to the reporter at the Telegraph. But he did not provide the reporter with facts as she needed. THE REPORTER IS NOT GOING TO DO ANYTHING NEGATIVE TOWARD YOU.

I made a joke out of Kilgallon and the reporter accepted that he is a jealous, crazy man. PLEASE DO NOT WORRY.

Brian will be there tomorrow. I saw him at the airport before he left and he is very pleased to be meeting you. I know all will be much better for all of us once he gets there.
Best regards,

Kilgallon made his position, attitude and actions eminently clear in another email of September twelfth. In the best tradition of John Wayne he was "a gonna do what he hada gonna do, pilgrim." This included dancing skeletons and newspaper slander. His ego could not stand to be hidden.

Hello to Everyone

I would like to respond in a positive manner to everyone's questions. However, all I wanted to do was to let you all know what Anamika had sent me, and you can come to your own conclusion.

All I have to say at this point is that Money talks and B.S. walks. We have one person that is heading to India. Passport and all shots taken care of and he will be there this week.

I do what I need to do. Funding arrives, from what ever source, Fantastic and those people or person funding will be making more money then they will know what to do with it.

I hope to see the deposit soon, and from the above statement you can understand my feeling.

Sincerely

Signed BobK

I met with Brian and his wife for breakfast the morning he left for India. We planned to keep in contact by email and I would forward information to the group. When I returned from meeting with Brian I found that Alan forwarded to me his most recent email from Anamika

Subject: Re: ALAN GIRVAN—ARE YOU OKAY
HELLO ALAN
WELL I AM ALRIGHT, BUT RECENTLY GOT KEEN (**she means knee**) INJURY FOR WHICH I HAD AN OPERATION, WELL YOU MUST BE AWARE THAT THE FUND HAS ALREADY BEEN

DELAY #27—Anamika operation

DESPATCHED FROM HERE. FIRST SET OF FUND I AM SENDING TO THOSE COMPANIES WHOME I AM STATING BELOW THEY ARE AS FOLLOWS:-
1. MR ALAN GIRVAN
2. MR DAVE BOWER
3. MR VINCENT PANITTERE
4. MR BRIAN GORDON
5. MR JACK FULTON

6. MR SCOTT PHILIP
7. MR KEVIN O ROURKE
8. MRS JODY
WELL ALL THIS PEOPLE WILLL GET FUND IN THEIR ACCOUNT BY 15TH OF

Funding Date # 39—September 15th

SEPTEMBER THAT IS MONDAY. AND REST OF THEM THEY ARE AS FOLLOWS:-

1. DR KILGALON
2 ARMADA'S HOLDINGS
3 TIMBER WOLF PRODUCTION
4. SILVERTOUCH
5. GIASSER
6. MAGICK
7. JJ CONCEPTS
8 SHAWN
9. KHOA NUGYEN
10. BIOTRON INTERNATIONAL

AND REST OF THEM WILL GET THE FUNDING BY THE END OF THIS MONTH.
SO YOU CAN UNDERSTAND AT LAST I DONE MY WORK. WELL I ALSO GOT A NEWS THAT SHAWN CALLED UP IN MY HOUSE AND THREATENED THAT HE WILL PUT ME BEHIND BARS JUST INFORM HIMTHAT HE WILL GET THE FUNDING BUT DUE TO SOME MISMANAGEMENT THIS PART FACILITY IS BEEN TAKEN. I DONT UNDERSTAND THAT WHEN I AM WORKING WITH ALL THIS ODDS BUT STILL TRYING THE LEVEL BEST I CAN DO TO COMPLETE YOUR DEAL WHY PEOPLE (MOST OF MY CLIENTS) ARE ALWAYS READY TO PUT ME BEHIND BARS, I THINK THIS IS MUST BE THE SYSTEM OF YOUR COUNTRY THAT PERSON WHO WORK FOR YOU IF INANY CASE OR BY SITUATION CANT COMPETET WITH COMMITMENT PUT HIM BEHIND BARS. NOW SOMETIMES I REPENT WHY I LEFT MY FAMILY FOR THIS KIND OF PEOPLE.

WELL MR BRIAN GORDON IS REACHING INDIA BY SUNDAY AND I WILL MEET HIM HOPE THAT ALL OF YOUR QUARIES AND DOUBTS WILL BE OVER AFTER I MEET HIM.

TAKE CARE
WITH BEST REGARDS
ANAMIKA BISWAS

At last we had Anamika's intentions in writing. In the second group were those we'd advised her not to fund as well as one company she insisted she would not fund. At this stage what she did with her money mattered less than that my company would be funded by September fifteenth. Maybe.

September 14

I spoke with Brian in his Kolkata hotel room on September fourteenth. He told me he was going to meet with Anamika and go over the bank documents with her. My notes of the conversation indicate he found Anamika "honorable." That he would get "the confirmation numbers today" and that Anamika felt "Kilgallon was behind the arrest."

The good news he told me was that within "twenty four to forty eight hours all will be substantiated with the bank." And, Brian explained that Anamika "could never move the funds because UBI wanted many banks between it and the U.S." He concluded "the Biswas family name has weight." He followed up with email.

Hi Vince;
Well I am here in Calcutta, at the KENILWORTH HOTEL, Tel: 91-3322823939 Room 316. I met Anamika about 2 hours ago, it is Sunday Morning here in Calcutta. It went very well, and we connected right away. We are supposed to meet again for dinner, I will have her sign the clean copies of my contract tonight, and she will be back again tomorrow morning with the confirmation codes and all related documentation. We had a great visit, she was hoping that, you could have come with me. She has routed the funds from Singapore to Canada, and then on to our banks in America. She has indicated that the funds will be in our bank by Tuesday, at the latest. I will know more when I see the tracking documents of the wire. But I do believe she is solid, and I know that we will do great business together. She has only committed to funding of the 8 people of which you are one. We will be discussing the realm of possibility for which of the other groups we should fund. I really like her, and I read her as

very honorable and honest. I am very excited about all of this. I will update with more when I get it. You are welcome to pass on this info only to those 6 other people out of the 8. I will also be sending those 6 people an email as well.

Thanks,
Brian

I forwarded the email to the clients who had contracts with Anamika and asked them not to discuss it with anyone outside the group. "There is nothing underhanded in this request. We simply want to maintain some order while Anamika and Brian determine next steps in the funding process for the remaining clients."

Next I reminded Brian to discuss additional clients to be funded which he should "keep in reserve for the appropriate time." And lastly I asked that "we need to know who filed the complaint against her from Canada and New Zealand. Who posed as the FBI, etc. All of the above in due course, after we confirm our funds are in our accounts."

During another call to him on the next morning (night in Kolkata) Brian told me he "will go to her office tomorrow to get the codes to verify the wires." By then he felt he would have the "confirmation numbers. The transfer has been made. No doubt." He explained that "banks credit funds at midnight" and "the full amount should reach the accounts of the eight clients by Tuesday."

Funding Date # 40—September 16th

He added that Anamika was "upbeat about coming to Vegas on September twenty eighth. We'll know all by tomorrow, who, when, what bank."

Scott a client from Pittsburgh who had a contract called. We hadn't heard anything from him during the entire process. He went about his business (online gaming) and didn't make waves or cause dissension, patiently waiting to see how the process played out. "It's hard to believe a lot of people will be financed," he said when getting the latest news.

Brian was so energized by his meeting with Anamika that he wrote to another colleague, "She is so full of life and very excited about working with me as a partner. I am so glad that I made the decision to come over here and do this in person. I have found her to be a very forthright and honorable person and someone that is not afraid to look me in the eye."

The information coming out of Kolkata kept on getting better. But, and there seemed to always be a "but" with Anamika, when I spoke to Brian on the sixteenth there was another delay.

He didn't go to the bank because of "other paperwork to do" regarding "folks who have screwed her." However he "spoke to the bank" and would "meet with the General Manager who confirmed all wires have gone. Will get numbers tomorrow." Brian confirmed he received his wire confirmation number. He said "all is fine as far as she knows. The bank acknowledged all en route" and that we should expect the money in the "next twenty four to forty eight hours."

Funding Date # 41—September 17th–18th

Anamika showed Brian the letters "Chris, Larry, Craig and Steve had faxed calling her a liar and a cheat; letters that went to her bank, trying to convince the bank she was a liar and a cheat. Steve (PB#3) says she took one million dollars from him."

He also said "the absolute 'outs' and the absolute 'ins' will be determined tomorrow." They also called the Kolkata Telegraph to set an appointment for an interview that would refute email from BobK (PB#1).

Our attempt to keep a lid on Brian's progress failed and soon the jungle drums gave out the news. Larry came forth with another pronunciamento, even though he did not get any information first hand.

September 17

Hello
This came in to a client recently (like today i think) and im not going to say who but i know he would not mind me sharing it

really doesnt say too much for actual dates but its nice to sees hes still active and her and brian are in direct contact.

also looks like shes eliminating some people but i think that is to be expected after the hassles shes been given

Also remember that she cant take advice well so that is a problem as well.

good luck to those who receive her graces

Larry

HELLO
WELL MY INTENSION IS TO FUND YOU, WHICH IS MY 110% INTEN-
SION AND I HAVE EVERYTHING FOR IT,

NOWADAYS YOU MUST BE KNOWING THAT MR BRIAN GORDAN IS IN
MY CITY AND I AM MEETING HIM EVERYDAY,

WELL YOU ALSO KNOW THAT I AM ASKING FROM YOU PEOPLE A
VERY LITTLE IN RETURN TO MY INVESTMENT FOR WHICH I SOLD
MY ALL ASSETS AND I HAVE ALREADY SPEND MY ALL PENNY TO
YOUR DEALS,

BUT IN RETURN I AM ASKING FROM YOU PEOPLE A VERY LITTLE
FAVOUR THAT MR GORDN WHO IS HERE PLEASE CALL THE PEOPLE
OF PRESS AND GIVE A PRESS RELEASE FOR HIS DEAL WHICH IS
LARGEST AS COMPARED TO ALL OF YOU AND THIS ANNOUNCE-
MENT WILL HELP ME TO GAIN BACK MY REPUTATION IN THE MAR-
KET OF MY COUNTRY WHICH I LIST FOR SOME OF YOU I DONT
WANT
TO TELL THE NAME.

WITH BEST REGARDS
ANAMIKA BISWAS

PB#2 advised Larry that he would "wait for a final outcome to this transaction at which point we will proceed accordingly." Another veiled, empty threat
from one of the PBers.

Anamika reached out to others in the group of eight. She wrote to Alan on
September seventeenth she was grateful for his support. But also advised him
she received "an email of threat from Larry." She asked that some press release
of support be issued to help stop whatever "reputation I lost ... comes back."

The morning of the seventeenth, Los Angeles time, I spoke with Brian. He
told me he "talked to the bank ... confirmed wire went." But the bank was
closed because it was Puja.

Holiday #4—Vishwakarma Puja (worship of machines and money oriented papers) plus a kite festival

He revealed that bank hours were noon to four and it took an hour to get there with traffic. "I appreciate her position," Brian said in describing the extent Anamika had to go to fulfill her responsibility to her clients. He felt "comfortable all went well and the funds were released through Canada to the U.S."

He planned to "review the paperwork at the bank tomorrow and get copies of all eight wire confirmations." The next day they would do a press conference with the print and electronic press.

Brian mentioned that "people in the hotel know Biswas; they know her and her family which gives great credibility to Anamika." He was planning on leaving Kolkata on Saturday, September twentieth and added "all in group of eight will have their paperwork and money by then. She's very, very real. She had her signature notarized by the Indian government. She has nothing to run from or hide."

September 18

But, all was not well in Kolkata when I spoke with Brian on the morning (LA time) of the eighteenth. Only five or six members of the press showed up and were "baffled why AB Exports would fund the group." He said he met Anamika's father who assured him that Anamika had wired the funds and they would "go tomorrow and open all the books." Brian admitted he could not "understand why it takes so long for electronic signals to hit our bank." Yet he said Anamika's father was "emphatic the money was sent." Jack also spoke with Brian that morning and left the conversation feeling he was "not as upbeat."

Jody's email from Anamika brought the "Jaws" music thrumming in our ears.

HELLO JODY
WELL HOPE THAT YOU ARE FINE TODAY, WELL I AM NOT TODAY I TOOK MY FATHER TO MEET BRIAN BUT THE ATMOSPHERE THAT HAPPENED THERE WAS NOT GOOD I AM SORRY THAT IT SEEMS TO ME NOW THAT AFTER YOU PEOPLE GET THE INVESTMENT IN YOUR BANK I WILL LEAVE EVERYTHING AND GO AND STAY IN HIMALAYAS OR IN ANY HILLY PLACE WHERE I CAN BE JUST ALONE

Poor Me Anamika #7

I DONT NEED MONEY OR FAME I JUST WANT TO SEE THAT YOU PEO-
PLE GOT YOUR FUNDING AND I WILL LEAVE THE WORLD BECAUSE I
DONT WANT TO SEE ANYONE SUFFER FOR ME, AND OVER INFRONT
OF MY EYES I AM SEEING BRIAN IS SUFFERING AS HE HAD FULL
NOTION THAT I AM EXPLOITING HIM OR RATHER I AM USEING HIM
FOR MY BENEFIT AND I HAVE NOT WIRED ANYONE OF YOU, THAT
BECAUSE I CANNOT TAKE HIM TO THE BANK YET, BUT BELIEVE ME
JODY I AM TAKING THE OATH OF MY MOTHER AND FATEHR THAT I
HAVE FUNDED YOU ALL BUT DUE TO SOME PERSONNAL PROBLEM I
COULD NOT ABLE TO TAKE TO BANK. THE PROBLEM I HAD WHICH
IS PREVENTING ME TO TAKE HIM TO BANK IS THAT I TOOK A LOAN
FROM BANK AND I TOLD THEM THE MOMENT MY CLIENTS WILL
ARRIVE FROM ABROAD I WILL PAY THE LOAN BACK TO THEM BUT
NOW I AM INCAPABLE OF DOING THAT SO I AM AVOIDING THEM
AND DONT WANT BRIAN TO GO TO THE BANK BUT TODAYS INCI-
DENT SHOWS THAT NONE OF YOU BELIEVE ME YOU ALL THINK
THAT I AM FRAUD, WELL THAT IS MY BADLUCK, NOW I REPENT WHY
I FORCED BRIAN TO GIVE PRESS RELEASE, BUT TODAYS SITUATION
WAS SUCH BAD THAT DONT HAD ANYOTEHR WAYS TO SOLVE IT.
WELL I KNOW OR NOW I UNDERSTAND THAT I AM INCAPABLE OF
DOING ANYTHING. WELL MAY BE AFTER TODAYS INCIDENT I WONT
MEET YOU ALL AS BRIAN LEFTS FOR AMERICA MY MEETING WITH
ALL OF YOU WILL END AND AFTER YOU GET FUNDINGWHICH WILL
BE IN YOU BANK IN TWO DAYS THE CHAPTER NAME ANAMIK-
ABISWAS WILL DIE.
TAKE CARE
GIVE YOUR CHILDREN MY BLESSINGS.
ANAMIKA BISWAS

As storm clouds threatened to bring the monsoon back to Kolkata, Larry
sent Brian an email asking for an update. First, he hoped Brian was "enjoying
the country and company." Next, he wondered "where my company's funding
stands" being anxious for some solid comfortable word. Then he asked the
magic words "… are there funds available? If so, who all is getting funded and
who isn't any longer?" Duh!

He admitted to writing "Anamika 5 days ago in the hopes of teaching her
how things are over here and how things were looked at from our point of

view ..." No doubt, this was the letter than Anamika took as a threat. I don't have a copy as he didn't share it with me.

As if that weren't enough, PB#2 added his over-valued two cents.

Brian:

Just an added note to Larry's comments since you are now seeing Anamika on a daily basis. As previously advised, Biotron continues to wait for the final outcome to Anamika's transaction. There are three outcome scenarios for Anamika, A. B. Exports and the Biswas Group of Companies, etc.—with, without and against:

a) With—Biotron will receive its full funding of $7.1 billion USD as per Anamika's commitment and we will work with her in accordance with our submitted Agreement.

b) Without—Biotron will receive 50% of its funding ($3.55 billion USD) as compensation and Biotron will withdraw its Agreement and proceed with its corporate agenda without Anamika.

c) Against—If Anamika does not honour either a) or b) above within the next 14 days, Biotron will initiate litigation against Anamika, her companies and all associated family members and their companies.

Scenarios a) and b) have already been offered and confirmed by Anamika, her legal counsel and her associates. Scenario c) is strictly a business decision and legal position that any company would initiate in light of the circumstances of the past 4-5 months and the undertakings of those that have provided affirmative correspondence to Biotron relative to a) and b) above.

I understand that Anamika may not fund certain projects that she has previously committed to fund. Should Biotron fall into this category and scenario a) is eliminated, we fully expect that Anamika will honour scenario b) and forward $3.55 billion USD in compensation immediately.

It should be noted that if Biotron proceeds with item c), such action will also include any persons and/or companies that have interfered with this transaction, provided illegal and improper advice to Anamika and were directly or indirectly involved with any circumvention of the committed funding or compensation package to Biotron.

I'm sure you will be able to clarify the content of this correspondence to Anamika. I look forward to receiving an update from you or a response directly from Anamika on this matter.

Regards,

Craig Fields

Then Steve advised all that he was eagerly awaiting a "timely" update from Brian as well.

On this same day BobK—our dancing skeleton, dirty trickster—was going for the gold. He took one last impotent shot at squeezing money out of Anamika. His email to her said he planned to file charges against her "for fraud, defamation of character, breaking of contract, non payment of settlements and a few more". He gave her forty eight hours to wire two billion five hundred million dollars ($2,500,000,000) to his account. Failure to do that he warned would result in his "corporate attorneys" taking action and "notification to the news media." Not bad per diem.

Without guidance or direction from the so-called "brokers" all of the companies were on their own—which arguably they should have been from the very beginning. Dealing directly with Anamika had been my position ever since I refused to rely on Larry and Chris for their crumbs of mostly useless information. I was surprised the others didn't act the same way, including the PBers who seemed content to carp and complain all the while remaining tethered to the umbilical cord of the group.

One clear sign of this new dynamic was Steve's supportive email to Anamika in which he criticized the tone and tenor of the dirty trickster. He was "appalled at its contents and wish to express my displeasure at your being subject to such." He wanted to "emphatically and irrevocably point out that this sort of uncalled for action is completely unacceptable and is not condoned in any shape or form." He concluded "Understanding the Subcontinent so very well, I do empathise with you in this regard …"

September 19

The conversation with Brian on the morning of the nineteenth did not improve the outlook for funding. Anamika's father spoke with Brian for a few minutes the previous day, told Brian he had to go to the bank but would return at twelve thirty to pick him up and they would return to the bank together. When I spoke with Brian it was six hours later and her father had not shown.

"He has a signed paper with bank confirmation numbers but he refuses to show it to me," Brian said. "They've not shown me they have one dime," he said before hanging up. Later that day Brian's wife called me to say he would stay in Kolkata until he "gets it done."

Anamika gave Dave an explanation for why Brian would not return home with the confirmation slips. According to Anamika, her bank manager "comes to Calcutta by train but due to certain problems of trains he could not able to reach here ..."

DELAY #28—Train problem delays bank manager

Later Jack called to advise me that Brian had received a "hand delivered letter from Anamika's father asking him to stay until Monday and promising to fax confirmation slips." Jack told me Brian will stay in India until Tuesday. What convinced Brian, he told Jack that morning was that Anamika's father "had looked me in the eye."

I also spoke with Kevin in Toronto that day. He confirmed Jack's report. Anamika's father will fax the confirmation slips and commitment letter. Apparently most, if not all of Anamika's money was coming from her father. "Her dad put his foot down when the yahoos contacted the bank," Kevin explained. Apparently the funds had been wired on September third and will arrive in Toronto on the twenty fifth. The letter to Brian, he continued, listed "eight companies already funded with the others on hold."

She gave more details to Alan.

HELLO ALAN,
WELL I CAN FEEL YOUR FEELING I DONT NEED ANY PRESS RELEASE FROM ANYONE OF YOUBECAUSE OUR INDIAN PRESS GOT SO ANNOYED AND DISAPPOINTED ON ME FOR SOME OF THE CLIENTS AND THEIR ATTACK OVER ME ON VARIOUS ASPECTS MADE THEM CONFUSED THAT INSPITE OF THE PRESS RELEASE OF YESTERDAY IT DIDNT CAME OUT AND THEIR NOT RESPONDING MODE INDICATES THAT IT WONT GET RELEASED, WELL THAT WILL HELP BRIAN A LOT AS HE IS GOING BACK WITHOUT CONFIRMATIONSLIPS OF ALL OF YOU BECAUSE THE DAY BRIAN REACHED HERE WAS SATURDAY THE WEEKEND 13TH OF SEPTEMBER 2003 THE NEXT DAY I MEET HIM THAT IS 14TH OF SEPTEMBER 2003 SUNDAY AND I TOLD HIM THAT I WILL TAKE HIM TO THE BANK ON WEDNESDAY 17TH OF SEPTEMBER 2003 BUT I WAS NOT AWARE THAT 17TH OF SEPTEMBER WE HAD VISHWAKARMA PUJA, WHERE WE WORSHIP MACHINES AND MON-

EYORIENTED PAPERS AND ALSO ON THAT DAY KITE FESTIVAL TAKES PLACE. SO OUR BANK MANAGER SINCE HE STAYS IN BURDAWN OUT SKIRT OF KOLKATA DIDNT CAME, SO I WAS UNABLE TO TAKE HIM TO BANK.

THE NEXT DAY WE HAD A PROBLEM WITH SHOW ORGANISER, WELL I DEFINE YOU I WAS ALREADY ORGANISING A SHOW IN WHICH I NEED THE HELP OF BRIAN SO WE CONDUCTED AN AGREEMENT BETWEENUS (MEANS BRIAN, ANDME) WITH THE ORGANISER THAT D S ASSOCIATES AND THERE I HAD A FIGHT WITH THOSE D S ASSOCIATES AS THEY WERE INTERPRETTING SOME WRONG INFORMATION TO BRIAN, SO AS I TOLD BRIAN THAT I WILL TAKE TO BANK ON 18TH AT 12:30PM IN THE NOON BUT FOR THAT PROBLEM OF MONEY THIS PEOPLE OF DS ASSOCIATES CLIMED THE TIME WENT OFF AND I REACHED IN THE HOTEL AT 2:30PM JUST IN THE TIME OF PRESS CONFERENCE, BY THAT TIME THEY HAD CANCELLED MOST OF THE PRESS AND ELECTRONICS MEDIA AND WE ARE INTERVIEWED BY THREE PAPERS WHO ALSO DIDNT TOOK THAT OUT TODAY. TODAY I TOLD BRIAN THAT MY FATEHR ON MY REQUEST CAME HERE TO MEET HIM AS BRIAN WAS INSTITNG TO MEET HIM, AND HE TOLD BRIAN THAT HE WILL TAKE HIM TO THE BANK BUT OUR BANK MANAGER WAS UNABLE TO REACH THE BANK AS THERE WAS CERTAIN PROBLEM OF RAILWAYS, SO TODAY ALSO WENT OFF, AND TOMORROW BRIAN IS GOING SO MY FATHER WENT AND MEET HIM AND TOLD HIM IF HE CAN STAY BACK TILL MONDAY AS TODAY WAS FRIDAY AND OUR WEEKEND STARTS AND NOTHING CAN HAPPEN BEFORE MONDAY, SO HE WENT TO REQUEST HIM IF HE CAN STAY BACK TILL MONDAY OR WE WILL FAX THOSE SLIPS ON MONDAY. AS BRIAN TOO SEEMS NOT TO BELIEVE ME AND MY FATEHR FOR THIS WIREING AND HE WANT TO SEE BY HIS EYES IN THE BANK SO I CAN GURANTEE YOU THAT AFTER GOING BACK FROM HERE THE LIST OF THE PEOPLE WHO DONT TRUST ME WILL INCREASE BY ONE, I KNOW ALAN I AM UNCAPABLE WOMEN BUT STILL TRYING TO HELP YOU

Poor me Anamika #8—an incapable woman

ALL HOPE THAT MY HELPING GOES OFF BY MONDAY AND AFTER THAT I WANT TO CLOSE THIS RELATION WITH ALL OF YOU AND I DONT WANT ANYRETURN FROM ANYONE OF YOU BECAUSE I AM INCAPABLE OF DEALING WITH YOU ALL BECAUSE BRIAN WAS MY

GUEST IN MY COUNTRY BUT I KNOW I COULD NOT ABLE TO TAKE-CARE OF HIM AND MAKE HIM HAPPY.
REQUESTING YOU TO WAIT TILL MONDAY FOR THE WIRE SLIP AND THEN I WILL WAVE YOU GOODBYE FOR EVER.
ANAMIKA BISWAS

September 20

On September twentieth, Brian transcribed the letter Mr. Biswas had given him only twenty four hours earlier. It read:
TO MR. BRIAN KENT GORDON
DATED-19/09/03

RESPECTED SIR
THIS IS TO INFORM YOU ASTHE MEMORANDUM OF YOUR TRAVEL THAT YOU REACHED HERE ON SATURDAY 13TH OF SEPTEMBER 2003 EVENING TO THE KELINWORTH HOTEL. MY DAUGHTER MIS ANAMIKA BISWAS, WHO IS YOUR INVESTOR MEET YOU ON THE 14TH OF SEPTEMBER 2003 SUNDAY. FROM THAT TIME YOU ARE BEING ATTENDED BY ANAMIKA BISWAS, SHE TOLD YOU THAT SHE WILL PROVIDE YOU WITH CONFIRMATION SLIPS ON WEDNESDAY THAT IS 17TH OF SEPTEMBER 2003, BUT THAT DAY WAS VISHWAKARAMA PUJA AND SO OUR BANK MANAGER DIDNT ARRIVE. THURSDAY WAS HER COMMITMENT TO GIVE YOU THE CONFIRMATION SLIPS BUT DUE TO SOME MISUNDERSTANDING AND DUE TO SOME PROBLEMS REGARDING HER SHOW SHE WAS UNABLE TO DO SO. ON THURSDAY AFTERNOON SHE MEET YOU AGAIN AT 2:30 P.M. FOR PRESS RELEASE. TODAY IS FRIDAY 19TH OF SEPTEMBER 2003 SHE WENT TO THE HOTEL TO MEET YOU LATER ON I JOIND HER, AS WE ARE SUPPOSE TO TAKE YOU TO THE BANK FOR GIVING YOU THE CONFIRMATION AND ALSO THE EXACT STATUS OF YOUR WIREING AND ALSO OTHER SEVEN COMPANIES;-THISTLE PRODUCTIONS, JA LAD, GLOBALSTAR, RESERVE OIL AND GAS, IMAGE ENTERTAINMENT, LSA AVIATION, KO GROUP AND COMPANY OF DAVE BOWER. BUT SINCE TODAY DUE TO SOME PROBLEMS OF RAILWAYS MY BANK MANAGER DIDNT ABLE TO REACH THE BANK FOR HIM I WATED FOR ENTIRE DAY OF BANKING HOURS, BUT ULTIMATELY I COULD NOT ABLE TO MEET HIM AS HE WAS NOT PRESENT TODAY, OVER THERE OUR BANKING INFRA-STRUCTURE IS SO POOR THAT YOU CANNOT ABLE TO DEAL WITH-OUT MANAGER, SO I WILL REQUEST IF YOU WANT THEN STAY BACK

TILL MONDAY TO TAKE YOUR SLIPS AS IT SEEMS THAT YOU DON'T TRUST ME AND MY DAUGHTER AS INSPITE OF ALL ODDS SHE WORKED FOR ALL OF YOU, IT IS VERY OBIVOUS THAT FOR A DEALING IN THE COMPANY LIKE YOU AND OTHER SEVEN NEED MUCH TIME TO COMPLETE FROM THE INFRASTRUCTURE OF KILKATA BUT SHE TOOK LESS TIME OF FIVE MONTHS.

SO I WILL HOPE THAT YOU WILL BLE TO COOPERATE WITH US AND WAIT IF YOU WANT TILL MONDAY OR YOU DEPART TOMORROW AND I WILL FAX THOSE TO YOU ON MONDAY THTA IS MY GURANTEE AND MY PROMISE. MAYBE I AM NOT THAT HIGH PROFILE BUSINESS PERSON LIKE YOU ARE BUT STILL I GOT REPUTATION IN MY MARKET OF INDIA.

THANKING YOU
MR ASHIT KUMAR BISWAS

Anamika and Steve traded a series of messages which demonstrated how fragile international communication could be even when both sides were speaking the same language to a degree. Anamika took umbrage with Stinson's sensitive email.

HELLO MR STINSON
WELL YOUR EMAIL SUBJECT WAS THAT YOU ARE EMBRASSED AND SHOCKED I DONT WHT YOU TRY TO SAY BY THIS—ARE YOU TRYING TO SAY YOU ARE EMBRASSED AND SHOCKED BY MY ATTITUDE OR YOU ARE SHOCKED BY THE BEHAVIOUR YOUR FELLOW COUNTRYMEN HAS DONE TO ME, WELL NEXT TIME WHEN YOU WRITE PLEASE STATETHAT CLEARLY.
WELL AS FAR AS MY OPINION IS CONCERNED I AM EMBRASSED AND SHOCKED TO KNOW AND SEE THAT PEOPLE FROM SOME OF THE WORLD RICHEST AND LARGEST ECONOMIC CENTRES ARE SO ILLBEHAVED.
AS YOU MUST BE AWARE THAT MR BRIAN GORDON OF GLOBAL STAR IS HERE PLEASE MAKE A POINT OF ASKING HIM THAT WHETHER ITS SOUNDS THAT I AM ILLBEHAVED TO HIM IN ANY WAYS, I HAVE DONE MY WORK OUT OF ALL THE ODDS I FACED, I DIDNT TURNED BACK AND ASKED HELP FROM ANYONE OF YOU BUT INSTEAD I ONLY ASKED FROM YOU ALL A BIT OF COOPERATION BECAUSE THE WORK

I AM DOING IS BIG THAT FUNDING ALL 24 CLIENTS WHICH AS CON-
CERN TO INDIAN WORKING HABITS AND MODE OF FUNCTIONING
NEEDS TIME THAT WHAT I HAVE DONE I ONLY ASKED TIME FORM
YOU ALL AND ALSO ASKED FROM ALL OF YOU TO SUPPORT ME,
WHICH I WILL DENEY THAT SOME OF YOU HAVE DONE BUT REST
DIDINT INSTEAD YOU PEOPLE HAD THREATENS ME THAT YOU WILL
DESTROY ME I DONT KNOW WHY BUT STILL FROM OF MY HEART I
AM DOING MY WOK MY FIRST SET OF INVESTMENT IS ABOUT TO
REACH THERE AND VERY SOON MY SECOND SET WILL REACH TO
YOU ALL BUT THAT DOESNT MEAN THAT YOU PEOPLE WILL ABUSE
ME AND I WILL TOLERATE IT BECAUSE I AM INVESTING YOU,
REMEMBER I AM INVESTING NOT PAYING BACK YOU LOANS, SO I
WILL ALSO ACEPT THAT YOU PEOPLE PLEASE BEHAVE WITH ME
DIPLOMATICALLY INSTEAD OF RUDELY.
WITH BEST REGARDS
ANAMIKA BISWAS

Steve responded with "… My disgust and embarrassment is directed
towards the project principal DEFINITELY NOT towards you whom I feel so
sorry for … Please note that no Canadian or American is a countryman of
mine—I am an Australian citizen, currently in New Zealand with my wife who
is also a director and the corporate secretary of AHI is a Filipino citizen. Most
of my working life has been in Asia …".

When I spoke with Brian on the morning (L.A. time) of the twentieth, he
told me he had received "an exciting letter from her father" who asked him to
stay until Monday when they'd go to the bank. Brian said he was "more pleased
to deal directly with her father as it's his money." He described Mr. Biswas as
"sincere, has nothing to hide. He guaranteed and promised to confirm by
Monday so that we can see when the money went out of his account."

Mr. Biswas revealed to Brian that he planned to move his family out of
India by the end of October. This bit of information plus the surprise letter
and personal plea contributed to the feeling that all was well.

Later that day Evalani, Brian's wife, called to tell me that Anamika had
received confirmation the funds left Singapore on Friday (September 19).
They were no longer in Singapore Anamika told Brian when she called.

September 21

Lo and behold! Anamika called me a little after nine on Sunday, September twenty first. She told me the "wires are done". The slips would be sent the next day.

Confirmation Slips Wired #10

But—yet another but. Since Brian's investment was about seven billion he had to show the Indian government that he had approval for his operation from the Panamanian and New York governments. "He needs to complete the paperwork before he gets his money," she told me.

DELAY#29—Government approval needed

I was pleased to hear her say that film production companies were welcomed "because they sell films and get money." I noted the call lasted seven minutes and twenty six seconds, just enough time to maintain excitement but not enough to get substantial information from her. Too many questions left unsaid.

Later that day Brian told me he'd met with Mr. Biswas at the hotel and knew a former CIA agent who "confirmed Biswas has money all over India in several banks." Had our not-so-diligent "brokers" known this and failed to tell us or were they ignorant as usual?

Brian also told me that the Reserve Bank of India, akin to the U.S. Federal Reserve, and the State Bank of India were not allowing release of his funds because the banks "were not satisfied with the paper work on his projects. They needed evidence of contracts where his projects were located." He felt this was because they were "nervous about allowing so much money to leave the country without an explanation." They also wanted concrete evidence that Mr. Biswas had the money and the authority to send it.

September 22

On the morning of September twenty second Brian told me he "will be stuck in mud for a while. The rest will be okay." He was going to forward the confirmation slips that night.

Apparently because there was a news story, the government got involved and needed "to see substantial stuff." He was going to show his documents to the Minister of External Affairs so he could give his approval to the Reserve

Bank for the release of the funds. "All else in clear and will get money," he assured me.

There was, however, an interesting wrinkle. Anamika leveraged Brian to give her forty percent of his profits instead of twenty five. So much for poor, frail, young Anamika.

Brian also provided another comforting bit of information. "The press people claim they have checked her out and she can provide the money." However, he couldn't totally hide his disappointment "Last night I thought all was cool and I was going to the bank. Then Mr. Biswas tells me he needs more government approval." Brian was angry that Anamika had confirmation the money went through Singapore, but he still couldn't get proof. Anamika was going to Delhi the next day for the approval.

Anamika Travels #2

Jack called several times that day. First he learned from Brian that "Anamika was a no show" and that Brian "has been warned to be careful. She's been speaking loudly around the hotel and not dressing like she has money." So? Seems to me the ostentatious display of wealth in a city like Kolkata or Rio, as another example, is open invitation to be robbed, kidnapped or killed.

Later he said Brian's project had been "red flagged to show how it would benefit the Indian people." Brian also told him that the "bank requires that we receive our confirmation slips."

All in all the situation didn't seem perilous. Brian's money would be delayed, but ours wouldn't. He certainly could satisfy the requests for information by the government. The money left Singapore on its way to Canada.

Jack was less than sanguine. "He needs to face the issue." were his cryptic parting words. While Jack was one of the seven companies with signed contracts with Anamika, his stance was more "trust but verify" than total belief. My stance was to give equal weight to both belief and verification.

Early on, when we discussed Anamika's motives for funding the group our usual questions were "if she doesn't have the money, why is she stringing us along. What does she get out of it?" Jack's position was that Anamika was conning others, maybe Indians, to invest in her company by showing them our business plans and thereby provide herself legitimacy.

Intellectually, Jack had a point. Anything was possible. But, if I didn't, couldn't or wouldn't see it, I took the position of doubting Thomas. I wanted to remain fixed on the positive.

September 23

Brian sent out an email stating that seven of the clients would get their funds in five days and he would get his in ten days.

Funding Date # 42—September 28th

Brian's wife told Jody that Brian is frustrated by the delay. We wanted Brian to go to Anamika's house, to speak with her father and let him know if we don't get funded we can't protect her from the other clients who want to sue.

Jack was concerned that "Brian has let Anamika deflect him. He's not able to face any issues. He doesn't know the bank manager's name and hasn't been to her office. She wouldn't take him. She's fair game after two weeks. I'm waiting another two weeks."

Beyond that, Jack was concerned that "Brian over states things. He wants the deal so bad he's twisting the facts. Brian said they don't look like they have money."

The news during my call with Brian was not any better. "I waited all day for her to come back at 11 AM with the contracts and heard nothing from her or her father."

On the chance I might find her, I called Anamika's house to learn from the housekeeper that Anamika's mother went to the hospital with a heart problem.

DELAY #30—Anamika's mother to hospital with heart problem

I contacted Anamika with the following:

Dear Anamika
I called your house this morning and was told by the man who answered that your mother was taken to the hospital with a heart problem. I hope it is not too serious and that she has a complete and fast recovery.
All of us in the group of 8 regret her illness and pray for her health.
HOWEVER—when you get this PLEASE SEND ME A COMPLETE UPDATE OF THE STATUS OF OUR FUNDS.

You can't possibly know how frustrating it has been for all of us who remain loyal to you but have been attacked constantly by the others—Larry, Chris, Craig, Reghu, Stinson, Bower, etc.—who are critical of you and don't trust you.

As I and others have helped you when you asked, it is now time for you to help us, as we desperately need your help.

SEND US CONFIRMATION SLIPS FOR THE FUNDS—we need to receive confirmation and the funds as soon as possible.

We need the confirmation, not because we don't trust you, but because that is the way business is conducted in the West. And, if you want to be credible and profitable in the West that is the way you need to conduct your business.

DO WHAT YOU SAY YOU WILL DO AT THE TIME YOU SAY YOU WILL DO IT.

That is the most important business rule in the West. Followed by:

IF THERE IS A DELAY OR PROBLEM, COMMUNICATE IMMEDIATELY.

That is what we do and what we EXPECT of our business associates and partners.

I continue to believe and respect you and look forward to a successful business relationship. I also look forward to your response as soon as possible.
Best regards,
Vincent Panettiere

Just when we thought all was well, BobK sent out an "advisory of litigation and criminal charges."

Please be advised of action forthcoming.

Dr. Robert D. Kilgallon of Americas Choice Inc. will be sending the United Press International, and other national news media, and the Telegraph in India all information and collected data on all events of Ms. Anamika Biswas and the Biswas Family fraudulent claims for funding, and causes for criminal charges, and international litigation of a single or class action suite …

This information includes all investigations, all communications, and transactions for immediate release and investigation. Additionally the United States Treasury Department has been given information on several violations of the Securities and Exchange Commissions laws regulating Investment, loans, and non licensed financial advice by individuals, that is contradictory to International Laws, and those suspected or are involved in such transactions.

I was told that I did not give enough time before taking action. You have been informed.

What happens from here on in is in the hands of the attorneys, federal law enforcement officer, and Interpol. I had given every opportunity for Ms. Biswas and her family to respond and those involved to respond and make amends. It never happened.

Those who have previously requested to be a part of this litigation are already included in this action.
BobK

If BobK made good on yet another of his empty threats no one knows. But, we do know that no story about his claims was ever printed or distributed.

Callous as it may seem, I was determined to get information about the confirmation numbers. Though I tried to keep focused on only the positive, there naturally were niggling doubts which had to be put to rest.

September 24

In my email to Anamika on September twenty fourth I hoped her mother had made a complete recovery, and then presented her with some options.

"In order to make your life easier, I wish to suggest the following with regard to the Confirmation/routing numbers for the wires your father said were sent on Sept. 3.

"1. If you have the receipts of the wires, I will call you and you can read them to me on the phone at a time and number you designate.

"2. You can call me at a time we designate. You called me last Sunday at 9am Los Angeles time, for example. You can call me three hours earlier (6am) any day of the week if that is convenient.

"3. My third suggestion is to make copies of the slips and send them to me via DHL. You can charge my account. If you don't have my number handy, I will send it to you again.

"I hope these suggestions lighten your burden.

I knew she had seen BobK's Litigation and criminal charges email and took it as an opportunity to remind Anamika that she needed to focus on those who consistently supported her.

".... We are not part of any law suit he may be planning, even though we received the email.

"HOWEVER WE NOW ARE YOUR ONLY FRIENDS IN THE GROUP.

"IT IS VERY, VERY, VERY IMPORTANT THAT BRIAN GETS THE CONFIRMATION NUMBERS WITHOUT DELAY, WITHOUT EXCUSES, ETC.

"IT IS VERY, VERY VERY IMPORTANT THAT YOU COMMUNICATE WITH US ON A VERY FREQUENT BASIS...."

In my daily morning phone call to Brian in Kolkata he told me of a discussion he had with a television reporter. Accordingly, the reporter told Brian if the Biswas' "did all as a joke they would cooperate to expose the Biswas" and get the attention of the proper ministers in India.

Back in cyberspace, Alan was challenging PB#1's advisory of litigation and criminal charges. PB#1's response was typically haughty "As I stated before it is out of my control. The corporate Attorneys are taking it from here." The corporate law practice in some "Dog Patch" Pennsylvania town must have suddenly become very lucrative.

Not to be ignored, Steve asked about the "current status of the AHI US$4.672 Billion bank transfer ..." and respectfully requested Anamika to "pay me the courtesy of addressing all outstanding issues forthwith."

I sent the Kolkata reporter a response to BobK's litigation advisory to head off any possibility of negative publicity that would interfere with our group getting funded. This was survival of the fittest time.

Dear Nisha:
I regret that once again you have been pestered by another email from "Dr" Kilgallon.

While my email address, and that of other supporters of Anamika, is included we do not support or sanction what many believe is Kilgallon's transparent attempt at extortion of Anamika and her family.

He is trying to obtain by threat and intimidation what he has no contractual right to obtain. Additionally, Kilgallon is trying to sabotage the funding of those who have contracts with Anamika. Kilgallon does not have a contract with Anamika. Thistle and other companies do.

Kilgallon's current email and others before it could clearly be identified as the childish and petty actions of a jealous, self involved, self important individual who uses his title—a PhD in molecular genetics—to give him an aura of expertise and superiority. Though his degree has never been confirmed and the university bestowing it is unknown.

Considering his business plan includes theme parks, a cargo line and various other enterprises not remotely connected with molecular genetics, the persistent wielding of this title—which he may have earned and be justly proud of—underscores his insecurity and accompanying disdain for those who are not instantly obeisant.

We can judge him by his past actions. As you know, he fabricated the alleged email from his computer "without his knowledge" to you and then cobbled together your response to make it appear as if the entire correspondence was legitimate.

His arrogant caveat to the group that he would never stoop to give the press any information only makes "me thinks the lady doth protest too much" a more apt description of his actions.

Unfortunately, being an expert in molecular genetics does not qualify one for being an expert in the jurisdiction of the Securities and Exchange Commission, which has authority only in the US; nor the US Treasury department. Furthermore on one of his numerous websites Kilgallon seeks to raise $15 million through, limited partnership units, for a mall, publishing company and a Great Lakes cruise line—all of which taken together may have some kind of molecular genetic structure, but it is not apparent to the naked eye.

I've taken enough of your time.

Hopefully you can give the doctor's email a suitable burial in your trash bin.

Best regards,
Vincent Panettiere

September 25

Email from Anamika on September twenty fifth informed me that her mother was in the ICU and would be transferred the next day. Once that happened Anamika said she "will fax you all the wire slips."

Meanwhile, Anamika was receiving frantic email from Reghuraj AKA Reghu the young man in Kerala state who initially sought her financing for his client in Toronto.

"We both are … in trouble now. Someone named Kilagon …" has filed suit "against you and me…. For real I don't know who is these people, Kilagaon, Henry, etc. I got so many threat emails its all because of you I'm facing it and I believe that, its because of a Honest work I did with U …"

Allen of Philadelphia contacted all in the group to "urge restraint" in regard to the "threats of lawsuit and criminal charges against the Biswas family." He felt that, as Brian was returning, all would be settled by the following Thursday, October second. Others didn't agree. PB#2 advised Allen that "Brian is not a communicator and never provides updates to the entire group … I think any updates at this point in time should come from the legal counsel for Anamika and the Biswas Group and from their bank(s)."

Allen couldn't leave it at that. He fired back blaming "our esteemed brokers, UN representatives, scam artists Chris Catlin and Larry Kronabach …" who he said had "sugar plums dancing in their heads" at the thought of all the money they would make and thereby didn't perform appropriate and timely due diligence on Anamika.

Jody continued her support of Anamika with an email to those who wanted to pursue litigation. She was most direct with "… it seems that those that wish to have vengeance would undoubtedly not have the means or the collateral to qualify for other more traditional funding." She left unsaid the fact that these same PBers also would not have the means to instigate an international law suit.

September 26

On September 26th, Nisha Lahiri replied to my email.

Hi, this is Nisha. Thanx for the email, letting me know about Dr. Kilgalon. Just keep me posted about your plans and how everything is going. Also, do you have any idea when Anamika is coming back to Calcutta?
Thanx

Nisha Lahiri,
The Telegraph

I continued to press Anamika for information about the location of the funds as well as the timetable for disbursement. Fully believing in her family difficulties, I knew it was a fine line to straddle, yet the months of delays and numerous crises prevented me from being completely understanding. Others gave her both barrels.

Dear Ms. Anamika Biswas
I had sent you an Email explaining that I was informed that you were no longer funding Americas Choice Inc. projects.

I had sent several Emails explaining that I had not contacted the Telegraph, as yet, requesting them to investigate you in the past.

Within that Email I explained that if the entire amount is not being funded that ACI would accept the original settlement of $2.5 billion as payment, and expected that payment to be made, or the entire amount if you wanted to still fund the projects, within 72 hours or we would file for litigation..

I allowed 6 days (144 hours) to pass and I heard nothing from you, nor was any deposit made. Since you refused to honor our business agreement and not make any contact with me I was forced to proceed with legal actions.

Your lack of communications and the emails I had gotten, second hand, from Brian indicating your decision not to fund ACI showed a disrespect from you and those involved with you, and a direct disregard to any agreements.

Our Corporate Attorneys are not just representing ACI, there are several other companies, (9 to be exact at this time) that you were going to fund, being represented.

Our corporate attorneys informed me that the only way for no legal action to occur is the direct deposit of either the 50% settlement amount of $2,500,000,000 USD be deposited into the account which will end our agreement, or the $5,000,000,000 USD be deposited into the account which will indicate that you still want to finance the projects.

Either of the deposits within a 24 hour time period, will end the ACI litigation and investigation. No excuses, no promises, no phone calls, only the direct deposit and transfer of funds within the next 24 hours..

I am sorry about your Mother being ill. As like you, I have physical family problems and I also have a very large business to operate.

You past record and actions, or rather your lack of actions has caused a great deal of damage, and pain (Financially, morally, and physically) to me personally and the Corporation has lost it professional standings in the community by marinating its faith in you, and your promises.

The only action acceptable from you now, is the deposit of the funds.

Sincerely

Robert Kilgallon

Of course Larry had to show he could play with the "big boys."

September 30

Hello
Well it took a bit of time but I finally got some information to release about Brian's trip to India

Brian may still few things more to add as he is not discussing things with me directly so we will have to wait and see if he sends out an update or not.

1.. Brian was received into Anamika and her fathers house and after a meeting or two was told that his project because of the size of the funding was not going to be funded as they were not able to comply with the amount comfortably.

Brian never visited Anamika's house

2.. The Father it seems is still very much a part of the selection process which seems to still be on going a bit although it was mentioned that 7 or 8 projects have been confirmed as moving forward to the funding stage.

3..It also seems that those who even spoke to Anamika such as myself and some others have been eliminated from the funding consideration and on this I say "NOT MUCH OF A LOSS" as I would never have really been comfortable accepting her money anyways as she is far too iffy and lax in her decisions for me.

Such high standards; her money not good enough

However congratulations to those who got her attention and who managed not to upset her as it seems those are the projects they are deciding upon and heavens knows that funding is tough enough to come by that when anyone does get the job done it is always very nice to see.

Again I am not moving forward with any press releases to defame her or her character, although I am taking legal action against her for her actions and inconsiderate attitude.

Another one without any funds to sue

Thats all i can find out for now and all I probably will be able to until she deides to confirm the funding as they get their end of things accomplished....
Thank you
Larry

I was gratified to receive Anamika's email on September thirtieth as it confirmed the importance of treating her with humanity and dignity.

HELLO MR VINCENT,
THANKS FOR ENQUIRING, WELL MY MOTHER IS FINE NOW SHE IS NOW OUT OF DANGER BUT HAS BEEN PRESCRIBED TO BE IN COMPLETE REST AND TENSION FREE.
I AM NOW IN DELHI TALKING TO ALL THE PEOPLE OF STATE LEVELS DISCUSSING ABOUT THE BRIAN GORDAN PROJECT AND SO FAR I

GOT GOOD RESPONSE FROM GOVERNMENT. WELL I THINK WITH THE PROCEDURE OF WORK WE WILL ABLE TO COMPLETE THIS MY 3RD OF OCTOBER 2003 AND WILL BE BACK BY 4TH OF OCTOBER2003 AND ON 6TH OF OCTOBER 2003 I WILL SEND ALL YOUR WIRE PAPERS BECAUSE THE PRECEDURE GOT STUCK FOR BRIANS PROJECT AND NOW WHEN IT IS MOVING POSITIVE THEN I WILL BE SENDING YOU ALL MY 6TH OF OCTOBER.
WELL I ALSO GOT FROM FEW OF YOUR EMAILS THAT FEW ARE FILING CASE AGAINST ME THAT IS LAWSUIT I WILL LIKE TO KNOW THEIR NAME AND ALSO AFTER YOU ALL GET FUNDING BY 6TH OF OCTOBER 2003 PLEASE TRY TO ASK

Funding Date # 43—October 6th

THOSE PERSON WHO IS FILEING CASE AGAINST ME TO PLEASE SEND ME A LETTER STATING THAT THEY DONT WANT ANYMORE FUNDING FROM ME BECAUSE I HAVE DONE DELAY SO THEY ARE FILEING CASE AGAINST ME.
PLEASE CONVEY THIS TO ALL I WILL GET BACK TO YOU AGAIN ON TOMORROW IF POSSIBLE.
ONCE AGAIN THANKS TO ALL OF YOU FOR ASKING ABOUT MY MOTHERS HEALTH AND ALSO FOR PRAYING FOR HER.
ANAMIKA BISWAS

I responded hoping that all would be successfully concluded in six days.

Dear Anamika
Thank you for your prompt reply to my email. I am pleased your mother is recovering and have informed the others.

There are four areas I wish to discuss with you.

1. COMMUNICATION—As I've mentioned, frequent communication is the best way for you to establish a solid relationship with those who support you. In this way you maintain their trust and credibility. That is why I am appreciative of your prompt reply.

2. FUNDING—While the delay is understandable—between your mother's illness and Brian's project—I hope that those of us who will be funded, receive

their funding before you send wire confirmations on Oct. 6. Though, at the very least we should be able to track the funds through the wire system.

This is very important because I am told your father told Brian the funds had been wired on Sept.3 and would take three weeks to to reach our accounts (approximately Sept. 24). Additionally, I also understand funds were supposed to have left Singapore at some time while Brian was in Kolkata.

These delays—understandable as they may be—do not help your credibility. For your sake—and I say this as a friend who has trusted you for many, many weeks—I hope the funds reach us from Singapore to Canada, etc. by Oct. 6.

3. REPORTER—A reporter contacted me and asked if you were back in Kolkata. I don't know how or if the reporter knew you were out of the city. I am not telling you the name of reporter, nor have I responded. Until funding is received and your credibility is proven without doubt, it does you no good to talk with reporters or hold press conferences.

I say this because I am more expert in publicity than anyone in the group—not because of the publicity I got for you, but as a result of more than 20 years experience.

The best publicity you can get is when 7 or 8 clients tell the world that you have funded them.

4. LAWSUIT—I believe those who are filing cases against you are primarily— Dr. Kilgallon and Craig Fields. Both have written email strongly suggesting their intentions. I don't know if Steve Stinson is involved with them, but he strongly supports their intentions. As I have declared myself as one of your supporters I have received little additional information.

I continue to send prayers for your mother's complete recovery.

I also pray to God that the funds arrive so that my belief and trust in you over these many weeks will not be a mistake.

I remain your friend and send you

Best regards,

Vincent Panettiere

And so ended the fifth month.

SEPTEMBER SCORE CARD		TOTALS
Funding Dates	9	43
(next funding date, we think Oct. 6)		
Delays	7	30
Funds Transfer Date	0	2
Draft/Tracking Numbers Sent	0	2
Holidays	1	4
Confirmation Slip Dates	1	10
Anamika Has Wired Funds	0	4
Anamika Travels	1	2
Poor Me Anamika	2	8

9. OCTOBER, 2003

CHARGES FLY, THE CENTER WOBBLES

As October began, law suits were on the horizon, but so was October sixth—our latest date for funding. We had come this far, what were another six days?

October 1

Naturally, those who had not received contracts from Anamika had other ideas. At least Steve was gentlemanly about it. Yet again, he sent Anamika an email "requesting you pay me the courtesy of addressing all outstanding issues forthwith." In fact his message to her of October first was similar to the message he sent on September twenty fourth.

Then, there was BobK, a real piece of work. His email of October first went to none other than President Bush!

The email was—count 'em—sixteen, I say sixteen, as in one, six, pages long!

The email also went to the President of India and the Indian Ambassador to the United States in Washington, D.C.!

He copied the reporter at the Kolkata Telegraph. Most likely this was the first and, I think it is safe to say, probably only time in her life when she received the same information at the same time as the presidents of the United States and India.

Accordingly, when the award is given for presumptuous, pretentious, pompous, self-serving egotism there is only one person who is most deserving and that is Bob K.

Included in the email were thirty one (31) emails from Anamika beginning on May twenty seventh and ending on September twenty fifth.

One interesting email included in the sixteen pages was from Sri M. K. Banerjee of the Reserve Bank of India. Considering the phony email which purportedly was sent to the Telegraph, this one from RBI could easily be a fake. Nevertheless, the email of July 4, 2003 informs BobK "As per guidelines remittances exceeding USD 100 million for investment abroad require prior approval from Ministry of Finance, Govt. of India. We are not aware whether MS Anamika Biswas and Others have obtained such permission. However, we inform you that we have not received any application for remittances."

His summation line to President George Bush et al was a whiny "Final note: No phone call, no deposits. Nothing!"

Now there's a compelling motivation for the President to drop Iraq, tax cuts, Medicare, the security and welfare of a few hundred million Americans and rush to the aid of PhD from PA just because he didn't get a phone call. What's a President for?

We don't know if the President ever responded.

Naturally, President Bush did not receive a copy of the infamous dancing skeletons email nor his phony "who me?" email to the Kolkata Telegraph.

After months of surprises, we received the greatest shock. Larry informed the group that as of "this morning October 1st, 2003 Action ventures is STOP-PING ALL CORRESPONDENCE with the Biswas and is CLOSING their part in this So Called Funding Affair." So that's what it is called?

To his clients he intimated future legal action and admitted "we (meaning he and Chris) have never been part of this deal right from the get go all because this lady decided she knows better than us on how things should or will proceed."

Hah! and double Hah! These guys knew enough **not** to confirm Anamika was qualified to invest before corralling twenty four companies desperate for financing. They knew enough **not** to go to India and meet her face to face. They knew enough **not** to do on-site due diligence. One was a student and the other on the dole. Nothing wrong with either, unless acting as "financial brokers" in a thirty three Billion dollar ($33Billion) deal. Some might call that hubris and others might call it fraudulent misrepresentation.

Larry complained about getting the "shaft" and he couldn't resist a remark of self pity, as in "… a few of the clients in the know are hiding facts for themselves so to me the heck with them too as I need nothing from them ever, so they can do as they wish."

But he was not beneath holding his hand out. "Best of luck to those of you who receive anything from this affair and if you do and wish to honor our fee agreement so be it and if you choose not to honor our agreements then I hope you enjoy your future."

He advised us in his "LAST LETTER FROM ACTION VENTURES" he was "moving on" except for any "legal action that we will soon be taking."

Hello Anamika

I have some information that I would like you to review Anamika if you could please and if you can afterwards to please send us some information on the status of each of our funding acceptance or disapprovals.

I am writing to you today not as J.J.'s Concept & Design as it appears that you have cancelled all interest in our project so we are going to request that you tear up any contracts and letters that you have concerning J.J.'S Concept & Design or keep them in case they are needed later in a court of law as evidence.

We were approached by you in April of this year through Chris Catlin and we told that you were seeking a multitude of projects for funding consideration and we answered your request in good faith.

We simply wished to have our projects reviewed and placed in front of you and if possible from that point on to get our projects funded and begin on our individual journey's.

I have tried to mention to you some of the western manners and procedures of investment and the expectations that we have and expect from any investor but it seems that you do not like or wish advice and that is ok too as it shows you have great character and integrity (intelligence) in these affairs.

However as you know you have promised alot of good people some funding for their companies and they have repeatedly asked you for some kind of proof of funding, as have I and chris, so that they can make serious plans.

Now I know that maybe we do business over here a bit different that you do but the bottom line is IF YOU MAKE A STATEMENT TO DO SOMETHING REPEATIDLY as you have, why then people want to trust and believe in you but they get nothing confirmed in return even after 7 months, it makes it very difficult to follow along any longer.

So to keep this short for you and easy for you to understand as we have "no new information" from you regarding the status of each clients progress or approvals or dissapprovals we are requesting FOR THE LAST TIME FROM MY COMPANY.

WILL YOU PLEASE SEND WORD TO EACH CLIENT DIRECTLY

the status of their projects as you see it today so that they can rejoice in funding appreciation or close the book on you and move on with their individual businesses and lives??

I am not too certain who you really are Anamika and at this point in my life I really do not care but I am going to tell you right up front that you have managed to almost completely destroy my good company name as an venture capital connection service just with your very inappropriate behavior and plain and simple

LACK OF ATTENTIVENESS TO PROCEDURES

as I work very very hard to avoid "problem investors" who like you have absolutely no respect for us as a broker service or as a client.

Now while we totally appreciate your indication that you are funding some of the projects and we wish you and the clients the very best if you indeed do fund some of them but as a brokers service I think it only fair to mention to you that I will be seeking some form of compensation in a court of law soon I hope, to bring an end to your capabilty to ruin company's, especially mine, at your own whim.

This is the LAST letter that you will ever receive from me on any subject and if I wish to discuss anything with you any further it will be inside a court room. Thank you for your time.

Larry

Brian was also struggling, along with all the others, to receive communication from Anamika on a consistent basis. "I am still behind you providing this funding, but you need to be clear with me to let me know whether or not it can be done. So I know whether or not to pursue other options."

While we were giving Anamika the benefit of many doubts, we gradually—some may say too late—realized Anamika could not be poked or prodded to do anything. Naturally, we were at a disadvantage. But then, what person or company about to receive a loan or financing from any entity is not at the mercy of the funder until the money is received? The idea that any of us could snap our fingers to instantly cause Anamika to do our bidding was egotistical and presumptuous. Though I'm sure it would be vehemently denied, inherent was a most definite soupcon of racism—a certain missionary zeal for taming the noble savage.

October 2

By October second, all gentlemanly pretexts were dropped by Steve—no more Mr. Nice Wonder From Down Under.

Dear Ms. Biswas,

In view of your continued refusal to communicate with Armada's Holdings International Pty. Ltd. (AHI), refusal to respond to our communiqués and failure to remit funds as you have committed to on more than one occasion, I am writing to inform you that unless you immediately SWIFT transfer the promised US$4.672 billion and provide proof of transfer from the remitting Bank you have left me no alternative than to join other disgruntled project principals in taking legal action against you.

It is most unfortunate that this has come to such an unsatisfactory situation and it is indeed with deep regret that AHI has to seek such redress. Should you fail to provide proof of transfer together with a detailed response by close of business in Calcutta today, 2nd October, 2003, AHI will join with the other project principals first thing tomorrow, 3rd October 2003 in instigating litigation as well as advising the relevant authorities of this unfortunate course of action.

Signed Steve Stinson

When Craig unloaded next, it seemed like an orchestrated barrage.

WITHOUT PREJUDICE

Ms. Anamika Biswas:

Please be advised that Biotron International Limited will be joining a class action lawsuit against you, A. B. Exports, the Biswas Group and other representatives thereof in order to seek settlement for your unfulfilled statements, claims and undertakings relative to the remittance of $7.1 billion USD to Biotron International Limited.

We have tried to assist you and co-operate with you in concluding this transaction but you have continually failed to complete the undertakings that you have committed to and have provided false statements and claims regarding the transfer of funds to the bank account of Biotron International Limited.

Over 130 pages of direct correspondence as well as other information and updates from third parties has been provided to our legal counsel and they have been instructed to initiate litigation proceedings immediately.

Without prejudice to our rights to pursue the remittance of $7.1 billion USD through legal litigation, we will provide you with 24 hours, from the date and time stated on this e-mail communication, to provide written confirmation that Anamika Biswas, A. B. Exports and the Biswas Group will undertake to honour their Offer of Compensation for 50% ($3.55 billion USD) of the total investment. This Offer of Compensation was issued by Mr. Anil Mitra, solicitor for the Biswas Group, on June 13, 2003 and was further confirmed by you, Anamika Biswas, on June 19, 2003 and on other dates thereafter. Your written confirmation and undertaking to honour the remittance of $3.55 billion USD to the bank account of Biotron International Limited must be notarized and, if accepted, registered in a court of law. The remittance of $3.55 billion USD can be made in one lump sum payment or it can be made by a sequence of payments on a weekly or monthly basis that will ultimately pay Biotron the full $3.55 billion USD. If you choose a schedule of payments, you must provide me with your proposed schedule within the next 24 hours from the date and time posted on this e-mail correspondence. If the submitted payment schedule is accepted, the first payment must be sent by SWIFT transfer by no later than 12:00 noon India time on Friday, October 3, 2003 and the transmitting bank must fax the confirmation directly to my attention at Biotron International Limited.

Please note, again, that this Offer of Pre-Litigation Settlement is provided without prejudice to our other legal rights to settlement as may be handed down by a court of law if a Pre-Litigation Agreement is not reached.

You now have an opportunity to settle this matter. Please govern yourself accordingly.

Signed Craig Fields

Some in the group who had stayed out of the feud came forth to declare their neutrality. Duane of EnTelServ told Anamika "I would also like for you to know EnTelServ has no plans on being part of any legal action against you or your family."

Buck, another client, also declared his support for her. "Anamika, I thought I'd let you know that we at our company have parted ways with Larry and do not support his position or attitude toward you. Deal with me as a separate entity from anyone else from here on."

While waiting for funding on October sixth, Jody and I thought of a way to solidify our relationship with Anamika. We decided that once we were funded we would go to India, meet with Anamika and prepare for a future working relationship.

Additionally, we felt announcing our intentions prior to funding might serve as an inducement for her to make sure all went smoothly. With all the disappointment that forty three unfulfilled funding dates brought us, we wanted to be as proactive as possible with every opportunity.

We explained to Anamika in an email of October second the reasons behind our trip.

"1. To meet you, introduce ourselves and get to know you better; 2. Discuss our projects and answer any questions you may have; 3. Discuss the films Jody and I want to produce in India; 4. Help with whatever legal problems you may be having—as we know the various characters in the group, we may be able to offer strategy and solutions; 5. Issue press releases, meet with the press and ANNOUNCE THAT WE HAVE BEEN FUNDED BY YOU."

We thought these were compelling, but never got a response from Anamika. Perhaps she was too busy determining how to respond to the onslaught of threats from the pompous ones.

Craig sent a high school taunt to Allen of Philadelphia "Well, as expected, Thursday has come and Thursday has gone and there has been no update from Brian and the matter is not settled. Enough said." Unfortunately we would hear more from him.

October 3

WITHOUT PREJUDICE

Ms. Anamika Biswas,
Further to my final demand letter to you yesterday, please be advised that Armada's Holdings International Pty. Ltd. will be joining a class action lawsuit against you, A. B. Exports, the Biswas Group and other representatives thereof in order to seek settlement for your unfulfilled statements, claims and under-takings relative to the remittance of US$4.672 billion to Armada's Holdings International Pty. Ltd.

We have tried to assist you and co-operate with you in bringing this transaction to a satisfactory conclusion but you have continually failed to complete the undertakings that you have committed to and have provided false statements and claims regarding the transfer of funds to the bank account of Armada's Holdings International Pty. Ltd.

Over 400 pages of direct correspondence as well as other information and updates from third parties has been provided to our legal counsel and they have been instructed to initiate litigation proceedings immediately.

Without prejudice to our rights to pursue the remittance of US$4.672 billion through legal litigation, we will provide you a further 24 hours, from the date and time stated on this e-mail communication, to provide written confirmation that Anamika Biswas, A. B. Exports and the Biswas Group will undertake to honour their Offer of Compensation for 50% (US$2.336 billion) of the total investment. This Offer of Compensation was issued by Mr. Anil Mitra, solicitor for the Biswas Group, on June 13, 2003 and was further confirmed by you, Anamika Biswas, on June 19, 2003 and on other dates thereafter. Your written confirmation and undertaking to honour the remittance of $2.336 billion USD to the bank account of Armada's Holdings International Pty. Ltd. must be notarized and, if accepted, registered in a court of law. The remittance of US$2.336 billion can be made in one lump sum payment or it can be made by a sequence of 20 payments on a weekly basis that will ultimately pay Armada's Holdings International Pty. Ltd. the full US$2.366 billion. If you choose a schedule of payments, you must provide me with your proposed schedule within the next 24 hours from the date and time posted on this e-mail correspondence. If the submitted payment schedule is accepted, the first payment must be sent by SWIFT transfer by no later than 12:00 noon India time on Friday, October 3, 2003 and the transmitting bank must fax the confirmation directly to my attention at Armada's Holdings International Pty. Ltd. on 1 708 575-8189

Please note, again, that this Offer of Pre-Litigation Settlement is provided without prejudice to our other legal rights to settlement as may be handed down by a court of law if a Pre-Litigation Agreement is not reached.

You now have the final opportunity to settle this matter. It is hoped you are now well informed and that you will act in an honourable manner to expedite it.

Most sincerely yours in hospitality,
Signed Steve Stinson

Just when we thought we would never receive another email from Larry again, up he pops with a slam at Brian. I was not copied on this email and received it from another client. My exclusion, while not hurtful, may be a sloppy oversight or … with Larry who knows.

His email to Brian on the third of October was full of self-serving petulance similar to what we had seen on many other occasions.

"Well Brian i am not too sure of where you are coming from any longer as your silence on your trip to India seems very wrong as if i remember correctly you went over there leaving in good faith and on good terms with most of us.

"Not sure who you are listening to or what you are thinking but personally i am the one fellow who has tried to help you out the best i can so far on your funding and it seems that for that i get not even the courtesy of a hi or what have you

"Well that is life Brian in the fast lane as i am sure you are well aware of and your perogative and as far as im concerned you and i have concluded all business together.

"However if you still want to work with linda and her funders if they turn and proove themselves real here in the next 5-7 weeks i say for you to go do as you wish on that.

"Other wise it has been a pleasure meeting you and for whatever went wrong no longer care."

As we've seen, Larry, who had a way with thoughts and words, always responded like an adult.

More and more we saw an orchestrated campaign of sabotage by the pompous ones. Sections of the "without prejudice" email contained similar or exact language which mirrored in honesty the language used to justify the invasion of Iraq. Instead of giving one last chance to get rid of WMD's the pompous ones were giving Anamika twenty four hours to wire them millions of dollars. Another front in that campaign began when Craig followed up on his October second "Notification of Litigation" email.

October 5

Ms. Anamika Biswas:
As you have chosen not to respond to our Offer of Pre-Litigation Settlement, we have advised our legal counsel to proceed accordingly with all legal applications of litigation against you, A. B. Exports, the Biswas group and other associates who have participated in providing commitments and undertakings relative to the remittance of $7.1 billion USD to Biotron International Limited.

The class action lawsuit will be filed in association with other select members of the group for which you made commitments for funding and compensation. Respective government officials and the media will be kept informed of the proceedings as your actions in this matter do have international repurcussions.

Signed Craig Fields

As if on cue, Steve sent an email about Anamika to the President of India as well as the Governor of the Reserve Bank of India and its regional director for West Bengal and, naturally, the reporter from the Kolkata Telegraph.

The Honourable Dr. Avul Pakir Jainulabdeen Abdul Kalam
President of India

Dear Dr. Abdul Kalam,
The warmest greetings to you from beautiful Christchurch, New Zealand!

I am Steve Stinson, the President, Chairman & Managing Director of the Armada's Group of Companies (AGC), International Developers, Operators and Consultants to the Hospitality, Tourism and Leisure Industries. One of our companies, the New Zealand incorporated Armada's Holdings International Pty. Ltd. (AHI) has been seeking US$4.672 billion funding for the AHI Project which consists of ten (10) concurrent facets detailed in order of priority with the following names and disbursement:

US$ 1.576 billion Puerto Princesa Resort, Palawan, Philippines;
US$ 740 million for Lake Tekapo Village Resort, New Zealand;
US$ 53 million for Dili Commercial, Hotel & Beach Resort, Timor-Leste;
US$ 131 million for YaoDing National Nature Park Resort, Sichuan, China;
US$ 80.522 million Schloss Langenzell Hotel & Resort, Heidelberg, Germany;
US$ 29.734 million Hofgut Mariahalden Hotel & Resort, Baden Baden, German;
US$ 17.744 million Schloss Lieser Hotel Development, Lieser, Germany;
US$ 682 million Ortigas Renaissance 5000, Pasig City, Metro Manila, Philippines;
US$ 743 million Christchurch CBD MXD, Christchurch, New Zealand; and,
US$ 619 million Cebu CBD MXD, Cebu, Philippines.

All facets of the AHI project fall within the accepted Infrastructure/ Humanitarian definitions of World Bank (WB), Asian Development Bank (ADB) and United Nations Development Programs (UNDP) as well as National Governments in each country detailed as each has a very large infrastructure and humanitarian component through urban water supply, transport, telecommunications, power, sewerage and waste management plus education, medical and health, employment, industrial, as well as economic, social, rural and tourism development.

Currently the status of the project is that all planning aspects and negotiations have been completed, contractors are on standby and upon closing of the committed funding, the actual acquisitions and construction will commence immediately. An amount of US$111.61 million has already been invested into the project to date.

It is most unfortunate that I am obliged to write to you on such a distasteful matter, but, in our quest for financing the AHI project, we were contacted, on 3rd May 2003, by a Ms. Anamika Biswas who allegedly is the Managing Director of A.B. Export Company, 84 Jatindra Mohan Avenue, Kolkata. 700005. India. Ms. Biswas informed us, through her brokers, that she and her family would fund US$4.672 Billion for the AHI project as an investor. AHI cooperated fully from the outset, as it was its intention to enter into a long term partnership with the Biswas Group, with full documentation submission being expedited:
~ AHI Application for US$4.672 Billion funding of 3rd May 2003;
~ AHI—AB Exports Contract of 3rd May 2003;
~ AHI—AB Exports NCND Agreement of 5th May 2003;
~ AHI Fax including NZ Overseas Investment Commission; and
~ AHI Summary Letter detailing responsibility for the loan of 11th June 2003.

All documentation was acknowledged as received and it was informed that closing procedures allegedly commenced.

AHI, however, was not the only project to be funded as some 22 to 23 other project principals were also to be funded to a total amount of in excess of US$23 Billion. Warning bells were ringing because when due diligence of Ms. Biswas and her family was requested and or followed up on, project principals were informed, in no uncertain terms by the Biswas, that it was an insult to them and that it seemed like they were not to be trusted. This reaction to routine business modus operandi appeared most unusual but allowances were made because of cultural differences and no offence was intended.

The funding of AHI's project and the others, went through several delaying phases. At first, it was advised that funding would be immediate in the week 5th to 9th May 2003 upon the release of a licence for A.B Exports being issued by the Reserve bank of India. Then it was informed there would be a slight delay until a visit by Ms. Biswas, her father and other family directors, so that they can get first hand information on all the projects, and those involved. This however never eventuated because of an alleged loss of US$2.5 billion in South Korea which had to be resolved by the family and their solicitor (a Mr. Anil Mitra M.Com. Law), and also Ms. Biswas' father became ill which caused additional problems. Ms. Biswas alleged Mr. Mitra was a member of the Calcutta Law Firm of Bose and Mitra but upon AHI's checking with this firm, the principals Mitra adamantly stated that he was not know to them nor was he associated with them in any way.

Because of the considerable delays in funding, a payment of 10% of the total amount was offered as additional compensation. As of this time, no project principal has received any compensation. More time passed and then on 14th June 2003, the family solicitor, Mr. Anil Mitra offered three options.
Quote....
1) WE CAN SEND YOU THE DHL AS WE ALREADY TOLD YOU ALONG WITH THE DRAFT OF 10%TO START THE WORK WITH AS THE DIRECTOR REACHES YOU.
(2) WE CAN OFFER YOU MOST WELL KNOWN GROUPS OF INDIA LIKE AMBANI, GOENKA, GODREJ AND MANY OTHERS IF YOU THINK THAT YOU HAVE DOUBT OF DEALING WITH BISWAS COMPANY, AND THESE COMPANIES CAN PROVIDE YOU FUNDS AS WELL AS PROOF ON THE FIRST MEETING WHICH BISWAS GROUP IS INCAPABLE OF AT THIS MOMENT.
(3) WE CAN OFFER YOU A COMPENSATION OF 50% OF THE TOTAL AMOUNT OF INVESTMENT WITHIN SEVEN DAYS AS COMPENSATION AND YOU FIND SOME ONE ELSE AS INVESTOR BECAUSE I THINK THIS IS THE FOURTH TIME BISWAS FAMILY ARE NOT CAPABLE OF KEEPING THEIR COMMITMENT, AND, I BELIEVE TO YOU PEOPLE BUSINESS IS MORE IMPORTANT THAN ANYTHING AS IT SHOULD BE BUT TO BISWAS FAMILY THEY THINK LIFE IS MORE IMPORTANT THAN ANYTHING WELL I APOLOGISE FOR THEIR THOUGHT I KNOW THIS FEELINGS HAS NO MEANING IN TODAY'S WORLD WHICH THEY ARE NOT

AWARE OFF AND THIS IS WHY BEING WEALTHY THEY ARE AWAY FROM LIMELIGHT OF THE WORLD.
…. Unquote

AHI opted for a variation of the first and third proposal which it considered to be a much fairer, equitable and workable arrangement of mutual benefit to both parties, namely:

- The Biswas Group remit via SWIFT/Telegraphic Transfer, the Ten Percent (10%) compensation, namely US$467.2 million [US$467,200,000.00] immediately to the account of Armada's Holdings International Pty. Ltd. Westpac Banking Corporation Christchurch New Zealand as per our previously submitted instructions that were provided to Mr. Somnath and Ms. Anamika and are reiterated below;
- In addition, within 14 days, the Biswas Group will remit via SWIFT/Telegraphic Transfer, an advance of Forty Percent (40%) of the Loan amount, namely US$1.869 billion [US$1,869,000,000.00] to the account of Armada's Holdings International Pty. Ltd. Westpac Banking Corporation Christchurch, New Zealand as per our previously submitted instructions. If the Biswas group is unable to travel to Christchurch, New Zealand within the next 30 days, this settlement offer of US$2.336 billion (being 10% US$467.2 million compensation plus the 40% advance of US$1.869 billion) would conclude our business relationship.
- If the Biswas Group is able to travel to Christchurch New Zealand within the next 30 days, WHICH IS WHAT WE WANT, to conclude the full funding transaction in the amount of US$4.672 billion [US$4,672,000,000.00], we will complete the transaction and they will then remit the Sixty Percent (60%) balance of the funding in the amount of US$2.803 billion [US$2,803,000,000.00]. At that time our long-term partnership will be consummated. Unfortunately, however, nothing has ever been paid or honoured as agreed to.

Several weeks passed and notification was received that Ms. Biswas was going to fund 100% of all the projects and that we were not to pursue other funding. On 8th August 2003, through a Mr. Vincent Panettiere of Thistle Productions in the USA, another project principal, a facsimile was received which was from Ms. Biswas which stated that AHI was to receive US$4.672 Billion through Bank Transfer on 13th August 2003. Again this commitment was not honoured and since then there has been nothing but delays and more incredulous excuses given. If any of the project principals objected or became somewhat agitated, Ms Biswas would notify project principals through intermediaries that should this persisted she would not fund anyone.

As of this date, AHI has waited for over 5 months for Ms. Biswas to honour her agreement for funding. It has been most courteous as well as tried to assist and co-operate with Ms. Biswas in bringing this transaction to a satisfactory conclusion but for reasons only known to her, she has continually failed to complete the undertakings that she has committed also providing false statements and claims regarding the transfer of funds to the bank account of AHI. As a result of this most unfortunate state of affairs, it has had an enormous negative impact on both AHI's and my personal credibility and integrity. Not only has it been challenged but also has been severely damaged because of us not being able to honour our commitments, which based upon the promises of Ms. Biswas and group, we entered into in good faith with our many creditors, bankers, acquisition property vendors, consultants, contractors and last but by no means least, our staff. In all, this has had far reaching direct implications on over 3,000 entities and individuals.

Full due process has been afforded Ms. Biswas to rectify the situation but she has not been availed of it. As such and as a desperate last resort, over 400 pages of direct correspondence as well as other information, updates and communiqués from third parties has been provided to AHI's legal counsel as AHI is now joining with the group of project principals who were promised funding but because of Ms. Biswas failure to honour the commitment are filing litigation against Ms. Biswas, her family and certain other individuals who have purposefully and maliciously sabotaged the funding as well as deliberately deceived to further their own interests at the expense and disadvantage of the remaining project principals.

It has always been AHI's intention to have a rock solid, long term business partnership with Ms. Biswas and everything possible has been done to achieve this end. The last thing AHI ever wanted was to have to litigate to have the commitments honoured. In recent times, many emails have been forwarded to Ms. Biswas which she has responded to failing to addresses the issues or has simply ignored them completely. Final notification of impending litigation has now been served. The following email addresses have been used by Ms. Biswas, her family and employees:

Anamika Biswas   anamika_biswas@hotmail.com

Anamika Biswas   moonmoonbiswas@yahoo.co.in
Anamika Biswas   munmun_2001_in@rediffmail.com
Akansha Agarwal   eximp_group_pioneer@yahoo.co.in
Anil Mitra   mitra_bose_soliciter_concern@yahoo.com
Somnath Biswas   sheer_e_bangal@yahoo.co.in
Niraj Biswas   sheer_e_bangal@yahoo.co.in

A selection of copy and pasted communiqués is attached to this Email as supporting exhibits of what has and has not transpired.

AHI, like many of the other project principals, does not want to have to instigate this litigation. If Ms. Biswas would honour her commitment, AHI, without prejudice, would withdraw its action as I am sure the other project principals would too also agree not to prosecute or file litigation. AHI has instructed its Counsel to wait until there has been a response from the other grieved project principals, and, if common sense cannot prevail with Ms. Biswas honouring her commitment, will then reluctantly proceed with litigation and other necessary action forthwith.

Humbly, Sir, I believe your influence may be most helpful in avoiding negative international publicity as well as preventing a distasteful and damaging action against the Biswas family, its businesses and the chosen associates who have attempted to pervert the course of honouring the commitment of funding.

Thank you for affording me your time and consideration in this matter.

Most respectfully and sincerely yours in hospitality,

Signed Steve Stinson

Reghu the young worker at an Internet café in Kerala was increasingly worried by the agitated state of Anamika's client group. In March 2003 he made the initial contact with her on behalf of Jerry a Canadian entrepreneur who paid him a modest stipend to troll the Internet looking for investors. After Reghu found Anamika and passed her along, with Jerry's permission, to Chris in Tasmania, Chris brought her to Larry who gathered the group.

Reghu sent a series of unanswered email to Anamika requesting information about the funds for Jerry and also pleading with her to do right by all her clients. By this time Reghu had become known to several in the group. I corresponded with him on Yahoo chat regularly until his obstinacy became too infuriating.

But, once Reghu learned of the possible law suits against Anamika he tried to cover his position. On October fifth, he contacted Kilgallon.

Hi Killagon
How are you, I am Reghuraj from India. I want to know is there my name in that list, I already heard that u were going to trouble Anamika and her 10 others, i would like to know, who were the others, is there my name or not,. If there is my name, also wants to know if there is my name, howmuch it is going to trouble me.…

bye and take care
Reghu,

The next day, Bob K deigned to answer Reghu with the patronizing tone of one convinced the noble savage could never be civilized.

October 6

Date: Mon, 6 Oct 2003 10:24:46–0400

Dear Reghuraj
First I would like to make something perfectly clear here. I am not the one that is making trouble for Ms. Anamika Biswas, and her 10 others. Ms. Anamika Biswas has caused all these problems, all on her own.

My company and many other businesses that she had promised and lied to, on her funding of many projects, is the reason she and many others will be facing litigation and possible criminal actions.

According to the Corporate attorneys, "The extent of your activity with Ms. Anamika Biswas and the Biswas Family and connected to the lies, deception, denials, and the eventual non funding of business projects will determine the course of action that will be taken against you.

Understand, that it is not just one business which is pursuing legal action but that of over 10 other businesses.

We had given Ms. Anamika Biswas every opportunity, over a 6+ month time period to graciously inform us that she was unable to fund any or all projects. She did not do so.

We offered our professional business advise and services to her which she refused. Collectively over 50+ years of experience.

We gave her our trust, and she abused it.

We even gave her notification that litigation and action will be taken unless she communicated with us, or at least live up to the Biswas agreement of the 50% settlement payment of all funds that were going to be invested. To which she ignored.

We have contacted the India government and the India Law Enforcement Agency and Interpol.

We had also made a last offer to Ms. Anamika Biswas to make the 50% settlement payments, and no action will occur. This was also relayed to the India Government. As of this date she or her family have done nothing.

The attorneys have the entire listing of those involved in this deception, lies, and broken agreements. If your name is on the list then you can thank Ms. Anamika Biswas, because it was her own actions, or lack of actions, that made it so.

Under the advise of the corporate attorneys, If you want to make a statement on your own behalf, in your involvement in this incident, then the attorneys and your justice system will take your cooperation into account.

Sincerely

Signed Robert Kilgallon

Jerry also learned about the pending litigation and advised Anamika on the sixth that "… I for one will not join any lawsuit, from day one I have kept to myself and only want my project funded."

Our funding date of October sixth arrived and once again I checked for an email or fax from Anamika with the wire confirmation numbers. Once again there was nothing.

I had been patient, understanding and believing into the seventh month. All was now slipping away. I decided to put constant pressure on Anamika, though not sure what it would accomplish. It was the only effort I could expend now.

Dear Anamika
In your last email to me, and the others with contracts, you said you would be returning from Delhi on Oct. 4 and would be sending us the confirmation slips on our Oct. 6

It is now 11:30am in Los Angeles on Oct. 6 and I have not received either an email or a fax from you.

Please provide me with specific details to update us.

IF YOU ARE HAVING PARTICULAR PROBLEMS GIVE US ALL OF THE DETAILS, RATHER THAN GENERALITIES.

With the details—whatever they are, no matter how difficult—we will be able to maintain our support and trust in you and the process.

I've spoken to Kevin, Alan, Jack, Scott, Brian and Jody this morning.

They are all patient and supportive.

We look forward to hearing from you and getting an update.

PLEASE SEND ME ANY NEW PHONE NUMBERS YOU MAY HAVE SO THAT I CAN BE IN BETTER COMMUNICATION.
I appreciate your assistance.

I called Anamika's house in Kolkata at ten thirty on the evening of October sixth. It would be approximately eleven thirty in the following morning there. I was told Anamika's father was in the hospital being operated on for gall stones!

DELAY #31—Father's operation for gall stones

I informed the group as follows:

"At about 10:30 pm Monday night I called Anamika's house and was told by the woman—not her mother—who answered that Anamika was out.

"When I asked to speak with her father, I was told he was "in the hospital" for a "serious operation", which later she identified as gall stones.

"Hopefully, I'll get an email from Anamika tonite as I asked her earlier today to provide an update.

"Stay tuned."

And, I contacted Anamika.

October 7

Dear Anamika
I learned last night in a call to your house that your father was in the hospital and scheduled for gall stone surgery.

I cannot fully describe the sympathy I have for you and your family which has endured so many ills during the last five months that we've been working together. It must seem like a bad dream.

I have alerted the group of 7 and they all convey their best wishes for the speedy recovery of your father and an end to all the misfortune that has befallen your family.

We hope that before too long, you will be able to update us on the status of the wired funds and provide confirmation numbers for the wires. Please advise.

I called Anamika's house on October seventh. When I heard the voice of a young woman answer, I greeted Anamika. Surprisingly the woman said, with bemusement, that she was Anandita, Anamika's sister. She remarked at the similarity in their voices and I had to agree. Anandita had recently arrived from Toronto be with her father. I inquired about his condition and was told

Mr. Biswas was in "critical condition" in the ICU. Anamika was in Mumbai (Bombay) on the fifth when their father was hospitalized.

I let Anamika's supporters know by email.

October 8

Hi

I spoke with Anamika's sister last night. She left her twins with her husband in Toronto to be with her father, who is now, she tells me, in critical condition in the ICU. She also returned to help Anamika who "is all alone" handling this latest family trauma.

Poor Me Anamika #9—all alone to handle family trauma

Apparently Mr. Biswas had major abdominal surgery, which included not only gall stones but a strangulated hernia, and all the additional abdominal problems that causes.

Anamika returned to Kolkata on Oct. 5 "and that is when the incident happened", she said referring to the day her father took ill and went to the hospital.

She thought her father would be home by Saturday.

Additionally, she told me Anamika returns home from the hospital late each night, but that she would ask her to call me and took my phone number. Film at 11.

I ended that email on a flippant note, amazed at the never ending hardships that Anamika and her family had endured. But, at the same time my thoughts were becoming more cynical toward Anamika than hopeful.

On October eighth one or more of the pompous ones posted a negative article on an Internet "Due Diligence Board" for "Performers, Non Performers and Scammers in Finance." My blood boiled as I read the latest attempt at character assassination by either BobK, Craig, Steve or Dave. It was vile, vindictive and libelous.

Even more reprehensible was the fact that the PBers who had created the libel then set about to give it legitimacy by referencing it, as an objective source, to those they wanted to negatively influence about Anamika.

Below is the actual posting anonymously (of course) by one of the four PBers.

Subject: Kolkata Scam New Twist in Business Plan Fraud
Posted By: pec371—Registered User
Posted At: (10/8/03 10:59 pm)

Due Diligence Asked for After the Fact
Kolkata, Calcutta—India
Los Cosa Nostra—International Financial Scamming Twist via the Internet
It seems the Indian mafia has implemented a unique twist on the normal financial investment scam common here in the US—Capture US Business Plans and showcase them to middle class Indian investors for cash.

This allegation is a total fantasy with not one shred of evidence except the bizarre conclusion of some barren imaginations

In a recent running of this scenario, the Biswas family of Kolkata obtained seventeen business models, for which they promised to invest over 4 billion dollars, thru a Canadian intermediary.

Factually wrong—24 businesses for investment of $33 Billion

It appears also that this family controls the local press, local government and has an insider in the Reserve Bank of India who can control international legal and private queries.

Most definitely don't control the press as I got the only publicity for them.

Recent press reports outline the extent of this families visions of wealth: "Calcutta Girl Set To Become Hollywood Mughal" www.weeklyvoice.com/ CNews ... sID=525424 after posting this in the local newspaper,

That story is an amalgam of several and printed in a weekly, Toronto-area newspaper for the local Indian community, which means the writer of the libel was Craig.

they followed with weeks upon weeks of constant delays and excuses of family deaths, power outages, licensing red tape

Again factually wrong. All those complaints came weeks before the article

and a myriad of other ludicrous stories. Upon contacting the referred law firm, the principals were informed that the particular individual referenced did not nor did he ever work at that law firm; this should have been evidenced when the email address while the same preface as the legal firm, ended in Yahoo.com. This family uses a front company A B Export Company—84 Jatindra Mohan Avenue Kolkata-700005 India; 91-33-25439793 and a long list of Board of Directors:

MS. ANAMIKA BISWAS
MR. NIRAJ BISWAS
MR. ASHIT KUMAR BISWAS
MR. AJIT BISWAS
MR. KUNAL BISWAS
MR. AMAR BISWAS
MR. AKASH BISWAS
MR. RAJIV BISWAS
MR. KARAN BISWAS
MR. SAHIL BISWAS
MR. PANKAJ BISWAS
MR. SOMENATH BISWAS

Their Banker References do not exist and the banks notified the family immediately upon any attempt to obtain information by the USA principals involved.

Mr. Sanyal from Bank of Boroda
Mr. Kamal Sood from United Bank of India
Mr. Govind Kumar from State Bank of India

"Watch for US and Canadian news releases on this situation in the near future"

While there may have been "news releases" written and disseminated all the threats of the PBers were as empty as the logic they used to write the scurrilous posting. Not one story about their travails appeared anywhere in the world.

When I read the posting, I contacted Anamika to give her a heads up.

Dear Anamika
I hope your father's health is improving and he returns home soon.

My reason for contacting you is as follows:
I have learned that certain clients—don't know who, but Larry is one of them—have hired lawyers to sue you for "non performance." Their basis for this is what they feel is your "commitment" made in various email messages. Personally, though not a lawyer, I dont think they have much of a case since there was no contractual commitment by you to fund Larry, Stinson, Craig, etc.

My suggestion to you—if at all possible—is to fund those or some of those who you have a contract with—as soon as possible. This will prove your legitimacy and good faith efforts and will deflect those who seek to hurt your reputation.

Your father told Brian the wires had been sent on Sept. 3. That is now five weeks ago. I am at loss to determine why the wires have not arrived by now.

Perhaps, when you contact me next, you can advise where the funds currently are located and when we will receive them.

Until then, our prayers for your parents health. I lost my father when I was 23 and mother at 26, so I know what a traumatic and tense time this must be for you.

I wish you and your family peace and good health.

Best regards,
Vincent Panettiere
Thistle Productions

    Kilgallon was the first to exploit the posting, but curiously did not copy President Bush..

October 11

Corruption in India

This was emailed to me. It is imperative that you read this. According to this web site information the banks in India and the news media are in league with a crime syndicate.

The Biswas family and their daughter Anamika Biswas are heading this organized crime unit, that is robbing billions from the honest businesses of India.

-----Original Message-----
From: <ezboard@ponyexpress.totality.com>
To: <americas@alltel.net>
Sent: Wednesday, October 08, 2003 9:10 PM
Subject: Dr. Robert Kilgallon—Thought you might like this ...

> I thought you might be interested in this conversation. It can be
> found at
>
http://pub122.ezboard.com/fduediligenceboardfrm18.showMessage?topicID
=277.topic

-----Original Message-----
From: Americas Choice
To: Action Ventures; Garey Webb; source one; linkexpress@juno.com; LILI LINDA; Christopher B. Catlin; k2unlimited@attbi.com; Craig S. Field; SJ Stinson
Cc: steve chen; anil bose; Niraj Biswas; Anamika Biswas; akansha agarwal
Sent: Friday, October 10, 2003 12:54 AM
Subject: Re: Emailing: fduediligenceboardfrm18.showMessagetopicID=277

Thanks Steve for the web site URL.
Craig and I were talking about why Anamika Biswas would go through all of this, and now we know their motive.
They take our Ideas, market them and run with the money. That is what I felt was going on with a few people I had been talking to. Ask for more details, and then nothing.

Linda, Garey and Greg excluded from them.

In case you did not get the web site this explains the Biswas story.
http://pub122.ezboard.com/fduediligenceboardfrm18.showMessage?topicID
=277.topic
Later
Signed Robert Kilgallon

Next to use the posting to his spurious advantage was the wonder from down under.

October 12

Office of Banking Ombudsmen
c/o Reserve Bank of India
15, Netaji Subhas Road,
Post Bag No. 552
Kolkata 700 001
India
Tel: 91 33 220-6222
Fax: 91 33 220-5899

TO WHOM IT MAY CONCERN

The warmest greetings to you from beautiful New Zealand!

This URL http://pub122.ezboard.com/fduediligenceboardfrm18.showMessage? topicID=277.topic was published on the internet obviously from a North American disgruntled Principal, and although one of the companies of the Armada's Group of Companies, Armada's Holdings International Pty. Ltd. (AHI) is in the process of bringing action against Ms. Biswas, A.B. Exports and the Biswas Group for their failure to honour investment commitments, there are some very serious and damning allegations made in this due diligence bulletin board posting against, amongst others:

Mr. Sanyal—Bank of Boroda;
Mr. Kamal Sood—United Bank of India; and.
Mr. Govind Kumar—State Bank of India.
I feel that these allegations regarding the banking sector could not possibly be true, but thought that I would bring it to your attention to afford you an opportunity to comment on the situation.

Our company Legal Counsel, who is also representing several other project principals from Canada and the United States of America who combined with us are owed in excess of US$18 billion, arrived in Calcutta yesterday and together with a retained local Calcutta reputable Law Firm is in the process of again trying to arrive at an amicable settlement before instigation criminal and litigation proceedings.

Your comments on this serious situation would be appreciated at the earliest. Thank you.

Most sincerely yours in hospitality,
Signed Steve Stinson

Sunday morning about 5:30 AM on October twelfth, I called Anamika's house and learned from the housekeeper that Mr. Biswas was still in the hospital. Anamika was not home and I asked to speak with her sister Anandita, but she was "staying with her in-laws. We'd not received any communication from Anamika since September and I was feeling uncomfortable with the thought that funding was slipping away. There were too many delays and too many crises. Besides one of Anamika's main email addresses was "over quota" so that messages from us were not delivered—another ominous sign.

October 13

The next day I received my first email from Anamika since September. It was a surprise. Whether it was the threat of law suit or simply her haphazard way of communicating we could not tell. However, it was appreciated and encouraging.

GOOD MORNING
    MR VINCENT, HELLO! HOPE THAT YOU ARE FINE AND ALSO MY ALL PATNERS...., I CONSIDER THEM SO INSPITE OF ALL NOTICE OF LIGITATION THEY SEND IT TO ME BY EMAIL WELL IT SEEMS THEY DON'T, WELL IT DOESNT MATTER TO ME AT ALL, BECAUSE MY DUTY IS TO SEND YOU THE FUND THAT WHAT I WILL DO NO MATTER WHAT YOU PEOPLE THINK ABOUT ME, BECAUSE I THINK WHEN I TOOK THE RESPONSIBILITY OF ALL OF YOURS DREAM TO FULFIL I MUST DO IT, WHAT EVER MAY BE THE SITUTATION. I HEARD THAT YOU CALLED IN MY HOUSE AND TALK WITH MY SISTER MAY BE YOU WILL BE SURPRISED WITH THE IDENTICAL VOICE, WELL MY FATHER'S CONDITION WAS SO SERIOUS THAT SHE HAD TO FLY HERE, WELL I ALSO CAME BACK FROM DELHI BUT I GOT GREEN SIGNAL FROM THE GOVERNMENT REGARDING THE INVESMENT OF GORDON AND FOR FURTHER SAFETY I SHOWED HIMM ALL OF YOUR

INVESTMENT THAT I AM DOING AND GOT GREEN SIGNAL FROM HIM.

TODAY MY FATHER GOT DISCHARGED FROM HOSPITAL AND TODAY NIGHT I AM FLYING BACK TO DELHI TO TAKE THE GREENSIGNAL IN WRITTEN FORMAT FROM MINISTRY OF FINANCE AND FROM MINISTRY OF EXTERNAL AFFAIRS. SO THAT YOU PEOPLE DON'T FACE ANY MORE PROBLEM.

WELL I AM FUNDING ALL THE 22 CLIENTS LEAVING KHOANU-GYUN, AND LARRY, I AMM FUNDING ALL 22 AT A TIME AFTER COMING BACK FROM DELHI ON 21ST OF OCTOBER 2003. THE FUNDS WILL BE SEND TO YOU ON 23RD OF OCTOBER 2003

Funding Date #44—October 23rd

AND CONFIRMATION SLIPS WILL BE SEND TO YOU BOTH BY FAX AND DHL AS BRIAN AGREEMENT IS WITH ME AND I HAVE DONE IT NOTORISED SO I WILL SEND IT BY DHL.

VINCENT PLEASE DO ME A LITTLE FAVOUR THAT IS PLEASE INFORM ALL THE CLIENTS THAT I DON'T WANT ANYRETURN FROM THEM AND NEITHER I WANT ANY PUBLICITY FROM ANYONE, YOU PEOPLE WAITED FOR SO LONG JUST WAIT TILL 23RD OF THIS MONTHS AND TAKE YOUR MONEY FROM.

THEN NEITHER THEY HAD TO PUT ANY NOTICE OF LIGITATION NEITHER THEY HAD TO KEEP ANYRELATION WITH ME. SPECIALLY TO MR CIAGE AND MR NEELY INFORM THE THAT THEY WILL GET THEIR FUND ON WHICH I WILL SEND FROM HERE ON 23RD OF THIS MONTH AND ALSO INFORM MR STINSON THAT THERE IS NO NEED TO BE SO TENSED HE WILL GET HIS FUND ON THE SAME DATE.

PLEASE ALSO ONFORM ALL THE CLIENTS THAT I WILL PAY THE COMMISSSION TO THE FUND SEEKERS THAT CHRIS, LARRY, AND SHAWN SO THEY DON'T HAVE TO PAY FROM MY BEHALF.

IF YOU ALL WANT TO CALL ME THEN PLEASE CALL ME IN THIS NUMBER AFTER TOMORROW 6:00PM OF INDIAN TIME THAT MEANS 14TH OF OCTOBER 2003 AFTER 6:00PM—9831358599.

PLEASE LET ME KNOW IF YOU OR ANY OF THE 22 CLIENTS HAVE ANYQUIRIES REGARING THE EMAIL

ANAMIKA BISWAS

I contacted Anamika to say how pleased we were to hear from her, but still had grave doubts about her funding those in the group who would cause her trouble and pain, not to mention any unnecessary legal problems.

Dear Anamika

I greatly appreciate receiving your email this morning, particularly the good news that your father is coming home from the hospital. Please convey to him that we in the group send our best wishes for his complete and speedy recovery.

Naturally, we are very pleased that you received a "green light" in Delhi. However, I am concerned about your plan to fund all 22 clients.

While, I realize what you do with your money is none of my business—as a friend who has believed and trusted in you over these five months, I hate the idea that any one would take advantage of your good nature. I hate the idea that anyone would intimidate and threaten you with legal action to blackmail you into funding them, when they have treated you with contempt and disrespect all this time. I would hate to see you lose your money, if there was a way to prevent it.

PLEASE RECONSIDER FUNDING ALL BUT—Brian, Kevin, me, Jody, Dave, Jack, Scott, Alan Girvan and Allen Stout.

MY SUGGESTION—After the above have been funded, re-examine the requests of the others.

Jody and I can fly to India to discuss this further, help you with legal issues, prepare documents, etc.

It is my considered opinion that you are under no obligation to fund Craig, Stinson, Macino (who has been listed as a fraudster) McNeely, etc. no matter what they send in email. Once they get the funds they will not be the kind of partners you want to have. I do believe they will take the money and run. Please be careful.

CAN YOU FORWARD TO ME ANY EMAIL THEY'VE SENT YOU THREATENING LEGAL ACTION SO THAT I CAN FURTHER ASSIST YOU?
If you can it will be a significant help.

It is my hope and prayer that we can continue moving forward so that we can develop a prosperous, successful and respectful business relationship.

Even more surprising, Anamika sent me three email messages in two days.

October 14

HELLO VINCENT
HOPE YOU AND ALL MY WELL WISHERS LIKE—JODY, BRIAN, ALAN, KEVIN JACK, DAVE AND MANY OTHERS ARE ALL FINE, THANKS FOR YOUR MESSAGE ABOUT MY FATHER I WILL SURELY CONVEY THIS TO HIM,
VINCENT I ALWAYS FROM BOTTOM OF MY HEART CONSIDERED YOU AND JODY AS BEST FRIENDS, I HAVE NO SHAME TO CONVEY MY FEELINGS TO YOU, YOU KNOW VINCENT I STARTED DOING BUSINESS BECAUSE FOR TWO REASON:- 1. TO HELP THOSE WHO NEED ME AS A FRIEND AND WHO COULD TREAT ME ALSO AS A FRIEND.
2:- TO BECOME FAMOUS IN MY OWN COUNTRY AND ALSO TO BE ABLE RECOGNIZED AS A INDIVIDUAL.
YOU KNOW THIS MONTH AN ASTROLOGER TOLD ME THAT I WOULD BE FAMOUS IN THIS MONTH BUT IT DOESNT HAPPEN, VINCENT I BECOME HAPPY WITH VERY LITTLE THINGS I DONT NEED MILLIONS OF MONEY TO BE HAPPY AS A BUSINESS WOMEN I NOW COUNT HOW WILL I GET BUSINESS AFTER I WILL FUND YOU ALL, AND THE WAY WHICH I GOT IS THAT BY THE PUBLICITY I WILL GET IF POSSBLE FROM YOU PEOPLE IN MY HOME TOWN, BUT NOW BY LOOKING TO THE PRESENT SITUTATION I REALIZED THAT I DONT WANT ANY HELP FROM ANY ONE OF YOU BECAUSE MY ASKING PUBLICITY FROM YOU ALL TENDS YOU TO BELIEVE THAT I AM EXPLOITING YOU ALL OR USEING YOU ALL AND I WILL NOT FUND YOUR BUSINESS THATS WHY MANY PEOPLE OUT 22CLIENTS TOLD ME THAT I AM USEING ALL OF YOUR NAME AND FAME AND ENTITY TO BECOME FAMOUS BUT I WILL NOT DO ANYTHING FOR YOUR BUSINESS BUT ONLY WAITING TO TAKE HELP FROM YOU. AS SOON AS I GET MY NAME I WILL LEAVE YOU ALL AND GO AWAY FROM YOUR REACH.
SO NOW I AM REQUESTING YOU ALL THAT PLEASE AFTER YOU GET THIS FUND END THIS RELATIONSHIP OF BUSINESS ORIENTATION HERE, THERE IS NO PROBLEM OF BEING FRIEND BUT PLEASE DONT THINK OF ANY PUBLICITY TO HELP ME.

THANKS FOR YOUR REPLY.
ANAMIKA BISWAS.

An hour later, Anamika sent another email. This time she had received the due diligence posting from Steve and Jerry.

ATTENTION:- MR VINCENT, ALANGIRVAN, BRIANGORDAN, SCOTTPHILIP, KEVIN OROURKE, ALLEN MANSFIELD, JODY AND MANY OTHERS;

RESPECTED SIR

THIS EMAIL WHICH I AM SENDING YOU IS NOT OF ANYEXCAUSES AND NEITHER OF ANIME PETITION, BUT IT IS MERELY ABOUT ASKING SOME QUESTIONES THAT I GOT FROM FEW OF MY EMAILS IN MY ACCOUNT OF anamila_biswas@hotmail.com; password 300920001, which i would like all of you to view an email send to me by MR STINSON ONE OF MY CLIENT AMONG YOU ALL AND ALSO AN EMAIL SEND TO BE BY JERRY ON 9TH OF OCTOBER ON SAME ACCOUNT OF HOTMAIL WHERE A NEWS THAT HAS BEEN PUBLISHED IN PAPERS REFFERS ME AS A MAFFIA AND FRAUD.

I DON'T K NOW WHO HAVE DONE IT, BUT JUST WANT TO KNOW FROM YOU ALL THAT I DIDNT WENT TO YOU IT IS YOUR FUND SEEKERS FOUND ME, I DIDNT TOOK ANY MONEY FROM YOU ALL FOR THIS FUNDING IT IS I WHO GOING TO GIVE YOU THE MONEY THEN WHEN DID I TOLD YOU THAT I HAD MY FAMILY PEOPLE WORKING IN RBI, IF THAT WOULD HAVE BEEN ABLE THEN YOUR FUNDINGS WILL NOT BE DELAYED.

I JUST WNAT TO ASK YOU ALL THATIF YOU PEOPLE THINK THT FOR MY PUBLICITY I CHOOSE YOU THEN PLEASE LET ME KNOW BY TODAY SO THAT I WILL CALL THE PRESS AND LET THEM KNOW THAT I AM NOT FUNDING YOU ALL FOR PUBLICITY.

I HOPE YOU ALL WILL AGREE THAT WITH THE MODE INDIAN INFRASTRUCTURE SPENDING SO MUCH WILL TAKE TIME THEN HOW COME YOU PEOPLE STARTED ANTI PUBLICITY AGAINST ME BY TELLING THAT I AM MAFFIA.

PLEASE THIS IS EARNEST REQUEST THAT YOU ALL 22 CLIENTS PLEASE TAKE A LITTLE PAIN TO ANSWER MY QUREIES:—THAT WHAT MADE YOU THINK I AM FRAUD?

IF THE ANSWER IS MY DELAY THEN I WOULD SUGGEST YOU THAT AFTER THIS FUNDING REACHES YOU I WILL ASK YOU TO COME TO INDIA AND BE HERE AND I WILL FIND FOR SOME CLIENTS AND I

WILL GIVE YOU MONEY BUT I WILL ASK YOU BY SITTING IN CAL-
CUTTA YOU PEOPLE WILL FUND THEM AND THEN IF YOU FEEL THAT
I HAVE TOLD YOU LIES I WILL BEAR ALL THE COSTING OR LOSSES
YOU HAVE HAD FACED FOR THIS DELAY.

I ALSO LIKE TO KNOW ALL OF YOUR IDEAS ABOUT ME AND ALSO
WHAT YOU WILL DO BECAUSE I HAVE DECIDED THAT AFTE FUND
REACHES YOU I WILL FILE AND APPLICATION IN RBI AND ALSO IN
SUPREME COURT TELLING THAT I LOST ALL MY MONEY AND WILL
DECLARE MYSELF AS BANKRUPCY SO THAT MY BUSINESS RELATION
AND SOCIAL RELATION WITH YOU ALL ENDS HERE.

I AM REQUESTING YOU ALL TO WAIT TILL 23RD THEN I WILL DO
WHAT EVER YOU ALL WILL ASK ME TO DO.

BUT PLEASE REPLY ME ALL OF YOUR OPINION BY TODAY.
ANAMIKA BISWAS

Suddenly, as rumors do, word got out that one of the clients with a contract
had received $1.5 million from Anamika. Whether or not this was another
high school prank, like the dancing skeletons and the email to the Kolkata
Telegraph, was not immediately apparent. I asked Anamika straight out, then
alerted the group.

To All
I spoke with Anamika this morning.

She confirmed what was in the email I forwarded to you yesterday that is—

She is in Delhi waiting to receive written approval for the funding; returning
on the 21st and funding on the 23rd.

I told her I'd heard her father say that the funds were sent on Sept. 3. She said
they were, and were in holding for tax clearance in Mumbai (Bombay) from
where they would go to Singapore. Then the government told them to stop the
transfer and they did, which brings us back to today.

I asked her if Dave Bower had contacted her and threatened her with exposure
if she did not pay him.

She said he had not.

I asked her if she paid him $1.5 million, as I heard he now claims.

She told me "I never paid a single penny."

Some folks like to swing cats by the tail, others throw wrenches to sabotage progress.

Nuff said.

Vince

I decided to set up a "sting" to smoke out whoever was behind the libelous posting on the Due Diligence website. Using an anonymous email address I replied to the posting with angry accusations. Lo and behold I got an answer. It was from Dave who had received a funding contract from Anamika. He had been agitating from the sidelines not willing to make any effort to work toward or mediate a successful conclusion. His position was always "give to me, do for me." His response on **October 15** was:

From: "David Bower" <n439foxtrot@hotmail.com>
To: <diogenes_66@hotmail.com>
Subject: Biswas Scam
Date: Wed, 15 Oct 2003 07:28:10–0500

I was a member of a group of 24 that was supposed to be funded by Biswas. I have a contract. Its not worth the paper its written on. I have waited almost 6 months and have received no money from them, and worse yet, no communications. What say you to this?

To which I replied in disguise on **October 16**

From: "Andy Romano" <diogenes_66@hotmail.com>
To: <n439foxtrot@hotmail.com>
Sent: Thursday, October 16, 2003 11:14 AM
Subject: Re: Biswas Scam

Where is your proof? Easy to slander an entire family and hide on the Internet, because you are a disappointed child.

You'd never have the guts to call a Caucasian male a member of the mafia.

Whatever lies have you told?

Easy to pick on a third world folks, then run away and hide.

If they have money why should they give it to you after your lying and slander?

Seems to be good cause to cancel your now even more worthless contract!

Dave continued to dialogue.

I have plenty of proof…. but who the hell are you to ask for it.. Andy Romano … i bet its ashit biswas in disquise. I wasn't the one that posted that by the way but I wish I had. These folks made over 45 committments to fund and never made one of them. We gave them the benefit of the doubt. Alas they chose to scam instead.

While we don't know if he posted the derogatory message or not, I often wonder why he rose to the bait and not the real culprit or culprits. Surely, they knew of the response made in defense of Anamika.

I contacted Anamika by phone. She told me written approval would arrive on Friday October seventeenth. I followed up with an email.

Dear Anamika
I was pleased to speak with you again this morning.

As we discussed, and in my opinion, your proposed funding should take place in several stages—at least two—so that you can blunt and discredit all the negative criticism that has been disseminated in the last few weeks.

Any government group, when made aware of the fact that you have funded six to eight companies will not seriously consider the criticism and complaints of the few who did not get funded. They will regard the allegations as "sour grapes"—jealousy. The critics will be discredited by their own complaints.

1. GROUP ONE—As you know, this first group consists of those who you have sent contracts by fax. It includes—Kevin, Alan Girvan, Jack Fulton, Scott Philp, me, Dave Bower and Brian—who will fund Jody.

As Jody does not have a contract with you, and as she has been one of your most loyal and trusting supporters, I suggest you send Jody's investment straight to her. She will provide you with her banking information before the 23rd. That is my first suggestion.

2. DAVE BOWER—As one of the contract holders, he has surprisingly been the most disloyal. First he alleged that you were on a U.S. State Department hot list—for doing what and what kind of list he did not disclose. Next he alleged you paid him $1.5 million so that he would not inform the newspapers. Last and most hurtful and slanderous was his posting on the EZBOARD due diligence bulletin board that you and your family were "mafia". His admission is below.

---

diogenes_66@hotmail.com

From: "David Bower" <n439foxtrot@hotmail.com>
To: <diogenes_66@hotmail.com>
Subject: Biswas Scam
Date: Wed, 15 Oct 2003 07:28:10–0500

I was a member of a group of 24 that was supposed to be funded by Biswas.I have a contract. Its not worth the paper its written on. I have waited almost 6 months and have received no money from them, and worse yet, no communications. What say you to this?

I set up the diogenes account on hotmail to flush out who sent the posting. Before fulfilling your contractual obligation to Bower, we should discuss how to approach him.

3. OTHER FUNDING—You need to reconsider funding—Craig, Stinson, Kilgallon, Macino. Partners who would first defame you and your family so that they can intimidate and extort funding from you will not make good partners and could easily lose all your investment. Think carefully about them until we have further discussion in India.

I look forward to your email, as we discussed, tomorrow morning and will call you with my comments.

I continue to support and trust you and look forward to a long and profitable relationship.

Best regards,

Intuiting that those who shout the loudest have the most to hide, Alan trolled the internet to discover some information to temper the rants of the pompous ones. With BobK he'd found information regarding some type of securities trading through a company registered in South Africa. The most interesting discovery was information about Steve and his ersatz military record. In order to get this information to the group, while creating a kind of "plausible denia-bility", I enlisted the services once again of "Andy Romano." He would be my source when I sent the group the information I found on the Internet about Stinson.

"The Coalition of Patriots for Military Honour http://www.cpmh.net/stinson _sj.html discovered discrepancies in Steve J. Stinson's purported military record. "Mr. Stinson, an Australian now residing near Christchurch New Zealand, has his own business page online at this link: www.armadas. com/sjscv.html. Full account on the site above.

"Note this particular paragraph:

"CPMH is only interested in exposing those frauds and charlatans who pose as military wannabes. However the question begging occasionally when imposters are discovered like Stinson using his military service in promoting his background, expertise and ability and some of that presentation is false, what about the rest of his Curriculum Vitae?

"IT'S IMPORTANT THAT THOSE WHO DO BUSINESS WITH PEOPLE CLAIMING ERRONEOUS MILITARY SERVICE IN THEIR RESUMES WILL ALSO QUALIFY THOSE AND OTHER BONA FIDES OFFERED, BEFORE PROCEEDING INTO A DEAL OR PARTNERSHIP."

Accordingly, I notified Anamika hoping this information would further dis-courage her from funding him and the others as I truly and deeply believed they would rip her off.

Next keeping up the plausible deniability mask, I "innocently" inquired, in an email to the group, about the meaning of this surprising email.

"What does this mean? Who cares if he's a fraud. Luckily I'm not funding him." I used the occasion to resend the original email from Andy Romano.

October 17

On the day Anamika was supposed to have received written approval for her investment I spoke again with Anamika. She told me that she had an appointment with the Ministry of External Affairs on Monday and that she would "get written permission" for her investments to eight clients.

October 19

I called Anamika on October nineteenth, which, with the time difference, was her Monday. Though the reception was poor, I was pleased to hear her tell me that she had received "approval in writing."

Anamika sent me an email later that day. We'd spoken two days before and planned to speak again on October eighteenth, but never did. As usual Anamika danced to her own sitar.

HELLO VINCENT
WELL I GOT THE PERMISSION BUT I WILL STAY IN DELHI FOR FUTURE DISCUSSION THAT WHEN I WILL GET RETURN FROM YOU ALL HOW WILL I INVEST THAT IN INDIA, FOR WHICH MY ARRIVAL TO KOLKATA WILL GHET DELAY FOR ONE DAY, AND ALSO MY DELAY WILL HAPPEN BECAUSE I ALSO NEED THE TAX REDUCTION PAPERS FROM GOVERNMENT. AS I HAVE TO SHOW ALL MY INVESTMENTS AS WHITE.

DELAY #32—have to show investments as "white" (legal)

HOPE THAT YOU WILL UNDERSTAND AND SO DO REST. WITH BEST WISHES—ANAMIKA BISWAS

I advised the group of this latest delay.

October 20

The next day her email to me explained why we never spoke again.

HELLO VINCENT
WELL YESTERDAY I TRIED TO SEND YOU AN EMAIL INTHIS NEW ID YOU SEND ME BUT IT RETURNED BACK TO ME, WELL I WILL TRY ONCE MORE. VINCENT WHILE COMING FROM KOLKATA I FORGOT

TO TAKE ORIGINAL CHARGER INHURRY INSTEAD OF MY PERTICU-
LAR CHARGER I TOOK THE WRONG

DELAY #33—brought wrong phone charger

ONE WITH ME SO I COULDNOT NOW WILL BE ABLE TO KEEP MY
CELL OPEN, PLEASE DONT MIND FOR IT. WELL TODAY I CHECKED
MY MAILBOX FOUND TWO MAIL ONE FROM ALLEN MANSFIELD
REGARDING KHOA PLEASE GO THROUGH IT FROM MY ACCOUNT—
moonmoonbiswas@yahoo.co.in 30091979(password) let me know what u
understood from it. well vincent i asked you to contact jerry the website email
sender of hotmail did u done it please let me know.

For some reason Anamika was entrusting me with the password to her
email account. But she was requesting I become a conduit to her other clients.
I still believed in the process and in her ability to fund us. I wanted to provide
her with reassurance and security so that she would be comfortable completing all the procedures required by the Indian government.

I read the email.

The same day (October twentieth) Anamika surfaced once again via an
email to one of her Midwest clients. She told of her plans to inform at least one
person in the group every day about the status of the funding. This day she was
in Delhi to get "permission from our government and for which I am at the
finishing stage of agreement with government regarding investments of all of
you and will be back in Calcutta with this permission on Tuesday after that
funds will be sended to all of you."

Craig was the only one of the pompous ones who offered a defense, but it
took him four days after the initial "Andy Romano" message to respond. Steve
was not heard from.

Andy Romano:
As a principal of one of the corporate participants in the Biswas transaction, I
have never requested nor deemed myself to be privy to the personal or corporate backgrounds of the other potential funding recipients in this matter.
Notwithstanding that such information is none of my business, I really don't
care. Having said that, receiving accusatory information on others from a third
party who has not identified himself, his company or the purpose of his correspondence, certainly raises reciprocal questions of credibility on the writer of
such correspondence.

Since you seem to have a keen interest in the background of others, perhaps you would be kind enough to provide us with a comprehensive introduction to yourself, your company and the objective and purpose of your findings on Mr. Stinson.

Signed Craig Fields

    Then Andy Romano set about responding to PB#2.

Mr. Fields
You confuse accusation with facts. I am not accusing, just passing on information that even Steve agreed was accurate, since he removed the false references from his website.

His admission of falsification is something you say is none of your business. You have such convenient and situational ethics. Would you want a convicted child molester to operate a day care center?.

Would you give credibility to someone who falsified (lied) about his qualifications to receive military medals—which many brave, honest men have fought and died to receive?

What other parts of his life and dealings has he lied about?

This reference on the website—which I did not write—goes to the honesty and integrity of an individual. How can he or she be trusted to be telling the truth. And, when they point the finger aren't four others pointing back at them.

I am against hypocrisy and sanctimony and those who would condone same. That's all you need to know about me.

    Naturally, Craig had to have the last word.

Andy Romano:
As previously stated, the information you have provided has no significance or interest to me or to the companies I am affiliated with. Since the association you have referenced, The Coalition of Patriots for Military Honour, along with the information you have distributed and you, yourself, cannot be properly

identified or authenticated, this is strictly a garbage in, garbage out scenario that can be filed with the Biswas' correspondence.

Good luck with whatever else you do.

Signed Craig Fields

Three weeks had passed since we were given the last funding date of October sixth. The time for entertaining interludes was over. I'd rattled their cages and had a bit of fun. Now I had to pay attention to the primary goal.

Nerves were fraying throughout the group and intra-group hostility erupted. One of the clients called others in the group "stupid dogs". He wanted his name taken off "the peanut gallery's list of people to give 'updates' to" and threatened to send additional email from the group to the Fairfax County Police Department.

Another client responded to Larry's October first email in a highly critical manner, calling it "revisionist at best and outright lies at worst." After disputing the facts in Larry's "apologia", he concluded that had it not been for Larry's and Chris' actions "we probably would have been funded by now ... you might find yourself on the receiving end of a lawsuit for fraud and harassment."

Larry was not shy about responding. But, never one to believe less is more, he provided all of us with insight into how the "brokers" were operating and relating to Anamika—just in case we didn't realize that from the tone, tenor and substance of his email.

"... as for me calling anamika a 'bitch' i think that was the polite stuff i called her as i called her a few good names...."

This is how you treat someone you want to provide billions?

"... shes not just a bitch many times ... shes a super rude one ... who respects nothing of what i have tried to do for her ..."

Huh? What he was doing was taking her money and cursing at her.

"... she has obviously upset me and many others and this lady made all the promises to fund the projects ... if you had any real gripes try directing it to at the right person or maybe you are too scared to??? ... you want to air anything out get a court order and we'll see who knows what."

Most amazing of all, Larry sent the above and more to <u>three</u> of Anamika's email addresses.

After seven months and forty four funding dates later, my patience was oozing out of me. Maybe I have a high threshold for pain, an addiction to fantasy or enlarged imagination. Now was the time for answers. I sent Anamika a list of questions on October twenty first at six thirty three in the morning.

October 21

CAN YOU ANSWER THE FOLLOWING QUESTIONS FOR ME?

1. You have written approval?
2. Was there a specific amount approved? Enough for the first 8 clients only? Or approval for more than 8 clients.
3. Did you get my email on DHL? What do you think of the idea of sending all the slips to me so that I can distribute to the others?
4. Did you get information on Jody's account number? Funds for Jody's deal go directly to her.
5. Are these the first 8 clients you will fund—Thistle (me), Kevin, Brian, Jody, Alan Girvan, Jack Fulton, Dave Bower and Scott Philp??
6. Will you send the funds by SWIFT? Will you provide us with your SWIFT number?
7. When do you plan to wire the funds?
8. Once the funds are wired, when do you want to meet with me and Jody?
9. Where would you want to meet us?

These are all the questions I would ask you on the phone. I appreciate whatever information you can provide.

Ten minutes later I responded to her inquiry about the email she had received from clients.

Dear Anamika
I read the Mansfield email and Khoa's response. Basically, its a discussion about the value of suing you. Khoa felt you made verbal promises and clients signed some documents at the beginning, but did not receive those same documents returned by you with your signature.

But, he feels that IF you do not have any money, all the documents and promises are meaningless and not worth the time and trouble to sue you. He trusts Chris and does not trust Larry at all.

(By the way, Larry is part of the Stinson, Craig and Kilgallon law suit)

I also reviewed Jerry's email from October 17 and will try to reach him by phone today yet again.

ONCE AGAIN, IT IS MY BELIEF THAT YOU NEED TO CAREFULLY RECONSIDER YOUR INVESTMENTS WITH THE REMAINING CLIENTS, NOW THAT YOU HAVE APPROVAL. IT IS NOT TOO LATE TO PROTECT YOUR INVESTMENTS.

Best regards,

Other clients were sending her messages of support and encouragement that masked their own growing doubts and fears. Jack told her "… I can only hope and pray that you do make good on your promises …" Another reminded her "… we have patiently awaited your completion. We need to know something."

Six days passed with no word from Anamika. She was supposed to be back from Delhi by the twentieth. On October twenty seventh I contacted Anamika regretting that we had not been in contact for several days but praising her for the flow of communication up to that time.

I pressed her for answers on the nine questions and also asked her to advise me if she had been contacted by any attorneys or received any legal documents instigated by the blowhards.

October 28

That night I managed to get her on the phone for a brief conversation. She said she was still in Delhi and would send email in "one hours time", but by seven thirty in the morning on October twenty eighth it had not arrived.

I relayed my latest contact with Anamika to the group adding "… The above are just the facts and there is no reason to regard them negatively. Will make sure I get some answers from her and let you know."

Clearly I was running on ego, if not empty. Why did I think I would succeed in penetrating the inner mechanism motivating Anamika Biswas when others—Larry, Chris, Shawn, Reghu, Brian, Kevin, even pompous threats, had not? The only answer was congenital, obsessive obstinacy.

Kevin, while not actively communicating with Anamika as he had a few months earlier, was still supportive and we kept him up to date.

October 29

I told Kevin in an email that, according to her father, Anamika was still in Delhi and would return the next day.

During my conversation that morning with Mr. Biswas I asked her father point blank, when they would wire the funds. In essence he said it was Anamika's business. "She is doing the business", he told me. His response was at odds with the relationship presented to Brian during his visit to Kolkata a few weeks earlier.

The Mr. Biswas Brian met indicated the majority of the money in Anamika's planned investment came from him. The Mr. Biswas I spoke with at his home phone number indicated a separation from Anamika who was acting independently. Did he not care how his money was being used? Was he so confident in Anamika that he could turn her loose with the vast majority of thirty three billion dollars?

However, the worst question in my mind after I hung up was this. Is the Mr. Biswas I spoke with on the phone, the same "Mr. Biswas" Brian met in his hotel? Was the man on the phone the same as the man who begged Brian to stay a little longer in Kolkata?

My far too fertile imagination conjured up the Indian version of Fagin with Anamika as an Indian Olivia Twist.

October 31

On the last day of October we got the answers to the list of nine questions sent to Anamika ten days earlier.

HELLO VINCENT
SORRY I WAS BIT ILL THATS WHY INSPITE OF KNOWING THAT YOU DIDINT GOT MY MAIL I COULDNOT ABLE TO CONTACT YOU.

DELAY #34—had some undisclosed illness

WELL LET ME ANSWER YOUR ALL QUESTIONS FIRST:—1. YES I GOT WRITTEN APPROVAL. 2. YES IN THIS IS WAS FIRSTLY STATED OF ALL 22 CLIENTS BUT LATER I SPECIFICLY TOLD THEM THAT FUNDING WILL BE DONE ON PART BASIS AND FIRST PART ARE YOU INCLUDED TO YOU ALL. 3. YES I GOT YOUR DHL EMAIL I WILL PREFER TO SEND YOU THE CONFIRMATION SLIPS INSTEAD OF SENDING THEM TO SPECI-FIED PERSON. 4. I GOT JODY ACCOUNT DETAILS. 5. I WILL SEND YOU CONFIRMATION SLIPS AFTER WIREING.. 6. I LIKE TO MEET YOU ALL

LEAVING BRIAN GORDON AS I MEAT HIM ALREADY.7. I LIKE MEET YOU ALL IN INDIA KOLKATA. 8. I WILL SEND YOU MY SWIFT CODE. 9. I WILL WIRE YOU THE MONEY BY THIS COMING WEEK AS THIS WEEK WAS FULL OF HOLIDAYS.

DELAY #35—week of holidays, Puja

I HOPE I HAVE ANSWERED ALL YOUR QUESTIONES.
ANAMIKA BISWAS

Anamika had answered all of our questions and planned on wiring the funds, yet we had to endure another week of delay on account of a week of holidays.

In my reply, I asked Anamika for a specific date when the funds will be wired and requested they be sent by SWIFT to avoid delay.

I also reminded her that while we believed the delays were not her fault they had caused numerous hardships from the dissolution of a marriage to threats of law suits as well as lost revenue and reputation. Our wait for funding would extend into November.

OCTOBER SCORE CARD		TOTALS
Funding Dates	1	44
(next funding date, we think Oct. 23)		
Delays	5	35
Funds Transfer Date	0	2
Draft/Tracking Numbers Sent	0	2
Holidays	1	5
Confirmation Slip Dates	0	9
Anamika Has Wired Funds	0	4
Anamika Travels	0	1
Poor Me Anamika	1	9

10. NOVEMBER, 2003

BEGINNING OF THE END

November began the eighth month of my involvement with Anamika and the group. My determination, and that of the loyalists who remained, was to have the process reach a final conclusion. We would be funded or we would have to continue searching elsewhere for financing.

November 1

Brian contacted her on the first. He had not heard from her directly since returning from India in September and asked for a status report. He also expressed the hope that she would continue to communicate with him. "After all we are supposed to be partners, and partners communicate with each other."

Jerry also contacted her in early November to express his disappointment that "we do not maintain a contact."

November 3

I spoke with Mr. Biswas and asked him what Anamika was doing. He told me "she's exporting, working and going to meetings." While he was not facile with English, he did not mention the funding of clients or the financial aspect of his relationship with her.

Anamika had another surprise for us.

November 4

HELLO MR VINCENT
WELL I AM ANINDITA GHOSH ELDER SISITER OF ANAMIKA BISWAS YOUR INVESTOR, WELL I WAS BEEN TOLD BY ANAMIKA TO CHECK HER MAIL BOX I GOT YOUR MAIL I CONVEYED THE SAME TO HER WELL IN REPLY SHE TOLD ME TO TELL YOU AS SHE IS STILL INCAPABLE OF GOING OUT OF HER HOUSE AS SHE IS HAVING DYERIA FOR LAST COUPLE OF DAYS AND TILL TODAT SHE HAD LOOSE MOTION OVER 60 TIMES IN A DAY AND SHE SHETURNRD INTO A

DELAY #36—Anamika has diarrhea and no strength

SKELETON AS SHE IS VERY THIN ROM BEGINING, SO SHE DONT HAVE ENOUGH STRENGTH TO SIT AND WRITE THE MAIL SO I AM DOING THAT, SHE TOLD ME TO TELL YOU THAT YOU BEING VERY SUPPORITIVE FROM VERY BEGINING WILL UNDERSTAND THAT THROUGH WHAT PHASE OF PROBLEMS SHE HAS GONE THROUGH SOMETIMES

HER FAMILY PROBLEM AND SOMETIMES THE PROBLEM CAUSED BY THE BANKS AND OTHER ENTITY RELATED TO THIS FINANCE.

WELL SHE TOLD ME TO TELL YOU THAT NEITH SHE IN THE PAST WANT ANYONE TO SUFFER FOR HER NEITHER SHE WILL ACEPT THAT ANYONR SUFFERED FOR NOW SO SHE IS REQUESTING TO ALL OF YOU (ALAN, JODY, BRIAN, VINCENT, JACK, KEVIN, ALANMANS-FIELD, AND TWO MORE I DONT REMEMBER THE NAME NOW BUT ALL TOTAL 9 PEOPLE WILL GET THE FUNDING IN THE FIRST HALF, SO SHE IS ASKING THAT ANYONE WHO IS GETTING SUED FOR HER MEANS FOR THE DELAY SHE CAUSED WILL BE PAYED BY HER TO SAFE GUARD THE CLIENT WHO IS SUFFERING FOR HER DELAY.

WELL MR VINCENT SHE TOLD ME TO TELL YOU THAT AS SOON AS SHE GETS BETTER SHE WILL NOT WASTE A SINGLE MINUTR BUT WILL SEND YOU THE FUND THROUGH SWIFT. I LIKETO SHARE A THING WITH YOU IF YOU PROMISE THAT YOU WONT CONVEY THIS TO MY PARENTS AND AS WELL AS TO ANAMIKA THOUGH I KNOW THAT SHE KNOWS IT AND THE SECREAT IS SHE IS HAVING TUBER-CLOSIS IN HER SPINAL COD. PLEASE MR VINCENT TRY TO KEEP IT

DELAY #37—Anamika has tuberculosis of the spine

SECREAT. BECAUSE NOW ANAMIKA AS SHEIS GIVING HER ALL ASSES-SETS TO YOU ALL I THOUGHT THAT YOU SHOULD KNOW IT THAT YOU PEOPLE WILL NOT HAVE TO GIVE HER RETURN BACK BECAUSE BY THAT SHE WONT BE ALIVE.

Poor Me Anamika #10—she will die before we can pay back her investment

HOPE YOU ALL ARE FINE, TAKE CARE AND TELL EVERYONE THAT SHE WILL PAY WHATEVER WILL BE REQUIRED FOR THE SUE.
THANKING YOU
ANINDITA GHOSH.

Oy! Whoever heard of tuberculosis of the spine? I checked with Jody and my wife Penny, both former nurses, and was assured that proper treatment would reverse the effects of tuberculosis, bring health and a long life.

I replied to Anindita and asked her to tell Anamika that we continued to support her and wished her a speedy recovery. While we appreciated her generosity and wanted her to invest "wisely" we also wanted her to know that we did not want her to give us <u>all</u> of her assets.

Anindita also contacted Brian on the same morning, about fourteen minutes later ...

HELLO MR. BRIAN K GORDON
WELL I KNOW THAT YOU CAME TO KOLKATA TO MEET MY SISITER ANAMIKA BISWAS YOUR FINANCER WELL I AM HER ELDER SISITER ANAINDITA GHOSH I STAY IN CANADA THATS WHY I COULD NOT ABLE TO MEET YOU. WELL I KNOW THAT WITH YOUR STAYING ANAMIKA BISWAS WENT TO DELHI AND SHE RETURNED LAST WEEK BECOZ IN THE MEANTIME SHE HAD TO COME AND METOO FROM-FROMCANADA AS OUR DADDY MR ASHIT KUMAR BISWAS HAD GONE THROUGH SUGERY. AFTER THAT SHE AGAIN WENT BACK AND RETURNED LAST WEEK BUT SINCE LAST WEEK WAS FULL OF HOLI-DAYS SHE COULD NOT ABLE TO PROCEDED AFTER THAT SHE IS NOW ILL AND SHE WILL SEND YOU THROUGH SWIFT CODE WITHIN VERY SHORT TIME. MR GORDON SHE KEPT VEERYTHING UPDATED TO MR VINCENT WHEN SHE WAS IN DELHI AND ALSO ON HER RETURN. MR GORDON I UNDERSTAND YOUR PROBLEMS BUT EVEN YOU WILL ADMIT THAT SHE WENT THROUGH A BIG BANG IN ALL THROUGH THIS PROCESS. MR BRIAN NEVER IN YOUR LIFE OR YOUR DREAMS THINK THAT WHEN SHE TOLD YOU THAT SHE WILL FUND YOU IT WONT CHANGE SO HER MISTAKE THAT SHE DIDINT KEPT YOU UPDATED BUT I WILL LIKE TO TELL THAT AS A PATNER WHICH I AM ASKING APOLOGY FOR THIS FROM YOU ON BEHALF OF HER.
WITH BEST REGARDS
ANAINDITA GHOSH

November 5

Some instinct guided me to call Anamika's sister Anindita at her house in Toronto on November fifth. Call it intuition, suspicion, mistrust, disbelief, coming to the end of my rope, etc. I called Toronto and Anindita answered. I introduced myself and asked her the thirty three billion dollar question. Had she sent me and Brian email the day before on Anamika's behalf?

Since Anamika's email address can be used with anyone in the world who has the password it was not beyond the realm of possibility that Anamika while sick asked her sister to communicate with her clients.

Anindita told me she "did not send" the email. She was also "very sorry to hear" that Anamika might have posed as her older sister to fool the group and told me she didn't know why her sister would do such a thing. "Are you sure?" she asked me repeatedly when I explained the events of the last eight months.

"Why are you believing her?" She asked the most important question. Anindita listened while I tried to bring her up to speed beginning with the Director's trip to Canada and her father being replaced by Uncle Niraj. She told me there is "no Uncle Niraj."

But, she explained she had not been to India for three years. She was not in touch with her family who were opposed to her immigrating to Canada with her husband in 1995.

When I related that Anamika indicated she could invest thirty three billion dollars in twenty four companies, Anindita was dumfounded. Her father was a "partner in a movie theater with his brothers" she told me and the family did not have that kind of money.

I also inquired about the health of her mother and she told me she didn't know if her mother was sick since she "very rarely" talks to her family.

Later that day I "talked" with Larry on Yahoo chat. I was snooping around to learn if he had any new information about the proposed law suits.

thistleent: all those top notch lawyers get back from India
action_ventures: u didn't hear?
action_ventures: from india?
action_ventures: the lawyers said a few weeks ago
action_ventures: that
action_ventures: she shas a few small companies
action_ventures: nothing worth mentioning
thistleent: no s—t!
thistleent: all this time
action_ventures: not enough
action_ventures: for what she said
thistleent: not 33 billion worth?
action_ventures: they said she isnt even worth pursuing
action_ventures: nope
action_ventures: not even close
thistleent: geez
action_ventures: apparently she is unbalanced
action_ventures: and trys this alot
thistleent: how do they know she tries this alot?
action_ventures: she has been instructed by the police to stop
action_ventures: not sure if she will

action_ventures: investigation i guess
action_ventures: they said they worked with a top law firm in calcutta
action_ventures: to find out what they needed to know
action_ventures: but to be honest
action_ventures: i was never told of the law firm that went over
thistleent: and the law firm told them she is unbalanced?
action_ventures: so this is second hand info
action_ventures: yes thats the report i got
thistleent: geez, after all this time
thistleent: so, if stinson didnt send law firm to India, someone had to contact a big law firm in calcutta
thistleent: sure would like to hear from—the law firm—so I can put this thing to rest
action_ventures: kilgallon s law firm.. thats why i am sceptible
thistleent: kilgallon's law firm contacted the calcutta law firm?
thistleent: and came back with the report?
thistleent: this is disappointing and not anything I envisioned—that she would be unblanced
action_ventures: yes me either
action_ventures: but what can one say
action_ventures: she is different thats for sure
thistleent: if, of course it is true
action_ventures: i think if i get rich
action_ventures: ill fly over and see her
thistleent: would love to know name of calcutta law firm
action_ventures: if shes that gbad off ill give her some loot
thistleent: nice of u
action_ventures: ya
action_ventures: why not
action_ventures: shes a very decent person
action_ventures: only meant well
thistleent: right
thistleent: anyway you can find out name of calcutta law firm
action_ventures: i can try but i doubt hell give it to me
action_ventures: ok
thistleent: getting back to anamika—I'm bummed out, as I've got a lot of emotional baggage tied up in her and her potential
action_ventures: yes
action_ventures: well iwish i had better news or cashto fly over

thistleent: would like to have definitive answers once and for all
action_ventures: but maybe brian can state some info
action_ventures: brians the only one
action_ventures: just a sec
thistleent: she answered all the questions I raised last week, now this week her sister says she has dyssentery and is too weak to wire funds
thistleent: what do I know
thistleent: k
action_ventures: ill try to find this letter
action_ventures: here it comes and this is for your eyes only ok
action_ventures: not to tell kilgalon i showed u please
thistleent: k

The following is the email BobK sent to his fellow litigants which Larry cut and pasted onto Yahoo instant messenger.

action_ventures: Hello gentlemen and ladies

Well I have just got done with John on the phone. From what I am gathering, from his conversation, is that it would not be worth anyone's time to pursue any litigation against Anamika Biswas and her family. At least the one we know. They have several small companies that generate a small profit. Anamika has psychological problems (at least that is what they have filed)

action_ventures: Collectively with all those involved, and what that family has in real-estate, investments, their businesses and such, they could not even pay the attorneys fees and court costs, which could last up to 12 years in court. It is highly suggested that we learn from our mistakes and look for other funding and write all this off to the school of hard knocks.

action_ventures: It seems that Anamika had tried this before and was hit with a major fine. That is why her father kicked her out of the house. Not sure but might be that litigation with Asian investors. As far as her being involved with organized crime, they did not even want to get into that bucket of worms, but could be true.

John said that ACI's retainer will cover the costs for the trip and such. I will take that off ACI taxes anyway. A little gift from ACI to you all.

action_ventures: He also said that he pity's all those who are still awaiting any funding. The police suggested that she ceases all activities, and notify those involved that they can not invest in anyone's business. John stated that this information stay within those who had filed for litigation and let the others find out for themselves.

BobK again shows his character

action_ventures: A bitter learning lesson. John and Mike will be getting with me on Thursday. They want to set up a co-operative investment consul. They will be happy to investigate (Due Diligence) on any individual or source of funding and those involved in such. US or World Wide. They told me that they would ask for only 1% of the amount funded, payable 30 days after funding, for their services.

action_ventures: They also said that many other law firms are getting involved and are weeding out the wanna bee's, scammers, and finding legitimate investors. A list is being developed on those not to trust.

An attorney can get more accomplished on diligence then an individual. Plus I feel that the price is right and I will mention this to any finder or broker that wants to utilize them. The fee might be tacked on to the total amount, or payable by the finder or broker.

Okay that is it for now.

End of BobK email

action_ventures: thats all i got....
thistleent: that was all from kilgallon?
action_ventures: yup
thistleent: who is John
action_ventures: the lawyer
action_ventures: one of them
thistleent: then, who them
action_ventures: his lawyer.. bob's
thistleent: k
action_ventures: thats all i know
thistleent: and this lawyer went or called to lawyers in India?

action_ventures: maybe if u get brian to open up i would love to know how it went for him
action_ventures: yes
thistleent: k
action_ventures: thanks vince
action_ventures: have a great week
thistleent: u 2
thistleent: and if you get any specifics on law firms in India, etc. please let me know
thistleent: am not sure I entirely believe kilgallon cause he is a trickster
action_ventures: k will do
action_ventures: yes me neither
action_ventures: hmmmm
thistleent: going back to dancing skeletons and the phony email from the newspaper in calcutta
action_ventures: a possible sad case there too
action_ventures: well brian knows thats all i know
thistleent: k, bye
action_ventures: k

Obviously, Anamika didn't know I'd spoken with Anindita. Lo and behold I received another email from Anindita the next day.

November 6

HELLO MR VINCENT AND ALL OTHER EIGHT CLIENTS.
WELL SIR THANKS FOR YOUR REPLY AND SUPPORT, BUT FOR THE CORRECTION PART ANAMIKA TOLD ME THAT SHE WILL SEND FUND TO ALLEN MANSFIELD ALSO AS SHE COULD NOT ABLE TO TRUST DAVE THAT MUCH FOR HIS GENORISITY HE SHOWED TO ANAMIKA, WELL SIR I ALSO KNOW THAT HER DISEASE THROUGH WHICH SHE IS SUFFERING HAS TREATMENT BUT THAT AGAIN DEPENDS ON THE MOTIVE OF THE PATIENT AS HOW SHE WILL TAKE THE TREATMENT AS ANAMIKA NEVER TAKES REST NEITHER SHE LOVES TO TAKE

Poor Me Anamika #11—she never rests

REST, SHE IS NOW THINKING OF DIFFERENT KIND BUSINESS SHE WILL DO AFTER SHE COMPLETETS HER INVESTMENT TO ALL OF YOU AND NOW SHE CONCLUDED TO HELICOPTER BUSINESS FOR WHICH SHE IS THINKING DAY AND NIGHT, EVEN SHE TALKS IN HER SLEEP

ABOUT HELICOPTERS AND WE ALL ARE VERYTENSED FOR HER IF THIS KIND OF BUSINESS ASPECTS HAPPENS TO HER THEN WE ARE AFRAID ABOUT HER FUTURE HEALTH.
SIR I WILL ASK HER THE APPROPRIATE DATE AS SOON AS HER FEVER GETS DOWN BIT FOR YOUR SWIFT.
WITH BEST REGARDS
ANINDITA GHOSH

Helicopters? On further review it was an appropriate choice. Anamika her self was a human helicopter full of constant, manic motion and noise.

Dear Anindita:
Thank you for your response. I think the helicopter business would be good for Anamika.

Please tell her not to take any chances UNTIL AFTER she wires us our funds.

I hope the fever breaks very soon and she wires the funds as soon as possible, because many of the group cannot accept any more delays—there have been too many, promises and promises but no money. I know it was not her fault, but if she really cares about us and sincerely wants to invest, we hope she will wire the funds very soon.
Thank you for your help.

I sent Anamika email detailing the information I received from Larry, but gave her no indication I was aware of the deceptive way she used her sister.

Dear Anamika
I hope you are getting better with each day and appreciate your sister's efforts to keep us informed.

I thought you would be pleased to hear that Kilgallon, Stinson, Field and others who planned to sue you have dropped their plans.

THE REASON—BobK's attorney reported back to him and the others that you are "unbalanced"; that you "have a few small companies, nothing worth mentioning" and as a result "she isn't worth pursuing." That "she's been instructed by the police to stop."

A top law firm in Calcutta provided the information. I don't know the name.

BobK's MEMO TO THE GROUP—"It would not be worth anyone's time to pursue any litigation against Anamika Biswas and her family. At least not the one we know. They have several small companies that generate a small profit. Anamika has psychological problems (according to the attorneys) Collectively, with all those involved and what that family has in real-estate, investments, their businesses and such, they could not even pay the attorneys fees and court costs which could last up to 12 years in court. It seems that Anamika has tried this before and was hit with a major fine. That is why her father kicked her out of the house. Not sure but might be that litigation with Asian investors. As far as being involved with organized crime, they did not even want to get into that bucket of worms, but could be true. The police suggested that she ceases all activities ... a bitter learning lesson."

You have no need for loyalty toward those who would try to hurt you by ruining your reputation. By cutting them lose, you also save yourself a considerable amount of money.

I STRONGLY SUGGEST YOU HAVE NO FURTHER COMMUNICATION WITH STINSON, KILGALLON, FIELDS AND THE OTHERS WHO WOULD SUE YOU. AND, DO NOT LET THEM KNOW THAT YOU ARE AWARE OF KILGALLON'S MEMO.

We who support you remain, Alan Girvan, Allen Stout, Jody, Brian, Kevin, Jack, Scott, me (Vincent) and your recent addition—Allen Mansfield.

We look forward to your health improving (very quickily I hope) so that you can wire the funds and we can begin a very successful business relationship.

It is very important that you contact me immediately with the date the funds are wired!!!

November 7

On the morning of November seventh, the phone rang while I was having my breakfast. It was Anamika calling at ten minutes after seven.

    More surprising than Anamika's early morning call was her revelation that her sister had visited India but returned home to Canada. In addition, someone was threatening her sister in Canada. That person was "saying he is

Vincent" and telling her sister that "fraud has been done". He also threatened the job of her brother-in-law. The call started "last Sunday" (Nov. 2) Anamika said, also advising me that her sister was "… very worried. Two men are going to her flat everyday."

Anamika said she'd learned all of this on November 7, the same day we were speaking!

Someone was lying. I spoke with Anindita two days earlier on November 5 and learned from her that she was not in touch with her family. Then an email from Anindita, while she supposedly was in India, arrives a day later even though Anindita denies sending me any email.

Now on November 7, Anamika indicates "someone saying he is Vincent" spoke with her sister. Were they now talking? Had Anindita used my call to make contact with Anamika?

Another surprise came when she asked me to "call Jerry and talk casually. Ask him if he sends anyone to my sister's apartment to have a conversation with members of my family." Jerry lived in Toronto and knew the area where Anindita lived.

Relieved that her suspicions were elsewhere, I told her I would call Jerry. Yet, as Anindita told me she was distant from her family, I wondered why the two sisters talked. Or, was Anamika possessed of some other worldly ESP?

I wanted more important information and changed the subject to the status of her funding. "Monday I will go to the bank," she said and funds would arrive "one to two days from Monday."

Funding dates #45 & 46—November 11th–12th.

Next I asked her about the investigation by the lawyer and she told me she was "shocked by the Kilgallon email."

When I hung up, there was little reason to believe that I had concluded my last conversation with Anamika … But, I had. I called Jerry.

Dear Anamika:
Thank you for your call this morning.

I spoke with Jerry a little bit after 9am—Los Angeles time—as you requested.

Jerry told me "the last time I talked with her father was two weeks ago when she was in Delhi." Another day he called and a woman he thought was your mother answered and then hung up.

About speaking with your sister he said: "The only time was when she first arrived in India and passed on my message to Anamika."

He told me he knew you had a sister because he learned she had twins in April, but doesn't know where your sister lives and didnt expect her back in Toronto until Christmas because she told Jerry she was staying in India for three months. Therefore he did not send anyone to her house.

He also said he did not understand why you didnt call him directly and he is waiting for your call.

Hope this helps.

Am very much looking forward to you wiring funds on Monday and that we receive the money in 1-2 days as you told me this morning.

I hope you can understand how hurt and frustrated some of us are who have supported you through all of your difficulties.

I hope you realize that you must keep your word and fund us on Monday.

We got cut off before we discussed the Kilgallon memo. I don't know what to think. If you don't have any funds then you've played a huge joke on us all.

If you do have funds you must wire them to save your credibility as a business woman and a human being.

THIS IS THE TIME AND YOU MUST DELIVER!!!!!!

I hope to hear from you very soon, either by email or phone. I will not be home this evening from 7pm—10pm, which is 8:30am—11:30am in India. You can call me on my Saturday at the same time as you called today.

I believe in you and truly want this relationship to work.

I also advised the seven Anamika loyalists of the phone call and her intention to fund the group within one to two days from Monday, October tenth.

I felt it necessary to delineate my "intentions" toward Anamika to the seven principals who remained. I told them on November seventh:

"I intend to keep in contact with Anamika in the event that there is a scintilla of a shred of a jot's worth of hope that she has enough $ to fund us … there are no illusions or expectations to roil our emotions. She is either wilier than any Republican congressman, covered in more Teflon than sainted Ronnie or a certifiable wacko. And maybe all three. Who knows, stranger things have happened and we may yet find WMDs in Iraq."

Anamika took offense at my strongly worded email which I sent after we spoke on the phone.

November 8

HELLO VINCENT
THANKS FOR THE HELP YOU DONE TO ME, WELL VINCENT I AM NOT JOCKING WITH ANY OF YOU, WELL I KNOW FOR MY DELAY PEOPLE STARTED THINKING THAT I AM JOCKING AND I EVEN KNOW THAT WHEN 100 PEOPLE IN A CROWD START BELIEVING IN A WORD THEN IT AUTOMATICALLY COMES TO THE MIND OF A MINORITYS THAT WHETHER MAJORITY IS RIGHT OR THEY ARE RIGHT SO I AM NOW ASKING YOU BOTH INCLUDING MY WELL WISHERS AND MY CRITICS TO WAIT TILL WEDNESDAY 12TH OF NOVEMBER 2003 FOR THE CALL FROM MY SIDE WHICH WILL CONFIRM YOU THAT WIREING HAS BEEN DONE, WIRE SLIPS HAS BEEN SEND THROUGH DHL AND YOU ALL WILL RECIEVE FAX TELLING YOU ALL YOUR CONFIRMATION NUMBERS AND SWIFT CODE OF MINE. THEN I WILL CALL YOU TO ASK WHAT YOUR FELLOW COUNTRY MEN INCLUDING KILGALLON FEEL ABOUT A WOMEN FROM INDIA.
WELL I CANNOT CALL YOU TODAY SORRY FOR THAT PLEASE CONVEY THIS MESSAGE TO JERRY AS I CANNOT ACESS FROM HERE TO MY HOTMAIL ACCOUNT SO THATS WHY I CANNOT CONTACT WITH JERRY, THAT HE WILL ALSO GET ALONG WITH YOU ALL.
TAKE CARE BYE—ANAMIKA BISWAS

On November eighth Anamika responded to a previous email from Alan. She told him that "you will have funding in month of November in two or three days from now." This confirmed her earlier dates of November eleventh or twelfth. Then she added, "… I promise you and all the clients I will not disappoint you or let you down. I will fulfill all your losses that you all suffered for me."

We all believed <u>this</u> time she would deliver.

Monday, November tenth arrived without any email from Anamika. I decided to keep pressing her for details and performance.

November 10

Dear Anamika:
When you called me last Friday—Nov. 7—you said you'd go to the bank on Monday (Nov. 10) to wire us our funds. At first you said we should get the funds in 2-3 days and then you said we should get the funds in 1-2 days from Monday.

One to two days from Monday is Wednesday, Nov. 12.

In your email to me of Saturday, Nov. 8 you said: "wait til Wednesday 12th of November 2003 for the call from my side which will confirm you that wireing has been done, wire slips has been send through DHL and you all will receive fax telling you all your confirmation numbers and SWIFT code of mine."

Does this mean you'll be wiring on Wednesday and then call me my Wednesday morning? If so, why did you tell me on the phone you would wire on Monday? We need to communicate very clearly with each other at this time because every time you delay your credibility gets less and less.

And you don't want to hurt those who have believed in you for so long. Please answer the following questions:

1. Did you wire the funds on Monday, Nov. 10?
1A—If yes, please advise status of confirmation slips, SWIFT number, etc.
1B. If no, explain why the funds weren't wired.

2. If the funds were wired have the confirmation slips been sent to me using my DHL account
2A. If the slips have been sent, provide me with the tracking number.
2B. If the slips have NOT been sent, tell me when they will be sent.

In your email of Nov. 8—you said you are not joking "with any of you".

We'll know for an absolute certainty that you are not joking when we receive the funds in our bank accounts. Until then....

Best regards,

Vincent
(still your friend, but I need you to do what you say you will do when you say you will do it)

I advised the group on Tuesday (Nov. 11) that Anamika had not responded to my previous email. Allen in Phoenix thanked me for the update and added "Even though the odds seem to be against us, all we can do is hope for the best."

Anamika finally replied the next day.

November 12

HELLO VINCENT
WELL THIS TIME I WONT ASK YOU HOWARE YOU BECAUSE IT SEEMS THAT YOU ARE NOT WELL AND ALSO VERY OFFENDED BY MY ATTI-TUDE OF DELAY

Poor Me Anamika #12—her delay has offended me

WELL I ADMIT IT IS MY FAULT AND I GOT A VERY GOOD SUPPORT FROM YOU FROM ALL THROUGH THIS 7MONTHS BUT STILL BY SOME HOW I COULD NOT ABLE TO KEEP PROMISES WHICH I MADE TO ALL OF YOU FOR VARIOUS REASONS SOME FOR MY OWN PROB-LEM AND SOME FOR THE PROBLEM ON THE SYSTEM OF OUR COUN-TRY WELL THAT TOO I TAKE AS MY DISABILITY AS I BELIEVE THAT WHEN ONE IS INEFFICIENT HE/SHE FACES THIS KIND OF PROBLEMS FOR HIS/HER INEFFICENCY, WELL I DONT BLAME ANYONE FOR MY DELAY EXCEPT MY

Poor Me Anamika #13—she is inefficient

DESTINY, AND NEITHER I WILL ASK YOU TO BELIEVE IN ME UNLESS YOU GET THE FUND IN YOUR ACCOUNT WELL I ADMIT THAT I TOLD YOU THAT I WILL WIRE ON MONDAY AND WHEN I TOLD IT WAS SUN-DAY THAT TIME I TOLD AS PER MY PRESUMPTION BUT WHEN MON-DAY CAME I GOT TO REALISE THAT IT WILL TAKE TIME TILL WEDNESDAY THAT WHY I WROTE THAT TO YOU.
WELL NOW I AM GETTING ON TO THE POINT THAT FUND WILL REACH TO YOU

Funding date #47—November 18th

ALL BY 18TH OF NOVEMBER 2003 AND IF I REAPTING ONCE MORE THAT AND IF IT FAILS THIS TIME THEN WHAT EVER YOU WILL DO TO ME REGARDING THIS LAWFULLY I WILL ACEPT THAT YOU CAN PUT ME BEHIND BARS. THIS IS MY

Poor Me Anamika #14—if she fails she'll willingly go to jail

LAST PROMISE WHICH I AM COMMITING YOU ALL BUT NOT ASKING YOU TO BELIEVE UNLESS YOU GET IT BUT THIS TIME IF I FAIL YOU CAN TAKE ANY STEP AGAINST ME I WILL NOT TELL YOU ANYTHING BECAUSE THIS I AM CONFIDENT FOR 1000% THAT I WILL SUCCEED.

WELL TILL I WILL NEITHER CALL YOU BECAUSE THIS TIME I NEED TO PULL MY SOCKS TO WIN THIS CHALLENGE. WELL I AM TAKING THIS TIME TO SEND THE FUND TO ALL 22 CLIENTS WHOSE CONFIRMATION SLIP WELL BE DESPATCHED TO YOU THROUGH YOUR DHL NUMBER ON 15TH WHICH I WILL CONVEY TO YOU THOUGH EMAIL ON 17TH MORNING. THIS IS REASON WHY I TOOK THIS TIME, WELL I DONT ASK YOU TO BELIEVE ME BUT I BEG YOU TO PLEASE OPEN YOUR MAILBOX ON 17TH SO THAT I CAN GET RID OF MY RESPONSIBILITY, WHICH I TOOK WRONGFULLY AS MY LIFE ONE OF THE BIGGEST WRONG DECISION. I KNOW I HAVE HURT YOU A LOT AND TO ALL OTHERS BUT AT THE SAME I THINK THAT YOU WILL UNDERSTAND THAT IN WHAT KIND OF

Poor Me Anamika #15—the infrastructure did her in

INFRASTRUCTURE I AM LIVING WELL I DONT ASK YOU TO SYMPATHY ME BECAUSE I DONT DESERVE IT FOR THIS DELAYS BUT STILL I CAN BEG YOU TO SEE TILL 17TH AS IN THE DAY I BELIEVE THAT TO A PERSON WHOME SO FAR YOU CALLED AS FRIEND WILL NOT DISHEARTEN YOU. THAT IS MY BELIEVE BUT I WONT ASK YOU TO BELIEVE BEFRE 17TH MORNING.
BYE
ANAMIKA BISWAS

Earlier she had conveyed much of the same information to Brian. To him she attributed the delay to "some election problems in Delhi". The funds would arrive about the seventeenth of November and the transmission slips would be sent "directly to Vincent through his DHL numbers." She challenged Brian with "… after 17th of November it will be your headache onwards to bring profit and I will relax because till now I worked very hard to build the pillars where you going to construct your dreamland."

That same day she gave Alan the same funding dates and also advised that the confirmation slips would be sent "to Vincent through his DHL numbers." But added a note of self pity "… as nowadays Vincent too don't want to believe in me I know this well I don't blame him for I blame my destiny …"

Part of my new approach to Anamika was to provide carrot and stick when warranted in the hope that in some way we would find the right combination to reach her, elicit responses and continue communication.

Dear Anamika

Thank you for your email. Now that I've received it, I am very well, indeed. I am NOT offended by the many delays. I am disappointed and disheartened— EVEN THOUGH I ACCEPT YOUR PERSONAL AND GOVERNMENTAL PROBLEMS.

This is a natural and normal response. Imagine holding a bowl of food in front of a hungry person and then pulling it back or leaving it within inches where he cannot reach it? Wouldn't that be frustrating, disappointing and disheartening?

So it is with your delays. However I still believe in you AND I/WE ARE STILL HUNGRY.

My email to you might have been avoided if you had communicated the delay ON MONDAY when you learned about it.

I've told you once before you have a responsibility to communicate to us on a timely basis—no matter what the circumstances as a result of these past numerous delays. That is the way we will determine your sincerity.

Make sure DHL picks up on Saturday the 15th and CALL ME WHEN THE PICK UP HAS BEEN MADE WITH THE TRACKING NUMBER.

Until then, I remain your friend sending you
Best regards,

Brian read Anamika's email, in which she blamed Delhi elections for the delay. The more I pondered the long list of excuses, the less I could accept this one. I was also determined to "call her" on all of her funding dates and excuses. If my constant pressure would be too great I risked the whole deal collapsing for all of us. However, for me, doing nothing and sitting idly by while Anamika's "destiny" worked its magic was not an option.

I asked her "What do elections in Delhi have to do with you delaying the funding which you said would be done on Monday Nov. 10, and would arrive in 1-2 days? You told me on the phone and in email you had WRITTEN approval, why should Delhi elections hold things up? IN ADDITION—in your email to me you say you will fund "all 22 clients". Why? The group of us—Jack, Brian, Kevin, Jody, Alan, Allen, Scott and ME has been the most loyal and supportive. Why would you reward those who speak against you and try to sue you? Is that being loyal to those whose loyalty and support has continued in spite of the delays—which by now are too numerous to count? The remaining clients by now have given up any hope that you will fund them and moved on to other financial resources. The 8 of us deserve your funding BEFORE any one else! I strongly suggest you make sure we are properly funded and then worry about the rest—if at all. And, forget all your high drama about going to jail. No one in our group of 8 has any intention of taking that action—and you know it! Take good care of us and we'll take good care of you." I signed it "Vincent—your impatient friend" and hoped for the best.

When I told Jerry about her plans to fund twenty two companies he was also surprised." I still have the opinion she is bringing in money from another source using her collateral or credit facilities," he said in his email.

Jody contacted Anamika and in her gentle Southern way conveyed not only her belief and trust but the "need for you to honor your word … I am continuing to support you, however I need the same back.…"

No one had heard from Anamika in two days. I applied more pressure.

November 14

Dear Anamika
I've sent you two emails and you have not responded. By now you should know that we need to have direct and frequent communication.

In your email of Nov. 12—you inform all of us—Jack, Alan Girvan, Kevin, Brian, Jody, Scott, Allen Stout and me (Vincent) that—"fund will reach you all by 18th of November 2003."

And that "I am taking this time to send the fund to all 22 clients … whose confirmation slip will be dispatched to you through your DHL number on 15th …"

Once again, I strongly suggest that you concentrate on funding ONLY those listed above. They are the ones who have supported you and cared about you and your family over these last seven months. Yet, you insist on ignoring your group of 8 friends to reward those who would slander your reputation and threaten you with financial ruin. Fund us first and worry about the rest later!

And that "I will convey to you through email on 17th morning …"

In order for you to "dispatch" the confirmation slips to me on the 15th of November, you will have needed to visit the bank before that date.

We all know that your banks are only open half a day on Saturday and I'm not sure if DHL picks up on Saturday.

HOWEVER—As your Friday Nov. 14 business day has concluded, my question remains: HAVE YOU GONE TO THE BANK YET?

If your answer is yes—you will receive the gratitude of 8 very appreciative people who will welcome you into their businesses with open arms and look forward to receiving email confirmation on Nov. 17.

If your answer is no—we will be very disappointed and your credibility will decrease another notch.

What is it? Yes, you've been to the bank; or No?

Best regards,
Vincent—still your friend, but needing your answer

Three days later, I contacted her again. This time instead of pressure I tried guilt, figuring it couldn't hurt.

November 17

Dear Anamika:
I, and the others in the group of 8, have believed in you and supported you throughout the obstacles and delays of the last few months.

I believed your email to me on Nov. 12 when you wrote "confirmation slip will be dispatched to you through your DHL number on 15th which I will convey to you through email on 17th morning ... please open your mailbox on 17th so that I can get rid of my responsiblity ..."

Remember writing that?

Today is Nov. 17. It is almost 8:30am and I have not received the email you promised regarding the DHL package with the confirmation slips. Nor have you responded to my earlier emails to you.

You suggest in your Nov. 12 email that I am offended. I am NOT offended, but I am disappointed and hurt by your failure to keep your word; and by the disrespectful way you've treated me and the others who have been loyal to you.

If and when we receive the funds by the Nov. 18th, as your email states, we will know you are honest, sincere and serious.

If we don't hear from you and do not receive the funds we will also know who you are.

I remain disappointed and hurt,

   Meanwhile Anamika told Jerry she would be "starting the fund transfer on the 18th or 19th" and would give him an exact date soon.
   I decided to call her on the confirmation slips.

November 18

Dear Anamika
I checked with DHL and no package has been sent to me from Kolkata.

You said you'd send the confirmation slips via my DHL account on Nov. 15.

Have the slips been sent on the 15th? If not, when were they sent?

Have the funds been wired? Let me know.

The time for joking is over. This is a serious business matter.

I want to believe in you, but you are making it VERY difficult.

Vincent

Despite the prodding and pleading it took Anamika seven days to contact us again.

November 19

HELLO VINCENT, ALANGRIVAN, JODY, BRIANGORDAN, KEVIN, JACK, AND OTHERS,

WELL I AM SORRY FOR ONE DAY DELAY BECAUSE AS PER MY EMAIL I WAS SUPPOSE TO INFORM YOU THAT FUND HAS BEEN WIRED BY 18TH, WHICH I AM DOING TODAY, WELL I HAVE WIRED ALL YOUR 9PEOPLE FUNDS AND

Anamika Has Wired Funds #5

REST13PEOPLE FUND WILL BE WIRED BY 22ND OF NOVEMBER, I HAVE DONE THE WIREING IN THIS WAY BECAUSE I KNOW YOU ALL SUPPORTED ME SO I WIRED YOUR FUND FIRST WHICH WILL REACH YOU BY 22ND OR 25TH OF NOVEMBER

Funding Dates # 48&49—November 22nd or 25th

2003 TO YOUR RESPECTIVE ACCOUNTS BECAUSE A WIRE FROM HERE AS PER BANK MODE OF CONDUCT TAKES 5 TO 7DAYS TO REACH YOUR RESPECTIVE ACCOUNTS FASTER THAN THIS I CANNOT DO BECAUSE EVERYPOINT I DEAL I NEED TO TAKE PERMISSION SO FASTER THAN THIS I CANNOT DO I KNOW ALL OF YOU SUPPORTED ME A LOT SO I AM ASKING APOLOGY FOR THIS DELAY BUT NOW THE WORK IS DONE, BUT I CANNOT FOWARD YOU THE CONFIRMATION SLIP BEFORE21ST OF NOVEMBER BECAUSE AS IT LEAVES DELHI WITH THE CONCENT OF MINISTER OF EXTERNAL AFFAIRS ALONG WITH THEIR PERMISSION I WILL FAX YOU THE CONFIRMATION SLIPS AS I AM MOVING DELHI TODAY NIGHT FOR

Anamika Travel #3

YOUR LAST FINISHING TOUCH OF WORK AFTER THAT ON 21ST OF NOVEMBER 2003 I WILL FAX YOU THE CONFIRMATION SLIP AND I WILL ALSO SEND YOU THE SLIPS ALONG WITH THE PERMNISSION LETTER IN DHL, BUT IN THE MEANTIME THE 21ST CAN ALSO GET REDUCED TO 20TH THAT IS TOMORROW IF I GET THE FOLLOWING INFORMATION FROM ALL OF YOU (MEANS ALL 9PEOPLE) BY TOMORROW OVER EMAILS AND THE INFORMATION IS IF I DONT GO IN THE PATNERSHIP WITH YOU ALL, BUT AS A INVESTOR AFTER GETTING THE MONEY WITHIN HOW MANY DAYS AND HOW WILL YOU ALL RETURN THE MONEY TO ME, PLEASE SEND THAT VERY VIVDLY TO ME IN MAIL BY TOMORROW MORNING SO THAT I CAN SUBMIT BECAUSE SO FAR THE BINDINGS THROUGH WHICH I AM RUNNING DONT ALLOW ME BOTH OFFICIALLY AND PERSONNALLY TO BE THE PATNER OF ALL OF YOUR COMPANIES.
AS EARLY AS POSSIBLE PLEASE SEND ME THE CHART WHICH WILL CLEARLY STATE HOW YOU WILL PAY ME AND IN WHICH WHICH MONTHS AND WITHIN HOW MUCH TIME YOU WILL COMPLETE RETURNING YOUR LOAN THAT IS MY MONEY WHICH I AM INVESTING. PLEASE TRY TO SEND ME THIS BY TOMORROW SO THAT I CAN SEND YOU YOUR DHL AND FAX ALSO BY TOMORROW.
THANKYOU
ANAMIKA BISWAS

This meant that within twenty four hours we had to provide Anamika with information detailing how and when she would get her return on investment in our companies. We all had those charts as part of our business plans, but the request at this late juncture was close to if not the last straw. However, if this was all that stood between us and funding it was easy to be motivated. All the loyalists sent her the information she requested, believing that she had wired the funds on November nineteenth.

Jack told her "Good to hear you are FINALLY making good on your commitment," while Brian pleaded for her to "please come through this time … please, please don't let us down."

I told her that I was delighted you have wired the funds and look forward to receiving them during the period Nov. 22-Nov.25 "as you indicated in your email."

This last week in the relationship with Anamika was perhaps the most stressful. Even those of us who took a "trust but verify" approach felt we were all so close. There didn't seem to be any imaginable obstacles left to prevent our being funded.

There was no contact from Anamika or funds in our accounts by November 22.

November 23

I spoke with Mr. Biswas on the twenty third. He told me "she's moved to a flat. I have no connection with her now. After coming back from Delhi she was very busy that's why she took a flat." Once again I asked about her business and he told me Anamika had been in the export business about "three to four years" and that he had "no connection" with her for the" last seven days."

On the night of November twenty third, Allen in Philadelphia was surprised by a phone call from Anamika. While he conveyed to her the clients "were gravely concerned" that none of the funds supposedly wired had reached their bank accounts, Anamika complained to him that her family was being "harassed". She even wanted a <u>letter</u> written from the group stating "non—harassment" as a policy.

In addition, Anamika told Allen that the eight principals would have to travel to India and visit with a government minister. Before he could get more details, the connection was broken.

The next morning I sent the group an update regarding my conversation with Mr. Biswas and Anamika's call to Allen.

I analyzed this latest maneuver by Anamika in the following way.

"Anamika has cozied up to Kevin, Brian, me and now Allen, going from one to the other as each in turn expressed interest in her and a willingness to help her. And when we became disturbed or upset at delay and excuses she moved to another who would give her the attention she wanted. In my amateur psychologist opinion Ms. Anamika is an adoration junkie."

I concluded that "if the funds … arrive in 5-7 days as her email to me on Nov. 19th indicated, then all will be well."

Jerry tried to get a response from her concluding "again a promise has gone unfulfilled."

November 26

Anamika had another surprise for us. On November twenty sixth she called Allen in Phoenix.

To All:
Anamika called Allen Stout this morning. It was a brief call, lasting only about 5 minutes.

She asked Allen to call those in the group of 9—i.e. those receiving this email to tell them the following:

1. The money is not in a position to be used by anyone.
2. The clients need to provide her with their "mortgage" papers showing each client owns 100% of his/her company—since she didn't know any of us except Brian and we don't know her.
3. If we couldn't or didn't provide the mortgage papers we had to go to India and meet with the Minister of Internal Affairs.

I've contacted Anamika to ask her for clarification of the above and advised her that no one would be available over the Thanksgiving Holiday. I've also asked her to provide the name of the Minister of Internal Affairs.

Monday I will contact the Indian consulate to find out once and for all criteria for an Indian citizen to invest abroad.

As you know on Nov. 19 she sent me an email which stated:
"... I wired your (the nine) fund first which will reach you by 22nd or 25th of November 2003 to your respective accounts because a wire from here as per bank mode of conduct takes 5 to 7 days to reach your respective accounts ..."

Am determined to play this out a bit more before getting contentious.

However she has two chances of receiving the above—slim and none.

Dear Anamika
Allen Stout informed me this morning that you had called him. We are both pleased that you called.

Before I get to the specifics of the call, let me say that I am NOT mad at you and you have NOT offended me. You are important to the growth and development of our companies as we are important to you.

As Allen has a hearing deficiency, he was unable to understand all of what you said. He did relay to me what he was able to hear. Which is—You told him the following:

1. Your investment funds are not in a position to be used by anyone.

2. You asked Allen to contact the 9 clients and tell them to provide you with "mortgage" papers showing each client owns 100% of his company—since you don't know us and we don't know you.

3. If we couldn't furnish the mortgage papers we had to come to India to meet with the Minister of Internal Affairs.

Please advise me if the above three points are what you conveyed to Allen and if there is anything else we need to know.

IN ADDITION—1. This is the Thanksgiving Holiday weekend in the U.S. It will be impossible for Allen to contact all the clients as many start the holiday early and their businesses are closed.

I will, however advise all through email that you called Allen.

2. Please provide me with the name of the Minister of Internal Affairs.

I look forward to receiving your response to the above.

Best regards,

Vincent

No one in our group ever heard from her again.

NOVEMBER SCORE CARD		TOTALS
Funding Dates	6	49
(final funding date Nov. 25)		
Delays	2	37
Funds Transfer Date	0	2
Draft/Tracking Numbers Sent	0	2
Holidays	0	5
Confirmation Slip Dates	0	9
Anamika Has Wired Funds	1	5
Anamika Travels	1	3
Poor Me Anamika	5	14

AFTERWORD

Breaking up is hard to do—as the old teen oriented song reminded us. At least for this teen it was. There is nothing more infuriating, and also motivating, for me than inconclusiveness. No answer demanded an answer. No reason demanded a reason. That my attitude might be traced to a trauma of infancy was irrelevant in early December.

Very simply I wanted what I wanted and I wanted it right now.

Except, of course, reality gradually pushed aside the demands of childhood. However, I was pleased to see my desire for a rationally explained conclusion was shared by others.

Reghu kept on sending Anamika email asking if she would be funding Jerry, but never received a response.

However, I was going to demand a response from Anamika. Sure.

December 2

Dear Anamika

For nearly 7 months I have believed in you and supported you—even though many in the group thought I was stupid and crazy to do so.

I endured their criticism of my support for you because I deeply and truly believed you were honest, serious and committed to investing in my company and in the other companies.

Recently you told us the wires had been sent and we would get our funds in "5-7 days" that meant about Nov. 22—Nov. 24. Today is December 2. No funds have been received.

You were supposed to send me the confirmation slips by DHL as well as your SWIFT code. No slips or code have been received.

You called Allen Mansfield and Allen Stout with requests that are clearly not necessary IF the funds had been wired, as you stated in your email to me of Nov. 19.

HOW COULD YOU TELL US THE FUNDS WERE WIRED AND 8 DAYS LATER SAY THE FUNDS COULDNT MOVE WHEN THEY WERE SUP-POSED TO BE IN OUR ACCOUNTS TWO DAYS EARLIER!!!????

Very soon, I'm afraid I'll be forced to withdraw all my support for you and my faith and belief in you will evaporate. It makes me very sad to write this as I thought we'd been communicating very well early in November—you called me, remember on Nov. 7.

I WANT A SERIOUS, HONEST AND BUSINESS-LIKE EXPLANATION FROM YOU. NO EXCUSES AND NO REQUESTS FOR MORE INFORMATION OR ASSISTANCE.

You said you got the approval in Delhi and the funds were sent about Nov. 17—destined to arrive in 5-7 days. Nothing!

Why have you stopped communicating with me?

Why have you led us on this merry chase for 7 months?

Tell me why—honestly and openly and sincerely without excuses and I will try to continue to support you.

If not …

Remember I am THE ONLY ONE who was able to get you publicity.

Remember I can work with you or against you.

I can help you improve your business career or not.

It's your choice.

Let me know.

NOW.

Best regards,
Vincent

December 7

Jody spoke with Anamika's father on December seventh regarding her promise of funds. Mr. Biswas told Jody "I don't know your business." He did tell Jody he would pass on the message that she called to Anamika.

Had this Mr. Biswas been the Mr. Biswas introduced to Brian in September; chances are he would know about Anamika's business.

Jerry continued his quest for funding in his email to Anamika on December tenth. He wanted a simple answer—was she going to fund him or not. He also refused to believe she had moved out of her father's house.

"Also, this ploy of your father saying you moved out of the house, is just that, a ploy to the harassment you are taking from the others. As I recall, you had said you had moved out early in the summer also. So please at least, tell me the truth."

December 15

On December fifteenth I decided to give Anindita another call in Toronto. She did not have much more to tell me except her son was sick and she talked with her in-laws. Once again I asked about Anamika's ability to invest such a huge sum of money. She told me her family "had never seen that much money" as of 1995 when she left India.

A week later I sent Anamika an email to all six of her email addresses.

December 22

Dear Anamika
No one has heard from you since Nov. 26 when you called Allen Stout.

All of us in the group of 8 who have believed in and supported you have started looking for financing elsewhere since it is by now obvious that you led us a merry chase for 8 months. I hope you had a good time and were thoroughly amused at our expense.

I am writing a book on the entire experience of trying to obtain funding from you—beginning in April 2003 to November 2003. I intend to use all the email, Instant Message transcripts and phone conversation notes sent or received from you and others as source material.

Should you have anything to say to explain or defend yourself, no matter what it is—to tell your side of the story, now is the time to express yourself.

If not … I wish you health and the hope you get all the help you need.

Best regards

Vincent Panettiere

In January, 2004 I sent her another email about the book, advising her that "I have completed the chapters for April and May and am now reviewing the material for June. It is not a pretty picture."

By surprise a writer from the Hindustan Times contacted me in mid-January. I'd first made contact with him in late June when he was a reporter for the Statesman in Kolkata. He had interviewed Anamika, but The Telegraph scooped him and his story was spiked.

Now he was following up with me to see how Anamika's "investment" had progressed. I used this opportunity to contact Anamika.

January 16

Dear Anamika
I regret that you have disappeared without any explanation—and more importantly without funding any of those who believed in you, cared for you and trusted you.

Yesterday the reporter who interviewed you in July for the Statesman contacted me. He is with the Hindustan Times. He wanted to know how the deal between you, me and my company Thistle Productions turned out. Did I have any new projects for India, etc.

What do I tell him?
Do I tell him you disappeared mysteriously?
Do I tell him you played games with us for 8 months
Do I tell him you are a fraud
Do I tell him you are a con artist
Do I tell him you are mentally unstable
Do I tell him that not only our group of 24, but many others
have been treated the same way by you.

WHAT DO I TELL HIM!

I am one of the few who believed in you and tried to help you all these months.

Why do you treat us so disrespectfully.

We deserve an explanation

We deserve the truth.

No more excuses

And finally—what do I tell your sister Anindita????

Let me know

Vincent Panettiere

I thought that my reference to her sister would elicit a response. It didn't.

March 4, 2004

Trying one more, and last, time to get satisfaction, I called Anindita again on March fourth.

She had visited India in February and told me that Anamika was "out of Kolkata". "She has some problem and is out of the house," she added.

Anindita, who revealed her father had "mentally gone down", met Anamika one day in February and when we spoke remained miffed that her younger sister didn't want to pose for a photo with her twin nephews.

Anindita was shockingly candid. "Everyone is sick of her. It is better for her to die. Then the family will be okay. She is totally mad."

Better that she die? Before I could utter words of conciliation she blurted out.

"Every court, every policeman knows her. She's sick! Everyone knows she's mad. My father got sick for her. If she is in trouble, let her be in trouble.

"She wasted your time, but not your money, that is the main thing. Whatever trouble she is in, let her be in trouble," Anindita repeated and we ended the conversation.

CONCLUSION

Earlier, in the preface, I advised that this book was not a cautionary tale. I will not present a tidy summation to warn the reader. This was my unique experience and I trust the reader to make an individual assessment. Nevertheless, there are several conclusions that can be drawn from the experiences of those eight months.

For some in the group the bottom line result was—no funding. What else, if anything, did we lose?

Most of us spent our time in hope and expectation sending and receiving email. A few had larger long distance phone bills. If I had not ordered twelve business plans printed and a dozen logo shirts in anticipation of meeting with the Directors of Anamika's investment group, my expenses would have been about four hundred dollars less. As an aside, the shirts were made in India which at the time I took as a positive omen.

Had I received funding from Anamika the money spent on shirts and business plans would have been incidental. I, however, would be acclaimed for my shrewd business sense—spending $400 to receive millions! Imagine! Amazing!

How many of the critics might spend four hundred dollars playing the slot machines during a weekend in Las Vegas? Or a day at Santa Anita? Or buying shares of some obscure but hot stock? How risky is that behavior?

Our bets, including those by the pompous blowhards, were on ourselves. The risk we took was to improve our companies, careers and lifestyles of our families. We ventured into the unknown as countless free-spirited Americans had done over decades.

Someone had to take a risk that a machine with wings could leave the ground, or that an assembly line was more efficient than building one car at a time. No one could see the value of sending packages overnight but FedEx sprang up. Until the Internet was born books came from the library or a book store, not amazon.com.

Some, who regard themselves as shrewd financial operators, will be quick to call us "stupid" or "naive" for wasting our time—never stopping to consider that it was our time, and not theirs, to do with as we wished.

Others would accuse us of being in denial, despite overwhelming evidence. Considering the numbers of Americans who still believe Iraq was behind 9/11 or that Iraq contained weapons of mass destruction, the ability to deny facts was not an attribute possessed by our group alone.

Other experts will intimate that we were not deserving of financing from anyone. "After all," they might reason, "if you were able to raise financing the traditional way you would have." Obviously this point of view, eschewing alternative methods for doing anything, would have prevented any cars other than black Model T's from ever being produced.

Critics more inclined to the role of judgmental parent might wag their fingers in our faces and proclaim "what do you expect, you wanted something for nothing." They might also never let us forget "if it's too good to be true, it usually is."

With all the abuse that might be heaped upon those of us who participated in the Anamika venture and particularly the few who staunchly defended her until the end of November, 2003 what actually did we lose? As it is not possible to lose what was never possessed, we have to consider the insight and experience gained.

An interesting social dynamic emerged. Had only one person spent eight fruitless months waiting for Anamika's largess, his frustration would have been consigned to anonymity.

With our group of twenty four, the desire for funding created a firestorm of hope which often obscured objective perception. More than anything we were looking to credit Anamika, not discredit her. Any ambiguous sign or shred of data was thrown into the melting pot of hope where it quickly lost specificity and was assimilated into group think.

As a result, because we had a burning desire to acquire funding, we did not look carefully at some telltale signs. Nor did we consider the sophomoric actions of some as being inimical to our collective goal.

In the sharp focus of hindsight there were indications questioning the substance and reality of potential funding from Anamika. Primarily, the brokers' casual, even lackadaisical approach to proving Anamika was financially sound. The lack of any incontrovertible proof at the onset of the funding process should have been an immediate stop sign. Yet, we were ready, willing, able and very eager to suspend disbelief, concentrating on the promise of "ABSOLUTELY NO FEE, 100% FINANCING" as Larry proclaimed in the first page of his email.

Those of us who were aware of the total amount of Anamika's funding commitment—$33 billion—were equally culpable and gullible. We all wanted funding so much that we refused to look at contravening evidence. All of us had the ability to check the latest edition of the New York Times or Wall Street Journal, compare the costs of some corporate mergers and thereby gain a clearer perspective of the reality of funds Anamika promised as well as those requested by various clients.

For example, the wonder from down under was to receive a bit less than $5 billion which equaled the amount the U.S. receives in fresh financing from foreign investors every two and a half days.

Larry was to receive $10 billion which was two thirds of the $15 billion the U.S. Export/Import Bank has the authority to issue.

Anamika was going to invest $33 billion in 24 unknown companies while Bank of America, the fifth largest bank in the United States merged with NationsBank, the third largest, for $57.7 billion.

With our noses pressed to the glass wall beyond which lay our hopes, plans and dreams not many of us had objective vision. What we could not see, we took on faith, clinging to the most recent positive expression. Sounds a bit like religion?

The trip to Toronto was delayed due to the illness of Anamika's father? No problem. Sudden illness is part of the human condition and consideration must be given. Another delay because of business problems in Korea? Frustrating but at least it proves the group is a player. Niraj's wife dies? Our empathic systems moved into overdrive.

At the time none of us kept specific count of the number of delays, which totaled nearly five per month over the eight month period. Had anyone kept track we might have realized that nearly one delay a week was more than happenstance.

The few that questioned Anamika's sincerity did so based on their own childish need to be satisfied rather than a quantitative approach.

Additionally, the forty nine funding dates Anamika gave us during the eight months average out to one every four days or approximately seven funding dates per month. With that frequency, perceived through the prism of hope and desire, we were continuously kept agitated, experiencing a constant cycle of hope and disappointment.

After revisiting the voluminous documents attesting to the hope and frustration during three fourths of 2003, I've reached additional conclusions.

Though I've never met Anamika in person and lack the interactive experience of Anindita, her sister, I don't believe Anamika is mad in the strict psychological definition.

It is my opinion that she craves the attention of older, understanding and nurturing men—her father being nearly fifty years older than she—to an addictive degree. Anamika dropped Chris once she learned he was twenty one and not thirty six as he claimed. Larry himself was a father and old enough so that Anamika would have gravitated to him had he not cursed her and been overly critical and patronizing. He never had a chance.

As a result, very soon after the "brokers" introduced Anamika to the clients she was communicating directly with Kevin and Brian. After Kevin pulled back and Brian returned from India, I was added. When I became more demanding, she went to Allen in Philadelphia and then Allen in Phoenix.

I also believe it is most unlikely, as the pompous ones alleged, that she was connected to what purports to be the Indian mafia. No self respecting "Don" would allow such a non-earner in his gang.

Nor do I know if she was flashing our business plans to embezzle other Indians. I do know that none of us gave Anamika any up front fees, nor did she request any.

Had this theory been true, and Anamika a Bengal grifter, as some in our group were convinced, surely a disgruntled client would have appeared to alert the Indian press. As we've seen demonstrated many times over, the press in many countries throughout the world will gladly jump at the chance to tear down someone they had previously built up. Indian journalists were no exception as I learned reading their online editions for many months.

My simple appraisal of Anamika is that she is delusional. So were many of us. If delusion were a crime, there would be no entertainment industry.

Looking back I have no regrets.

Without Anamika I could never have written this book.

APPENDIX

APPENDIX 1
THE 12 MOST COMMON EXCUSES USED BY SWINDLERS FOR NOT RETURNING YOUR MONEY*

Not sure you've been conned?
This Is What May Have Happened:
• You have received profits on time, perhaps more than once; Or
• You have paid a fee up front to a "broker" who promises you funding for your company; Or
• You have invited others to join the investment on the basis of your results. (Now you have become a middleman to a fraud.)
• The time comes for the 3rd or 4th disbursement of profits, but there are delays.
• You are told the profits have been delayed, or you cannot get your money back, because:

1. Bank error. The Trader (substitute whatever title applies) will fix the mess and re-submit.

2. Bank officer encrypted the wrong transfer code and the funds were returned by one of the correspondent banks. The Trader will fix the mess and re-submit.

3. The Trader has pneumonia (the flu, broke his leg, whatever) and is in the hospital. The funds will be disbursed as soon as he gets out.

4. The Trader's mother (father, uncle, sister, wife …) is in the hospital (dead, heart-attack …). The funds will be disbursed as soon as he gets back.

5. The bank is going through an annual audit and/or a bank merger, so all transfers are temporarily frozen.

6. One of the investors contacted the bank and asked a lot of questions. The bank is angry and has frozen all disbursements.

---

*   Reproduced with the permission of Annie Mcguire's <u>www.fraudaid.com</u>

7. The Trader has gone to an important banking conference and the funds will be disbursed when he returns.

8. The SEC (FBI, Treasury Dept., Banking Commission, whatever) is performing an unwarranted investigation of the investment. Funds will be transferred as soon as they are satisfied.

9. The Trader is in Europe (Asia, Middle East, Moscow ...) trying to settle a problem caused by (any number of things) and it may be a while before funds can be disbursed.

10. There is no trading after about the middle of November until the middle of January because those are not international banking days for trading.

11. The currency market is down, the exchange rate has shifted, the fall in the Japanese stock market, the September 11th tragedy, etc. has made conditions unfavorable for profitable trading at the moment. We will have to wait until international conditions are more favorable.

12. The fund is now full and we are not accepting any more applications. The fund is now in the process of developing profits and disbursements will begin soon.

Not one of these excuses is acceptable

Any one of them is cause for you to be suspicious

APPENDIX 2
WHAT A CON ARTIST WON'T TELL YOU*

A con artist will tell you everything and anything you want to hear—up to the point where you start asking pointed questions. These are the questions a con artist will not answer, or will answer with false information, or lull you with excuses, and then flee the scene.

1. May I have your business license number?
2. Do you belong to the Chamber of Commerce?
3. What is the name of your banker so I can verify your statements?
4. May I have your broker's license number?
5. Would you mind going with me to speak with my bank officer?
6. What state/country agencies are you registered with?
7. What sort of references can you provide?
8. Can you give me addresses where I can see samples of your work?
9. Do you mind if I get a second opinion?
10. May I call your embassy about that?
11. Do you mind if I check with the local authorities?
12. May I have your contractor's license number?
13. Do you mind if I call the AMA (American Medical Association)?
14. Do you mind if I call the ABA (American Bar Association)?
15. Do you mind if I call the Banking Commission?
16. Will you show your Trustee papers to my lawyer?
17. May I call your local Chamber of Commerce?

---

*   Reproduced with the permission of Annie Mcguire's www.fraudaid.com

APPENDIX 3
NIGERIAN SCAM LETTERS:
THEY ARE NOT ONLY INTERNATIONAL IN
SCOPE, BUT CAN BE DEADLY!*

Not all scams referred to as "Nigerian" are currently emanating from Nigeria*. They are not only international in scope, but can be deadly.

Nigerian Scam Letters, or 419's, appear in email boxes all over the world. They appear on fax machines, and are delivered by the postman. They offer opportunity, adventure, travel, and lots and lots of money.

These popular schemes are called "Nigerian" because that is where they originated, namely in the former capitol city of Lagos. Nowadays there is ample evidence that the scam is being perpetrated by swindlers worldwide. 419'ers are located in England, Canada, Asia, and throughout Europe and the U.S.

4-1-9: Four-One-Nine is the Nigerian criminal code for a scam that is not only widespread but deadly. One receives an unsolicited email, snail mail, or fax stating that millions of US dollars need to be removed from Nigeria (or some other country, usually in West Africa) and you have been selected by government, banking officials, or surviving relatives to assist.

"But there will be just a few expenses"
"Naturally, you will be amply rewarded for your assistance by retaining a percentage of the funds transferred; however, in order to facilitate the procedure your financial assistance is required up front."

---

*   Reproduced with the permission of Annie Mcguire's www.fraudaid.com

This phrase is couched in other words, soft persuasive words, that impel the victim to begin sending money and gifts (for bribes) that are supposedly needed to release the funds from the fingers of greedy officials.

Sometimes convincing a victim to hand over all his money (or at least an overwhelming portion of his savings) isn't enough—there have been instances of victims who have gone to Africa to meet with the supposed Nigerian officials, only to end up mugged, badly beaten, and even dead. The victim's cash and credit cards are taken (to be sold on the international market), and anything whatsoever of value is ripped from the victim's person. Victims beaten, killed … or missing … graves in the jungle?

And then there is this from the U.S. Secret Service site:
"Victims are almost always requested to travel to Nigeria or a border country to complete a transaction. Individuals are often told that a visa will not be necessary to enter the country. The Nigerian con artists may then bribe airport officials to pass the victims through Immigration and Customs. Because it is a serious offense in Nigeria to enter without a valid visa, the victim's illegal entry may be used by the fraudsters as leverage to coerce the victims into releasing funds. Violence and threats of physical harm may be employed to further pressure victims. In June of 1995, an American was murdered in Lagos, Nigeria, while pursuing a 4-1-9 scam, and numerous other foreign nationals have been reported as missing."

APPENDIX 4
HOW TO REPORT A NIGERIAN
SCAM LETTER*

What to do if you receive a Nigerian Scam Letter

Many people merely throw the letter in the trash, or forward it to friends to share a laugh. That would be fine if everyone thought the letters laughable. The truth is that people in desperate financial situations will cling to even the most outrageous source of hope for relief.

As pointed out in on the previous page, it is an accumulation of evidence that gives law enforcement the edge.

The owner of the 419 Coalition web site, C. A. Pascale, has generously allowed Annie Mcguire to copy the instructions for responsible action for the receipt of a Nigerian Scam Letter. They are as follows:

What to Do For Everybody Everywhere

If you have NOT suffered a financial loss, so the matter is not urgent, you may alternatively SNAILMAIL the Scam documents you have received to the United States Secret Service, Financial Crimes Division, 419 Task Force, 950 H Street, Washington, DC, 20001-4518, USA. But be sure to mark your documents "No Financial Loss—For Your Database." Or, you may EMAIL the Task Force at 419fcd@usss.treas.gov.

If the contact from the 419ers was via email: write their email provider at their "abuse" address (abuse@yahoo.com, abuse@onebox.com etc.) and include the

---

*   Reproduced with the permission of Annie Mcguire's www.fraudaid.com

419er message with its headers; complain about the 419 message; and ask that the account be shut down.

Some 419'ers give different email addresses in the body of their mail than the one they sent from, so you should complain to "abuse" etc. at those email providers as well. If you wish, file a complaint with the Nigerian Embassy or High Commission in your nation.

The 419 Coalition web site has been around for a long time. The information provided well worth the visit.

Here are some excerpts from the site:
"A Five Billion US$ (as of 1996, much more now) worldwide Scam which has run since the early 1980's under Successive Governments of Nigeria. It is also referred to as "Advance Fee Fraud", "419 Fraud" (Four-One-Nine) after the relevant section of the Criminal Code of Nigeria, and "The Nigerian Connection" (mostly in Europe). However, it is usually called plain old "419" even by the Nigerians themselves."

"Most 419 letters and emails originate from or are traceable back to Nigeria. However, some originate from other nations, mostly also West African nations such as Ghana, Togo, Liberia, Sierra Leone, Ivory Coast (Cote D'Ivoire) etc. In most cases 419 emails from other nations are also Nigerian in that the "Home Office" of the 419ers involved is Nigeria regardless of the source of the contact materials. But there are occasionally some "local" copycats trying to emulate the success of the Nigerians. These folks tend not to last too long actually operating out of nations other than Nigeria, but they do try."

REPORTING A NIGERIAN SCAM LETTER FOR:

UNITED STATES CITIZENS OR RESIDENTS

1. No Financial Loss:
If you are a United States Citizen or Resident and have not suffered a financial loss print "No Financial Loss—For Your Database" in a white space* on the

---

* Please try to avoid writing over signatures, addresses, phone numbers, bank account numbers or fax machine info data at the top and/or bottom of the document.

documents you received and fax them to the US Secret Service Task Force handling Scam matters at one of the following fax numbers:

Fax: 202-406-6930
Fax: 202-406-5031
Actual hard copy of the 419er document(s) is required to add your 419er's information to the Task Force Database for legal reasons; merely telling Task Force about it will NOT suffice.

NOTE: Since the Task Force is very busy dealing with cases in which there have been financial losses, it is NOT customary for them to contact you in cases where there has been No Loss. But it is very important that you get your 419er's data into the Task Force Database, so DO send it along.

2. Financial Loss:
If you are a United States Citizen or Resident, and have suffered a financial loss:
Don't worry; you are not in any trouble.
Make a copy of each of the documents you have received and/or sent
Print "Financial Loss—Contact Me ASAP" on the copies and fax those copies with a cover letter and your telephone number(s) to the Task Force at

202-406-6930 or 202-406-5031
A Secret Service Agent will call you back as soon as possible to discuss the matter with you.
If you are not contacted by a Special Agent soon enough to suit you, call the Task Force Voice at 202-406-5850 and tell the Operator (or voicemail) that it's Urgent, you want to speak with an Agent as soon as possible. Don't forget to give your name and telephone number(s)

REPORTING A NIGERIAN SCAM LETTER FOR

UNITED KINGDOM

For those in the UK with NO financial loss, examples of Internet '419' Advance Fee Fraud should be forwarded to your local fraud squad for investigation, whose location is obtainable through your local police station. Please quote 'NCIS West African Organised Crime Section' in your correspondence with them and under no circumstances reply to these criminals.

In addition to the above, if you HAVE lost money and there is a UK connection to the 419 operation, the NCIS wishes to speak directly with you as soon as possible. Persons who Have actually lost money to such scams can contact NCIS at: victim@spring39.demon.co.uk or by phone at 020 7238 8012.

NCIS also notes that 419 emails are very common, and it is possible that you may receive others in the future. Please do not send them direct to NCIS unless there is a loss, but as well as transmitting them direct to your local fraud squad, please send a copy to the Internet Service Provider (ISP's) from where the 419er email has originated. These emails to the ISP's should be addressed to: abuse@"the ISP's name" (for example abuse@yahoo.com, abuse@hotmail.com, abuse@onebox.com). By this method the ISP's will be able to quickly terminate the accounts that abuse their systems.

Anyone OUTSIDE the UK receiving such a letter or email with a UK connection is advised to notify your Own Nation's National Law Enforcement Agency and your Own Nation's Foreign Office; to NOT reply to the 419er communication; and to forward the 419er correspondence to the National Criminal Intelligence Service, PO Box 8000, London SE11 5EN, or by e-mail.

Also please email 419 letters, materials, and other relevant data to Task Force Main in DC or fax it to them at 202-406-6930 (US) if you prefer. Please be SURE to state if there is any US Connection to your 419ers' operations, particularly if there is US Banking Data on them. Please mark the materials Loss (or No Loss as the case may be)—For Your Database.

REPORTING A NIGERIAN SCAM LETTER FOR

SOUTH AFRICA

Please contact Captain SC Schambriel of Commercial Crime, Head Office, at telephone number (012) 339 1203 or fax the information to him at (012) 339 1202.

Also please fax the Scam documents, especially Nigerian Scammer banking data, to the US Task Force at 202-406-6930 appropriately marked South Africa—Loss (or No Loss as the case may be)—For Your Database. Please be SURE to state if there is any US Connection to your 419ers' operations, particularly if there is US Banking Data on them. You may also email such relevant data to Task Force Main in DC if you prefer to do it that way.

The South African Police Service maintains a 419 Scams/Nigerian Letters Alert on their website. For a look at a short Anti-419 Pamphlet issued by and available from the South African Police Service. Check there.

REPORTING A NIGERIAN SCAM LETTER FOR

CANADA

Although there is a 419 investigative team of the RCMP based in Ottawa, this is NOT where citizens should direct complaints or inquiries. Regional Offices of the RCMP Commercial Crime Branch are the appropriate places to direct inquiries or data. The phone/fax numbers of the nearest CCB office are available from any detachment of the RCMP/GRC. Data forwarded to the Regional CCB office is used to establish regional statistics and will be sent to the Central Team.

Also, in Canada, The Phonebusters National Call Centre (PNCC) is a joint partnership involving the Ontario Provincial Police and the Royal Canadian Mounted Police. Phonebusters is very interested in receiving copies of any 'new' versions of Nigerian letter schemes particularly those involving Canadian mailing addresses or telephone numbers. You can email such 419 letters to them at WAFL@phonebusters.com

And please do fax hardcopy of your 419ers data, especially Nigerian Scammer Banking Data to the US Task Force, appropriately marked with Canada, Loss (or No Loss as the Case May Be), No US Connection, For Your Database, at 202-406-6930. You may also email such data to Task Force Main in DC if you prefer.

If there IS a US Connection, please Follow These Instructions for Canada AND ALSO follow the instructions for US Citizens and Residents given above.

You may also access the Royal Canadian Mounted Police Website (RCMP/GRC) which contains a section on the Nigerian Scam. 419-06/canada

REPORTING A NIGERIAN SCAM LETTER FOR

AUSTRALIA

According to the West African Crime Section (WAOCS) in the UK, Australians are to report 419 matters In Australia to their local police and to the Australian West African Organized Crime Section at er-waoc@afp.gov.au

And please do fax hardcopy of your 419ers data, especially Nigerian Scammer Banking Data to the US Task Force, appropriately marked with Australia, Loss (or No Loss as the Case May Be), No US Connection, For Your Database, at 202-406-6930. You may also email such data to Task Force Main in DC if you prefer.

If there IS a US Connection, please Follow These Instructions for Australia AND follow the instructions for US Citizens and Residents.

978-0-595-38567-6
0-595-38567-2